W9-BYW-118

40 Short Stories

A Portable Anthology

40
Short Stories

A Portable Anthology

Sixth Edition

Edited by
BEVERLY LAWN
Emerita, Adelphi University

JOANNE DIAZ
Illinois Wesleyan University

bedford/st.martin's
Macmillan Learning
BOSTON | NEW YORK

Vice President: Leasa Burton
Program Director, English: Stacey Purviance
Senior Program Manager: John E. Sullivan III
Director of Content Development: Jane Knetzger
Executive Development Manager: Maura Shea
Development Editor: Cari Goldfine
Director of Media Editorial: Adam Whitehurst
Marketing Manager: Vivian Garcia
Director, Content Management Enhancement: Tracey Kuehn
Senior Managing Editor: Michael Granger
Senior Manager of Publishing Services: Andrea Cava
Senior Content Project Manager: Pamela Lawson
Senior Workflow Project Manager: Paul Rohloff
Production Supervisor: Robert Cherry
Director of Design, Content Management: Diana Blume
Cover Design: William Boardman
Director, Rights and Permissions: Hilary Newman
Text Permissions Researcher: Arthur Johnson
Photo Permissions Editor: Angie Boehler
Director of Digital Production: Keri deManigold
Advanced Media Project Manager: Allison Hart
Project Management: Lumina Datamatics, Inc.
Project Manager: Misbah Ansari
Editorial Services: Lumina Datamatics, Inc.
Copyeditor: Michael Goldstein
Composition: Lumina Datamatics, Inc.
Cover Image: Jose A. Bernat Bacete/Getty Images
Printing and Binding: LSC Communications

Copyright © 2021, 2017, 2013, 2009 by Bedford/ St. Martin's.

All rights reserved. No part of this book may be reproduced, stored in a retrieval system, or transmitted in any form or by any means, electronic, mechanical, photocopying, recording, or otherwise, except as may be permitted by law or expressly permitted in writing by the Publisher.

Library of Congress Control Number: 2020937109
ISBN 978-1-319-21570-5

Printed in the United States of America.

3 4 5 6 25 24 23

For information, write: Bedford/St. Martin's, 75 Arlington Street, Boston, MA 02116

Acknowledgments
Text acknowledgments and copyrights appear at the back of the book on pages 467–68, which constitute an extension of the copyright page. Art acknowledgments and copyrights appear on the same page as the art selections they cover.

Preface for Instructors

The sixth edition of *40 Short Stories: A Portable Anthology*, like its predecessors, is a compact collection of highly regarded, very teachable stories by respected authors. Stories of depth, power, and recognized artistry are included in a balance of the traditional and the contemporary. Exciting writers such as Chimamanda Ngozi Adichie, Neel Patel, and Ted Chiang—all born after 1965—join those who forged, and now represent, the classic tradition, among them Anton Chekhov, Nathaniel Hawthorne, Katherine Mansfield, and Edgar Allan Poe. The sixth edition includes more contemporary stories than previous editions; fully twenty percent of the selections were published in the past 20 years, within the lifetime of most students likely to be reading this edition in a college course, including Ramona Ausubel's "You Can Find Love Now," Meron Hadero's "The Suitcase," and Grace Oluseyi's "A Modern Marriage."

As the short story tradition has broadened, the valuable has become more various. While instructors want a strong representation of the classic tradition, they also consistently ask for a collection that offers wide cultural and artistic variety. Accordingly, while most of our authors lived or now live in the United States, one-quarter were born or now live in other countries: Antigua, Austria-Hungary, Canada, Colombia, England, Ethiopia, Ireland, New Zealand, Nigeria, and Russia.

The sixth edition, like the five that preceded it, preserves the editorial features that have always defined *40 Short Stories* and benefits instructors and students by being inexpensive, easy to read, and light to carry. While assembling a vibrant short story collection has always been our paramount purpose, we also seek to help students understand and appreciate, without intrusive critical breaks, writers' imagination and skills. The format is simple and designed to be useful in a wide variety of teaching situations, from general introduction-to-literature and short fiction courses to creative writing workshops and composition classes. The stories are arranged chronologically by date of the authors' birth, to suggest the evolution of the short story tradition, with the date of publication appearing at the end of each story to further locate the fiction within historical contexts. Apart from occasional footnotes within the stories, critical assistance is placed at the back of the book, so as not to be obtrusive or immediately influence close reading. This critical apparatus includes biographical notes on the authors in the anthology; a glossary of literary terms; a section on how to read short stories closely; and a section on how to write about short fiction.

NEW TO THE SIXTH EDITION

The publisher conducted a nationwide survey of instructors who had used the fifth edition and also canvassed a significant number of instructors who taught with other fiction anthologies. The comments and suggestions of all these teachers encouraged us to make the following updates and improvements to the sixth edition:

Thirteen new stories, many of them fresh and recent. While many instructors who used the fifth edition requested that the new edition include fresh, recent selections, they also wished to maintain the anthology's balance of contemporary and classic fiction that has proven to be appealing to students. With this in mind, we have replaced thirteen of the forty stories. Popular fifth-edition authors including Sandra Cisneros, Gabriel García Márquez, Franz Kafka, Margaret Atwood, and Lauren Groff remain in the sixth edition. Authors entirely new to *40 Short Stories* include celebrated contemporary writers such as George Saunders, ZZ Packer, Ted Chiang, and Neel Patel—all of whose reputations as exemplary writers of fiction have only increased since the fifth edition was published—and classic writers including Virginia Woolf, Tille Olsen, and John Cheever.

A full-length student essay. Newly added to the coverage of critical writing about fiction, a full-length, annotated student literary analysis of Nathaniel Hawthorne's "Young Goodman Browne" provides students with a quality model of writing about fiction.

The Nobel Prize–winning Peruvian novelist Mario Vargas Llosa reminds us that fiction has the awesome power to develop and liberate the imagination of the writer and reader. We hope the stories we have chosen and the assistance we have provided help open the imagination of your students to fiction's power.

ACKNOWLEDGMENTS

We are grateful to the instructors who responded so thoughtfully to our queries about their experience with the fifth edition: Chad Barlett, Mount Hood Community College; Maryam Barrie, Washtenaw Community College; James Brennan, Quinsigamond Community College; Gannon Daniels, Glendale Community College; James Decker, Illinois Central College; Cara Diaconoff, Bellevue College; Stacey Donohue, Central Oregon Community College; Richard Hancuff, Misericordia University; Kevin Leaverton, Central Washington University; Myra Mendible, Florida Gulf Coast University; Thor Polukoshko, Langara College; Erin Robb, Langara College; Marianne Taylor, Kirkwood Community College; Susan Tenon, Lakeland Community College; and Robert Vettese, Southern Maine Community College.

We also remain thankful to all those who have reviewed earlier editions of the book, going back to the turn of the millennium. They have all left their mark on earlier editions of *40 Short Stories*.

In addition to his review of *40 Short Stories*, we are grateful to Robert Vettese for his contributions to the instructor resources that accompany this edition (available for download on the Macmillan Learning catalog).

Our deep thanks to all those at Bedford/St. Martin's who devoted their professional knowledge and skill to the creation of this book: Leasa Burton, Vice President Editorial, Humanities; Stacey Purviance, Program Director for English; John Sullivan, Senior Program Manager, Readers and Literature; Maura Shea, Executive Development Editor; and especially our editor for this edition, Cari Goldfine, for all her suggestions and last-minute problem-solving. In the production department, thanks go to Pamela Lawson, Senior Content Project Manager, and Misbah Ansari, Project Manager at Lumina Datamatics. We are grateful to Hilary Newman, Director, Rights and Permissions and to Arthur Johnson, Text Permissions Researcher, who cleared the permissions for the sixth edition.

Joanne Diaz prepared all sections of this revised sixth edition. She thanks Brandi Reissenweber and Grace Talusan for their advice on the new table of contents. She would also like to thank Megan Baker and Erin Burnison for their help with manuscript preparation.

— Beverly Lawn and Joanne Diaz

Bedford/St. Martin's Puts You First

From day one, our goal has been simple: to provide inspiring resources that are grounded in best practices for teaching reading and writing. For more than 35 years, Bedford/St. Martin's has partnered with the field, listening to teachers, scholars, and students about the support writers need. We are committed to helping every writing instructor make the most of our resources.

HOW CAN WE HELP *YOU*?

- Our editors can align our resources to your outcomes through correlation and transition guides for your syllabus. Just ask us.
- Our sales representatives specialize in helping you find the right materials to support your course goals.
- Our learning solutions and product specialists help you make the most of the digital resources you choose for your course.
- Our *Bits* blog on the Bedford/St. Martin's English Community (**community.macmillan.com**) publishes fresh teaching ideas weekly. You'll also find easily downloadable professional resources and links to author webinars on our community site.

Contact your Bedford/St. Martin's sales representative, or visit **macmillanlearning.com** to learn more.

PRINT AND DIGITAL OPTIONS FOR *40 SHORT STORIES*

Choose the format that works best for your course, and ask about our packaging options that offer savings for students.

Print

- *Paperback.* To order the sixth edition, use ISBN 978-1-319-21570-5. To order *40 Short Stories* (print) packaged with Achieve, use ISBN 978-1-319-37903-2.

Digital

- *Achieve for Writer's Help.* Achieve puts student writing at the center of your course and keeps revision at the core, with a dedicated composition space that guides students through drafting, peer review, plagiarism prevention, reflection, and revision. Developed to support best practices in commenting on student drafts, Achieve is a flexible, integrated suite of tools for designing and facilitating writing assignments, paired with actionable insights that make students' progress towards outcomes clear and measurable. With trusted content from the widely used Hacker or Lunsford handbooks, Writer's Help takes students through first-year writing and beyond. For details, visit **macmillanlearning .com/college/us/englishdigital**.
- *Popular e-book formats.* For details about our e-book partners, visit **macmillanlearning.com/ebooks**.
- *Inclusive Access.* Enable every student to receive their course materials through your LMS on the first day of class. Macmillan Learning's Inclusive Access program is the easiest, most affordable way to ensure all students have access to quality educational resources. Find out more at **macmillanlearning.com /inclusiveaccess**.

YOUR COURSE, YOUR WAY

No two literature or writing programs or classrooms are exactly alike. Our Curriculum Solutions team works with you to design custom options that provide the resources your students need. (Options below require enrollment minimums.)

- *ForeWords for English.* Customize any print resource to fit the focus of your course or program by choosing from a range of prepared topics, such as Sentence Guides for Academic Writers.
- *Macmillan Author Program (MAP).* Add excerpts or package acclaimed works from Macmillan's trade imprints to connect students with prominent authors and public conversations. A list of popular examples or academic themes is available upon request.
- *Mix and Match.* With our simplest solution, you can add up to 50 pages of curated content to your Bedford/St. Martin's text. Contact your sales representative for additional details.

- *Bedford Select.* Build your own print anthology from a database of more than 800 selections, or build a handbook and add your own materials to create your ideal text. Package with any Bedford/St. Martin's text for additional savings. Visit **macmillanlearning.com/bedfordselect**.

INSTRUCTOR RESOURCES

You have a lot to do in your course. We want to make it easy for you to find the support you need—and to get it quickly.

Instructor Resources for *40 Short Stories*, Sixth Edition, include sample syllabi and a transition guide for the edition, and are available as PDFs that can be downloaded from **macmillanlearning.com**.

Contents

Other Ways into the Stories: Alternative Contents

ELEMENTS OF FICTION

PLOT

CHARACTER

SETTING

POINT OF VIEW

STYLE, TONE, IRONY

SYMBOL AND METAPHOR

THEMATIC GROUPINGS

ARTISTIC EXPRESSION

CULTURAL CONFRONTATIONS

CULTURAL DIFFERENCES

FAMILIES

INNOCENCE AND EXPERIENCE

JOURNEYS

LOVE AND HATE

THE LURE OF THE FORBIDDEN

MYTH AND ARCHETYPE

STORIES FROM AROUND THE WORLD

SUSPENSE AND TERROR

YOUTH AND AGE

Young Goodman Brown

NATHANIEL HAWTHORNE

[1804–1864]

Young Goodman Brown came forth at sunset into the street at Salem village; but put his head back, after crossing the threshold, to exchange a parting kiss with his young wife. And Faith, as the wife was aptly named, thrust her own pretty head into the street, letting the wind play with the pink ribbons of her cap while she called to Goodman Brown.

"Dearest heart," whispered she, softly and rather sadly, when her lips were close to his ear, "prithee put off your journey until sunrise and sleep in your own bed to-night. A lone woman is troubled with such dreams and such thoughts that she's afeared of herself sometimes. Pray tarry with me this night, dear husband, of all nights in the year."

"My love and my Faith," replied young Goodman Brown, "of all nights in the year, this one night must I tarry away from thee. My journey, as thou callest it, forth and back again, must needs be done 'twixt now and sunrise. What, my sweet, pretty wife, dost thou doubt me already, and we but three months married?"

"Then God bless you!" said Faith, with the pink ribbons, "and may you find all well when you come back."

"Amen!" cried Goodman Brown. "Say thy prayers, dear Faith, and go to bed at dusk, and no harm will come to thee."

So they parted; and the young man pursued his way until, being about to turn the corner by the meeting-house, he looked back and saw the head of Faith still peeping after him with a melancholy air, in spite of her pink ribbons.

"Poor little Faith!" thought he, for his heart smote him. "What a wretch am I to leave her on such an errand! She talks of dreams, too. Methought as she spoke there was trouble in her face, as if a dream had warned her what work is to be done to-night. But no, no;

't would kill her to think it. Well, she's a blessed angel on earth, and after this one night I'll cling to her skirts and follow her to heaven."

With this excellent resolve for the future, Goodman Brown felt himself justified in making more haste on his present evil purpose. He had taken a dreary road, darkened by all the gloomiest trees of the forest, which barely stood aside to let the narrow path creep through, and closed immediately behind. It was all as lonely as could be; and there is this peculiarity in such a solitude, that the traveller knows not who may be concealed by the innumerable trunks and the thick boughs overhead; so that with lonely footsteps he may yet be passing through an unseen multitude.

"There may be a devilish Indian behind every tree," said Goodman Brown to himself; and he glanced fearfully behind him as he added, "What if the devil himself should be at my very elbow!"

His head being turned back, he passed a crook of the road, and, looking forward again, beheld the figure of a man, in grave and decent attire, seated at the foot of an old tree. He arose at Goodman Brown's approach and walked onward side by side with him.

"You are late, Goodman Brown," said he. "The clock of the Old South was striking as I came through Boston, and that is full fifteen minutes agone."

"Faith kept me back a while," replied the young man, with a tremor in his voice, caused by the sudden appearance of his companion, though not wholly unexpected.

It was now deep dusk in the forest, and deepest in that part of it where these two were journeying. As nearly as could be discerned, the second traveller was about fifty years old, apparently in the same rank of life as Goodman Brown, and bearing a considerable resemblance to him, though perhaps more in expression than features. Still they might have been taken for father and son. And yet, though the elder person was as simply clad as the younger, and as simple in manner too, he had an indescribable air of one who knew the world, and who would not have felt abashed at the governor's dinner table or in King William's court, were it possible that his affairs should call him thither. But the only thing about him that could be fixed upon as remarkable was his staff, which bore the likeness of a great black snake, so curiously wrought that it might almost be seen to twist and wriggle itself like a living serpent. This, of course, must have been an ocular deception, assisted by the uncertain light.

"Come, Goodman Brown," cried his fellow-traveller, "this is a dull pace for the beginning of a journey. Take my staff, if you are so soon weary."

"Friend," said the other, exchanging his slow pace for a full stop, "having kept covenant by meeting thee here, it is my purpose now to return whence I came. I have scruples touching the matter thou wot'st of."

"Sayest thou so?" replied he of the serpent, smiling apart. "Let us walk on, nevertheless, reasoning as we go; and if I convince thee not thou shalt turn back. We are but a little way in the forest yet."

"Too far! too far!" exclaimed the goodman, unconsciously resuming his walk. "My father never went into the woods on such an errand, nor his father before him. We have been a race of honest men and good Christians since the days of the martyrs; and shall I be the first of the name of Brown that ever took this path and kept—"

"Such company, thou wouldst say," observed the elder person, interpreting his pause. "Well said, Goodman Brown! I have been as well acquainted with your family as with ever a one among the Puritans; and that's no trifle to say. I helped your grandfather, the constable, when he lashed the Quaker woman so smartly through the streets of Salem; and it was I that brought your father a pitch-pine knot, kindled at my own hearth, to set fire to an Indian village, in King Philip's war.[1] They were my good friends, both; and many a pleasant walk have we had along this path, and returned merrily after midnight. I would fain be friends with you for their sake."

"If it be as thou sayest," replied Goodman Brown, "I marvel they never spoke of these matters; or, verily, I marvel not, seeing that the least rumor of the sort would have driven them from New England. We are a people of prayer, and good works to boot, and abide no such wickedness."

"Wickedness or not," said the traveller with the twisted staff, "I have a very general acquaintance here in New England. The deacons of many a church have drunk the communion wine with me; the selectmen of divers towns make me their chairman; and a majority of the Great and General Court are firm supporters of my interest. The governor and I, too—But these are state secrets."

[1]King Philip, a Wampanoag chief, waged war against the New England colonists (1675–76).

"Can this be so?" cried Goodman Brown, with a stare of amazement at his undisturbed companion. "Howbeit, I have nothing to do with the governor and council; they have their own ways, and are no rule for a simple husbandman like me. But, were I to go on with thee, how should I meet the eye of that good old man, our minister, at Salem village? Oh, his voice would make me tremble both Sabbath day and lecture day."

Thus far the elder traveller had listened with due gravity; but now burst into a fit of irrepressible mirth, shaking himself so violently that his snake-like staff actually seemed to wriggle in sympathy.

"Ha! ha! ha!" shouted he again and again; then composing himself, "Well, go on, Goodman Brown, go on; but, prithee, don't kill me with laughing."

"Well, then, to end the matter at once," said Goodman Brown, considerably nettled, "there is my wife, Faith. It would break her dear little heart; and I'd rather break my own."

"Nay, if that be the case," answered the other, "e'en go thy ways, Goodman Brown. I would not for twenty old women like the one hobbling before us that Faith should come to any harm."

As he spoke he pointed his staff at a female figure on the path, in whom Goodman Brown recognized a very pious and exemplary dame, who had taught him his catechism in youth, and was still his moral and spiritual adviser, jointly with the minister and Deacon Gookin.

"A marvel, truly that Goody Cloyse should be so far in the wilderness at nightfall," said he. "But with your leave, friend, I shall take a cut through the woods until we have left this Christian woman behind. Being a stranger to you, she might ask whom I was consorting with and whither I was going."

"Be it so," said his fellow-traveller. "Betake you to the woods, and let me keep the path."

Accordingly the young man turned aside, but took care to watch his companion, who advanced softly along the road until he had come within a staff's length of the old dame. She, meanwhile, was making the best of her way, with singular speed for so aged a woman, and mumbling some indistinct words—a prayer, doubtless—as she went. The traveller put forth his staff and touched her withered neck with what seemed the serpent's tail.

"The devil!" screamed the pious old lady.

"Then Goody Cloyse knows her old friend?" observed the traveller, confronting her and leaning on his writhing stick.

"Ah, forsooth, and is it your worship indeed?" cried the good dame. "Yea, truly is it, and in the very image of my old gossip, Goodman Brown, the grandfather of the silly fellow that now is. But—would your worship believe it?—my broomstick hath strangely disappeared, stolen, as I suspect, by that unhanged witch, Goody Cory, and that, too, when I was all anointed with the juice of smallage, and cinquefoil, and wolf's bane—"[2]

"Mingled with fine wheat and the fat of a new-born babe," said the shape of old Goodman Brown.

"Ah, your worship knows the recipe," cried the old lady, cackling aloud. "So, as I was saying, being all ready for the meeting, and no horse to ride on, I made up my mind to foot it; for they tell me there is a nice young man to be taken into communion to-night. But now your good worship will lend me your arm, and we shall be there in a twinkling."

"That can hardly be," answered her friend. "I may not spare you my arm, Goody Cloyse; but here is my staff, if you will."

So saying, he threw it down at her feet, where, perhaps, it assumed life, being one of the rods which its owner had formerly lent to the Egyptian magi. Of this fact, however, Goodman Brown could not take cognizance. He had cast up his eyes in astonishment, and, looking down again, beheld neither Goody Cloyse nor the serpentine staff, but his fellow-traveller alone, who waited for him as calmly as if nothing had happened.

"That old woman taught me my catechism," said the young man; and there was a world of meaning in this simple comment.

They continued to walk onward, while the elder traveller exhorted his companion to make good speed and persevere in the path, discoursing so aptly that his arguments seemed rather to spring up in the bosom of his auditor than to be suggested by himself. As they went, he plucked a branch of maple to serve for a walking stick, and began to strip it of the twigs and little boughs, which were wet with

[2]Three plants sometimes associated with witchcraft. Smallage refers to varieties of parsley and celery; cinquefoil to plants with compound leaves, each having five leaflets; wolf's bane to plants with dull green leaves and yellow foliage, sometimes called winter wheat or aconite.

evening dew. The moment his fingers touched them they became strangely withered and dried up as with a week's sunshine. Thus the pair proceeded, at a good free pace, until suddenly, in a gloomy hollow of the road, Goodman Brown sat himself down on the stump of a tree and refused to go any farther.

"Friend," he said, stubbornly, "my mind is made up. Not another step will I budge on this errand. What if a wretched old woman do choose to go to the devil when I thought she was going to heaven: is that any reason why I should quit my dear Faith and go after her?"

"You will think better of this by and by," said his acquaintance, composedly. "Sit here and rest yourself a while; and when you feel like moving again, there is my staff to help you along."

Without more words, he threw his companion the maple stick, and was as speedily out of sight as if he had vanished into the deepening gloom. The young man sat a few moments by the roadside, applauding himself greatly, and thinking with how clear a conscience he should meet the minister in his morning walk, nor shrink from the eye of good old Deacon Gookin. And what calm sleep would be his that very night, which was to have been spent so wickedly, but so purely and sweetly now, in the arms of Faith! Amidst these pleasant and praiseworthy meditations, Goodman Brown heard the tramp of horses along the road, and deemed it advisable to conceal himself within the verge of the forest, conscious of the guilty purpose that had brought him thither, though now so happily turned from it.

On came the hoof tramps and the voices of the riders, two grave old voices, conversing soberly as they drew near. These mingled sounds appeared to pass along the road, within a few yards of the young man's hiding-place; but, owing doubtless to the depth of the gloom at that particular spot, neither the travellers nor their steeds were visible. Though their figures brushed the small boughs by the wayside, it could not be seen that they intercepted, even for a moment, the faint gleam from the strip of bright sky athwart which they must have passed. Goodman Brown alternately crouched and stood on tiptoe, pulling aside the branches and thrusting forth his head as far as he durst without discerning so much as a shadow. It vexed him the more, because he could have sworn, were such a thing possible, that he recognized the voices of the minister and Deacon Gookin, jogging along quietly, as they were wont to do, when bound to some ordination or ecclesiastical council. While yet within hearing, one of the riders stopped to pluck a switch.

"Of the two, reverend sir," said the voice like the deacon's, "I had rather miss an ordination dinner than to-night's meeting. They tell me that some of our community are to be here from Falmouth and beyond, and others from Connecticut and Rhode Island, besides several of the Indian powwows, who, after their fashion, know almost as much deviltry as the best of us. Moreover, there is a goodly young woman to be taken into communion."

"Mighty well, Deacon Gookin!" replied the solemn old tones of the minister. "Spur up, or we shall be late. Nothing can be done, you know, until I get on the ground."

The hoofs clattered again; and the voices, talking so strangely in the empty air, passed on through the forest, where no church had ever been gathered or solitary Christian prayed. Whither, then, could these holy men be journeying so deep into the heathen wilderness? Young Goodman Brown caught hold of a tree for support, being ready to sink down on the ground, faint and overburdened with the heavy sickness of his heart. He looked up to the sky, doubting whether there really was a heaven above him. Yet there was the blue arch, and the stars brightening in it.

"With heaven above and Faith below, I will yet stand firm against the devil!" cried Goodman Brown.

While he still gazed upward into the deep arch of the firmament and had lifted his hands to pray, a cloud, though no wind was stirring, hurried across the zenith and hid the brightening stars. The blue sky was still visible, except directly overhead, where this black mass of cloud was sweeping swiftly northward. Aloft in the air, as if from the depths of the cloud, came a confused and doubtful sound of voices. Once the listener fancied that he could distinguish the accents of towns-people of his own, men and women, both pious and ungodly, many of whom he had met at the communion table, and had seen others rioting at the tavern. The next moment, so indistinct were the sounds, he doubted whether he had heard aught but the murmur of the old forest, whispering without a wind. Then came a stronger swell of those familiar tones, heard daily in the sunshine at Salem village, but never until now from a cloud of night. There was one voice, of a young woman, uttering lamentations, yet with an uncertain sorrow, and entreating for some favor, which, perhaps, it would grieve her to obtain; and all the unseen multitude, both saints and sinners, seemed to encourage her onward.

"Faith!" shouted Goodman Brown, in a voice of agony and desperation; and the echoes of the forest mocked him, crying, "Faith! Faith!" as if bewildered wretches were seeking her all through the wilderness.

The cry of grief, rage, and terror was yet piercing the night, when the unhappy husband held his breath for a response. There was a scream, drowned immediately in a louder murmur of voices, fading into far-off laughter, as the dark cloud swept away, leaving the clear and silent sky above Goodman Brown. But something fluttered lightly down through the air and caught on the branch of a tree. The young man seized it, and beheld a pink ribbon.

"My Faith is gone!" cried he after one stupefied moment. "There is no good on earth; and sin is but a name. Come, devil; for to thee is this world given."

And, maddened with despair, so that he laughed loud and long, did Goodman Brown grasp his staff and set forth again, at such a rate that he seemed to fly along the forest path rather than to walk or run. The road grew wilder and drearier and more faintly traced, and vanished at length, leaving him in the heart of the dark wilderness, still rushing onward with the instinct that guides mortal man to evil. The whole forest was peopled with frightful sounds—the creaking of the trees, the howling of wild beasts, and the yell of Indians; while sometimes the wind tolled like a distant church bell, and sometimes gave a broad roar around the traveller, as if all Nature were laughing him to scorn. But he was himself the chief horror of the scene, and shrank not from its other horrors.

"Ha! ha! ha!" roared Goodman Brown when the wind laughed at him. "Let us hear which will laugh loudest. Think not to frighten me with your deviltry. Come witch, come wizard, come Indian powwow, come devil himself, and here comes Goodman Brown. You may as well fear him as he fear you."

In truth, all through the haunted forest there could be nothing more frightful than the figure of Goodman Brown. On he flew among the black pines, brandishing his staff with frenzied gestures, now giving vent to an inspiration of horrid blasphemy, and now shouting forth such laughter as set all the echoes of the forest laughing like demons around him. The fiend in his own shape is less hideous than when he rages in the breast of man. Thus sped the demoniac on his course, until, quivering among the trees, he saw a red light before him, as when the felled trunks and branches of a clearing have been set on fire, and throw up their lurid blaze against the sky, at the hour of midnight. He paused, in a lull of the tempest that had driven him onward, and heard the swell of what seemed a hymn, rolling solemnly from a distance with the weight of many voices. He knew the tune; it was a familiar one in the choir of the village meeting-house. The verse died heavily away, and was lengthened by a chorus, not of human voices, but of all the sounds of the benighted wilderness pealing in awful harmony together. Goodman Brown cried out, and his cry was lost to his own ear by its unison with the cry of the desert.

In the interval of silence he stole forward until the light glared full upon his eyes. At one extremity of an open space, hemmed in by the dark wall of the forest, arose a rock, bearing some rude, natural resemblance either to an altar or a pulpit, and surrounded by four blazing pines, their tops aflame, their stems untouched, like candles at an evening meeting. The mass of foliage that had overgrown the summit of the rock was all on fire, blazing high into the night and fitfully illuminating the whole field. Each pendent twig and leafy festoon was in a blaze. As the red light arose and fell, a numerous congregation alternately shone forth, then disappeared in shadow, and again grew, as it were, out of the darkness, peopling the heart of the solitary woods at once.

"A grave and dark-clad company," quoth Goodman Brown.

In truth they were such. Among them, quivering to and fro between gloom and splendor, appeared faces that would be seen next day at the council board of the province, and others which, Sabbath after Sabbath, looked devoutly heavenward, and benignantly over the crowded pews, from the holiest pulpits in the land. Some affirm that the lady of the governor was there. At least there were high dames well known to her, and wives of honored husbands, and widows, a great multitude, and ancient maidens, all of excellent repute, and fair young girls, who trembled lest their mothers should espy them. Either the sudden gleams of light flashing over the obscure field bedazzled Goodman Brown, or he recognized a score of the church members of Salem village famous for their especial sanctity. Good old Deacon Gookin had arrived, and waited at the skirts of that venerable saint, his revered pastor. But, irreverently consorting with these grave, reputable, and pious people, these elders of the church, these chaste dames and dewy virgins, there were men of dissolute lives and women of spotted fame, wretches given over to all mean and filthy vice, and suspected even of horrid crimes. It was strange to see that the good shrank not from the wicked, nor were the sinners abashed by the saints. Scattered also among their pale-faced enemies were the Indian priests, or powwows, who had often scared their native forest with more hideous incantations than any known to English witchcraft.

"But where is Faith?" thought Goodman Brown; and, as hope came into his heart, he trembled.

Another verse of the hymn arose, a slow and mournful strain, such as the pious love, but joined to words which expressed all that our nature can conceive of sin, and darkly hinted at far more. Unfathomable to mere mortals is the lore of fiends. Verse after verse was sung; and still the chorus of the desert swelled between like the deepest tone of a mighty organ; and with the final peal of that dreadful anthem there came a sound, as if the roaring wind, the rushing streams, the howling beasts, and every other voice of the unconcerted wilderness were mingling and according with the voice of guilty man in homage to the prince of all. The four blazing pines threw up a loftier flame, and obscurely discovered shapes and visages of horror on the smoke wreaths above the impious assembly. At the same moment the fire on the rock shot redly forth and formed a flowing arch above its base, where now appeared a figure. With reverence be it spoken, the figure bore no slight similitude, both in garb and manner, to some grave divine of the New England churches.

"Bring forth the converts!" cried a voice that echoed through the field and rolled into the forest.

At the word, Goodman Brown stepped forth from the shadow of the trees and approached the congregation, with whom he felt a loathful brotherhood by the sympathy of all that was wicked in his heart. He could have well-nigh sworn that the shape of his own dead father beckoned him to advance, looking downward from a smoke wreath, while a woman, with dim features of despair, threw out her hand to warn him back. Was it his mother? But he had no power to retreat one step, nor to resist, even in thought, when the minister and good old Deacon Gookin seized his arms and led him to the blazing rock. Thither came also the slender form of a veiled female, led between Goody Cloyse, that pious teacher of the catechism, and Martha Carrier, who had received the devil's promise to be queen of hell. A rampant hag was she. And there stood the proselytes beneath the canopy of fire.

"Welcome, my children," said the dark figure, "to the communion of your race. Ye have found thus young your nature and your destiny. My children, look behind you!"

They turned; and flashing forth, as it were, in a sheet of flame, the fiend worshippers were seen; the smile of welcome gleamed darkly on every visage.

"There," resumed the sable form, "are all whom ye have reverenced from youth. Ye deemed them holier than yourselves and shrank from your own sin, contrasting it with their lives of righteousness and prayerful aspirations heavenward. Yet here are they all in my worshipping assembly. This night it shall be granted you to know their secret deeds: how hoary-bearded elders of the church have whispered wanton words to the young maids of their households; how many a woman, eager for widows' weeds, has given her husband a drink at bedtime and let him sleep his last sleep in her bosom; how beardless youths have made haste to inherit their fathers' wealth; and how fair damsels—blush not, sweet ones—have dug little graves in the garden, and bidden me, the sole guest, to an infant's funeral. By the sympathy of your human hearts for sin ye shall scent out all the places—whether in church, bedchamber, street, field, or forest—where crime has been committed, and shall exult to behold the whole earth one stain of guilt, one mighty blood spot. Far more than this. It shall be yours to penetrate, in every bosom, the deep mystery of sin, the fountain of all wicked arts, and which inexhaustibly supplies more evil impulses than human power—than my power at its utmost—can make manifest in deeds. And now, my children, look upon each other."

They did so; and, by the blaze of the hell-kindled torches, the wretched man beheld his Faith, and the wife her husband, trembling before that unhallowed altar.

"Lo, there ye stand, my children," said the figure, in a deep and solemn tone, almost sad with its despairing awfulness, as if his once angelic nature could yet mourn for our miserable race. "Depending upon one another's hearts, ye had still hoped that virtue were not all a dream. Now are ye undeceived. Evil is the nature of mankind. Evil must be your only happiness. Welcome again, my children, to the communion of your race."

"Welcome," repeated the fiend worshippers, in one cry of despair and triumph.

And there they stood, the only pair, as it seemed, who were yet hesitating on the verge of wickedness in this dark world. A basin was hallowed, naturally, in the rock. Did it contain water, reddened by the lurid light? or was it blood? or, perchance, a liquid flame? Herein did the shape of evil dip his hand and prepare to lay the mark of baptism upon their foreheads, that they might be partakers of the mystery of sin, more conscious of the secret guilt of others, both in deed and thought, than they could now be of their own. The husband cast one look at his pale wife, and Faith at him. What polluted wretches would the next glance show them to each other, shuddering alike at what they disclosed and what they saw!

"Faith! Faith!" cried the husband, "look up to heaven, and resist the wicked one."

Whether Faith obeyed he knew not. Hardly had he spoken when he found himself amid calm night and solitude, listening to a roar of the wind which died heavily away through the forest. He staggered against the rock, and felt it chill and damp; while a hanging twig, that had been all on fire, besprinkled his cheek with the coldest dew.

The next morning young Goodman Brown came slowly into the street of Salem village, staring around him like a bewildered man. The good old minister was taking a walk along the graveyard to get an appetite for breakfast and meditate his sermon, and bestowed a blessing, as he passed, on Goodman Brown. He shrank from the venerable saint as if to avoid an anathema. Old Deacon Gookin was at domestic worship, and the holy words of his prayer were heard through the open window. "What God doth the wizard pray to?" quoth Goodman Brown. Goody Cloyse, that excellent old Christian, stood in the early sunshine at her own lattice, catechizing a little girl who had brought her a pint of morning's milk. Goodman Brown snatched away the child as from the grasp of the fiend himself. Turning the corner by the meeting-house, he spied the head of Faith, with the pink ribbons, gazing anxiously forth, and bursting into such joy at sight of him that she skipped along the street and almost kissed her husband before the whole village. But Goodman Brown looked sternly and sadly into her face, and passed on without a greeting.

Had Goodman Brown fallen asleep in the forest and only dreamed a wild dream of a witch-meeting?

Be it so if you will; but, alas! it was a dream of evil omen for young Goodman Brown. A stern, a sad, a darkly meditative, a distrustful, if not a desperate man did he become from the night of that fearful dream. On the Sabbath day, when the congregation were singing a holy psalm, he could not listen because an anthem of sin rushed loudly upon his ear and drowned all the blessed strain. When the minister spoke from the pulpit with power and fervid eloquence, and, with his hand on the open Bible, of the sacred truths of our religion, and of saint-like lives and triumphant deaths, and of future bliss or misery unutterable, then did Goodman Brown turn pale, dreading lest the roof should thunder down upon the gray blasphemer and his hearers. Often, awaking suddenly at midnight, he shrank from the bosom of Faith; and at morning or eventide, when the family knelt down at prayer, he scowled and muttered to himself, and gazed sternly at his wife, and turned away. And when he had lived long, and was borne to his grave a hoary corpse, followed by Faith, an aged woman, and children and grandchildren, a goodly procession, besides neighbors not a few, they carved no hopeful verse upon his tombstone, for his dying hour was gloom.

1835

The Cask of Amontillado

EDGAR ALLAN POE

[1809–1849]

The thousand injuries of Fortunato I had borne as I best could; but when he ventured upon insult, I vowed revenge. You, who so well know the nature of my soul, will not suppose, however, that I gave utterance to a threat. *At length* I would be avenged; this was a point definitely settled—but the very definitiveness with which it was resolved precluded the idea of risk. I must not only punish, but punish with impunity. A wrong is unredressed when retribution overtakes its redresser. It is equally unredressed when the avenger fails to make himself felt as such to him who has done the wrong.

It must be understood, that neither by word nor deed had I given Fortunato cause to doubt my good-will. I continued, as was my wont, to smile in his face, and he did not perceive that my smile *now* was at the thought of his immolation.

He had a weak point—this Fortunato—although in other regards he was a man to be respected and even feared. He prided himself on his connoisseurship in wine. Few Italians have the true virtuoso spirit. For the most part their enthusiasm is adopted to suit the time and opportunity—to practise imposture upon the British and Austrian *millionnaires*. In painting and gemmary Fortunato, like his countrymen, was a quack—but in the matter of old wines he was sincere. In this respect I did not differ from him materially: I was skilful in the Italian vintages myself, and bought largely whenever I could.

It was about dusk, one evening during the supreme madness of the carnival season, that I encountered my friend. He accosted me with excessive warmth, for he had been drinking much. The man wore motley. He had on a tight-fitting parti-striped dress, and his head was surmounted by the conical cap and bells. I was so pleased to see him, that I thought I should never have done wringing his hand.

I said to him: "My dear Fortunato, you are luckily met. How remarkably well you are looking to-day! But I have received a pipe[1] of what passes for Amontillado, and I have my doubts."

"How?" said he. "Amontillado? A pipe? Impossible! And in the middle of the carnival!"

"I have my doubts," I replied; "and I was silly enough to pay the full Amontillado price without consulting you in the matter. You were not to be found, and I was fearful of losing a bargain."

"Amontillado!"

"I have my doubts."

"Amontillado!"

"And I must satisfy them."

"Amontillado!"

"As you are engaged, I am on my way to Luchesi. If any one has a critical turn, it is he. He will tell me——"

"Luchesi cannot tell Amontillado from Sherry."

"And yet some fools will have it that his taste is a match for your own."

"Come, let us go."

"Whither?"

"To your vaults."

"My friend, no; I will not impose upon your good nature. I perceive you have an engagement. Luchesi——"

"I have no engagement;—come."

"My friend, no. It is not the engagement, but the severe cold with which I perceive you are afflicted. The vaults are insufferably damp. They are encrusted with nitre."[2]

"Let us go, nevertheless. The cold is merely nothing. Amontillado! You have been imposed upon. And as for Luchesi, he cannot distinguish Sherry from Amontillado."

Thus speaking, Fortunato possessed himself of my arm. Putting on a mask of black silk, and drawing a *roquelaire*[3] closely about my person, I suffered him to hurry me to my palazzo.

There were no attendants at home; they had absconded to make merry in honor of the time. I had told them that I should not return

[1]A large cask.
[2]Potassium nitrate, or saltpeter; believed at the end of the eighteenth century to be an element in air and plants.
[3]A cloak.

until the morning, and had given them explicit orders not to stir from the house. These orders were sufficient, I well knew, to insure their immediate disappearance, one and all, as soon as my back was turned.

I took from their sconces two flambeaux, and giving one to Fortunato, bowed him through several suites of rooms to the archway that led into the vaults. I passed down a long and winding staircase, requesting him to be cautious as he followed. We came at length to the foot of the descent, and stood together on the damp ground of the catacombs of the Montresors.

The gait of my friend was unsteady, and the bells upon his cap jingled as he strode.

"The pipe?" said he.

"It is farther on," said I; "but observe the white web-work which gleams from these cavern walls."

He turned toward me, and looked into my eyes with two filmy orbs that distilled the rheum of intoxication.

"Nitre?" he asked, at length.

"Nitre," I replied. "How long have you had that cough?"

"Ugh! ugh! ugh!—ugh! ugh! ugh!—ugh! ugh! ugh!—ugh! ugh! ugh!—ugh! ugh! ugh!"

My poor friend found it impossible to reply for many minutes.

"It is nothing," he said, at last.

"Come," I said, with decision, "we will go back; your health is precious. You are rich, respected, admired, beloved; you are happy, as once I was. You are a man to be missed. For me it is no matter. We will go back; you will be ill, and I cannot be responsible. Besides, there is Luchesi —"

"Enough," he said; "the cough is a mere nothing; it will not kill me. I shall not die of a cough."

"True—true," I replied; "and, indeed, I had no intention of alarming you unnecessarily; but you should use all proper caution. A draught of this Medoc will defend us from the damps."

Here I knocked off the neck of a bottle which I drew from a long row of its fellows that lay upon the mould.

"Drink," I said, presenting him the wine.

He raised it to his lips with a leer. He paused and nodded to me familiarly, while his bells jingled.

"I drink," he said, "to the buried that repose around us."

"And I to your long life."

He again took my arm, and we proceeded.

"These vaults," he said, "are extensive."

"The Montresors," I replied, "were a great and numerous family."

"I forget your arms."

"A huge human foot d'or,[4] in a field azure; the foot crushes a serpent rampant whose fangs are imbedded in the heel."

"And the motto?"

"Nemo me impune lacessit."[5]

"Good!" he said.

The wine sparkled in his eyes and the bells jingled. My own fancy grew warm with the Medoc. We had passed through walls of piled bones, with casks and puncheons intermingling into the inmost recesses of the catacombs. I paused again, and this time I made bold to seize Fortunato by an arm above the elbow.

"The nitre!" I said; "see, it increases. It hangs like moss upon the vaults. We are below the river's bed. The drops of moisture trickle among the bones. Come, we will go back ere it is too late. Your cough——"

"It is nothing," he said; "let us go on. But first, another draught of the Medoc."

I broke and reached him a flagon of De Grâve. He emptied it at a breath. His eyes flashed with a fierce light. He laughed and threw the bottle upward with a gesticulation I did not understand.

I looked at him in surprise. He repeated the movement—a grotesque one.

"You do not comprehend?" he said.

"Not I," I replied.

"Then you are not of the brotherhood."

"How?"

"You are not of the masons."

"Yes, yes," I said; "yes, yes."

"You? Impossible! A mason?"

"A mason," I replied.

"A sign," he said.

"It is this," I answered, producing a trowel from beneath the folds of my *roquelaire*.

"You jest," he exclaimed, recoiling a few paces. "But let us proceed to the Amontillado."

[4]Of gold.

[5]"No one wounds me with impunity"; the motto of the Scottish royal arms.

"Be it so," I said, replacing the tool beneath the cloak, and again offering him my arm. He leaned upon it heavily. We continued our route in search of the Amontillado. We passed through a range of low arches, descended, passed on, and descending again, arrived at a deep crypt, in which the foulness of the air caused our flambeaux rather to glow than flame.

At the most remote end of the crypt there appeared another less spacious. Its walls had been lined with human remains, piled to the vault overhead, in the fashion of the great catacombs of Paris. Three sides of this interior crypt were still ornamented in this manner. From the fourth the bones had been thrown down, and lay promiscuously upon the earth, forming at one point a mound of some size. Within the wall thus exposed by the displacing of the bones, we perceived a still interior recess, in depth about four feet, in width three, in height six or seven. It seemed to have been constructed for no especial use within itself, but formed merely the interval between two of the colossal supports of the roof of the catacombs, and was backed by one of their circumscribing walls of solid granite.

It was in vain that Fortunato, uplifting his dull torch, endeavored to pry into the depth of the recess. Its termination the feeble light did not enable us to see.

"Proceed," I said; "herein is the Amontillado. As for Luchesi——"

"He is an ignoramus," interrupted my friend, as he stepped unsteadily forward, while I followed immediately at his heels. In an instant he had reached the extremity of the niche, and finding his progress arrested by the rock, stood stupidly bewildered. A moment more and I had fettered him to the granite. In its surface were two iron staples, distant from each other about two feet, horizontally. From one of these depended a short chain, from the other a padlock. Throwing the links about his waist, it was but the work of a few seconds to secure it. He was too much astounded to resist. Withdrawing the key I stepped back from the recess.

"Pass your hand," I said, "over the wall; you cannot help feeling the nitre. Indeed it is *very* damp. Once more let me *implore* you to return. No? Then I must positively leave you. But I must first render you all the little attentions in my power."

"The Amontillado!" ejaculated my friend, not yet recovered from his astonishment.

"True," I replied; "the Amontillado."

As I said these words I busied myself among the pile of bones of which I have before spoken. Throwing them aside, I soon uncovered a quantity of building stone and mortar. With these materials and with the aid of my trowel, I began vigorously to wall up the entrance of the niche.

I had scarcely laid the first tier of the masonry when I discovered that the intoxication of Fortunato had in a great measure worn off. The earliest indication I had of this was a low moaning cry from the depth of the recess. It was *not* the cry of a drunken man. There was then a long and obstinate silence. I laid the second tier, and the third, and the fourth; and then I heard the furious vibrations of the chain. The noise lasted for several minutes, during which, that I might hearken to it with the more satisfaction, I ceased my labors and sat down upon the bones. When at last the clanking subsided, I resumed the trowel, and finished without interruption the fifth, the sixth, and the seventh tier. The wall was now nearly upon a level with my breast. I again paused, and holding the flambeaux over the masonwork, threw a few feeble rays upon the figure within.

A succession of loud and shrill screams, bursting suddenly from the throat of the chained form, seemed to thrust me violently back. For a brief moment I hesitated—I trembled. Unsheathing my rapier, I began to grope with it about the recess; but the thought of an instant reassured me. I placed my hand upon the solid fabric of the catacombs, and felt satisfied. I reapproached the wall. I replied to the yells of him who clamored. I reechoed—I aided—I surpassed them in volume and in strength. I did this, and the clamorer grew still.

It was now midnight, and my task was drawing to a close. I had completed the eighth, the ninth, and the tenth tier. I had finished a portion of the last and the eleventh; there remained but a single stone to be fitted and plastered in. I struggled with its weight; I placed it partially in its destined position. But now there came from out the niche a low laugh that erected the hairs upon my head. It was succeeded by a sad voice, which I had difficulty in recognizing as that of the noble Fortunato. The voice said—

"Ha! ha! ha!—he! he!—a very good joke indeed—an excellent jest. We will have many a rich laugh about it at the palazzo—he! he! he!—over our wine—he! he! he!"

"The Amontillado!" I said.

"He! he! he!—he! he! he!—yes, the Amontillado. But is it not getting late? Will not they be awaiting us at the palazzo, the Lady Fortunato and the rest? Let us be gone."

"Yes," I said, "let us be gone."

"For the love of God, Montresor!"

"Yes," I said, "for the love of God!"

But to these words I hearkened in vain for a reply. I grew impatient. I called aloud:

"Fortunato!"

No answer. I called again:

"Fortunato!"

No answer still, I thrust a torch through the remaining aperture and let it fall within. There came forth in return only a jingling of the bells. My heart grew sick—on account of the dampness of the catacombs. I hastened to make an end of my labor. I forced the last stone into its position; I plastered it up. Against the new masonry I reerected the old rampart of bones. For the half of a century no mortal has disturbed them. *In pace requiescat!*[6]

1846

[6]May he rest in peace (Latin).

An Occurrence at Owl Creek Bridge

AMBROSE BIERCE

[1842–1914]

I

A man stood upon a railroad bridge in Northern Alabama, looking down into the swift waters twenty feet below. The man's hands were behind his back, the wrists bound with a cord. A rope loosely encircled his neck. It was attached to a stout cross-timber above his head, and the slack fell to the level of his knees. Some loose boards laid upon the sleepers supporting the metals of the railway supplied a footing for him and his executioners—two private soldiers of the Federal army, directed by a sergeant, who in civil life may have been a deputy sheriff. At a short remove upon the same temporary platform was an officer in the uniform of his rank, armed. He was a captain. A sentinel at each end of the bridge stood with his rifle in the position known as "support," that is to say, vertical in front of the left shoulder, the hammer resting on the forearm thrown straight across the chest—a formal and unnatural position, enforcing an erect carriage of the body. It did not appear to be the duty of these two men to know what was occurring at the centre of the bridge; they merely blockaded the two ends of the foot plank which traversed it.

Beyond one of the sentinels nobody was in sight; the railroad ran straight away into a forest for a hundred yards, then, curving, was lost to view. Doubtless there was an outpost further along. The other bank of the stream was open ground—a gentle acclivity crowned with a stockade of vertical tree trunks, loop-holed for rifles, with a single embrasure through which protruded the muzzle of a brass cannon commanding the bridge. Midway of the slope between bridge and fort were the spectators—a single company of infantry in line, at "parade rest," the butts of the rifles on the ground, the barrels inclining slightly backward against the right shoulder, the hands crossed upon the stock. A lieutenant stood at the right of the line, the point of his sword upon the ground, his left hand resting upon his right. Excepting the group of four at the centre of the bridge not a man moved. The company faced the bridge, staring stonily, motionless. The sentinels, facing the banks of the stream, might have been statues to adorn the bridge. The captain stood with folded arms, silent, observing the work of his subordinates but making no sign. Death is a dignitary who, when he comes announced, is to be received with formal manifestations of respect, even by those most familiar with him. In the code of military etiquette silence and fixity are forms of deference.

The man who was engaged in being hanged was apparently about thirty-five years of age. He was a civilian, if one might judge from his dress, which was that of a planter. His features were good—a straight nose, firm mouth, broad forehead, from which his long, dark hair was combed straight back, falling behind his ears to the collar of his well-fitted frock coat. He wore a moustache and pointed beard, but no whiskers; his eyes were large and dark grey and had a kindly expression which one would hardly have expected in one whose neck was in the hemp. Evidently this was no vulgar assassin. The liberal military code makes provision for hanging many kinds of people, and gentlemen are not excluded.

The preparations being complete, the two private soldiers stepped aside and each drew away the plank upon which he had been standing. The sergeant turned to the captain, saluted and placed himself immediately behind that officer, who in turn moved apart one pace. These movements left the condemned man and the sergeant standing on the two ends of the same plank, which spanned three of the cross-ties of the bridge. The end upon which the civilian stood almost, but not quite, reached a fourth. This plank had been held in place by the weight of the captain; it was now held by that of the sergeant. At a signal from the former, the latter would step aside, the plank would tilt and the condemned man go down between two ties. The arrangement commended itself to his judgment as simple and effective. His face had not been covered nor his eyes bandaged. He looked a moment at his "unsteadfast footing," then let his gaze wander to the swirling water of the stream racing madly beneath his feet. A piece of dancing driftwood caught his attention and his eyes followed it down the current. How slowly it appeared to move! What a sluggish stream!

He closed his eyes in order to fix his last thoughts upon his wife and children. The water, touched to gold by the early sun, the brooding mists under the banks at some distance down the stream, the fort, the soldiers, the piece of driftwood—all had distracted him. And now he became conscious of a new disturbance. Striking through the thought of his dear ones was a sound which he could neither ignore nor understand, a sharp, distinct, metallic percussion like the stroke of a blacksmith's hammer upon the anvil; it had the same ringing quality. He wondered what it was, and whether immeasurably distant or near by—it seemed both. Its recurrence was regular, but as slow as the tolling of a death knell. He awaited each stroke with impatience and—he knew not why—apprehension. The intervals of silence grew progressively longer; the delays became maddening. With their greater infrequency the sounds increased in strength and sharpness. They hurt his ear like the thrust of a knife; he feared he would shriek. What he heard was the ticking of his watch.

He unclosed his eyes and saw again the water below him. "If I could free my hands," he thought, "I might throw off the noose and spring into the stream. By diving I could evade the bullets, and, swimming vigorously, reach the bank, take to the woods, and get away home. My home, thank God, is as yet outside their lines; my wife and little ones are still beyond the invader's farthest advance."

As these thoughts, which have here to be set down in words, were flashed into the doomed man's brain rather than evolved from it, the captain nodded to the sergeant. The sergeant stepped aside.

II

Peyton Farquhar was a well-to-do planter, of an old and highly respected Alabama family. Being a slave owner, and, like other slave owners, a politician, he was naturally an original secessionist and ardently devoted to the Southern cause. Circumstances of an imperious nature which it is unnecessary to relate here, had prevented him from taking service with the gallant army which had fought the disastrous campaigns ending with the fall of Corinth,[1] and he chafed under the inglorious restraint, longing for the release of his energies, the larger life of the soldier, the opportunity for distinction. That opportunity, he felt, would come, as it comes to all in war time. Meanwhile he did what

[1]The Battle of Corinth, Mississippi (October 3–4, 1862) ended in a decisive victory for the Union forces over the Confederate forces.

he could. No service was too humble for him to perform in aid of the South, no adventure too perilous for him to undertake if consistent with the character of a civilian who was at heart a soldier, and who in good faith and without too much qualification assented to at least a part of the frankly villainous dictum that all is fair in love and war.

One evening while Farquhar and his wife were sitting on a rustic bench near the entrance to his grounds, a grey-clad soldier rode up to the gate and asked for a drink of water. Mrs. Farquhar was only too happy to serve him with her own white hands. While she was gone to fetch the water, her husband approached the dusty horseman and inquired eagerly for news from the front.

"The Yanks are repairing the railroads," said the man, "and are getting ready for another advance. They have reached the Owl Creek bridge, put it in order, and built a stockade on the other bank. The commandant has issued an order, which is posted everywhere, declaring that any civilian caught interfering with the railroad, its bridges, tunnels, or trains, will be summarily hanged. I saw the order."

"How far is it to the Owl Creek bridge?" Farquhar asked.

"About thirty miles."

"Is there no force on this side the creek?"

"Only a picket post half a mile out, on the railroad, and a single sentinel at this end of the bridge."

"Suppose a man—a civilian and student of hanging—should elude the picket post and perhaps get the better of the sentinel," said Farquhar, smiling, "what could he accomplish?"

The soldier reflected. "I was there a month ago," he replied. "I observed that the flood of last winter had lodged a great quantity of driftwood against the wooden pier at this end of the bridge. It is now dry and would burn like tow."

The lady had now brought the water, which the soldier drank. He thanked her ceremoniously, bowed to her husband, and rode away. An hour later, after nightfall, he repassed the plantation, going northward in the direction from which he had come. He was a Federal scout.

III

As Peyton Farquhar fell straight downward through the bridge, he lost consciousness and was as one already dead. From this state he was awakened—ages later, it seemed to him—by the pain of a sharp pressure upon his throat, followed by a sense of suffocation. Keen, poignant agonies seemed to shoot from his neck downward through every fibre of his body and limbs. These pains appeared to flash along well-defined lines of ramification, and to beat with an inconceivably rapid periodicity. They seemed like streams of pulsating fire heating him to an intolerable temperature. As to his head, he was conscious of nothing but a feeling of fullness—of congestion. These sensations were unaccompanied by thought. The intellectual part of his nature was already effaced; he had power only to feel, and feeling was torment. He was conscious of motion. Encompassed in a luminous cloud, of which he was now merely the fiery heart, without material substance, he swung through unthinkable arcs of oscillation, like a vast pendulum. Then all at once, with terrible suddenness, the light about him shot upward with the noise of a loud splash; a frightful roaring was in his ears, and all was cold and dark. The power of thought was restored; he knew that the rope had broken and he had fallen into the stream. There was no additional strangulation; the noose about his neck was already suffocating him, and kept the water from his lungs. To die of hanging at the bottom of a river—the idea seemed to him ludicrous. He opened his eyes in the blackness and saw above him a gleam of light, but how distant, how inaccessible! He was still sinking, for the light became fainter and fainter until it was a mere glimmer. Then it began to grow and brighten, and he knew that he was rising toward the surface—knew it with reluctance, for he was now very comfortable. "To be hanged and drowned," he thought, "that is not so bad; but I do not wish to be shot. No; I will not be shot; that is not fair."

He was not conscious of an effort, but a sharp pain in his wrist apprised him that he was trying to free his hands. He gave the struggle his attention, as an idler might observe the feat of a juggler, without interest in the outcome. What splendid effort!—what magnificent, what superhuman strength! Ah, that was a fine endeavor! Bravo! The cord fell away; his arms parted and floated upward, the hands dimly seen on each side in the growing light. He watched them with a new interest as first one and then the other pounced upon the noose at his neck. They tore it away and thrust it fiercely aside, its undulations resembling those of a water-snake. "Put it back, put it back!" He thought he shouted these words to his hands, for the undoing of the noose had been succeeded by the direst pang which he had yet experienced. His neck ached horribly; his brain was on fire; his heart, which had been fluttering faintly, gave a great leap, trying to force itself out at his mouth. His whole body was racked and wrenched with an insupportable anguish! But his disobedient hands gave no heed to the command. They beat the water vigorously with quick, downward strokes, forcing him to the surface. He felt his head emerge; his eyes were blinded by the sunlight; his chest expanded convulsively, and with a supreme and crowning agony his lungs engulfed a great draught of air, which instantly he expelled in a shriek!

He was now in full possession of his physical senses. They were, indeed, preternaturally keen and alert. Something in the awful disturbance of his organic system had so exalted and refined them that they made record of things never before perceived. He felt the ripples upon his face and heard their separate sounds as they struck. He looked at the forest on the bank of the stream, saw the individual trees, the leaves and the veining of each leaf—saw the very insects upon them, the locusts, the brilliant-bodied flies, the grey spiders stretching their webs from twig to twig. He noted the prismatic colors in all the dew-drops upon a million blades of grass. The humming of the gnats that danced above the eddies of the stream, the beating of the dragon flies' wings, the strokes of the water spiders' legs, like oars which had lifted their boat—all these made audible music. A fish slid along beneath his eyes and he heard the rush of its body parting the water.

He had come to the surface facing down the stream; in a moment the visible world seemed to wheel slowly round, himself the pivotal point, and he saw the bridge, the fort, the soldiers upon the bridge, the captain, the sergeant, the two privates, his executioners. They were in silhouette against the blue sky. They shouted and gesticulated, pointing at him; the captain had drawn his pistol, but did not fire; the others were unarmed. Their movements were grotesque and horrible, their forms gigantic.

Suddenly he heard a sharp report and something struck the water smartly within a few inches of his head, spattering his face with spray. He heard a second report, and saw one of the sentinels with his rifle at his shoulder, a light cloud of blue smoke rising from the muzzle. The man in the water saw the eye of the man on the bridge gazing into his own through the sights of the rifle. He observed that it was a grey eye, and remembered having read that grey eyes were keenest and that all famous marksmen had them. Nevertheless, this one had missed.

A counter swirl had caught Farquhar and turned him half round; he was again looking into the forest on the bank opposite the fort. The sound of a clear, high voice in a monotonous singsong now rang out behind him and came across the water with a distinctness that pierced and subdued all other sounds, even the beating of the ripples in his ears. Although no soldier, he had frequented camps enough to know the dread significance of that deliberate, drawling, aspirated chant; the lieutenant on shore was taking a part in the morning's work. How coldly and pitilessly—with what an even, calm intonation, presaging and enforcing tranquility in the men—with what accurately-measured intervals fell those cruel words:

"Attention, company. . . . Shoulder arms. . . . Ready. . . . Aim. . . . Fire."

Farquhar dived—dived as deeply as he could. The water roared in his ears like the voice of Niagara, yet he heard the dulled thunder of the volley, and rising again toward the surface, met shining bits of metal, singularly flattened, oscillating slowly downward. Some of them touched him on the face and hands, then fell away, continuing their descent. One lodged between his collar and neck; it was uncomfortably warm, and he snatched it out.

As he rose to the surface, gasping for breath, he saw that he had been a long time under water; he was perceptibly farther down stream—nearer to safety. The soldiers had almost finished reloading; the metal ramrods flashed all at once in the sunshine as they were drawn from the barrels, turned in the air, and thrust into their sockets. The two sentinels fired again, independently and ineffectually.

The hunted man saw all this over his shoulder; he was now swimming vigorously with the current. His brain was as energetic as his arms and legs; he thought with the rapidity of lightning.

"The officer," he reasoned, "will not make the martinet's error a second time. It is as easy to dodge a volley as a single shot. He has probably already given the command to fire at will. God help me, I cannot dodge them all!"

An appalling splash within two yards of him, followed by a loud rushing sound, *diminuendo*, which seemed to travel back through the air to the fort and died in an explosion which stirred the very river to its deeps! A rising sheet of water, which curved over him, fell down upon him, blinded him, strangled him! The cannon had taken a hand in the game. As he shook his head free from the commotion of the smitten water, he heard the deflected shot humming through the air ahead, and in an instant it was cracking and smashing the branches in the forest beyond.

"They will not do that again," he thought; "the next time they will use a charge of grape. I must keep my eye upon the gun; the smoke will apprise me—the report arrives too late; it lags behind the missile. It is a good gun."

Suddenly he felt himself whirled round and round—spinning like a top. The water, the banks, the forest, the now distant bridge, fort, and men—all were commingled and blurred. Objects were represented by their colors only; circular horizontal streaks of color—that was all he saw. He had been caught in a vortex and was being whirled on with a velocity of advance and gyration which made him giddy and sick. In a few moments he was flung upon the gravel at the foot of the left bank of the stream—the southern bank—and behind a projecting point which concealed him from his enemies. The sudden arrest of his motion, the abrasion of one of his hands on the gravel, restored him and he wept with delight. He dug his fingers into the sand, threw it over himself in handfuls and audibly blessed it. It looked like gold, like diamonds, rubies, emeralds; he could think of nothing beautiful which it did not resemble. The trees upon the bank were giant garden plants; he noted a definite order in their arrangement, inhaled the fragrance of their blooms. A strange, roseate light shone through the spaces among their trunks, and the wind made in their branches the music of æolian harps. He had no wish to perfect his escape, was content to remain in that enchanting spot until retaken.

A whizz and rattle of grapeshot among the branches high above his head roused him from his dream. The baffled cannoneer had fired him a random farewell. He sprang to his feet, rushed up the sloping bank, and plunged into the forest.

All that day he travelled, laying his course by the rounding sun. The forest seemed interminable; nowhere did he discover a break in it, not even a woodman's road. He had not known that he lived in so wild a region. There was something uncanny in the revelation.

By nightfall he was fatigued, footsore, famishing. The thought of his wife and children urged him on. At last he found a road which led him in what he knew to be the right direction. It was as wide and straight as a city street, yet it seemed untravelled. No fields bordered it, no dwelling anywhere. Not so much as the barking of a dog suggested human habitation. The black bodies of the great trees formed a straight wall on both sides, terminating on the horizon in a point, like a diagram in a lesson in perspective. Overhead, as he looked up through this rift in the wood, shone great golden stars looking unfamiliar and grouped in strange constellations. He was sure they were arranged in some order which had a secret and malign significance. The wood on either side was full of singular noises, among which—once, twice, and again—he distinctly heard whispers in an unknown tongue.

His neck was in pain, and, lifting his hand to it, he found it horribly swollen. He knew that it had a circle of black where the rope had bruised it. His eyes felt congested; he could no longer close them. His tongue was swollen with thirst; he relieved its fever by thrusting it forward from between his teeth into the cool air. How softly the turf had carpeted the untravelled avenue! He could no longer feel the roadway beneath his feet!

Doubtless, despite his suffering, he fell asleep while walking, for now he sees another scene—perhaps he has merely recovered from a delirium. He stands at the gate of his own home. All is as he left it, and all bright and beautiful in the morning sunshine. He must have travelled the entire night. As he pushes open the gate and passes up the wide white walk, he sees a flutter of female garments; his wife, looking fresh and cool and sweet, steps down from the verandah to meet him. At the bottom of the steps she stands waiting, with a smile of ineffable joy, an attitude of matchless grace and dignity. Ah, how beautiful she is! He springs forward with extended arms. As he is about to clasp her, he feels a stunning blow upon the back of the neck; a blinding white light blazes all about him, with a sound like the shock of a cannon—then all is darkness and silence!

Peyton Farquhar was dead; his body, with a broken neck, swung gently from side to side beneath the timbers of the Owl Creek bridge.

1891

The Story of an Hour

KATE CHOPIN

[1851–1904]

Knowing that Mrs. Mallard was afflicted with a heart trouble, great care was taken to break to her as gently as possible the news of her husband's death.

It was her sister Josephine who told her, in broken sentences; veiled hints that revealed in half concealing. Her husband's friend Richards was there, too, near her. It was he who had been in the newspaper office when intelligence of the railroad disaster was received, with Brently Mallard's name leading the list of "killed." He had only taken the time to assure himself of its truth by a second telegram, and had hastened to forestall any less careful, less tender friend in bearing the sad message.

She did not hear the story as many women have heard the same, with a paralyzed inability to accept its significance. She wept at once, with sudden, wild abandonment, in her sister's arms. When the storm of grief had spent itself she went away to her room alone. She would have no one follow her.

There stood, facing the open window, a comfortable, roomy armchair. Into this she sank, pressed down by a physical exhaustion that haunted her body and seemed to reach into her soul.

She could see in the open square before her house the tops of trees that were all aquiver with the new spring life. The delicious breath of rain was in the air. In the street below a peddler was crying his wares. The notes of a distant song which some one was singing reached her faintly, and countless sparrows were twittering in the eaves.

There were patches of blue sky showing here and there through the clouds that had met and piled one above the other in the west facing her window.

She sat with her head thrown back upon the cushion of the chair, quite motionless, except when a sob came up into her throat and shook her, as a child who had cried itself to sleep continues to sob in its dreams.

She was young, with a fair, calm face, whose lines bespoke repression and even a certain strength. But now there was a dull stare in her eyes, whose gaze was fixed away off yonder on one of those patches of blue sky. It was not a glance of reflection, but rather indicated a suspension of intelligent thought.

There was something coming to her and she was waiting for it, fearfully. What was it? She did not know; it was too subtle and elusive to name. But she felt it, creeping out of the sky, reaching toward her through the sounds, the scents, the color that filled the air.

Now her bosom rose and fell tumultuously. She was beginning to recognize this thing that was approaching to possess her, and she was striving to beat it back with her will—as powerless as her two white slender hands would have been.

When she abandoned herself a little whispered word escaped her slightly parted lips. She said it over and over under her breath: "free, free, free!" The vacant stare and the look of terror that had followed it went from her eyes. They stayed keen and bright. Her pulses beat fast, and the coursing blood warmed and relaxed every inch of her body.

She did not stop to ask if it were or were not a monstrous joy that held her. A clear and exalted perception enabled her to dismiss the suggestion as trivial.

She knew that she would weep again when she saw the kind, tender hands folded in death; the face that had never looked save with love upon her, fixed and gray and dead. But she saw beyond that bitter moment a long procession of years to come that would belong to her absolutely. And she opened and spread her arms out to them in welcome.

There would be no one to live for her during those coming years: she would live for herself. There would be no powerful will bending hers in that blind persistence with which men and women believe they have a right to impose a private will upon a fellow-creature. A kind intention or a cruel intention made the act seem no less a crime as she looked upon it in that brief moment of illumination.

And yet she had loved him—sometimes. Often she had not. What did it matter! What could love, the unsolved mystery, count for in face of this possession of self-assertion which she suddenly recognized as the strongest impulse of her being!

"Free! Body and soul free!" she kept whispering.

Josephine was kneeling before the closed door with her lips to the keyhole, imploring for admission. "Louise, open the door! I beg; open the door—you will make yourself ill. What are you doing, Louise? For heaven's sake open the door."

"Go away. I am not making myself ill." No; she was drinking in a very elixir of life through that open window.

Her fancy was running riot along those days ahead of her. Spring days, and summer days, and all sorts of days that would be her own. She breathed a quick prayer that life might be long. It was only yesterday she had thought with a shudder that life might be long.

She arose at length and opened the door to her sister's importunities. There was a feverish triumph in her eyes, and she carried herself unwittingly like a goddess of Victory. She clasped her sister's waist, and together they descended the stairs. Richards stood waiting for them at the bottom.

Some one was opening the front door with a latchkey. It was Brently Mallard who entered, a little travel-stained, composedly carrying his gripsack and umbrella. He had been far from the scene of accident, and did not even know there had been one. He stood amazed at Josephine's piercing cry; at Richards' quick motion to screen him from the view of his wife.

But Richards was too late.

When the doctors came they said she had died of heart disease—of joy that kills.

1894

The Lady with the Dog

ANTON CHEKHOV

[1860–1904]

I

It was said that a new person had appeared on the sea-front: a lady with a little dog. Dmitri Dmitritch Gurov, who had by then been a fortnight at Yalta, and so was fairly at home there, had begun to take an interest in new arrivals. Sitting in Verney's pavilion, he saw, walking on the sea-front, a fair-haired young lady of medium height, wearing a *béret*; a white Pomeranian dog was running behind her.

And afterwards he met her in the public gardens and in the square several times a day. She was walking alone, always wearing the same *béret*, and always with the same white dog; no one knew who she was, and every one called her simply "the lady with the dog."

"If she is here alone without a husband or friends, it wouldn't be amiss to make her acquaintance," Gurov reflected.

He was under forty, but he had a daughter already twelve years old, and two sons at school. He had been married young, when he was a student in his second year, and by now his wife seemed half as old again as he. She was a tall, erect woman with dark eyebrows, staid and dignified, and, as she said of herself, intellectual. She read a great deal, used phonetic spelling, called her husband, not Dmitri, but Dimitri, and he secretly considered her unintelligent, narrow, inelegant, was afraid of her, and did not like to be at home. He had begun being unfaithful to her long ago—had been unfaithful to her often, and, probably on that account, almost always spoke ill of women, and when they were talked about in his presence, used to call them "the lower race."

Translated by Constance Garnett, 1899.

It seemed to him that he had been so schooled by bitter experience that he might call them what he liked, and yet he could not get on for two days together without "the lower race." In the society of men he was bored and not himself, with them he was cold and uncommunicative; but when he was in the company of women he felt free, and knew what to say to them and how to behave; and he was at ease with them even when he was silent. In his appearance, in his character, in his whole nature, there was something attractive and elusive which allured women and disposed them in his favour; he knew that, and some force seemed to draw him, too, to them.

Experience often repeated, truly bitter experience, had taught him long ago that with decent people, especially Moscow people—always slow to move and irresolute—every intimacy, which at first so agreeably diversifies life and appears a light and charming adventure, inevitably grows into a regular problem of extreme intricacy, and in the long run the situation becomes unbearable. But at every fresh meeting with an interesting woman this experience seemed to slip out of his memory, and he was eager for life, and everything seemed simple and amusing.

One evening he was dining in the gardens, and the lady in the *béret* came up slowly to take the next table. Her expression, her gait, her dress, and the way she did her hair told him that she was a lady, that she was married, that she was in Yalta for the first time and alone, and that she was dull there. . . . The stories told of the immorality in such places as Yalta are to a great extent untrue; he despised them, and knew that such stories were for the most part made up by persons who would themselves have been glad to sin if they had been able; but when the lady sat down at the next table three paces from him, he remembered these tales of easy conquests, of trips to the mountains, and the tempting thought of a swift, fleeting love affair, a romance with an unknown woman, whose name he did not know, suddenly took possession of him.

He beckoned coaxingly to the Pomeranian, and when the dog came up to him he shook his finger at it. The Pomeranian growled: Gurov shook his finger at it again.

The lady looked at him and at once dropped her eyes.

"He doesn't bite," she said, and blushed.

"May I give him a bone?" he asked; and when she nodded he asked courteously, "Have you been long in Yalta?"

"Five days."

"And I have already dragged out a fortnight here."

There was a brief silence.

"Time goes fast, and yet it is so dull here!" she said, not looking at him.

"That's only the fashion to say it is dull here. A provincial will live in Belyov or Zhidra and not be dull, and when he comes here it's 'Oh, the dullness! Oh, the dust!' One would think he came from Grenada."

She laughed. Then both continued eating in silence, like strangers, but after dinner they walked side by side; and there sprang up between them the light jesting conversation of people who are free and satisfied, to whom it does not matter where they go or what they talk about. They walked and talked of the strange light on the sea: the water was of a soft warm lilac hue, and there was a golden streak from the moon upon it. They talked of how sultry it was after a hot day. Gurov told her that he came from Moscow, that he had taken his degree in Arts, but had a post in a bank; that he had trained as an opera-singer, but had given it up, that he owned two houses in Moscow. . . . And from her he learnt that she had grown up in Petersburg, but had lived in S—— since her marriage two years before, that she was staying another month in Yalta, and that her husband, who needed a holiday too, might perhaps come and fetch her. She was not sure whether her husband had a post in a Crown Department or under the Provincial Council—and was amused by her own ignorance. And Gurov learnt, too, that she was called Anna Sergeyevna.

Afterwards he thought about her in his room at the hotel—thought she would certainly meet him next day; it would be sure to happen. As he got into bed he thought how lately she had been a girl at school, doing lessons like his own daughter; he recalled the diffidence, the angularity, that was still manifest in her laugh and her manner of talking with a stranger. This must have been the first time in her life she had been alone in surroundings in which she was followed, looked at, and spoken to merely from a secret motive which she could hardly fail to guess. He recalled her slender, delicate neck, her lovely grey eyes.

"There's something pathetic about her, anyway," he thought, and fell asleep.

II

A week had passed since they had made acquaintance. It was a holiday. It was sultry indoors, while in the street the wind whirled the dust round and round, and blew people's hats off. It was a thirsty day, and Gurov often went into the pavilion, and pressed Anna Sergeyevna to have syrup and water or an ice. One did not know what to do with oneself.

In the evening when the wind had dropped a little, they went out on the groyne[1] to see the steamer come in. There were a great many people walking about the harbour; they had gathered to welcome some one, bringing bouquets. And two peculiarities of a well-dressed Yalta crowd were very conspicuous: the elderly ladies were dressed like young ones, and there were great numbers of generals.

Owing to the roughness of the sea, the steamer arrived late, after the sun had set, and it was a long time turning about before it reached the groyne. Anna Sergeyevna looked through her lorgnette at the steamer and the passengers as though looking for acquaintances, and when she turned to Gurov her eyes were shining. She talked a great deal and asked disconnected questions, forgetting next moment what she had asked; then she dropped her lorgnette in the crush.

The festive crowd began to disperse; it was too dark to see people's faces. The wind had completely dropped, but Gurov and Anna Sergeyevna still stood as though waiting to see some one else come from the steamer. Anna Sergeyevna was silent now, and sniffed the flowers without looking at Gurov.

"The weather is better this evening," he said. "Where shall we go now? Shall we drive somewhere?"

She made no answer.

Then he looked at her intently, and all at once put his arm round her and kissed her on the lips, and breathed in the moisture and the fragrance of the flowers; and he immediately looked round him, anxiously wondering whether any one had seen them.

"Let us go to your hotel," he said softly. And both walked quickly.

The room was close and smelt of the scent she had bought at the Japanese shop. Gurov looked at her and thought: "What different people one meets in the world!" From the past he preserved memories of careless, good-natured women, who loved cheerfully and were grateful to him for the happiness he gave them, however brief it might be; and of women like his wife who loved without any genuine feeling, with superfluous phrases, affectedly, hysterically, with an expression that suggested that it was not love nor passion, but

[1]A wall or jetty built out from a shore to control erosion.

something more significant; and of two or three others, very beautiful, cold women, on whose faces he had caught a glimpse of a rapacious expression—an obstinate desire to snatch from life more than it could give, and these were capricious, unreflecting, domineering, unintelligent women not in their first youth, and when Gurov grew cold to them their beauty excited his hatred, and the lace on their linen seemed to him like scales.

But in this case there was still the diffidence, the angularity of inexperienced youth, an awkward feeling; and there was a sense of consternation as though some one had suddenly knocked at the door. The attitude of Anna Sergeyevna—"the lady with the dog"—to what had happened was somehow peculiar, very grave, as though it were her fall—so it seemed, and it was strange and inappropriate. Her face dropped and faded, and on both sides of it her long hair hung down mournfully; she mused in a dejected attitude like "the woman who was a sinner" in an old-fashioned picture.

"It's wrong," she said. "You will be the first to despise me now."

There was a water-melon on the table. Gurov cut himself a slice and began eating it without haste. There followed at least half an hour of silence.

Anna Sergeyevna was touching; there was about her the purity of a good, simple woman who had seen little of life. The solitary candle burning on the table threw a faint light on her face, yet it was clear that she was very unhappy.

"How could I despise you?" asked Gurov. "You don't know what you are saying."

"God forgive me," she said, and her eyes filled with tears. "It's awful."

"You seem to feel you need to be forgiven."

"Forgiven? No. I am a bad, low woman; I despise myself and don't attempt to justify myself. It's not my husband but myself I have deceived. And not only just now; I have been deceiving myself for a long time. My husband may be a good, honest man, but he is a flunkey! I don't know what he does there, what his work is, but I know he is a flunkey! I was twenty when I was married to him. I have been tormented by curiosity; I wanted something better. 'There must be a different sort of life,' I said to myself. I wanted to live! To live, to live! . . . I was fired by curiosity . . . you don't understand it, but, I swear to God, I could not control myself; something happened to me: I could not be restrained. I told my husband I was ill, and came here. . . . And here I have been walking about as though I were dazed, like a mad creature; . . . and now I have become a vulgar, contemptible woman whom any one may despise."

Gurov felt bored already, listening to her. He was irritated by the naïve tone, by this remorse, so unexpected and inopportune; but for the tears in her eyes, he might have thought she was jesting or playing a part.

"I don't understand," he said softly. "What is it you want?"

She hid her face on his breast and pressed close to him.

"Believe me, believe me, I beseech you . . ." she said. "I love a pure, honest life, and sin is loathsome to me. I don't know what I am doing. Simple people say: 'The Evil One has beguiled me.' And I may say of myself now that the Evil One has beguiled me."

"Hush, hush! . . ." he muttered.

He looked at her fixed, scared eyes, kissed her, talked softly and affectionately, and by degrees she was comforted, and her gaiety returned; they both began laughing.

Afterwards when they went out there was not a soul on the sea-front. The town with its cypresses had quite a deathlike air, but the sea still broke noisily on the shore; a single barge was rocking on the waves, and a lantern was blinking sleepily on it.

They found a cab and drove to Oreanda.

"I found out your surname in the hall just now: it was written on the board—Von Diderits," said Gurov. "Is your husband a German?"

"No; I believe his grandfather was a German, but he is an Orthodox Russian himself."

At Oreanda they sat on a seat not far from the church, looked down at the sea, and were silent. Yalta was hardly visible through the morning mist; white clouds stood motionless on the mountain-tops. The leaves did not stir on the trees, grasshoppers chirruped, and the monotonous hollow sound of the sea rising up from below, spoke of the peace, of the eternal sleep awaiting us. So it must have sounded when there was no Yalta, no Oreanda here; so it sounds now, and it will sound as indifferently and monotonously when we are all no more. And in this constancy, in this complete indifference to the life and death of each of us, there lies hid, perhaps, a pledge of our eternal salvation, of the unceasing movement of life upon earth, of unceasing progress towards perfection. Sitting beside a young woman who in the dawn seemed so lovely, soothed and spellbound in these magical surroundings—the sea, mountains, clouds, the open sky—Gurov thought how in reality everything is beautiful in this world when one reflects: everything except what we think or do ourselves when we forget our human dignity and the higher aims of our existence.

A man walked up to them—probably a keeper—looked at them and walked away. And this detail seemed mysterious and beautiful, too. They saw a steamer come from Theodosia, with its lights out in the glow of dawn.

"There is dew on the grass," said Anna Sergeyevna, after a silence.

"Yes. It's time to go home."

They went back to the town.

Then they met every day at twelve o'clock on the sea-front, lunched and dined together, went for walks, admired the sea. She complained that she slept badly, that her heart throbbed violently; asked the same questions, troubled now by jealousy and now by the fear that he did not respect her sufficiently. And often in the square or gardens, when there was no one near them, he suddenly drew her to him and kissed her passionately. Complete idleness, these kisses in broad daylight while he looked round in dread of some one's seeing them, the heat, the smell of the sea, and the continual passing to and fro before him of idle, well-dressed, well-fed people, made a new man of him; he told Anna Sergeyevna how beautiful she was, how fascinating. He was impatiently passionate, he would not move a step away from her, while she was often pensive and continually urged him to confess that he did not respect her, did not love her in the least, and thought of her as nothing but a common woman. Rather late almost every evening they drove somewhere out of town, to Oreanda or to the waterfall; and the expedition was always a success, the scenery invariably impressed them as grand and beautiful.

They were expecting her husband to come, but a letter came from him, saying that there was something wrong with his eyes, and he entreated his wife to come home as quickly as possible. Anna Sergeyevna made haste to go.

"It's a good thing I am going away," she said to Gurov. "It's the finger of destiny!"

She went by coach and he went with her. They were driving the whole day. When she had got into a compartment of the express, and when the second bell had rung, she said:

"Let me look at you once more . . . look at you once again. That's right."

She did not shed tears, but was so sad that she seemed ill, and her face was quivering.

"I shall remember you . . . think of you," she said. "God be with you; be happy. Don't remember evil against me. We are parting forever—it must be so, for we ought never to have met. Well, God be with you."

The train moved off rapidly, its lights soon vanished from sight, and a minute later there was no sound of it, as though everything had conspired together to end as quickly as possible that sweet delirium, that madness. Left alone on the platform, and gazing into the dark distance, Gurov listened to the chirrup of the grasshoppers and the hum of the telegraph wires, feeling as though he had only just waked up. And he thought, musing, that there had been another episode or adventure in his life, and it, too, was at an end, and nothing was left of it but a memory. . . . He was moved, sad, and conscious of a slight remorse. This young woman whom he would never meet again had not been happy with him; he was genuinely warm and affectionate with her, but yet in his manner, his tone, and his caresses there had been a shade of light irony, the coarse condescension of a happy man who was, besides, almost twice her age. All the time she had called him kind, exceptional, lofty; obviously he had seemed to her different from what he really was, so he had unintentionally deceived her. . . .

Here at the station was already a scent of autumn; it was a cold evening.

"It's time for me to go north," thought Gurov as he left the platform. "High time!"

III

At home in Moscow everything was in its winter routine; the stoves were heated, and in the morning it was still dark when the children were having breakfast and getting ready for school, and the nurse would light the lamp for a short time. The frosts had begun already. When the first snow has fallen, on the first day of sledge-driving it is pleasant to see the white earth, the white roofs, to draw soft, delicious breath, and the season brings back the days of one's youth. The old limes and birches, white with hoar-frost, have a good-natured expression; they are nearer to one's heart than cypresses and palms, and near them one doesn't want to be thinking of the sea and the mountains.

Gurov was Moscow born; he arrived in Moscow on a fine frosty day, and when he put on his fur coat and warm gloves, and walked along Petrovka, and when on Saturday evening he heard the ringing of the bells, his recent trip and the places he had seen lost all charm for him. Little by little he became absorbed in Moscow life, greedily read three newspapers a day, and declared he did not read the Moscow papers on principle! He already felt a longing to go to restaurants, clubs, dinner-parties, anniversary celebrations, and he felt flattered at entertaining distinguished lawyers and artists, and at playing cards with a professor at the doctors' club. He could already eat a whole plateful of salt fish and cabbage. . . .

In another month, he fancied, the image of Anna Sergeyevna would be shrouded in a mist in his memory, and only from time to time would visit him in his dreams with a touching smile as others did. But more than a month passed, real winter had come, and everything was still clear in his memory as though he had parted with Anna Sergeyevna only the day before. And his memories glowed more and more vividly. When in the evening stillness he heard from his study the voices of his children, preparing their lessons, or when he listened to a song or the organ at the restaurant, or the storm howled in the chimney, suddenly everything would rise up in his memory: what had happened on the groyne, and the early morning with the mist on the mountains, and the steamer coming from Theodosia, and the kisses. He would pace a long time about his room, remembering it all and smiling; then his memories passed into dreams, and in his fancy the past was mingled with what was to come. Anna Sergeyevna did not visit him in dreams, but followed him about everywhere like a shadow and haunted him. When he shut his eyes he saw her as though she were living before him, and she seemed to him lovelier, younger, tenderer than she was; and he imagined himself finer than he had been in Yalta. In the evenings she peeped out at him from the bookcase, from the fireplace, from the corner—he heard her breathing, the caressing rustle of her dress. In the street he watched the women, looking for some one like her.

He was tormented by an intense desire to confide his memories to some one. But in his home it was impossible to talk of his love, and he had no one outside; he could not talk to his tenants nor to any one at the bank. And what had he to talk of? Had he been in love, then? Had there been anything beautiful, poetical, or edifying or simply interesting in his relations with Anna Sergeyevna? And there was nothing for him but to talk vaguely of love, of woman, and no one guessed what it meant; only his wife twitched her black eyebrows, and said: "The part of a lady-killer does not suit you at all, Dimitri."

One evening, coming out of the doctors' club with an official with whom he had been playing cards, he could not resist saying:

"If only you knew what a fascinating woman I made the acquaintance of in Yalta!"

The official got into his sledge and was driving away, but turned suddenly and shouted:

"Dmitri Dmitritch!"

"What?"

"You were right this evening: the sturgeon was a bit too strong!"

These words, so ordinary, for some reason moved Gurov to indignation, and struck him as degrading and unclean. What savage manners, what people! What senseless nights, what uninteresting, uneventful days! The rage for card-playing, the gluttony, the drunkenness, the continual talk always about the same thing. Useless pursuits and conversations always about the same things absorb the better part of one's time, the better part of one's strength, and in the end there is left a life grovelling and curtailed, worthless and trivial, and there is no escaping or getting away from it—just as though one were in a madhouse or a prison.

Gurov did not sleep all night, and was filled with indignation. And he had a headache all next day. And the next night he slept badly; he sat up in bed, thinking, or paced up and down his room. He was sick of his children, sick of the bank; he had no desire to go anywhere or to talk of anything.

In the holidays in December he prepared for a journey, and told his wife he was going to Petersburg to do something in the interests of a young friend—and he set off for S——. What for? He did not very well know himself. He wanted to see Anna Sergeyevna and to talk with her—to arrange a meeting, if possible.

He reached S—— in the morning, and took the best room at the hotel, in which the floor was covered with grey army cloth, and on the table was an inkstand, grey with dust and adorned with a figure on horseback, with its hat in its hand and its head broken off.

The hotel porter gave him the necessary information; Von Diderits lived in a house of his own in Old Gontcharny Street—it was not far from the hotel: he was rich and lived in good style, and had his own horses; every one in the town knew him. The porter pronounced the name "Dridirits."

Gurov went without haste to Old Gontcharny Street and found the house. Just opposite the house stretched a long grey fence adorned with nails.

"One would run away from a fence like that," thought Gurov, looking from the fence to the windows of the house and back again.

He considered: to-day was a holiday, and the husband would probably be at home. And in any case it would be tactless to go into the house and upset her. If he were to send her a note it might fall into her husband's hands, and then it might ruin everything. The best thing was to trust to chance. And he kept walking up and down the street by the fence, waiting for the chance. He saw a beggar go in at the gate and dogs fly at him; then an hour later he heard a piano, and the sounds were faint and indistinct. Probably it was Anna Sergeyevna playing. The front door suddenly opened, and an old woman came out, followed by the familiar white Pomeranian. Gurov was on the point of calling to the dog, but his heart began beating violently, and in his excitement he could not remember the dog's name.

He walked up and down, and loathed the grey fence more and more, and by now he thought irritably that Anna Sergeyevna had forgotten him, and was perhaps already amusing herself with some one else, and that that was very natural in a young woman who had nothing to look at from morning till night but that confounded fence. He went back to his hotel room and sat for a long while on the sofa, not knowing what to do, then he had dinner and a long nap.

"How stupid and worrying it is!" he thought when he woke and looked at the dark windows: it was already evening. "Here I've had a good sleep for some reason. What shall I do in the night?"

He sat on the bed, which was covered by a cheap grey blanket, such as one sees in hospitals, and he taunted himself in his vexation:

"So much for the lady with the dog . . . so much for the adventure. . . . You're in a nice fix. . . ."

That morning at the station a poster in large letters had caught his eye. *The Geisha* was to be performed for the first time. He thought of this and went to the theatre.

"It's quite possible she may go to the first performance," he thought.

The theatre was full. As in all provincial theatres, there was a fog above the chandelier, the gallery was noisy and restless; in the front row the local dandies were standing up before the beginning of the performance, with their hands behind them; in the Governor's box the Governor's daughter, wearing a boa, was sitting in the front seat, while the Governor himself lurked modestly behind the curtain with only his hands visible; the orchestra was a long time tuning up; the stage curtain swayed. All the time the audience were coming in and taking their seats Gurov looked at them eagerly.

Anna Sergeyevna, too, came in. She sat down in the third row, and when Gurov looked at her his heart contracted, and he understood clearly that for him there was in the whole world no creature so near, so precious, and so important to him; she, this little woman, in no way remarkable, lost in a provincial crowd, with a vulgar lorgnette in her hand, filled his whole life now, was his sorrow and his joy, the one happiness that he now desired for himself, and to the sounds of the inferior orchestra, of the wretched provincial violins, he thought how lovely she was. He thought and dreamed.

A young man with small side-whiskers, tall and stooping, came in with Anna Sergeyevna and sat down beside her; he bent his head at every step and seemed to be continually bowing. Most likely this was the husband whom at Yalta, in a rush of bitter feeling, she had called a flunkey. And there really was in his long figure, his side-whiskers, and the small bald patch on his head, something of the flunkey's obsequiousness; his smile was sugary, and in his buttonhole there was some badge of distinction like the number on a waiter.

During the first interval the husband went away to smoke; she remained alone in her stall. Gurov, who was sitting in the stalls, too, went up to her and said in a trembling voice, with a forced smile:

"Good-evening."

She glanced at him and turned pale, then glanced again with horror, unable to believe her eyes, and tightly gripped the fan and the lorgnette in her hands, evidently struggling with herself not to faint. Both were silent. She was sitting, he was standing, frightened by her confusion and not venturing to sit down beside her. The violins and the flute began tuning up. He felt suddenly frightened; it seemed as though all the people in the boxes were looking at them. She got up and went quickly to the door; he followed her, and both walked senselessly along passages, and up and down stairs, and figures in legal, scholastic, and civil service uniforms, all wearing badges, flitted before their eyes. They caught glimpses of ladies, of fur coats hanging on pegs; the draughts blew on them, bringing a smell of stale tobacco. And Gurov, whose heart was beating violently, thought:

"Oh, heavens! Why are these people here and this orchestra! . . ."

And at that instant he recalled how when he had seen Anna Sergeyevna off at the station he had thought that everything was over and they would never meet again. But how far they were still from the end!

On the narrow, gloomy staircase over which was written "To the Amphitheatre," she stopped.

"How you have frightened me!" she said, breathing hard, still pale and overwhelmed. "Oh, how you have frightened me! I am half dead. Why have you come? Why?"

"But do understand, Anna, do understand . . ." he said hastily in a low voice. "I entreat you to understand. . . ."

She looked at him with dread, with entreaty, with love; she looked at him intently, to keep his features more distinctly in her memory.

"I am so unhappy," she went on, not heeding him. "I have thought of nothing but you all the time; I live only in the thought of you. And I wanted to forget, to forget you; but why, oh, why, have you come?"

On the landing above them two schoolboys were smoking and looking down, but that was nothing to Gurov; he drew Anna Sergeyevna to him, and began kissing her face, her cheeks, and her hands.

"What are you doing, what are you doing!" she cried in horror, pushing him away. "We are mad. Go away to-day; go away at once. . . . I beseech you by all that is sacred, I implore you. . . . There are people coming this way!"

Some one was coming up the stairs.

"You must go away," Anna Sergeyevna went on in a whisper. "Do you hear, Dmitri Dmitritch? I will come and see you in Moscow. I have never been happy; I am miserable now, and I never, never shall be happy, never! Don't make me suffer still more! I swear I'll come to Moscow. But now let us part. My precious, good, dear one, we must part!"

She pressed his hand and began rapidly going downstairs, looking round at him, and from her eyes he could see that she really was unhappy. Gurov stood for a little while, listened, then, when all sound had died away, he found his coat and left the theatre.

IV

And Anna Sergeyevna began coming to see him in Moscow. Once in two or three months she left S——, telling her husband that she was going to consult a doctor about an internal complaint—and her husband believed her, and did not believe her. In Moscow she stayed at the Slaviansky Bazaar hotel, and at once sent a man in a red cap to Gurov. Gurov went to see her, and no one in Moscow knew of it.

Once he was going to see her in this way on a winter morning (the messenger had come the evening before when he was out). With him walked his daughter, whom he wanted to take to school: it was on the way. Snow was falling in big wet flakes.

"It's three degrees above freezing-point, and yet it is snowing," said Gurov to his daughter. "The thaw is only on the surface of the earth; there is quite a different temperature at a greater height in the atmosphere."

"And why are there no thunderstorms in the winter, father?"

He explained that, too. He talked, thinking all the while that he was going to see *her*, and no living soul knew of it, and probably never would know. He had two lives: one, open, seen and known by all who cared to know, full of relative truth and of relative falsehood, exactly like the lives of his friends and acquaintances; and another life running its course in secret. And through some strange, perhaps accidental, conjunction of circumstances, everything that was essential, of interest and of value to him, everything in which he was sincere and did not deceive himself, everything that made the kernel of his life, was hidden from other people; and all that was false in him, the sheath in which he hid himself to conceal the truth—such, for instance, as his work in the bank, his discussions at the club, his "lower race," his presence with his wife at anniversary festivities—all that was open. And he judged of others by himself, not believing in what he saw, and always believing that every man had his real, most interesting life under the cover of secrecy and under the cover of night. All personal life rested on secrecy, and possibly it was partly on that account that civilised man was so nervously anxious that personal privacy should be respected.

After leaving his daughter at school, Gurov went on to the Slaviansky Bazaar. He took off his fur coat below, went upstairs, and softly knocked at the door. Anna Sergeyevna, wearing his favourite grey dress, exhausted by the journey and the suspense, had been expecting him since the evening before. She was pale; she looked at him, and did not smile, and he had hardly come in when she fell on his breast. Their kiss was slow and prolonged, as though they had not met for two years.

"Well, how are you getting on there?" he asked. "What news?"

"Wait; I'll tell you directly. . . . I can't talk."

She could not speak; she was crying. She turned away from him, and pressed her handkerchief to her eyes.

"Let her have her cry out. I'll sit down and wait," he thought, and he sat down in an arm-chair.

Then he rang and asked for tea to be brought him, and while he drank his tea she remained standing at the window with her back to him. She was crying from emotion, from the miserable consciousness that their life was so hard for them; they could only meet in secret, hiding themselves from people, like thieves! Was not their life shattered?

"Come, do stop!" he said.

It was evident to him that this love of theirs would not soon be over, that he could not see the end of it. Anna Sergeyevna grew more and more attached to him. She adored him, and it was unthinkable to say to her that it was bound to have an end some day; besides, she would not have believed it!

He went up to her and took her by the shoulders to say something affectionate and cheering, and at that moment he saw himself in the looking-glass.

His hair was already beginning to turn grey. And it seemed strange to him that he had grown so much older, so much plainer during the last few years. The shoulders on which his hands rested were warm and quivering. He felt compassion for this life, still so warm and lovely, but probably already not far from beginning to fade and wither like his own. Why did she love him so much? He always seemed to women different from what he was, and they loved in him not himself, but the man created by their imagination, whom they had been eagerly seeking all their lives; and afterwards, when they noticed their mistake, they loved him all the same. And not one of them had been happy with him. Time passed, he had made their acquaintance, got on with them, parted, but he had never once loved; it was anything you like, but not love.

And only now when his head was grey he had fallen properly, really in love—for the first time in his life.

Anna Sergeyevna and he loved each other like people very close and akin, like husband and wife, like tender friends; it seemed to them that fate itself had meant them for one another, and they could not understand why he had a wife and she a husband; and it was as though they were a pair of birds of passage, caught and forced to live in different cages. They forgave each other for what they were ashamed of in their past, they forgave everything in the present, and felt that this love of theirs had changed them both.

In moments of depression in the past he had comforted himself with any arguments that came into his mind, but now he no longer cared for arguments; he felt profound compassion, he wanted to be sincere and tender. . . .

"Don't cry, my darling," he said. "You've had your cry; that's enough. . . . Let us talk now, let us think of some plan."

Then they spent a long while taking counsel together, talked of how to avoid the necessity for secrecy, for deception, for living in different towns and not seeing each other for long at a time. How could they be free from this intolerable bondage?

"How? How?" he asked, clutching his head. "How?"

And it seemed as though in a little while the solution would be found, and then a new and splendid life would begin; and it was clear to both of them that they had still a long, long road before them, and that the most complicated and difficult part of it was only just beginning.

1899

The Yellow Wallpaper

CHARLOTTE PERKINS GILMAN

[1860–1935]

It is very seldom that mere ordinary people like John and myself secure ancestral halls for the summer.

A colonial mansion, a hereditary estate, I would say a haunted house and reach the height of romantic felicity—but that would be asking too much of fate!

Still I will proudly declare that there is something queer about it.

Else, why should it be let so cheaply? And why have stood so long untenanted?

John laughs at me, of course, but one expects that in marriage.

John is practical in the extreme. He has no patience with faith, an intense horror of superstition, and he scoffs openly at any talk of things not to be felt and seen and put down in figures.

John is a physician, and *perhaps*—(I would not say it to a living soul, of course, but this is dead paper and a great relief to my mind)—*perhaps* that is one reason I do not get well faster.

You see, he does not believe I am sick!

And what can one do?

If a physician of high standing, and one's own husband, assures friends and relatives that there is really nothing the matter with one but temporary nervous depression—a slight hysterical tendency—what is one to do?

My brother is also a physician, and also of high standing, and he says the same thing.

So I take phosphates or phosphites—whichever it is, and tonics, and journeys, and air, and exercise, and am absolutely forbidden to "work" until I am well again.

Personally, I disagree with their ideas.

Personally, I believe that congenial work, with excitement and change, would do me good.

But what is one to do?

I did write for a while in spite of them; but it *does* exhaust me a good deal—having to be so sly about it, or else meet with heavy opposition.

I sometimes fancy that in my condition if I had less opposition and more society and stimulus—but John says the very worst thing I can do is to think about my condition, and I confess it always makes me feel bad.

So I will let it alone and talk about the house.

The most beautiful place! It is quite alone, standing well back from the road, quite three miles from the village. It makes me think of English places that you read about, for there are hedges and walls and gates that lock, and lots of separate little houses for the gardeners and people.

There is a *delicious* garden! I never saw such a garden—large and shady, full of box-bordered paths, and lined with long grape-covered arbors with seats under them.

There were greenhouses, too, but they are all broken now.

There was some legal trouble, I believe, something about the heirs and co-heirs; anyhow, the place has been empty for years.

That spoils my ghostliness, I am afraid, but I don't care—there is something strange about the house—I can feel it.

I even said so to John one moonlight evening, but he said what I felt was a *draught*, and shut the window.

I get unreasonably angry with John sometimes. I'm sure I never used to be so sensitive. I think it is due to this nervous condition.

But John says if I feel so, I shall neglect proper self-control; so I take pains to control myself—before him, at least, and that makes me very tired.

I don't like our room a bit. I wanted one downstairs that opened on the piazza and had roses all over the window, and such pretty old-fashioned chintz hangings! but John would not hear of it.

He said there was only one window and not room for two beds, and no near room for him if he took another.

He is very careful and loving, and hardly lets me stir without special direction.

I have a schedule prescription for each hour in the day; he takes all care from me, and so I feel basely ungrateful not to value it more.

He said we came here solely on my account, that I was to have perfect rest and all the air I could get. "Your exercise depends on your strength, my dear," said he, "and your food somewhat on your appetite; but air you can absorb all the time." So we took the nursery at the top of the house.

It is a big, airy room, the whole floor nearly, with windows that look all ways, and air and sunshine galore. It was nursery first and then playroom and gymnasium, I should judge; for the windows are barred for little children, and there are rings and things in the walls.

The paint and paper look as if a boys' school had used it. It is stripped off—the paper—in great patches all around the head of my bed, about as far as I can reach, and in a great place on the other side of the room low down. I never saw a worse paper in my life.

One of those sprawling flamboyant patterns committing every artistic sin.

It is dull enough to confuse the eye in following, pronounced enough to constantly irritate and provoke study, and when you follow the lame uncertain curves for a little distance they suddenly commit suicide—plunge off at outrageous angles, destroy themselves in unheard of contradictions.

The color is repellant, almost revolting; a smouldering unclean yellow, strangely faded by the slow-turning sunlight.

It is a dull yet lurid orange in some places, a sickly sulphur tint in others.

No wonder the children hated it! I should hate it myself if I had to live in this room long.

There comes John, and I must put this away,—he hates to have me write a word.

We have been here two weeks, and I haven't felt like writing before, since that first day.

I am sitting by the window now, up in this atrocious nursery, and there is nothing to hinder my writing as much as I please, save lack of strength.

John is away all day, and even some nights when his cases are serious.

I am glad my case is not serious!

But these nervous troubles are dreadfully depressing.

John does not know how much I really suffer. He knows there is no *reason* to suffer, and that satisfies him.

Of course it is only nervousness. It does weigh on me so not to do my duty in any way!

I meant to be such a help to John, such a real rest and comfort, and here I am a comparative burden already!

Nobody would believe what an effort it is to do what little I am able,—to dress and entertain, and order things.

It is fortunate Mary is so good with the baby. Such a dear baby!

And yet I *cannot* be with him, it makes me so nervous.

I suppose John never was nervous in his life. He laughs at me so about this wallpaper!

At first he meant to repaper the room, but afterward he said that I was letting it get the better of me, and that nothing was worse for a nervous patient than to give way to such fancies.

He said that after the wallpaper was changed it would be the heavy bedstead, and then the barred windows, and then that gate at the head of the stairs, and so on.

"You know the place is doing you good," he said, "and really, dear, I don't care to renovate the house just for a three months' rental."

"Then do let us go downstairs," I said, "there are such pretty rooms there."

Then he took me in his arms and called me a blessed little goose, and said he would go down cellar, if I wished, and have it whitewashed into the bargain.

But he is right enough about the beds and windows and things.

It is an airy and comfortable room as anyone need wish, and, of course, I would not be so silly as to make him uncomfortable just for a whim.

I'm really getting quite fond of the big room, all but that horrid paper.

Out of one window I can see the garden, those mysterious deep-shaded arbors, the riotous old-fashioned flowers, and bushes and gnarly trees.

Out of another I get a lovely view of the bay and a little private wharf belonging to the estate. There is a beautiful shaded lane that runs down there from the house. I always fancy I see people walking in these numerous paths and arbors, but John has cautioned me not to give way to fancy in the least. He says that with my imaginative power and habit of story-making, a nervous weakness like mine is sure to lead to all manner of excited fancies, and that I ought to use my will and good sense to check the tendency. So I try.

I think sometimes that if I were only well enough to write a little it would relieve the press of ideas and rest me.

But I find I get pretty tired when I try.

It is so discouraging not to have any advice and companionship about my work. When I get really well, John says we will ask Cousin Henry and Julia down for a long visit; but he says he would as soon put fireworks in my pillow-case as to let me have those stimulating people about now.

I wish I could get well faster.

But I must not think about that. This paper looks to me as if it *knew* what a vicious influence it had!

There is a recurrent spot where the pattern lolls like a broken neck and two bulbous eyes stare at you upside down.

I get positively angry with the impertinence of it and the everlastingness. Up and down and sideways they crawl, and those absurd, unblinking eyes are everywhere. There is one place where two breadths didn't match, and the eyes go all up and down the line, one a little higher than the other.

I never saw so much expression in an inanimate thing before, and we all know how much expression they have! I used to lie awake as a child and get more entertainment and terror out of blank walls and plain furniture than most children could find in a toy-store.

I remember what a kindly wink the knobs of our big, old bureau used to have, and there was one chair that always seemed like a strong friend.

I used to feel that if any of the other things looked too fierce I could always hop into that chair and be safe.

The furniture in this room is no worse than inharmonious, however, for we had to bring it all from downstairs. I suppose when this was used as a playroom they had to take the nursery things out, and no wonder! I never saw such ravages as the children have made here.

The wallpaper, as I said before, is torn off in spots, and it sticketh closer than a brother—they must have had perseverance as well as hatred.

Then the floor is scratched and gouged and splintered, the plaster itself is dug out here and there, and this great heavy bed, which is all we found in the room, looks as if it had been through the wars.

But I don't mind it a bit—only the paper.

There comes John's sister. Such a dear girl as she is, and so careful of me! I must not let her find me writing.

She is a perfect and enthusiastic housekeeper, and hopes for no better profession. I verily believe she thinks it is the writing which made me sick!

But I can write when she is out, and see her a long way off from these windows.

There is one that commands the road, a lovely shaded winding road, and one that just looks off over the country. A lovely country, too, full of great elms and velvet meadows.

This wallpaper has a kind of sub-pattern in a different shade, a particularly irritating one, for you can only see it in certain lights, and not clearly then.

But in the places where it isn't faded and where the sun is just so—I can see a strange, provoking, formless sort of figure, that seems to skulk about behind that silly and conspicuous front design.

There's sister on the stairs!

Well, the Fourth of July is over! The people are all gone and I am tired out. John thought it might do me good to see a little company, so we just had mother and Nellie and the children down for a week.

Of course I didn't do a thing. Jennie sees to everything now.

But it tired me all the same.

John says if I don't pick up faster he shall send me to Weir Mitchell[1] in the fall.

But I don't want to go there at all. I had a friend who was in his hands once, and she says he is just like John and my brother, only more so!

Besides, it is such an undertaking to go so far.

I don't feel as if it was worthwhile to turn my hand over for anything, and I'm getting dreadfully fretful and querulous.

I cry at nothing, and cry most of the time.

Of course I don't when John is here, or anybody else, but when I am alone.

And I am alone a good deal just now. John is kept in town very often by serious cases, and Jennie is good and lets me alone when I want her to.

So I walk a little in the garden or down that lovely lane, sit on the porch under the roses, and lie down up here a good deal.

I'm getting really fond of the room in spite of the wallpaper. Perhaps *because* of the wallpaper.

It dwells in my mind so!

[1]Dr. S. Weir Mitchell (1829–1914) was an American neurologist and author who advocated "rest cures" for nervous illnesses.

I lie here on this great immovable bed—it is nailed down, I believe—and follow that pattern about by the hour. It is as good as gymnastics, I assure you. I start, we'll say, at the bottom, down in the corner over there where it has not been touched, and I determine for the thousandth time that I *will* follow that pointless pattern to some sort of a conclusion.

I know a little of the principle of design, and I know this thing was not arranged on any laws of radiation, or alternation, or repetition, or symmetry, or anything else that I ever heard of.

It is repeated, of course, by the breadths, but not otherwise.

Looked at in one way each breadth stands alone, the bloated curves and flourishes—a kind of "debased Romanesque" with *delirium tremens*—go waddling up and down in isolated columns of fatuity.

But, on the other hand, they connect diagonally, and the sprawling outlines run off in great slanting waves of optic horror, like a lot of wallowing sea-weeds in full chase.

The whole thing goes horizontally, too, at least it seems so, and I exhaust myself in trying to distinguish the order of its going in that direction.

They have used a horizontal breadth for a frieze, and that adds wonderfully to the confusion.

There is one end of the room where it is almost intact, and there, when the crosslights fade and the low sun shines directly upon it, I can almost fancy radiation after all,—the interminable grotesques seem to form around a common centre and rush off in headlong plunges of equal distraction.

It makes me tired to follow it. I will take a nap I guess.

I don't know why I should write this.

I don't want to.

I don't feel able.

And I know John would think it absurd. But I *must* say what I feel and think in some way—it is such a relief!

But the effort is getting to be greater than the relief.

Half the time now I am awfully lazy, and lie down ever so much.

John says I mustn't lose my strength, and has me take cod liver oil and lots of tonics and things, to say nothing of ale and wine and rare meat.

Dear John! He loves me very dearly, and hates to have me sick. I tried to have a real earnest reasonable talk with him the other day, and tell him how I wish he would let me go and make a visit to Cousin Henry and Julia.

But he said I wasn't able to go, nor able to stand it after I got there; and I did not make out a very good case for myself, for I was crying before I had finished.

It is getting to be a great effort for me to think straight. Just this nervous weakness I suppose.

And dear John gathered me up in his arms, and just carried me upstairs and laid me on the bed, and sat by me and read to me till it tired my head.

He said I was his darling and his comfort and all he had, and that I must take care of myself for his sake, and keep well.

He says no one but myself can help me out of it, that I must use my will and self-control and not let any silly fancies run away with me.

There's one comfort, the baby is well and happy, and does not have to occupy this nursery with the horrid wallpaper.

If we had not used it, that blessed child would have! What a fortunate escape! Why, I wouldn't have a child of mine, an impressionable little thing, live in such a room for worlds.

I never thought of it before, but it is lucky that John kept me here after all, I can stand it so much easier than a baby, you see.

Of course I never mention it to them any more—I am too wise, but I keep watch of it all the same.

There are things in the wallpaper that nobody knows but me, or ever will.

Behind that outside pattern the dim shapes get clearer every day.

It is always the same shape, only very numerous.

And it is like a woman stooping down and creeping about behind that pattern. I don't like it a bit. I wonder—I begin to think—I wish John would take me away from here!

It is so hard to talk with John about my case, because he is so wise, and because he loves me so.

But I tried it last night.

It was moonlight. The moon shines in all around just as the sun does.

I hate to see it sometimes, it creeps so slowly, and always comes in by one window or another.

John was asleep and I hated to waken him, so I kept still and watched the moonlight on that undulating wallpaper till I felt creepy.

The faint figure behind seemed to shake the pattern, just as if she wanted to get out.

I got up softly and went to feel and see if the paper *did* move, and when I came back John was awake.

"What is it, little girl?" he said. "Don't go walking about like that—you'll get cold."

I thought it was a good time to talk, so I told him that I really was not gaining here, and that I wished he would take me away.

"Why, darling!" said he, "our lease will be up in three weeks, and I can't see how to leave before.

"The repairs are not done at home, and I cannot possibly leave town just now. Of course if you were in any danger, I could and would, but you really are better, dear, whether you can see it or not. I am a doctor, dear, and I know. You are gaining flesh and color, your appetite is better, I feel really much easier about you."

"I don't weigh a bit more," said I, "nor as much; and my appetite may be better in the evening when you are here but it is worse in the morning when you are away!"

"Bless her little heart!" said he with a big hug, "she shall be as sick as she pleases! But now let's improve the shining hours by going to sleep, and talk about it in the morning!"

"And you won't go away?" I asked gloomily.

"Why, how can I, dear? It is only three weeks more and then we will take a nice little trip of a few days while Jennie is getting the house ready. Really dear you are better!"

"Better in body perhaps —" I began, and stopped short, for he sat up straight and looked at me with such a stern, reproachful look that I could not say another word.

"My darling," said he, "I beg you, for my sake and for our child's sake, as well as for your own, that you will never for one instant let that idea enter your mind! There is nothing so dangerous, so fascinating, to a temperament like yours. It is a false and foolish fancy. Can you trust me as a physician when I tell you so?"

So of course I said no more on that score, and we went to sleep before long. He thought I was asleep first, but I wasn't, and lay there for hours trying to decide whether that front pattern and the back pattern really did move together or separately.

On a pattern like this, by daylight, there is a lack of sequence, a defiance of law, that is a constant irritant to a normal mind.

The color is hideous enough, and unreliable enough, and infuriating enough, but the pattern is torturing.

You think you have mastered it, but just as you get well underway in following, it turns a back-somersault and there you are. It slaps you in the face, knocks you down, and tramples upon you. It is like a bad dream.

The outside pattern is a florid arabesque, reminding one of a fungus. If you can imagine a toadstool in joints, an interminable string of toadstools, budding and sprouting in endless convolutions—why, that is something like it.

That is, sometimes!

There is one marked peculiarity about this paper, a thing nobody seems to notice but myself, and that is that it changes as the light changes.

When the sun shoots in through the east window—I always watch for that first long, straight ray—it changes so quickly that I never can quite believe it.

That is why I watch it always.

By moonlight—the moon shines in all night when there is a moon—I wouldn't know it was the same paper.

At night in any kind of light, in twilight, candlelight, lamplight, and worst of all by moonlight, it becomes bars! The outside pattern I mean, and the woman behind it is as plain as can be.

I didn't realize for a long time what the thing was that showed behind, that dim sub-pattern, but now I am quite sure it is a woman.

By daylight she is subdued, quiet. I fancy it is the pattern that keeps her so still. It is so puzzling. It keeps me quiet by the hour.

I lie down ever so much now. John says it is good for me, and to sleep all I can.

Indeed he started the habit by making me lie down for an hour after each meal.

It is a very bad habit I am convinced, for you see I don't sleep.

And that cultivates deceit, for I don't tell them I'm awake—O, no!

The fact is I am getting a little afraid of John.

He seems very queer sometimes, and even Jennie has an inexplicable look.

It strikes me occasionally, just as a scientific hypothesis,—that perhaps it is the paper!

I have watched John when he did not know I was looking, and come into the room suddenly on the most innocent excuses, and

I've caught him several times *looking at the paper*! And Jennie too. I caught Jennie with her hand on it once.

She didn't know I was in the room, and when I asked her in a quiet, a very quiet voice, with the most restrained manner possible, what she was doing with the paper—she turned around as if she had been caught stealing, and looked quite angry—asked me why I should frighten her so!

Then she said that the paper stained everything it touched, that she had found yellow smooches on all my clothes and John's, and she wished we would be more careful!

Did not that sound innocent? But I know she was studying that pattern, and I am determined that nobody shall find it out but myself!

Life is very much more exciting now than it used to be. You see I have something more to expect, to look forward to, to watch. I really do eat better, and am more quiet than I was.

John is so pleased to see me improve! He laughed a little the other day, and said I seemed to be flourishing in spite of my wallpaper.

I turned it off with a laugh. I had no intention of telling him it was *because* of the wallpaper—he would make fun of me. He might even want to take me away.

I don't want to leave now until I have found it out. There is a week more, and I think that will be enough.

I'm feeling ever so much better! I don't sleep much at night, for it is so interesting to watch developments; but I sleep a good deal in the daytime.

In the daytime it is tiresome and perplexing.

There are always new shoots on the fungus, and new shades of yellow all over it. I cannot keep count of them, though I have tried conscientiously.

It is the strangest yellow, that wallpaper! It makes me think of all the yellow things I ever saw—not beautiful ones like buttercups, but old foul, bad yellow things.

But there is something else about that paper—the smell! I noticed it the moment we came into the room, but with so much air and sun it was not bad. Now we have had a week of fog and rain, and whether the windows are open or not, the smell is here.

It creeps all over the house.

I find it hovering in the dining-room, skulking in the parlor, hiding in the hall, lying in wait for me on the stairs.

It gets into my hair.

Even when I go to ride, if I turn my head suddenly and surprise it—there is that smell!

Such a peculiar odor, too! I have spent hours in trying to analyze it, to find what it smelled like.

It is not bad—at first, and very gentle, but quite the subtlest, most enduring odor I ever met.

In this damp weather it is awful, I wake up in the night and find it hanging over me.

It used to disturb me at first. I thought seriously of burning the house—to reach the smell.

But now I am used to it. The only thing I can think of that it is like is the *color* of the paper! A yellow smell.

There is a very funny mark on this wall, low down, near the mop-board. A streak that runs round the room. It goes behind every piece of furniture, except the bed, a long, straight, even *smooch*, as if it had been rubbed over and over.

I wonder how it was done and who did it, and what they did it for. Round and round and round—round and round and round—it makes me dizzy!

I really have discovered something at last.

Through watching so much at night, when it changes so, I have finally found out.

The front pattern *does* move—and no wonder! The woman behind shakes it!

Sometimes I think there are a great many women behind, and sometimes only one, and she crawls around fast, and her crawling shakes it all over.

Then in the very bright spots she keeps still, and in the very shady spots she just takes hold of the bars and shakes them hard.

And she is all the time trying to climb through. But nobody could climb through that pattern—it strangles so; I think that is why it has so many heads.

They get through, and then the pattern strangles them off and turns them upside down, and makes their eyes white!

If those heads were covered or taken off it would not be half so bad.

I think that woman gets out in the daytime!

And I'll tell you why—privately—I've seen her!

I can see her out of every one of my windows!

It is the same woman, I know, for she is always creeping, and most women do not creep by daylight.

I see her in that long shaded lane, creeping up and down. I see her in those dark grape arbors, creeping all around the garden.

I see her on that long road under the trees, creeping along, and when a carriage comes she hides under the blackberry vines.

I don't blame her a bit. It must be very humiliating to be caught creeping by daylight!

I always lock the door when I creep by daylight. I can't do it at night, for I know John would suspect something at once.

And John is so queer now, that I don't want to irritate him. I wish he would take another room! Besides, I don't want anybody to get that woman out at night but myself.

I often wonder if I could see her out of all the windows at once.

But, turn as fast as I can, I can only see out of one at one time.

And though I always see her, she *may* be able to creep faster than I can turn!

I have watched her sometimes away off in the open country, creeping as fast as a cloud shadow in a high wind.

If only that top pattern could be gotten off from the under one! I mean to try it, little by little.

I have found out another funny thing, but I shan't tell it this time! It does not do to trust people too much.

There are only two more days to get this paper off, and I believe John is beginning to notice. I don't like the look in his eyes.

And I heard him ask Jennie a lot of professional questions about me. She had a very good report to give.

She said I slept a good deal in the daytime.

John knows I don't sleep very well at night, for all I'm so quiet!

He asked me all sorts of questions too, and pretended to be very loving and kind.

As if I couldn't see through him!

Still, I don't wonder he acts so, sleeping under this paper for three months.

It only interests me, but I feel sure John and Jennie are secretly affected by it.

Hurrah! This is the last day, but it is enough. John is to stay in town over night, and won't be out until this evening.

Jennie wanted to sleep with me—the sly thing! But I told her I should undoubtedly rest better for a night all alone.

That was clever, for really I wasn't alone a bit! As soon as it was moonlight and that poor thing began to crawl and shake the pattern, I got up and ran to help her.

I pulled and she shook, I shook and she pulled, and before morning we had peeled off yards of that paper.

A strip about as high as my head and half around the room.

And then when the sun came and that awful pattern began to laugh at me, I declared I would finish it to-day!

We go away to-morrow, and they are moving all my furniture down again to leave things as they were before.

Jennie looked at the wall in amazement, but I told her merrily that I did it out of pure spite at the vicious thing.

She laughed and said she wouldn't mind doing it herself, but I must not get tired.

How she betrayed herself that time!

But I am here, and no person touches this paper but me,—not *alive*!

She tried to get me out of the room—it was too patent! But I said it was so quiet and empty and clean now that I believed I would lie down again and sleep all I could, and not to wake me even for dinner—I would call when I woke.

So now she is gone, and the servants are gone, and the things are gone, and there is nothing left but that great bedstead nailed down, with the canvas mattress we found on it.

We shall sleep downstairs to-night, and take the boat home tomorrow.

I quite enjoy the room, now it is bare again.

How those children did tear about here!

This bedstead is fairly gnawed!

But I must get to work.

I have locked the door and thrown the key down into the front path.

I don't want to go out, and I don't want to have anybody come in, till John comes.

I want to astonish him.

I've got a rope up here that even Jennie did not find. If that woman does get out, and tries to get away, I can tie her!

But I forgot I could not reach far without anything to stand on!

This bed will *not* move!

I tried to lift and push it until I was lame, and then I got so angry I bit off a little piece at one corner—but it hurt my teeth.

Then I peeled off all the paper I could reach standing on the floor. It sticks horribly and the pattern just enjoys it! All those strangled heads and bulbous eyes and waddling fungus growths just shriek with derision!

I am getting angry enough to do something desperate. To jump out of the window would be admirable exercise, but the bars are too strong even to try.

Besides I wouldn't do it. Of course not. I know well enough that a step like that is improper and might be misconstrued.

I don't like to *look* out of the windows even—there are so many of those creeping women, and they creep so fast.

I wonder if they all come out of that wallpaper as I did?

But I am securely fastened now by my well-hidden rope—you don't get *me* out in the road there!

I suppose I shall have to get back behind the pattern when it comes night, and that is hard!

It is so pleasant to be out in this great room and creep around as I please!

I don't want to go outside. I won't, even if Jennie asks me to.

For outside you have to creep on the ground, and everything is green instead of yellow.

But here I can creep smoothly on the floor, and my shoulder just fits in that long smooch around the wall, so I cannot lose my way.

Why, there's John at the door!

It is no use, young man, you can't open it!

How he does call and pound!

Now he's crying for an axe.

It would be a shame to break down that beautiful door!

"John dear!" said I in the gentlest voice, "the key is down by the front steps, under a plantain leaf!"

That silenced him for a few moments.

Then he said—very quietly indeed, "Open the door, my darling!"

"I can't," said I. "The key is down by the front door under a plantain leaf!"

And then I said it again, several times, very gently and slowly, and said it so often that he had to go and see, and he got it of course, and came in. He stopped short by the door.

"What is the matter?" he cried. "For God's sake, what are you doing!"

I kept on creeping just the same, but I looked at him over my shoulder.

"I've got out at last," said I, "in spite of you and Jane. And I've pulled off most of the paper, so you can't put me back!"

Now why should that man have fainted? But he did, and right across my path by the wall, so that I had to creep over him every time!

1892

Araby

JAMES JOYCE
[1882–1941]

North Richmond Street, being blind, was a quiet street except at the hour when the Christian Brothers' School set the boys free. An un-inhabited house of two storeys stood at the blind end, detached from its neighbours in a square ground. The other houses of the street, conscious of decent lives within them, gazed at one another with brown imperturbable faces.

The former tenant of our house, a priest, had died in the back drawing-room. Air, musty from having been long enclosed, hung in all the rooms, and the waste room behind the kitchen was littered with old useless papers. Among these I found a few paper-covered books, the pages of which were curled and damp: *The Abbot,* by Walter Scott, *The Devout Communicant,* and *The Memoirs of Vidocq.* I liked the last best because its leaves were yellow. The wild garden behind the house contained a central apple-tree and a few straggling bushes under one of which I found the late tenant's rusty bicycle-pump. He had been a very charitable priest; in his will he had left all his money to institutions and the furniture of his house to his sister.

When the short days of winter came dusk fell before we had well eaten our dinners. When we met in the street the houses had grown sombre. The space of sky above us was the colour of ever-changing violet and towards it the lamps of the street lifted their feeble lanterns. The cold air stung us and we played till our bodies glowed. Our shouts echoed in the silent street. The career of our play brought us through the dark muddy lanes behind the houses where we ran the gauntlet of the rough tribes from the cottages, to the back doors of the dark dripping gardens where odours arose from the ashpits, to the dark odorous stables where a coachman smoothed and combed the horse or shook music from the buckled harness.

When we returned to the street light from the kitchen windows had filled the areas. If my uncle was seen turning the corner we hid in the shadow until we had seen him safely housed. Or if Mangan's sister came out on the doorstep to call her brother in to his tea we watched her from our shadow peer up and down the street. We waited to see whether she would remain or go in and, if she remained, we left our shadow and walked up to Mangan's steps resignedly. She was waiting for us, her figure defined by the light from the half-opened door. Her brother always teased her before he obeyed and I stood by the railings looking at her. Her dress swung as she moved her body and the soft rope of her hair tossed from side to side.

Every morning I lay on the floor in the front parlour watching her door. The blind was pulled down to within an inch of the sash so that I could not be seen. When she came out on the doorstep my heart leaped. I ran to the hall, seized my books, and followed her. I kept her brown figure always in my eye and, when we came near the point at which our ways diverged, I quickened my pace and passed her. This happened morning after morning. I had never spoken to her, except for a few casual words, and yet her name was like a summons to all my foolish blood.

Her image accompanied me even in places the most hostile to romance. On Saturday evenings when my aunt went marketing I had to go to carry some of the parcels. We walked through the flaring streets, jostled by drunken men and bargaining women, amid the curses of labourers, the shrill litanies of shop-boys who stood on guard by the barrel of pigs' cheeks, the nasal chanting of street-singers, who sang a *come-all-you* about O'Donovan Rossa,[1] or a ballad about the troubles in our native land. These noises converged in a single sensation of life for me: I imagined that I bore my chalice safely through a throng of foes. Her name sprang to my lips at moments in strange prayers and praises which I myself did not understand. My eyes were often full of tears (I could not tell why) and at times a flood from my heart seemed to pour itself out into my bosom. I thought little of the future. I did not know whether I would ever speak to her or not or, if I spoke to her, how I could tell her of

[1]Jeremiah O'Donovan (1831–1915) was nicknamed "Dynamite Rossa" for his militant pursuit of Irish independence.

my confused adoration. But my body was like a harp and her words and gestures were like fingers running upon the wires.

One evening I went into the back drawing-room in which the priest had died. It was a dark rainy evening and there was no sound in the house. Through one of the broken panes I heard the rain impinge upon the earth, the fine incessant needles of water playing in the sodden beds. Some distant lamp or lighted window gleamed below me. I was thankful that I could see so little. All my senses seemed to desire to veil themselves and, feeling that I was about to slip from them, I pressed the palms of my hands together until they trembled, murmuring: *"O love! O love!"* many times.

At last she spoke to me. When she addressed the first words to me I was so confused that I did not know what to answer. She asked me was I going to *Araby*. I forgot whether I answered yes or no. It would be a splendid bazaar, she said she would love to go.

"And why can't you?" I asked.

While she spoke she turned a silver bracelet round and round her wrist. She could not go, she said, because there would be a retreat that week in her convent. Her brother and two other boys were fighting for their caps and I was alone at the railings. She held one of the spikes, bowing her head towards me. The light from the lamp opposite our door caught the white curve of her neck, lit up her hair that rested there and, falling, lit up the hand upon the railing. It fell over one side of her dress and caught the white border of a petticoat, just visible as she stood at ease.

"It's well for you," she said.

"If I go," I said, "I will bring you something."

What innumerable follies laid waste my waking and sleeping thoughts after that evening! I wished to annihilate the tedious intervening days. I chafed against the work of school. At night in my bedroom and by day in the classroom her image came between me and the page I strove to read. The syllables of the word *Araby* were called to me through the silence in which my soul luxuriated and cast an Eastern enchantment over me. I asked for leave to go to the bazaar on Saturday night. My aunt was surprised and hoped it was not some Freemason affair. I answered few questions in class. I watched my master's face pass from amiability to sternness; he hoped I was not beginning to idle. I could not call my wandering thoughts together. I had hardly any patience with the serious work of life which, now that it stood between me and my desire, seemed to me child's play, ugly monotonous child's play.

On Saturday morning I reminded my uncle that I wished to go to the bazaar in the evening. He was fussing at the hallstand, looking for the hat-brush, and answered me curtly:

"Yes, boy, I know."

As he was in the hall I could not go into the front parlour and lie at the window. I left the house in bad humour and walked slowly towards the school. The air was pitilessly raw and already my heart misgave me.

When I came home to dinner my uncle had not yet been home. Still it was early. I sat staring at the clock for some time and, when its ticking began to irritate me, I left the room. I mounted the staircase and gained the upper part of the house. The high cold empty gloomy rooms liberated me and I went from room to room singing. From the front window I saw my companions playing below in the street. Their cries reached me weakened and indistinct and, leaning my forehead against the cool glass, I looked over at the dark house where she lived. I may have stood there for an hour, seeing nothing but the brown-clad figure cast by my imagination, touched discreetly by the lamplight at the curved neck, at the hand upon the railings and at the border below the dress.

When I came downstairs again I found Mrs. Mercer sitting at the fire. She was an old garrulous woman, a pawnbroker's widow, who collected used stamps for some pious purpose. I had to endure the gossip of the tea-table. The meal was prolonged beyond an hour and still my uncle did not come. Mrs. Mercer stood up to go: she was sorry she couldn't wait any longer, but it was after eight o'clock and she did not like to be out late, as the night air was bad for her. When she had gone I began to walk up and down the room, clenching my fists. My aunt said:

"I'm afraid you may put off your bazaar for this night of Our Lord."

At nine o'clock I heard my uncle's latchkey in the halldoor. I heard him talking to himself and heard the hallstand rocking when it had received the weight of his overcoat. I could interpret these signs. When he was midway through his dinner I asked him to give me the money to go to the bazaar. He had forgotten.

"The people are in bed and after their first sleep now," he said.

I did not smile. My aunt said to him energetically:

"Can't you give him the money and let him go? You've kept him late enough as it is."

My uncle said he was very sorry he had forgotten. He said he believed in the old saying: "All work and no play makes Jack a dull boy." He asked me where I was going and, when I had told him a second time he asked me did I know *The Arab's Farewell to his Steed.*[2] When I left the kitchen he was about to recite the opening lines of the piece to my aunt.

I held a florin[3] tightly in my hand as I strode down Buckingham Street towards the station. The sight of the streets thronged with buyers and glaring with gas recalled to me the purpose of my journey. I took my seat in a third-class carriage of a deserted train. After an intolerable delay the train moved out of the station slowly. It crept onward among ruinous houses and over the twinkling river. At Westland Row Station a crowd of people pressed to the carriage doors; but the porters moved them back, saying that it was a special train for the bazaar. I remained alone in the bare carriage. In a few minutes the train drew up beside an improvised wooden platform. I passed out on to the road and saw by the lighted dial of a clock that it was ten minutes to ten. In front of me was a large building which displayed the magical name.

I could not find any sixpenny entrance and, fearing that the bazaar would be closed, I passed in quickly through a turnstile, handing a shilling to a weary-looking man. I found myself in a big hall girdled at half its height by a gallery. Nearly all the stalls were closed and the greater part of the hall was in darkness. I recognised a silence like that which pervades a church after a service. I walked into the centre of the bazaar timidly. A few people were gathered about the stalls which were still open. Before a curtain, over which the words *Café Chantant* were written in coloured lamps, two men were counting money on a salver. I listened to the fall of the coins.

Remembering with difficulty why I had come I went over to one of the stalls and examined porcelain vases and flowered tea-sets. At the door of the stall a young lady was talking and laughing with two young gentlemen. I remarked their English accents and listened vaguely to their conversation.

"O, I never said such a thing!"

[2]A nostalgic poem by Caroline Norton (1808–1877).

[3]A silver coin worth two shillings.

"O, but you did!"

"O, but I didn't!"

"Didn't she say that?"

"Yes. I heard her."

"O, there's a . . . fib!"

Observing me the young lady came over and asked me did I wish to buy anything. The tone of her voice was not encouraging; she seemed to have spoken to me out of a sense of duty. I looked humbly at the great jars that stood like eastern guards at either side of the dark entrance to the stall and murmured:

"No, thank you."

The young lady changed the position of one of the vases and went back to the two young men. They began to talk of the same subject. Once or twice the young lady glanced at me over her shoulder.

I lingered before her stall, though I knew my stay was useless, to make my interest in her wares seem the more real. Then I turned away slowly and walked down the middle of the bazaar. I allowed the two pennies to fall against the sixpence in my pocket. I heard a voice call from one end of the gallery that the light was out. The upper part of the hall was now completely dark.

Gazing up into the darkness I saw myself as a creature driven and derided by vanity; and my eyes burned with anguish and anger.

1914

Kew Gardens

VIRGINIA WOOLF
[1882–1941]

From the oval-shaped flower bed there rose perhaps a hundred stalks spreading into heart-shaped or tongue-shaped leaves half way up and unfurling at the tip red or blue or yellow petals marked with spots of colour raised upon the surface; and from the red, blue, or yellow gloom of the throat emerged a straight bar, rough with gold dust and slightly clubbed at the end. The petals were voluminous enough to be stirred by the summer breeze, and when they moved, the red, blue, and yellow lights passed one over the other, staining an inch of the brown earth beneath with a spot of the most intricate colour. The light fell either upon the smooth grey back of a pebble, or, the shell of a snail with its brown, circular veins, or falling into a raindrop, it expanded with such intensity of red, blue, and yellow the thin walls of water that one expected them to burst and disappear. Instead, the drop was left in a second silver grey once more, and the light now settled upon the flesh of a leaf, revealing the branching thread of fibre beneath the surface, and again it moved on and spread its illumination in the vast green spaces beneath the dome of the heart-shaped and tongue-shaped leaves. Then the breeze stirred rather more briskly overhead and the colour was flashed into the air above, into the eyes of the men and women who walk in Kew Gardens in July.

The figures of these men and women straggled past the flower bed with a curiously irregular movement not unlike that of the white and blue butterflies who crossed the turf in zig-zag flights from bed to bed. The man was about six inches in front of the woman, strolling carelessly, while she bore on with greater purpose, only turning her head now and then to see that the children were not too far behind. The man kept this distance in front of the woman purposely, though perhaps unconsciously, for he wished to go on with his thoughts.

"Fifteen years ago I came here with Lily," he thought. "We sat somewhere over there by a lake, and I begged her to marry me all through the hot afternoon. How the dragonfly kept circling round us: how clearly I see the dragon-fly and her shoe with the square silver buckle at the toe. All the time I spoke I saw her shoe and when it moved impatiently I knew without looking up what she was going to say: the whole of her seemed to be in her shoe. And my love, my desire, were in the dragonfly; for some reason I thought that if it settled there, on that leaf, the broad one with the red flower in the middle of it, if the dragon fly settled on the leaf she would say 'Yes' at once. But the dragonfly went round and round: it never settled anywhere—of course not, happily not, or I shouldn't be walking here with Eleanor and the children—Tell me, Eleanor, d'you ever think of the past?"

"Why do you ask, Simon?"

"Because I've been thinking of the past. I've been thinking of Lily, the woman I might have married . . . Well, why are you silent? Do you mind my thinking of the past?"

"Why should I mind, Simon? Doesn't one always think of the past, in a garden with men and women lying under the trees? Aren't they one's past, all that remains of it, those men and women, those ghosts lying under the trees, . . . one's happiness, one's reality?"

"For me, a square silver shoe-buckle and a dragonfly—"

"For me, a kiss. Imagine six little girls sitting before their easels twenty years ago, down by the side of a lake, painting the water-lilies, the first red water-lilies I'd ever seen. And suddenly a kiss, there on the back of my neck. And my hand shook all the afternoon so that I couldn't paint. I took out my watch and marked the hour when I would allow myself to think of the kiss for five minutes only—it was so precious—the kiss of an old grey-haired woman with a wart on her nose, the mother of all my kisses all my life. Come, Caroline, come, Hubert."

They walked on past the flowerbed, now walking four abreast, and soon diminished in size among the trees and looked half transparent as the sunlight and shade swam over their backs in large trembling irregular patches.

In the oval flower bed the snail, whose shell had been stained red, blue, and yellow for the space of two minutes or so, now appeared to be moving very slightly in its shell, and next began to labour over the crumbs of loose earth which broke away and rolled down as it passed over them. It appeared to have a definite goal in front of it, differing in this respect from the singular high-stepping angular green insect who attempted to cross in front of it, and waited for a second with its antennae trembling as if in deliberation, and then stepped off as rapidly and strangely in the opposite direction. Brown cliffs with deep green lakes in the hollows, flat, blade-like trees that waved from root to tip, round boulders of grey stone, vast crumpled surfaces of a thin crackling texture—all these objects lay across the snail's progress between one stalk and another to his goal. Before he had decided whether to circumvent the arched tent of a dead leaf or to breast it there came past the bed the feet of other human beings.

This time they were both men. The younger of the two wore an expression of perhaps unnatural calm; he raised his eyes and fixed them very steadily in front of him while his companion spoke, and directly his companion had done speaking he looked on the ground again and sometimes opened his lips only after a long pause and sometimes did not open them at all. The elder man had a curiously uneven and shaky method of walking, jerking his hand forward and throwing up his head abruptly, rather in the manner of an impatient carriage horse tired of waiting outside a house; but in the man these gestures were irresolute and pointless. He talked almost incessantly; he smiled to himself and again began to talk, as if the smile had been an answer. He was talking about spirits—the spirits of the dead, who, according to him, were even now telling him all sorts of odd things about their experiences in Heaven.

"Heaven was known to the ancients as Thessaly, William, and now, with this war, the spirit matter is rolling between the hills like thunder." He paused, seemed to listen, smiled, jerked his head, and continued: —

"You have a small electric battery and a piece of rubber to insulate the wire—isolate?—insulate?—well, we'll skip the details, no good going into details that wouldn't be understood—and in short the little machine stands in any convenient position by the head of the bed, we will say, on a neat mahogany stand. All arrangements being properly fixed by workmen under my direction, the widow applies her ear and summons the spirit by sign as agreed. Women! Widows! Women in black—"

Here he seemed to have caught sight of a woman's dress in the distance, which in the shade looked a purple black. He took off his hat, placed his hand upon his heart, and hurried towards her muttering and gesticulating feverishly. But William caught him by the sleeve and touched a flower with the tip of his walking-stick in order to divert the old man's attention. After looking at it for a moment in some confusion the old man bent his ear to it and seemed to answer a voice speaking from it, for he began talking about the forests of Uruguay which he had visited hundreds of years ago in company with the most beautiful young woman in Europe. He could be heard murmuring about forests of Uruguay blanketed with the wax petals of tropical roses, nightingales, sea beaches, mermaids, and women drowned at sea, as he suffered himself to be moved on by William, upon whose face the look of stoical patience grew slowly deeper and deeper.

Following his steps so closely as to be slightly puzzled by his gestures came two elderly women of the lower middle class, one stout and ponderous, the other rosy-cheeked and nimble. Like most people of their station they were frankly fascinated by any signs of eccentricity betokening a disordered brain, especially in the well-to-do; but they were too far off to be certain whether the gestures were merely eccentric or genuinely mad. After they had scrutinised the old man's back in silence for a moment and given each other a queer, sly look, they went on energetically piecing together their very complicated dialogue:

"Nell, Bert, Lot, Cess, Phil, Pa, he says, I says, she says, I says, I says, I says—"

"My Bert, Sis, Bill, Grandad, the old man, sugar,

Sugar, flour, kippers, greens,
Sugar, sugar, sugar."

The ponderous woman looked through the pattern of falling words at the flowers standing cool, firm, and upright in the earth, with a curious expression. She saw them as a sleeper waking from a heavy sleep sees a brass candlestick reflecting the light in an unfamiliar way, and closes his eyes and opens them, and seeing the brass candlestick again, finally starts broad awake and stares at the candlestick with all his powers. So the heavy woman came to a standstill opposite the oval-shaped flower bed, and ceased even to pretend to listen to what the other woman was saying. She stood there letting the words fall over her, swaying the top part of her body slowly backwards and forwards, looking at the flowers. Then she suggested that they should find a seat and have their tea.

The snail had now considered every possible method of reaching his goal without going round the dead leaf or climbing over it. Let alone the effort needed for climbing a leaf, he was doubtful whether the thin texture which vibrated with such an alarming crackle when touched even by the tip of his horns would bear his weight; and this determined him finally to creep beneath it, for there was a point where the leaf curved high enough from the ground to admit him. He had just inserted his head in the opening and was taking stock of the high brown roof and was getting used to the cool brown light when two other people came past outside on the turf. This time they were both young, a young man and a young woman. They were both in the prime of youth, or even in that season which precedes the prime of youth, the season before the smooth pink folds of the flower have burst their gummy case, when the wings of the butterfly, though fully grown, are motionless in the sun.

"Lucky it isn't Friday," he observed.

"Why? D'you believe in luck?"

"They make you pay sixpence on Friday."

"What's sixpence anyway? Isn't it worth sixpence?"

"What's 'it'—what do you mean by 'it'?"

"O anything—I mean—you know what I mean."

Long pauses came between each of these remarks, they were uttered in toneless and monotonous voices. The couple stood still on the edge of the flowerbed, and together pressed the end of her parasol deep down into the soft earth. The action and the fact that his hand rested on the top of hers expressed their feelings in a strange way, as these short insignificant words also expressed something, words with short wings for their heavy body of meaning, inadequate to carry them far and thus alighting awkwardly upon the very common objects that surrounded them and were to their inexperienced touch so massive, but who knows (so they thought as they pressed the parasol into the earth) what precipices aren't concealed in them, or what slopes of ice don't shine in the sun on the other side? Who knows? Who has ever seen this before? Even when she wondered what sort of tea they gave you at Kew, he felt that something loomed up behind her words, and stood vast and solid behind them; and the mist very slowly rose and uncovered—O Heavens, what were those shapes?—little white tables, and waitresses who looked first at her and then at him; and there was a bill that he would pay with a real two shilling piece, and it was real, all real, he assured himself, fingering the coin in his pocket, real to everyone except to him and to her; even to him it began to seem real; and then—but it was too exciting to stand and think any longer, and he pulled the parasol out of the earth with a jerk and was impatient to find the place where one had tea with other people, like other people.

"Come along Trissie; it's time we had our tea."

"Wherever *does* one have one's tea?" she asked with the oddest thrill of excitement in her voice, looking vaguely round and letting herself be drawn on down the grass path, trailing her parasol, turning her head this way and that way, forgetting her tea, wishing to go down there and then down there, remembering orchids and cranes among wild flowers, a Chinese pagoda and a crimson-crested bird; but he bore her on.

Thus one couple after another with much the same irregular and aimless movement passed the flower bed and were enveloped in layer after layer of green blue vapour, in which at first their bodies had substance and a dash of colour, but later both substance and colour dissolved in the green blue atmosphere. How hot it was! So hot that even the thrush chose to hop, like a mechanical bird, in the shadow of the flowers, with long pauses between one movement and the next; instead of rambling vaguely the white butterflies danced one above another, making with their white shifting flakes the outline of a shattered marble column above the tallest flowers; the glass roofs of the palm house shone as if a whole market full of shiny green umbrellas had opened in the sun; and in the drone of the aeroplane the voice of the summer sky murmured its fierce soul. Yellow and black, pink and snow white, shapes of all these colours, men, women, and children were spotted for a second upon the horizon, and then, seeing the breadth of yellow that lay upon the grass, they wavered and sought shade beneath the trees, dissolving like drops of water in the yellow and green atmosphere, staining it faintly with red and blue. It seemed as if all gross and heavy bodies had sunk down in the heat motionless and lay huddled upon the ground, but their voices went wavering from them as if they were flames lolling from the thick waxen bodies of candles. Voices, yes, voices, wordless voices, breaking the silence suddenly with such depth of contentment, such passion of desire, or, in the voices of children, such freshness of surprise; breaking the silence? But there was no silence; all the time the motor omnibuses were turning their wheels and changing their gear; like a vast nest of Chinese boxes all of wrought steel turning ceaselessly one within another the city murmured; on the top of which the voices cried aloud and the petals of myriads of flowers flashed their colours into the air.

1919

A Hunger Artist

FRANZ KAFKA
[1883–1924]

During these last decades the interest in professional fasting has markedly diminished. It used to pay very well to stage such great performances under one's own management, but today that is quite impossible. We live in a different world now. At one time the whole town took a lively interest in the hunger artist; from day to day of his fast the excitement mounted; everybody wanted to see him at least once a day; there were people who bought season tickets for the last few days and sat from morning till night in front of his small barred cage; even in the nighttime there were visiting hours, when the whole effect was heightened by torch flares; on fine days the cage was set out in the open air, and then it was the children's special treat to see the hunger artist; for their elders he was often just a joke that happened to be in fashion, but the children stood openmouthed, holding each other's hands for greater security, marveling at him as he sat there pallid in black tights, with his ribs sticking out so prominently, not even on a seat but down among straw on the ground, sometimes giving a courteous nod, answering questions with a constrained smile, or perhaps stretching an arm through the bars so that one might feel how thin it was, and then again withdrawing deep into himself, paying no attention to anyone or anything, not even to the all-important striking of the clock that was the only piece of furniture in his cage, but merely staring into vacancy with half-shut eyes, now and then taking a sip from a tiny glass of water to moisten his lips.

Besides casual onlookers there were also relays of permanent watchers selected by the public, usually butchers, strangely enough, and it was their task to watch the hunger artist day and night, three of

Translated by Willa and Edwin Muir, 1948.

them at a time, in case he should have some secret recourse to nourishment. This was nothing but a formality, instituted to reassure the masses, for the initiates knew well enough that during his fast the artist would never in any circumstances, not even under forcible compulsion, swallow the smallest morsel of food; the honor of his profession forbade it. Not every watcher, of course, was capable of understanding this, there were often groups of night watchers who were very lax in carrying out their duties and deliberately huddled together in a retired corner to play cards with great absorption, obviously intending to give the hunger artist the chance of a little refreshment, which they supposed he could draw from some private hoard. Nothing annoyed the artist more than such watchers; they made him miserable; they made his fast seem unendurable; sometimes he mastered his feebleness sufficiently to sing during their watch for as long as he could keep going, to show them how unjust their suspicions were. But that was of little use; they only wondered at his cleverness in being able to fill his mouth even while singing. Much more to his taste were the watchers who sat close up to the bars, who were not content with the dim night lighting of the hall but focused him in the full glare of the electric pocket torch given them by the impresario. The harsh light did not trouble him at all, in any case he could never sleep properly, and he could always drowse a little, whatever the light, at any hour, even when the hall was thronged with noisy onlookers. He was quite happy at the prospect of spending a sleepless night with such watchers; he was ready to exchange jokes with them, to tell them stories out of his nomadic life, anything at all to keep them awake and demonstrate to them again that he had no eatables in his cage and that he was fasting as not one of them could fast. But his happiest moment was when the morning came and an enormous breakfast was brought them, at his expense, on which they flung themselves with the keen appetite of healthy men after a weary night of wakefulness. Of course there were people who argued that this breakfast was an unfair attempt to bribe the watchers, but that was going rather too far, and when they were invited to take on a night's vigil without a breakfast, merely for the sake of the cause, they made themselves scarce, although they stuck stubbornly to their suspicions.

Such suspicions, anyhow, were a necessary accompaniment to the profession of fasting. No one could possibly watch the hunger artist continuously, day and night, and so no one could produce first-hand evidence that the fast had really been rigorous and continuous; only the artist himself could know that, he was therefore bound to be the sole completely satisfied spectator of his own fast. Yet for other reasons he was never satisfied; it was not perhaps mere fasting that had brought him to such skeleton thinness that many people had regretfully to keep away from his exhibitions, because the sight of him was too much for them, perhaps it was dissatisfaction with himself that had worn him down. For he alone knew, what no other initiate knew, how easy it was to fast. It was the easiest thing in the world. He made no secret of this, yet people did not believe him, at the best they set him down as modest, most of them, however, thought he was out for publicity or else was some kind of cheat who found it easy to fast because he had discovered a way of making it easy, and then had the impudence to admit the fact, more or less. He had to put up with all that, and in the course of time had got used to it, but his inner dissatisfaction always rankled, and never yet, after any term of fasting—this must be granted to his credit—had he left the cage of his own free will. The longest period of fasting was fixed by his impresario at forty days, beyond that term he was not allowed to go, not even in great cities, and there was good reason for it, too. Experience had proved that for about forty days the interest of the public could be stimulated by a steadily increasing pressure of advertisement, but after that the town began to lose interest, sympathetic support began notably to fall off; there were of course local variations as between one town and another or one country and another, but as a general rule forty days marked the limit. So on the fortieth day the flower-bedecked cage was opened, enthusiastic spectators filled the hall, a military band played, two doctors entered the cage to measure the results of the fast, which were announced through a megaphone, and finally two young ladies appeared, blissful at having been selected for the honor, to help the hunger artist down the few steps leading to a small table on which was spread a carefully chosen invalid repast. And at this very moment the artist always turned stubborn. True, he would entrust his bony arms to the outstretched helping hands of the ladies bending over him, but stand up he would not. Why stop fasting at this particular moment, after forty days of it? He had held out for a long time, an illimitably long time; why stop now, when he was in his best fasting form, or rather, not yet quite in his best fasting form? Why should he be cheated of the fame he would get for fasting longer, for being not only the record hunger artist of all time, which presumably he was already, but for beating his own record by a performance beyond human imagination, since he felt that there were no limits to his capacity for fasting? His public pretended to admire him so much, why should it have so little patience with him; if he could endure fasting longer, why shouldn't the public endure it? Besides, he was tired, he was comfortable sitting in the straw, and now he was supposed to lift himself to his full height and go down to a meal the very thought of which gave him a nausea that only the presence of the ladies kept him from betraying, and even that with an effort. And he looked up into the eyes of the ladies who were apparently so friendly and in reality so cruel, and shook his head, which felt too heavy on its strengthless neck. But then there happened yet again what always happened. The impresario came forward, without a word—for the band made speech impossible—lifted his arms in the air above the artist, as if inviting Heaven to look down upon its creature here in the straw, this suffering martyr, which indeed he was, although in quite another sense; grasped him around the emaciated waist, with exaggerated caution, so that the frail condition he was in might be appreciated; and committed him to the care of the blenching ladies, not without secretly giving him a shaking so that his legs and body tottered and swayed. The artist now submitted completely; his head lolled on his breast as if it had landed there by chance; his body was hollowed out; his legs in a spasm of self-preservation clung close to each other at the knees, yet scraped on the ground as if it were not really solid ground, as if they were only trying to find solid ground; and the whole weight of his body, a featherweight after all, relapsed onto one of the ladies, who, looking around for help and panting a little—this post of honor was not at all what she had expected it to be—first stretched her neck as far as she could to keep her face at least free from contact with the artist, then finding this impossible, and her more fortunate companion not coming to her aid but merely holding extended in her own trembling hand the little bunch of knucklebones that was the artist's, to the great delight of the spectators burst into tears and had to be replaced by an attendant who had long been stationed in readiness. Then came the food, a little of which the impresario managed to get between the artist's lips, while he sat in a kind of half-fainting trance, to the accompaniment of cheerful patter designed to distract the public's attention from the artist's condition; after that, a toast was drunk to the public, supposedly prompted by a whisper from the artist in the impresario's ear; the band confirmed it with a mighty flourish, the spectators melted away, and no one had any cause to be dissatisfied with the proceedings, no one except the hunger artist himself, he only, as always.

So he lived for many years, with small regular intervals of recuperation, in visible glory, honored by the world, yet in spite of that troubled in spirit, and all the more troubled because no one would take his trouble seriously. What comfort could he possibly need? What more could he possibly wish for? And if some good-natured person, feeling sorry for him, tried to console him by pointing out that his melancholy was probably caused by fasting, it could happen, especially when he had been fasting for some time, that he reacted with an outburst of fury and to the general alarm began to shake the bars of his cage like a wild animal. Yet the impresario had a way of punishing these outbreaks which he rather enjoyed putting into operation. He would apologize publicly for the artist's behavior, which was only to be excused, he admitted, because of the irritability caused by fasting; a condition hardly to be understood by well-fed people; then by natural transition he went on to mention the artist's equally incomprehensible boast that he could fast for much longer than he was doing; he praised the high ambition, the good will, the great self-denial undoubtedly implicit in such a statement; and then quite simply countered it by bringing out photographs, which were also on sale to the public, showing the artist on the fortieth day of a fast lying in bed almost dead from exhaustion. This perversion of the truth, familiar to the artist though it was, always unnerved him afresh and proved too much for him. What was a consequence of the premature ending of his fast was here presented as the cause of it! To fight against this lack of understanding, against a whole world of non-understanding, was impossible. Time and again in good faith he stood by the bars listening to the impresario, but as soon as the photographs appeared he always let go and sank with a groan back onto his straw, and the reassured public could once more come close and gaze at him.

A few years later when the witnesses of such scenes called them to mind, they often failed to understand themselves at all. For meanwhile the aforementioned change in public interest had set in; it seemed to happen almost overnight; there may have been profound causes for it, but who was going to bother about that; at any rate the pampered hunger artist suddenly found himself deserted one fine day by the amusement-seekers, who went streaming past him to other more-favored attractions. For the last time the impresario hurried him over half Europe to discover whether the old interest might still survive here and there; all in vain; everywhere, as if by secret agreement, a positive revulsion from professional fasting was in evidence. Of course it could not really have sprung up so suddenly as all that, and many premonitory symptoms which had not been sufficiently remarked or suppressed during the rush and glitter of success now came retrospectively to mind, but it was now too late to take any countermeasures. Fasting would surely come into fashion again at some future date, yet that was no comfort for those living in the present. What, then, was the hunger artist to do? He had been applauded by thousands in his time and could hardly come down to showing himself in a street booth at village fairs, and as for adopting another profession, he was not only too old for that but too fanatically devoted to fasting. So he took leave of the impresario, his partner in an unparalleled career, and hired himself to a large circus; in order to spare his own feelings he avoided reading the conditions of his contract.

A large circus with its enormous traffic in replacing and recruiting men, animals, and apparatus can always find a use for people at any time, even for a hunger artist, provided of course that he does not ask too much, and in this particular case anyhow it was not only the artist who was taken on but his famous and long-known name as well, indeed considering the peculiar nature of his performance, which was not impaired by advancing age, it could not be objected that here was an artist past his prime, no longer at the height of his professional skill, seeking a refuge in some quiet corner of a circus; on the contrary, the hunger artist averred that he could fast as well as ever, which was entirely credible, he even alleged that if he were allowed to fast as he liked, and this was at once promised him without more ado, he could astound the world by establishing a record never yet achieved, a statement that certainly provoked a smile among the other professionals, since it left out of account the change in public opinion, which the hunger artist in his zeal conveniently forgot.

He had not, however, actually lost his sense of the real situation and took it as a matter of course that he and his cage should be stationed, not in the middle of the ring as a main attraction, but outside, near the animal cages, on a site that was after all easily accessible. Large and gaily painted placards made a frame for the cage and announced what was to be seen inside it. When the public came thronging out in the intervals to see the animals, they could hardly avoid passing the hunger artist's cage and stopping there for a moment, perhaps they might even have stayed longer had not those pressing behind them in the narrow gangway, who did not understand why they should be held up on their way toward the excitements of the menagerie, made it impossible for anyone to stand gazing quietly for any length of time. And that was the reason why the hunger artist, who had of course been looking forward to these visiting hours as the main achievement of his life, began instead to shrink from them. At first he could hardly wait for the intervals; it was exhilarating to watch the crowds come streaming his way, until only too soon—not even the most obstinate self-deception, clung to almost consciously, could hold out against the fact—the conviction was borne in upon him that these people, most of them, to judge from their actions, again and again, without exception, were all on their way to the menagerie. And the first sight of them from the distance remained the best. For when they reached his cage he was at once deafened by the storm of shouting and abuse that arose from the two contending factions, which renewed themselves continuously, of those who wanted to stop and stare at him—he soon began to dislike them more than the others—not out of real interest but only out of obstinate self-assertiveness, and those who wanted to go straight on to the animals. When the first great rush was past, the stragglers came along, and these, whom nothing could have prevented from stopping to look at him as long as they had breath, raced past with long strides, hardly even glancing at him, in their haste to get to the menagerie in time. And all too rarely did it happen that he had a stroke of luck, when some father of a family fetched up before him with his children, pointed a finger at the hunger artist, and explained at length what the phenomenon meant, telling stories of earlier years when he himself had watched similar but much more thrilling performances, and the children, still rather uncomprehending, since neither inside nor outside school had they been sufficiently prepared for this lesson—what did they care about fasting?—yet showed by the brightness of their intent eyes that new and better times might be coming. Perhaps, said the hunger artist to himself many a time, things would be a little better if his cage were set not quite so near the menagerie. That made it too easy for people to make their choice, to say nothing of what he suffered from the stench of the menagerie, the animals' restlessness by night, the carrying past of raw lumps of flesh for the beasts of prey, the roaring at feeding times, which depressed him continually. But he did not dare to lodge a complaint with the management; after all, he had the animals to thank for the troops of people who passed his cage, among whom there might always be one here and there to take an interest in him, and who could tell where they might seclude him if he called attention to his existence and thereby to the fact that, strictly speaking, he was only an impediment on the way to the menagerie.

A small impediment, to be sure, one that grew steadily less. People grew familiar with the strange idea that they could be expected, in times like these, to take an interest in a hunger artist, and with this familiarity the verdict went out against him. He might fast as much as he could, and he did so; but nothing could save him now, people passed him by. Just try to explain to anyone the art of fasting! Anyone who has no feeling for it cannot be made to understand it. The fine placards grew dirty and illegible, they were torn down; the little notice board telling the number of fast days achieved, which at first was changed carefully every day, had long stayed at the same figure, for after the first few weeks even this small task seemed pointless to the staff; and so the artist simply fasted on and on, as he had once dreamed of doing, and it was no trouble to him, just as he had always foretold, but no one counted the days, no one, not even the artist himself, knew what records he was already breaking, and his heart grew heavy. And when once in a while some leisurely passer-by stopped, made merry over the old figure on the board, and spoke of swindling, that was in its way the stupidest lie ever invented by indifference and inborn malice, since it was not the hunger artist who was cheating, he was working honestly, but the world was cheating him of his reward.

Many more days went by, however, and that too came to an end. An overseer's eye fell on the cage one day and he asked the attendants why this perfectly good cage should be left standing there unused with dirty straw inside it; nobody knew, until one man, helped out by the notice board, remembered about the hunger artist. They poked into the straw with sticks and found him in it. "Are you still fasting?" asked the overseer, "when on earth do you mean to stop?" "Forgive me, everybody," whispered the hunger artist; only the overseer, who had his ear to the bars, understood him. "Of course," said the overseer, and tapped his forehead with a finger to let the attendants know what state the man was in, "we forgive you." "I always wanted you to admire my fasting," said the hunger artist. "We do admire it," said the overseer, affably. "But you shouldn't admire it," said the hunger artist. "Well then we don't admire it," said the overseer, "but why shouldn't we admire it?" "Because I have to fast, I can't help it," said the hunger artist. "What a fellow you are," said the overseer, "and why can't you help it?" "Because," said the hunger artist, lifting his head a little and speaking, with his lips pursed, as if for a kiss, right into the overseer's ear, so that no syllable might be lost, "because I couldn't find the food I liked. If I had found it, believe me, I should have made no fuss and stuffed myself like you or anyone else." These were his last words, but in his dimming eyes remained the firm though no longer proud persuasion that he was still continuing to fast.

"Well, clear this out now!" said the overseer, and they buried the hunger artist, straw and all. Into the cage they put a young panther. Even the most insensitive felt it refreshing to see this wild creature leaping around the cage that had so long been dreary. The panther was all right. The food he liked was brought him without hesitation by the attendants; he seemed not even to miss his freedom; his noble body, furnished almost to the bursting point with all that it needed, seemed to carry freedom around with it too; somewhere in his jaws it seemed to lurk; and the joy of life streamed with such ardent passion from his throat that for the onlookers it was not easy to stand the shock of it. But they braced themselves, crowded around the cage, and did not want ever to move away.

1922

Miss Brill

KATHERINE MANSFIELD

[1888–1923]

Although it was so brilliantly fine—the blue sky powdered with gold and great spots of light like white wine splashed over the Jardins Publiques—Miss Brill was glad that she had decided on her fur. The air was motionless, but when you opened your mouth there was just a faint chill, like a chill from a glass of iced water before you sip, and now and again a leaf came drifting—from nowhere, from the sky. Miss Brill put up her hand and touched her fur. Dear little thing! It was nice to feel it again. She had taken it out of its box that afternoon, shaken out the moth-powder, given it a good brush, and rubbed the life back into the dim little eyes. "What has been happening to me?" said the sad little eyes. Oh, how sweet it was to see them snap at her again from the red eiderdown! . . . But the nose, which was of some black composition, wasn't at all firm. It must have had a knock, somehow. Never mind—a little dab of black sealing-wax when the time came—when it was absolutely necessary. . . . Little rogue! Yes, she really felt like that about it. Little rogue biting its tail just by her left ear. She could have taken it off and laid it on her lap and stroked it. She felt a tingling in her hands and arms, but that came from walking, she supposed. And when she breathed, something light and sad—no, not sad, exactly—something gentle seemed to move in her bosom.

There were a number of people out this afternoon, far more than last Sunday. And the band sounded louder and gayer. That was because the Season had begun. For although the band played all the year round on Sundays, out of season it was never the same. It was like some one playing with only the family to listen; it didn't care how it played if there weren't any strangers present. Wasn't the conductor wearing a new coat, too? She was sure it was new. He scraped with his foot and flapped his arms like a rooster about to crow, and the bandsmen sitting in the green rotunda blew out their cheeks and glared at the music. Now there came a little "flutey" bit—very pretty!—a little chain of bright drops. She was sure it would be repeated. It was; she lifted her head and smiled.

Only two people shared her "special" seat: a fine old man in a velvet coat, his hands clasped over a huge carved walking-stick, and a big old woman, sitting upright, with a roll of knitting on her embroidered apron. They did not speak. This was disappointing, for Miss Brill always looked forward to the conversation. She had become really quite expert, she thought, at listening as though she didn't listen, at sitting in other people's lives just for a minute while they talked round her.

She glanced, sideways, at the old couple. Perhaps they would go soon. Last Sunday, too, hadn't been as interesting as usual. An Englishman and his wife, he wearing a dreadful Panama hat and she button boots. And she'd gone on the whole time about how she ought to wear spectacles; she knew she needed them; but that it was no good getting any; they'd be sure to break and they'd never keep on. And he'd been so patient. He'd suggested everything—gold rims, the kind that curved round your ears, little pads inside the bridge. No, nothing would please her. "They'll always be sliding down my nose!" Miss Brill had wanted to shake her.

The old people sat on the bench, still as statues. Never mind, there was always the crowd to watch. To and fro, in front of the flower-beds and the band rotunda, the couples and groups paraded, stopped to talk, to greet, to buy a handful of flowers from the old beggar who had his tray fixed to the railings. Little children ran among them, swooping and laughing; little boys with big white silk bows under their chins, little girls, little French dolls, dressed up in velvet and lace. And sometimes a tiny staggerer came suddenly rocking into the open from under the trees, stopped, stared, as suddenly sat down "flop," until its small high-stepping mother, like a young hen, rushed scolding to its rescue. Other people sat on the benches and green chairs, but they were nearly always the same, Sunday after Sunday, and—Miss Brill had often noticed—there was something funny about nearly all of them. They were odd, silent, nearly all old, and from the way they stared they looked as though they'd just come from dark little rooms or even—even cupboards!

Behind the rotunda the slender trees with yellow leaves down drooping, and through them just a line of sea, and beyond the blue sky with gold-veined clouds.

Tum-tum-tum tiddle-um! tiddle-um! tum tiddley-um tum ta! blew the band.

Two young girls in red came by and two young soldiers in blue met them, and they laughed and paired and went off arm-in-arm. Two peasant women with funny straw hats passed, gravely, leading beautiful smoke-coloured donkeys. A cold, pale nun hurried by. A beautiful woman came along and dropped her bunch of violets, and a little boy ran after to hand them to her, and she took them and threw them away as if they'd been poisoned. Dear me! Miss Brill didn't know whether to admire that or not! And now an ermine toque and a gentleman in grey met just in front of her. He was tall, stiff, dignified, and she was wearing the ermine toque she'd bought when her hair was yellow. Now everything, her hair, her face, even her eyes, was the same colour as the shabby ermine, and her hand, in its cleaned glove, lifted to dab her lips, was a tiny yellowish paw. Oh, she was so pleased to see him—delighted! She rather thought they were going to meet that afternoon. She described where she'd been—everywhere, here, there, along by the sea. The day was so charming—didn't he agree? And wouldn't he, perhaps? . . . But he shook his head, lighted a cigarette, slowly breathed a great deep puff into her face, and, even while she was still talking and laughing, flicked the match away and walked on. The ermine toque was alone; she smiled more brightly than ever. But even the band seemed to know what she was feeling and played more softly, played tenderly, and the drum beat, "The Brute! The Brute!" over and over. What would she do? What was going to happen now? But as Miss Brill wondered, the ermine toque turned, raised her hand as though she'd seen some one else, much nicer, just over there, and pattered away. And the band changed again and played more quickly, more gaily than ever, and the old couple on Miss Brill's seat got up and marched away, and such a funny old man with long whiskers hobbled along in time to the music and was nearly knocked over by four girls walking abreast.

Oh, how fascinating it was! How she enjoyed it! How she loved sitting here, watching it all! It was like a play. It was exactly like a play. Who could believe the sky at the back wasn't painted? But it wasn't till a little brown dog trotted on solemn and then slowly trotted off, like a little "theatre" dog, a little dog that had been drugged, that Miss Brill discovered what it was that made it so exciting. They were all on the stage. They weren't only the audience, not only looking on; they were acting. Even she had a part and came every Sunday. No doubt somebody would have noticed if she hadn't been there; she was part of the performance after all. How strange she'd never thought of it like that before! And yet it explained why she made such a point of starting from home at just the same time each week—so as not to be late for the performance—and it also explained why she had quite a queer, shy feeling at telling her English pupils how she spent her Sunday afternoons. No wonder! Miss Brill nearly laughed out loud. She was on the stage. She thought of the old invalid gentleman to whom she read the newspaper four afternoons a week while he slept in the garden. She had got quite used to the frail head on the cotton pillow, the hollowed eyes, the open mouth and the high pinched nose. If he'd been dead she mightn't have noticed for weeks; she wouldn't have minded. But suddenly he knew he was having the paper read to him by an actress! "An actress!" The old head lifted; two points of light quivered in the old eyes. "An actress—are ye?" And Miss Brill smoothed the newspaper as though it were the manuscript of her part and said gently: "Yes, I have been an actress for a long time."

The band had been having a rest. Now they started again. And what they played was warm, sunny, yet there was just a faint chill—something, what was it?—not sadness—no, not sadness—a something that made you want to sing. The tune lifted, lifted, the light shone; and it seemed to Miss Brill that in another moment all of them, all the whole company, would begin singing. The young ones, the laughing ones who were moving together, they would begin, and the men's voices, very resolute and brave, would join them. And then she too, she too, and the others on the benches—they would come in with a kind of accompaniment—something low, that scarcely rose or fell, something so beautiful—moving. . . . And Miss Brill's eyes filled with tears and she looked smiling at all the other members of the company. Yes, we understand, we understand, she thought—though what they understood she didn't know.

Just at that moment a boy and a girl came and sat down where the old couple had been. They were beautifully dressed; they were in love. The hero and heroine, of course, just arrived from his father's yacht. And still soundlessly singing, still with that trembling smile, Miss Brill prepared to listen.

"No, not now," said the girl. "Not here, I can't."

"But why? Because of that stupid old thing at the end there?" asked the boy. "Why does she come here at all—who wants her? Why doesn't she keep her silly old mug at home?"

"It's her fu-fur which is so funny," giggled the girl. "It's exactly like a fried whiting."

"Ah, be off with you!" said the boy in an angry whisper. Then: "Tell me, ma petite chérie—"

"No, not here," said the girl. "Not *yet*."

On her way home she usually bought a slice of honey-cake at the baker's. It was her Sunday treat. Sometimes there was an almond in her slice, sometimes not. It made a great difference. If there was an almond it was like carrying home a tiny present—a surprise—something that might very well not have been there. She hurried on the almond Sundays and struck the match for the kettle in quite a dashing way.

But to-day she passed the baker's by, climbed the stairs, went into the little dark room—her room like a cupboard—and sat down on the red eiderdown. She sat there for a long time. The box that the fur came out of was on the bed. She unclasped the necklet quickly; quickly, without looking, laid it inside. But when she put the lid on she thought she heard something crying.

1920

A Rose for Emily

WILLIAM FAULKNER
[1897–1962]

1

When Miss Emily Grierson died, our whole town went to her funeral: the men through a sort of respectful affection for a fallen monument, the women mostly out of curiosity to see the inside of her house, which no one save an old manservant—a combined gardener and cook—had seen in at least ten years.

It was a big, squarish frame house that had once been white, decorated with cupolas and spires and scrolled balconies in the heavily lightsome style of the seventies, set on what had once been our most select street. But garages and cotton gins had encroached and obliterated even the august names of that neighborhood; only Miss Emily's house was left, lifting its stubborn and coquettish decay above the cotton wagons and the gasoline pumps—an eyesore among eyesores. And now Miss Emily had gone to join the representatives of those august names where they lay in the cedar-bemused cemetery among the ranked and anonymous graves of Union and Confederate soldiers who fell at the battle of Jefferson.

Alive, Miss Emily had been a tradition, a duty, and a care; a sort of hereditary obligation upon the town, dating from that day in 1894 when Colonel Sartoris, the mayor—he who fathered the edict that no Negro woman should appear on the streets without an apron—remitted her taxes, the dispensation dating from the death of her father on into perpetuity. Not that Miss Emily would have accepted charity. Colonel Sartoris invented an involved tale to the effect that Miss Emily's father had loaned money to the town, which the town, as a matter of business, preferred this way of repaying. Only a man of Colonel Sartoris's generation and thought could have invented it, and only a woman could have believed it.

When the next generation, with its more modern ideas, became mayors and aldermen, this arrangement created some little dissatisfaction. On the first of the year they mailed her a tax notice. February came, and there was no reply. They wrote her a formal letter, asking her to call at the sheriff's office at her convenience. A week later the mayor wrote her himself, offering to call or to send his car for her, and received in reply a note on paper of an archaic shape, in a thin, flowing calligraphy in faded ink, to the effect that she no longer went out at all. The tax notice was also enclosed, without comment.

They called a special meeting of the Board of Aldermen. A deputation waited upon her, knocked at the door through which no visitor had passed since she ceased giving china-painting lessons eight or ten years earlier. They were admitted by the old Negro into a dim hall from which a stairway mounted into still more shadow. It smelled of dust and disuse—a close, dank smell. The Negro led them into the parlor. It was furnished in heavy, leather-covered furniture. When the Negro opened the blinds of one window, they could see that the leather was cracked; and when they sat down, a faint dust rose sluggishly about their thighs, spinning with slow motes in the single sun-ray. On a tarnished gilt easel before the fireplace stood a crayon portrait of Miss Emily's father.

They rose when she entered—a small, fat woman in black, with a thin gold chain descending to her waist and vanishing into her belt, leaning on an ebony cane with a tarnished gold head. Her skeleton was small and spare; perhaps that was why what would have been merely plumpness in another was obesity in her. She looked bloated, like a body long submerged in motionless water, and of that pallid hue. Her eyes, lost in the fatty ridges of her face, looked like two small pieces of coal pressed into a lump of dough as they moved from one face to another while the visitors stated their errand.

She did not ask them to sit. She just stood in the door and listened quietly until the spokesman came to a stumbling halt. Then they could hear the invisible watch ticking at the end of the gold chain.

Her voice was dry and cold. "I have no taxes in Jefferson. Colonel Sartoris explained it to me. Perhaps one of you can gain access to the city records and satisfy yourselves."

"But we have. We are the city authorities, Miss Emily. Didn't you get a notice from the sheriff, signed by him?"

"I received a paper, yes," Miss Emily said. "Perhaps he considers himself the sheriff. . . . I have no taxes in Jefferson."

"But there is nothing on the books to show that, you see. We must go by the —"

"See Colonel Sartoris. I have no taxes in Jefferson."

"But, Miss Emily —"

"See Colonel Sartoris." (Colonel Sartoris had been dead almost ten years.) "I have no taxes in Jefferson. Tobe!" The Negro appeared. "Show these gentlemen out."

2

So she vanquished them, horse and foot, just as she had vanquished their fathers thirty years before about the smell. That was two years after her father's death and a short time after her sweetheart—the one we believed would marry her—had deserted her. After her father's death she went out very little; after her sweetheart went away, people hardly saw her at all. A few of the ladies had the temerity to call, but were not received, and the only sign of life about the place was the Negro man—a young man then—going in and out with a market basket.

"Just as if a man—any man—could keep a kitchen properly," the ladies said; so they were not surprised when the smell developed. It was another link between the gross, teeming world and the high and mighty Griersons.

A neighbor, a woman, complained to the mayor, Judge Stevens, eighty years old.

"But what will you have me do about it, madam?" he said.

"Why, send her word to stop it," the woman said. "Isn't there a law?"

"I'm sure that won't be necessary," Judge Stevens said. "It's probably just a snake or a rat that nigger of hers killed in the yard. I'll speak to him about it."

The next day he received two more complaints, one from a man who came in diffident deprecation. "We really must do something about it, Judge. I'd be the last one in the world to bother Miss Emily, but we've got to do something." That night the Board of Aldermen met—three graybeards and one younger man, a member of the rising generation.

"It's simple enough," he said. "Send her word to have her place cleaned up. Give her a certain time to do it in, and if she don't. . . ."

"Dammit, sir," Judge Stevens said, "will you accuse a lady to her face of smelling bad?"

So the next night, after midnight, four men crossed Miss Emily's lawn and slunk about the house like burglars, sniffing along the base of the brickwork and at the cellar openings while one of them performed a regular sowing motion with his hand out of a sack slung from his shoulder. They broke open the cellar door and sprinkled lime there, and in all the outbuildings. As they recrossed the lawn, a window that had been dark was lighted and Miss Emily sat in it, the light behind her, and her upright torso motionless as that of an idol. They crept quietly across the lawn and into the shadow of the locusts that lined the street. After a week or two the smell went away.

That was when people had begun to feel really sorry for her. People in our town, remembering how old lady Wyatt, her great-aunt, had gone completely crazy at last, believed that the Griersons held themselves a little too high for what they really were. None of the young men were quite good enough for Miss Emily and such. We had long thought of them as a tableau. Miss Emily a slender figure in white in the background, her father a spraddled silhouette in the foreground, his back to her and clutching a horsewhip, the two of them framed by the backflung front door. So when she got to be thirty and was still single, we were not pleased exactly, but vindicated; even with insanity in the family she wouldn't have turned down all of her chances if they had really materialized.

When her father died, it got about that the house was all that was left to her; and in a way, people were glad. At last they could pity Miss Emily. Being left alone, and a pauper, she had become humanized. Now she too would know the old thrill and the old despair of a penny more or less.

The day after his death all the ladies prepared to call at the house and offer condolence and aid, as is our custom. Miss Emily met them at the door, dressed as usual and with no trace of grief on her face. She told them that her father was not dead. She did that for three days, with the ministers calling on her, and the doctors, trying to persuade her to let them dispose of the body. Just as they were about to resort to law and force, she broke down, and they buried her father quickly.

We did not say she was crazy then. We believed she had to do that. We remembered all the young men her father had driven away, and we knew that with nothing left, she would have to cling to that which had robbed her, as people will.

3

She was sick for a long time. When we saw her again, her hair was cut short, making her look like a girl, with a vague resemblance to those angels in colored church windows—sort of tragic and serene.

The town had just let the contracts for paving the sidewalks, and in the summer after her father's death they began the work. The construction company came with niggers and mules and machinery, and a foreman named Homer Barron, a Yankee—a big, dark, ready man, with a big voice and eyes lighter than his face. The little boys would follow in groups to hear him cuss the niggers, and the niggers singing in time to the rise and fall of picks. Pretty soon he knew everybody in town. Whenever you heard a lot of laughing anywhere about the square, Homer Barron would be in the center of the group. Presently, we began to see him and Miss Emily on Sunday afternoons driving in the yellow-wheeled buggy and the matched team of bays from the livery stable.

At first we were glad that Miss Emily would have an interest, because the ladies all said, "Of course a Grierson would not think seriously of a Northerner, a day laborer." But there were still others, older people, who said that even grief could not cause a real lady to forget *noblesse oblige*—without calling it *noblesse oblige*. They just said, "Poor Emily. Her kinsfolk should come to her." She had some kin in Alabama; but years ago her father had fallen out with them over the estate of old lady Wyatt, the crazy woman, and there was no communication between the two families. They had not even been represented at the funeral.

And as soon as the old people said, "Poor Emily," the whispering began. "Do you suppose it's really so?" they said to one another. "Of course it is. What else could. . . ." This behind their hands; rustling of craned silk and satin behind jalousies closed upon the sun of Sunday afternoon as the thin, swift clop-clop-clop of the matched team passed: "Poor Emily."

She carried her head high enough—even when we believed that she was fallen. It was as if she demanded more than ever the recognition of her dignity as the last Grierson; as if it had wanted that touch of earthiness to reaffirm her imperviousness. Like when she bought the rat poison, the arsenic. That was over a year after they had begun to say "Poor Emily," and while the two female cousins were visiting her.

"I want some poison," she said to the druggist. She was over thirty then, still a slight woman, though thinner than usual, with cold, haughty black eyes in a face the flesh of which was strained across the temples and about the eye-sockets as you imagine a lighthouse-keeper's face ought to look. "I want some poison," she said.

"Yes, Miss Emily. What kind? For rats and such? I'd recom——"

"I want the best you have. I don't care what kind."

The druggist named several. "They'll kill anything up to an elephant. But what you want is——"

"Arsenic," Miss Emily said. "Is that a good one?"

"Is . . . arsenic? Yes, ma'am. But what you want——"

"I want arsenic."

The druggist looked down at her. She looked back at him, erect, her face like a strained flag. "Why, of course," the druggist said. "If that's what you want. But the law requires you to tell what you are going to use it for."

Miss Emily just stared at him, her head tilted back in order to look him eye for eye, until he looked away and went and got the arsenic and wrapped it up. The Negro delivery boy brought her the package: the druggist didn't come back. When she opened the package at home there was written on the box, under the skull and bones: "For rats."

4

So the next day we all said, "She will kill herself"; and we said it would be the best thing. When she had first begun to be seen with Homer Barron, we had said, "She will marry him." Then we said, "She will persuade him yet," because Homer himself had remarked—he liked men, and it was known that he drank with the younger men in the Elks' Club—that he was not a marrying man. Later we said, "Poor Emily" behind the jalousies as they passed on Sunday afternoon in the glittering buggy, Miss Emily with her head high and Homer Barron with his hat cocked and a cigar in his teeth, reins and whip in a yellow glove.

Then some of the ladies began to say that it was a disgrace to the town and a bad example to the young people. The men did not want to interfere; but at last the ladies forced the Baptist minister—Miss Emily's people were Episcopal—to call upon her. He would never divulge what happened during that interview, but he refused to go back again. The next Sunday they again drove about the streets, and the following day the minister's wife wrote to Miss Emily's relations in Alabama.

So she had blood-kin under her roof again and we sat back to watch developments. At first nothing happened. Then we were sure that they were to be married. We learned that Miss Emily had been to the jeweler's and ordered a man's toilet set in silver, with the letters H.B. on each piece. Two days later we learned that she had bought a complete outfit of men's clothing, including a nightshirt, and we said, "They are married." We were really glad. We were glad because the two female cousins were even more Grierson than Miss Emily had ever been.

So we were not surprised when Homer Barron—the streets had been finished some time since—was gone. We were a little disappointed that there was not a public blowing-off, but we believed that he had gone on to prepare for Miss Emily's coming, or to give her a chance to get rid of the cousins. (By that time it was a cabal, and we were all Miss Emily's allies to help circumvent the cousins.) Sure enough, after another week they departed. And, as we had expected all along, within three days Homer Barron was back in town. A neighbor saw the Negro man admit him at the kitchen door at dusk one evening.

And that was the last we saw of Homer Barron. And of Miss Emily for some time. The Negro man went in and out with the market basket, but the front door remained closed. Now and then we would see her at the window for a moment, as the men did that night when they sprinkled the lime, but for almost six months she did not appear on the streets. Then we knew that this was to be expected too; as if that quality of her father which had thwarted her woman's life so many times had been too virulent and too furious to die.

When we next saw Miss Emily, she had grown fat and her hair was turning gray. During the next few years it grew grayer and grayer until it attained an even pepper-and-salt iron-gray, when it ceased turning. Up to the day of her death at seventy-four it was still that vigorous iron-gray, like the hair of an active man.

From that time on her front door remained closed, save during a period of six or seven years, when she was about forty, during which she gave lessons in china-painting. She fitted up a studio in one of the downstairs rooms, where the daughters and granddaughters of Colonel Sartoris's contemporaries were sent to her with the same regularity and in the same spirit that they were sent to church on Sundays with a twenty-five-cent piece for the collection plate. Meanwhile her taxes had been remitted.

Then the newer generation became the backbone and the spirit of the town, and the painting pupils grew up and fell away and did not send their children to her with boxes of color and tedious brushes and pictures cut from the ladies' magazines. The front door closed upon the last one and remained closed for good. When the town got free postal delivery, Miss Emily alone refused to let them fasten the metal numbers above her door and attach a mailbox to it. She would not listen to them.

Daily, monthly, yearly we watched the Negro grow grayer and more stooped, going in and out with the market basket. Each December we sent her a tax notice, which would be returned by the post office a week later, unclaimed. Now and then we would see her in one of the downstairs windows—she had evidently shut up the top floor of the house—like the carven torso of an idol in a niche, looking or not looking at us, we could never tell which. Thus she passed from generation to generation—dear, inescapable, impervious, tranquil, and perverse.

And so she died. Fell ill in the house filled with dust and shadows, with only a doddering Negro man to wait on her. We did not even know she was sick; we had long since given up trying to get any information from the Negro. He talked to no one, probably not even to her, for his voice had grown harsh and rusty, as if from disuse.

She died in one of the downstairs rooms, in a heavy walnut bed with a curtain, her gray head propped on a pillow yellow and moldy with age and lack of sunlight.

5

The Negro met the first of the ladies at the front door and let them in, with their hushed, sibilant voices and their quick, curious glances, and then he disappeared. He walked right through the house and out the back and was not seen again.

The two female cousins came at once. They held the funeral on the second day, with the town coming to look at Miss Emily beneath a mass of bought flowers, with the crayon face of her father musing profoundly above the bier and the ladies sibilant and macabre; and the very old men—some in their brushed Confederate uniforms—on the porch and the lawn, talking of Miss Emily as if she had been a contemporary of theirs, believing that they had danced with her and courted her perhaps, confusing time with its mathematical progression, as the old do, to whom all the past is not a diminishing road but, instead, a huge meadow which no winter ever quite touches, divided from them now by the narrow bottleneck of the most recent decade of years.

Already we knew that there was one room in that region above stairs which no one had seen in forty years, and which would have to be forced. They waited until Miss Emily was decently in the ground before they opened it.

The violence of breaking down the door seemed to fill this room with pervading dust. A thin, acrid pall as of the tomb seemed to lie everywhere upon this room decked and furnished as for a bridal; upon the valance curtains of faded rose color, upon the rose-shaded lights, upon the dressing table, upon the delicate array of crystal and the man's toilet things backed with tarnished silver, silver so tarnished that the monogram was obscured. Among them lay a collar and tie, as if they had just been removed, which, lifted, left upon the surface a pale crescent in the dust. Upon a chair hung the suit, carefully folded; beneath it the two mute shoes and the discarded socks.

The man himself lay in the bed.

For a long while we just stood there, looking down at the profound and fleshless grin. The body had apparently once lain in the attitude of an embrace, but now the long sleep that outlasts love, that conquers even the grimace of love, had cuckolded him. What was left of him, rotted beneath what was left of the nightshirt, had become inextricable from the bed in which he lay; and upon him and upon the pillow beside him lay that even coating of the patient and biding dust.

Then we noticed that in the second pillow was the indentation of a head. One of us lifted something from it, and leaning forward, that faint and invisible dust dry and acrid in the nostrils, we saw a long strand of iron-gray hair.

1931

Hills Like White Elephants

ERNEST HEMINGWAY

[1899–1961]

The hills across the valley of the Ebro were long and white. On this side there was no shade and no trees and the station was between two lines of rails in the sun. Close against the side of the station there was the warm shadow of the building and a curtain, made of strings of bamboo beads, hung across the open door into the bar, to keep out flies. The American and the girl with him sat at a table in the shade, outside the building. It was very hot and the express from Barcelona would come in forty minutes. It stopped at this junction for two minutes and went on to Madrid.

"What should we drink?" the girl asked. She had taken off her hat and put it on the table.

"It's pretty hot," the man said.

"Let's drink beer."

"*Dos cervezas*," the man said into the curtain.

"Big ones?" a woman asked from the doorway.

"Yes. Two big ones."

The woman brought two glasses of beer and two felt pads. She put the felt pads and the beer glasses on the table and looked at the man and the girl. The girl was looking off at the line of hills. They were white in the sun and the country was brown and dry.

"They look like white elephants," she said.

"I've never seen one," the man drank his beer.

"No, you wouldn't have."

"I might have," the man said. "Just because you say I wouldn't have doesn't prove anything."

The girl looked at the bead curtain. "They've painted something on it," she said. "What does it say?"

"Anis del Toro. It's a drink."

"Could we try it?"

The man called "Listen" through the curtain. The woman came out from the bar.

"Four reales."[1]

"We want two Anis del Toro."

"With water?"

"Do you want it with water?"

"I don't know," the girl said. "Is it good with water?"

"It's all right."

"You want them with water?" asked the woman.

"Yes, with water."

"It tastes like licorice," the girl said and put the glass down.

"That's the way with everything."

"Yes," said the girl. "Everything tastes of licorice. Especially all the things you've waited so long for, like absinthe."

"Oh, cut it out."

"You started it," the girl said. "I was being amused. I was having a fine time."

"Well, let's try and have a fine time."

"All right. I was trying. I said the mountains looked like white elephants. Wasn't that bright?"

"That was bright."

"I wanted to try this new drink: That's all we do, isn't it—look at things and try new drinks?"

"I guess so."

The girl looked across at the hills.

"They're lovely hills," she said. "They don't really look like white elephants. I just meant the coloring of their skin through the trees."

"Should we have another drink?"

"All right."

The warm wind blew the bead curtain against the table.

"The beer's nice and cool," the man said.

"It's lovely," the girl said.

"It's really an awfully simple operation, Jig," the man said. "It's not really an operation at all."

The girl looked at the ground the table legs rested on.

"I know you wouldn't mind it, Jig. It's really not anything. It's just to let the air in."

The girl did not say anything.

[1]Spanish silver coins.

"I'll go with you and I'll stay with you all the time. They just let the air in and then it's all perfectly natural."

"Then what will we do afterward?"

"We'll be fine afterward. Just like we were before."

"What makes you think so?"

"That's the only thing that bothers us. It's the only thing that's made us unhappy."

The girl looked at the bead curtain, put her hand out, and took hold of two of the strings of beads.

"And you think then we'll be all right and be happy."

"I know we will. You don't have to be afraid. I've known lots of people that have done it."

"So have I," said the girl. "And afterward they were all so happy."

"Well," the man said, "if you don't want to you don't have to. I wouldn't have you do it if you didn't want to. But I know it's perfectly simple."

"And you really want to?"

"I think it's the best thing to do. But I don't want you to do it if you don't really want to."

"And if I do it you'll be happy and things will be like they were and you'll love me?"

"I love you now. You know I love you."

"I know. But if I do it, then it will be nice again if I say things are like white elephants, and you'll like it?"

"I'll love it. I love it now but I just can't think about it. You know how I get when I worry."

"If I do it you won't ever worry?"

"I won't worry about that because it's perfectly simple."

"Then I'll do it. Because I don't care about me."

"What do you mean?"

"I don't care about me."

"Well, I care about you."

"Oh, yes. But I don't care about me. And I'll do it and then everything will be fine."

"I don't want you to do it if you feel that way."

The girl stood up and walked to the end of the station. Across, on the other side, were fields of grain and trees along the banks of the Ebro. Far away, beyond the river, were mountains. The shadow of a cloud moved across the field of grain and she saw the river through the trees.

"And we could have all this," she said. "And we could have everything and every day we make it more impossible."

"What did you say?"

"I said we could have everything."

"We can have everything."

"No, we can't."

"We can have the whole world."

"No, we can't."

"We can go everywhere."

"No, we can't. It isn't ours any more."

"It's ours."

"No, it isn't. And once they take it away, you never get it back."

"But they haven't taken it away."

"We'll wait and see."

"Come on back in the shade," he said. "You mustn't feel that way."

"I don't feel any way," the girl said. "I just know things."

"I don't want you to do anything that you don't want to do——"

"Nor that isn't good for me," she said. "I know. Could we have another beer?"

"All right. But you've got to realize——"

"I realize," the girl said. "Can't we maybe stop talking?"

They sat down at the table and the girl looked across at the hills on the dry side of the valley and the man looked at her and at the table.

"You've got to realize," he said, "that I don't want you to do it if you don't want to. I'm perfectly willing to go through with it if it means anything to you."

"Doesn't it mean anything to you? We could get along."

"Of course it does. But I don't want anybody but you. I don't want any one else. And I know it's perfectly simple."

"Yes, you know it's perfectly simple."

"It's all right for you to say that, but I do know it."

"Would you do something for me now?"

"I'd do anything for you."

"Would you please please please please please please please stop talking?"

He did not say anything but looked at the bags against the wall of the station. There were labels on them from all the hotels where they had spent nights.

"But I don't want you to," he said, "I don't care anything about it."

"I'll scream," the girl said.

The woman came out through the curtains with two glasses of beer and put them down on the damp felt pads. "The train comes in five minutes," she said.

"What did she say?" asked the girl.

"That the train is coming in five minutes."

The girl smiled brightly at the woman, to thank her.

"I'd better take the bags over to the other side of the station," the man said. She smiled at him.

"All right. Then come back and we'll finish the beer."

He picked up the two heavy bags and carried them around the station to the other tracks. He looked up the tracks but could not see the train. Coming back, he walked through the barroom, where people waiting for the train were drinking. He drank an Anis at the bar and looked at the people. They were all waiting reasonably for the train. He went out through the bead curtain. She was sitting at the table and smiled at him.

"Do you feel better?" he asked.

"I feel fine," she said. "There's nothing wrong with me. I feel fine."

1927

I Stand Here Ironing

TILLIE OLSEN
[1912–2007]

I stand here ironing, and what you asked me moves tormented back and forth with the iron.

"I wish you would manage the time to come in and talk with me about your daughter. I'm sure you can help me understand her. She's a youngster who needs help and whom I'm deeply interested in helping."

"Who needs help." . . . Even if I came, what good would it do? You think because I am her mother I have a key, or that in some way you could use me as a key? She has lived for nineteen years. There is all that life that has happened outside of me, beyond me.

And when is there time to remember, to sift, to weigh, to estimate, to total? I will start and there will be an interruption and I will have to gather it all together again. Or I will become engulfed with all I did or did not do, with what should have been and what cannot be helped.

She was a beautiful baby. The first and only one of our five that was beautiful at birth. You do not guess how new and uneasy her tenancy in her now-loveliness. You did not know her all those years she was thought homely, or see her poring over her baby pictures, making me tell her over and over how beautiful she had been—and would be, I would tell her—and was now, to the seeing eye. But the seeing eyes were few or nonexistent. Including mine.

I nursed her. They feel that's important nowadays, I nursed all the children, but with her, with all the fierce rigidity of first motherhood, I did like the books then said. Though her cries battered me to trembling and my breasts ached with swollenness, I waited till the clock decreed.

Why do I put that first? I do not even know if it matters, or if it explains anything.

She was a beautiful baby. She blew shining bubbles of sound. She loved motion, loved light, loved color and music and textures. She would lie on the floor in her blue overalls patting the surface so hard in ecstasy her hands and feet would blur. She was a miracle to me, but when she was eight months old I had to leave her daytimes with the woman downstairs to whom she was no miracle at all, for I worked or looked for work and for Emily's father, who "could no longer endure" (he wrote in his good-bye note) "sharing want with us."

I was nineteen. It was the pre-relief, pre-WPA[1] world of the depression. I would start running as soon as I got off the streetcar, running up the stairs, the place smelling sour, and awake or asleep to startle awake, when she saw me she would break into a clogged weeping that could not be comforted, a weeping I can hear yet.

After a while I found a job hashing at night so I could be with her days, and it was better. But it came to where I had to bring her to his family and leave her.

It took a long time to raise the money for her fare back. Then she got chicken pox and I had to wait longer. When she finally came, I hardly knew her, walking quick and nervous like her father, looking like her father, thin, and dressed in a shoddy red that yellowed her skin and glared at the pockmarks. All the baby loveliness gone.

She was two. Old enough for nursery school they said, and I did not know then what I know now—the fatigue of the long day, and the lacerations of group life in the kinds of nurseries that are only parking places for children.

Except that it would have made no difference if I had known. It was the only place there was. It was the only way we could be together, the only way I could hold a job.

And even without knowing, I knew. I knew the teacher that was evil because all these years it has curdled into my memory, the little boy hunched in the corner, her rasp, "why aren't you outside, because Alvin hits you? that's no reason, go out, scaredy." I knew Emily hated it even if she did not clutch and implore "don't go Mommy" like the other children, mornings.

She always had a reason why we should stay home. Momma, you look sick. Momma, I feel sick. Momma, the teachers aren't there

[1]The Works Progress Administration (1935–1943) employed millions of unemployed people to work on public works projects during the Great Depression as part of the New Deal.

today, they're sick. Momma, we can't go, there was a fire there last night. Momma, it's a holiday today, no school, they told me.

But never a direct protest, never rebellion. I think of our others in their three-, four-year-oldness—the explosions, the tempers, the denunciations, the demands—and I feel suddenly ill. I put the iron down. What in me demanded that goodness in her? And what was the cost, the cost to her of such goodness?

The old man living in the back once said in his gentle way: "You should smile at Emily more when you look at her." What *was* in my face when I looked at her? I loved her. There were all the acts of love.

It was only with the others I remembered what he said, and it was the face of joy, and not of care or tightness or worry I turned to them—too late for Emily. She does not smile easily, let alone almost always as her brothers and sisters do. Her face is closed and sombre, but when she wants, how fluid. You must have seen it in her pantomimes, you spoke of her rare gift for comedy on the stage that rouses laughter out of the audience so dear they applaud and applaud and do not want to let her go.

Where does it come from, that comedy? There was none of it in her when she came back to me that second time, after I had to send her away again. She had a new daddy now to learn to love, and I think perhaps it was a better time.

Except when we left her alone nights, telling ourselves she was old enough.

"Can't you go some other time, Mommy, like tomorrow?" she would ask. "Will it be just a little while you'll be gone? Do you promise?"

The time we came back, the front door open, the clock on the floor in the hall. She rigid awake. "It wasn't just a little while. I didn't cry. Three times I called you, just three times, and then I ran downstairs to open the door so you could come faster. The clock talked loud. I threw it away, it scared me what it talked."

She said the clock talked loud again that night I went to the hospital to have Susan. She was delirious with the fever that comes before red measles, but she was fully conscious all the week I was gone and the week after we were home when she could not come near the new baby or me.

She did not get well. She stayed skeleton thin, not wanting to eat, and night after night she had nightmares. She would call for me, and I would rouse from exhaustion to sleepily call back: "You're all right, darling, go to sleep, it's just a dream," and if she still called, in a sterner voice, "now go to sleep, Emily, there's nothing to hurt you." Twice, only twice, when I had to get up for Susan anyhow, I went in to sit with her.

Now when it is too late (as if she would let me hold her and comfort her like I do the others) I get up and go to her at once at her moan or restless stirring. "Are you awake, Emily? Can I get you something?" And the answer is always the same: "No, I'm all right, go back to sleep, Mother."

They persuaded me at the clinic to send her away to a convalescent home in the country where "she can have the kind of food and care you can't manage for her, and you'll be free to concentrate on the new baby." They still send children to that place. I see pictures on the society page of sleek young women planning affairs to raise money for it, or dancing at the affairs, or decorating Easter eggs or filling Christmas stockings for the children.

They never have a picture of the children so I do not know if the girls still wear those gigantic red bows and the ravaged looks on the every other Sunday when parents can come to visit "unless otherwise notified"—as we were notified the first six weeks.

Oh it is a handsome place, green lawns and tall trees and fluted flower beds. High up on the balconies of each cottage the children stand, the girls in their red bows and white dresses, the boys in white suits and giant red ties. The parents stand below shrieking up to be heard and the children shriek down to be heard, and between them the invisible wall "Not To Be Contaminated by Parental Germs or Physical Affection."

There was a tiny girl who always stood hand in hand with Emily. Her parents never came. One visit she was gone. "They moved her to Rose Cottage," Emily shouted in explanation. "They don't like you to love anybody here."

She wrote once a week, the labored writing of a seven-year-old. "I am fine. How is the baby. If I write my leter nicly I will have a star. Love." There never was a star. We wrote every other day, letters she could never hold or keep but only hear read—once. "We simply do not have room for children to keep any personal possessions," they patiently explained when we pieced one Sunday's shrieking together to plead how much it would mean to Emily, who loved so to keep things, to be allowed to keep her letters and cards.

Each visit she looked frailer. "She isn't eating," they told us.

(They had runny eggs for breakfast or mush with lumps, Emily said later, I'd hold it in my mouth and not swallow. Nothing ever tasted good, just when they had chicken.)

It took us eight months to get her released home, and only the fact that she gained back so little of her seven lost pounds convinced the social worker.

I used to try to hold and love her after she came back, but her body would stay stiff, and after a while she'd push away. She ate little. Food sickened her, and I think much of life too. Oh she had physical lightness and brightness, twinkling by on skates, bouncing like a ball up and down up and down over the jump rope, skimming over the hill; but these were momentary.

She fretted about her appearance, thin and dark and foreign-looking at a time when every little girl was supposed to look or thought she should look a chubby blonde replica of Shirley Temple. The doorbell sometimes rang for her, but no one seemed to come and play in the house or to be a best friend. Maybe because we moved so much.

There was a boy she loved painfully through two school semesters. Months later she told me how she had taken pennies from my purse to buy him candy. "Licorice was his favorite and I brought him some every day, but he still liked Jennifer better'n me. Why, Mommy?" The kind of question for which there is no answer.

School was a worry for her. She was not glib or quick in a world where glibness and quickness were easily confused with ability to learn. To her overworked and exasperated teachers she was an over-conscientious "slow learner" who kept trying to catch up and was absent entirely too often.

I let her be absent, though sometimes the illness was imaginary. How different from my now-strictness about attendance with the others. I wasn't working. We had a new baby. I was home anyhow. Sometimes, after Susan grew old enough, I would keep her home from school, too, to have them all together.

Mostly Emily had asthma, and her breathing, harsh and labored, would fill the house with a curiously tranquil sound. I would bring the two old dresser mirrors and her boxes of collections to her bed. She would select beads and single earrings, bottle tops and shells, dried flowers and pebbles, old postcards and scraps, all sorts of oddments; then she and Susan would play Kingdom, setting up landscapes and furniture, peopling them with action.

Those were the only times of peaceful companionship between her and Susan. I have edged away from it, that poisonous feeling between them, that terrible balancing of hurts and needs I had to do between the two, and did so badly, those earlier years.

Oh there were conflicts between the others too, each one human, needing, demanding, hurting, taking—but only between Emily and Susan, no, Emily toward Susan that corroding resentment. It seems so obvious on the surface, yet it is not obvious; Susan, the second child, Susan, golden- and curly-haired and chubby, quick and articulate and assured, everything in appearance and manner Emily was not; Susan, not able to resist Emily's precious things, losing or sometimes clumsily breaking them; Susan telling jokes and riddles to company for applause while Emily sat silent (to say to me later: that was *my* riddle, Mother, I told it to Susan); Susan, who for all the five years' difference in age was just a year behind Emily in developing physically.

I am glad for that slow physical development that widened the difference between her and her contemporaries, though she suffered over it. She was too vulnerable for that terrible world of youthful competition, of preening and parading, of constant measuring of yourself against every other, of envy, "If I had that copper hair," "If I had that skin. . . ." She tormented herself enough about not looking like the others, there was enough of unsureness, the having to be conscious of words before you speak, the constant caring—what are they thinking of me? without having it all magnified by the merciless physical drives.

Ronnie is calling. He is wet and I change him. It is rare there is such a cry now. That time of motherhood is almost behind me when the ear is not one's own but must always be racked and listening for the child cry, the child call. We sit for a while and I hold him, looking out over the city spread in charcoal with its soft aisles of light. "*Shoogily*," he breathes and curls closer. I carry him back to bed, asleep. *Shoogily*. A funny word, a family word, inherited from Emily, invented by her to say: *comfort*.

In this and other ways she leaves her seal, I say aloud. And startle at my saying it. What do I mean? What did I start to gather together, to try and make coherent? I was at the terrible, growing years. War years. I do not remember them well. I was working, there were four smaller ones now, there was not time for her. She had to help be a mother, and housekeeper, and shopper. She had to get her seal. Mornings of crisis and near hysteria trying to get lunches packed, hair combed, coats and shoes found, everyone to school or Child

Care on time, the baby ready for transportation. And always the paper scribbled on by a smaller one, the book looked at by Susan then mislaid, the homework not done. Running out to that huge school where she was one, she was lost, she was a drop; suffering over the unpreparedness, stammering and unsure in her classes.

There was so little time left at night after the kids were bedded down. She would struggle over books, always eating (it was in those years she developed her enormous appetite that is legendary in our family) and I would be ironing, or preparing food for the next day, or writing V-mail[2] to Bill, or tending the baby. Sometimes, to make me laugh, or out of her despair, she would imitate happenings or types at school.

I think I said once: "Why don't you do something like this in the school amateur show?" One morning she phoned me at work, hardly understandable through the weeping: "Mother, I did it. I won, I won; they gave me first prize; they clapped and clapped and wouldn't let me go."

Now suddenly she was Somebody, and as imprisoned in her difference as she had been in anonymity.

She began to be asked to perform at other high schools, even in colleges, then at city and statewide affairs. The first one we went to, I only recognized her that first moment when thin, shy, she almost drowned herself into the curtains. Then: Was this Emily? The control, the command, the convulsing and deadly clowning, the spell, then the roaring, stamping audience, unwilling to let this rare and precious laughter out of their lives.

Afterwards: You ought to do something about her with a gift like that—but without money or knowing how, what does one do? We have left it all to her, and the gift has so often eddied inside, clogged and clotted, as been used and growing.

She is coming. She runs up the stairs two at a time with her light graceful step, and I know she is happy tonight. Whatever it was that occasioned your call did not happen today.

"Aren't you ever going to finish the ironing, Mother? Whistler[3] painted his mother in a rocker. I'd have to paint mine standing over an ironing board." This is one of her communicative nights and she

[2]Victory mail, a system of microfilming letters in order to save space on cargo ships during World War II.

[3]James McNeill Whistler (1834–1903), an American painter. His most famous painting, *Arrangement in Grey and Black No. 1,* is also known as *Whistler's Mother.*

tells me everything and nothing as she fixes herself a plate of food out of the icebox.

She is so lovely. Why did you want me to come in at all? Why were you concerned? She will find her way.

She starts up the stairs to bed. "Don't get me up with the rest in the morning." "But I thought you were having midterms." "Oh, those," she comes back in, kisses me, and says quite lightly, "in a couple of years when we'll all be atom-dead they won't matter a bit."

She has said it before. She *believes* it. But because I have been dredging the past, and all that compounds a human being is so heavy and meaningful in me, I cannot endure it tonight.

I will never total it all. I will never come in to say: She was a child seldom smiled at. Her father left me before she was a year old. I had to work her first six years when there was work, or I sent her home and to his relatives. There were years she had care she hated. She was dark and thin and foreign-looking in a world where the prestige went to blondeness and curly hair and dimples, she was slow where glibness was prized. She was a child of anxious, not proud, love. We were poor and could not afford for her the soil of easy growth. I was a young mother, I was a distracted mother. There were other children pushing up, demanding. Her younger sister seemed all that she was not. There were years she did not want me to touch her. She kept too much in herself, her life was such she had to keep too much in herself. My wisdom came too late. She has much to her and probably little will come of it. She is a child of her age, of depression, of war, of fear.

Let her be. So all that is in her will not bloom—but in how many does it? There is still enough left to live by. Only help her to know—help make it so there is cause for her to know—that she is more than this dress on the ironing board, helpless before the iron.

1961

The Swimmer

JOHN CHEEVER

[1912–2007]

It was one of those midsummer Sundays when everyone sits around saying, "I *drank* too much last night." You might have heard it whispered by the parishioners leaving church, heard it from the lips of the priest himself, struggling with his cassock in the *vestiarium*,[1] heard it from the golf links and the tennis courts, heard it from the wildlife preserve where the leader of the Audubon group was suffering from a terrible hangover. "I *drank* too much," said Donald Westerhazy. "We all *drank* too much," said Lucinda Merrill. "It must have been the wine," said Helen Westerhazy. "I *drank* too much of that claret."

This was at the edge of the Westerhazys' pool. The pool, fed by an artesian well with a high iron content, was a pale shade of green. It was a fine day. In the west there was a massive stand of cumulus cloud so like a city seen from a distance—from the bow of an approaching ship—that it might have had a name. Lisbon. Hackensack. The sun was hot. Neddy Merrill sat by the green water, one hand in it, one around a glass of gin. He was a slender man—he seemed to have the especial slenderness of youth—and while he was far from young he had slid down his banister that morning and given the bronze backside of Aphrodite on the hall table a smack, as he jogged toward the smell of coffee in his dining room. He might have been compared to a summer's day, particularly the last hours of one, and while he lacked a tennis racket or a sail bag the impression was definitely one of youth, sport, and clement weather. He had been swimming and now he was breathing deeply, stertorously as if he could gulp into his lungs the components of that moment, the heat

[1]A wardrobe.

of the sun, the intenseness of his pleasure. It all seemed to flow into his chest. His own house stood in Bullet Park, eight miles to the south, where his four beautiful daughters would have had their lunch and might be playing tennis. Then it occurred to him that by taking a dogleg to the southwest he could reach his home by water.

His life was not confining and the delight he took in this observation could not be explained by its suggestion of escape. He seemed to see, with a cartographer's eye, that string of swimming pools, that quasi-subterranean stream that curved across the county. He had made a discovery, a contribution to modern geography; he would name the stream Lucinda after his wife. He was not a practical joker nor was he a fool but he was determinedly original and had a vague and modest idea of himself as a legendary figure. The day was beautiful and it seemed to him that a long swim might enlarge and celebrate its beauty.

He took off a sweater that was hung over his shoulders and dove in. He had an inexplicable contempt for men who did not hurl themselves into pools. He swam a choppy crawl, breathing either with every stroke or every fourth stroke and counting somewhere well in the back of his mind the one-two one-two of a flutter kick. It was not a serviceable stroke for long distances but the domestication of swimming had saddled the sport with some customs and in his part of the world a crawl was customary. To be embraced and sustained by the light green water was less a pleasure, it seemed, than the resumption of a natural condition, and he would have liked to swim without trunks, but this was not possible, considering his project. He hoisted himself up on the far curb—he never used the ladder—and started across the lawn. When Lucinda asked where he was going he said he was going to swim home.

The only maps and charts he had to go by were remembered or imaginary but these were clear enough. First there were the Grahams, the Hammers, the Lears, the Howlands, and the Crosscups. He would cross Ditmar Street to the Bunkers and come, after a short portage, to the Levys, the Welchers, and the public pool in Lancaster. Then there were the Hallorans, the Sachses, the Biswangers, Shirley Adams, the Gilmartins, and the Clydes. The day was lovely, and that he lived in a world so generously supplied with water seemed like a clemency, a beneficence. His heart was high and he ran across the grass. Making his way home by an uncommon route gave him the feeling that he was a pilgrim, an explorer, a man with a destiny, and he knew that he would find friends all along the way; friends would line the banks of the Lucinda River.

He went through a hedge that separated the Westerhazys' land from the Grahams', walked under some flowering apple trees, passed the shed that housed their pump and filter, and came out at the Grahams' pool. "Why, Neddy," Mrs. Graham said, "what a marvelous surprise. I've been trying to get you on the phone all morning. Here, let me get you a drink." He saw then, like any explorer, that the hospitable customs and traditions of the natives would have to be handled with diplomacy if he was ever going to reach his destination. He did not want to mystify or seem rude to the Grahams nor did he have the time to linger there. He swam the length of their pool and joined them in the sun and was rescued, a few minutes later, by the arrival of two carloads of friends from Connecticut. During the uproarious reunions he was able to slip away. He went down by the front of the Grahams' house, stepped over a thorny hedge, and crossed a vacant lot to the Hammers'. Mrs. Hammer, looking up from her roses, saw him swim by although she wasn't quite sure who it was. The Lears heard him splashing past the open windows of their living room. The Howlands and the Crosscups were away. After leaving the Hoelands' he crossed Ditmar Street and started for the Bunkers', where he could hear, even at that distance, the noise of a party.

The water refracted the sound of voices and laughter and seemed to suspend it in midair. The Bunkers' pool was on a rise and he climbed some stairs to a terrace where twenty-five or thirty men and women were drinking. The only person in the water was Rusty Towers, who floated there on a rubber raft. Oh, how bonny and lush were the banks of the Lucinda River! Prosperous men and women gathered by the sapphire- colored waters while caterer's men in white coats passed them cold gin. Overhead a red de Haviland trainer was circling around and around and around in the sky with something like the glee of a child in a swing. Ned felt a passing affection for the scene, a tenderness for the gathering, as if it was something he might touch. In the distance he heard thunder. As soon as Enid Bunker saw him she began to scream: "Oh, look who's here! What a marvelous surprise! When Lucinda said that you couldn't come I thought I'd *die*." She made her way to him through the crowd, and when they had finished kissing she led him to the bar, a progress that was slowed by the fact that he stopped to kiss eight or ten other women and shake the hands of as many men. A smiling bartender he had seen at a hundred parties gave him a gin and tonic and he stood by the bar for a moment, anxious not to get stuck in any conversation that would delay his voyage. When he seemed about to be surrounded he dove in and swam close to the side to avoid colliding with Rusty's raft. At the far end of the pool he bypassed the Tomlinsons with a broad smile and jogged up the garden path. The gravel cut his feet but this was the only unpleasantness. The party was confined to the pool, and as he went toward the house he heard the brilliant, watery sound of voices fade, heard the noise of a radio from the Bunkers' kitchen, where someone was listening to a ball game. Sunday afternoon. He made his way through the parked cars and down the grassy border of their driveway to Alewives Lane. He did not want to be seen on the road in his bathing trunks but there was no traffic and he made the short distance to the Levys' driveway, marked with a PRIVATE PROPERTY sign and a green tube for *The New York Times*. All the doors and windows of the big house were open but there were no signs of life; not even a dog barked. He went around the side of the house to the pool and saw that the Levys had only recently left. Glasses and bottles and dishes of nuts were on a table at the deep end, where there was a bathhouse or gazebo, hung with Japanese lanterns. After swimming the pool he got himself a glass and poured a drink. It was his fourth or fifth drink and he had swum nearly half the length of the Lucinda River. He felt tired, clean, and pleased at that moment to be alone; pleased with everything.

It would storm. The stand of cumulus cloud—that city—had risen and darkened, and while he sat there he heard the percussiveness of thunder again. The de Haviland trainer was still circling overhead and it seemed to Ned that he could almost hear the pilot laugh with pleasure in the afternoon; but when there was another peal of thunder he took off for home. A train whistle blew and he wondered what time it had gotten to be. Four? Five? He thought of the provincial station at that hour, where a waiter, his tuxedo concealed by a raincoat, a dwarf with some flowers wrapped in newspaper, and a woman who had been crying would be waiting for the local. It was suddenly growing dark; it was that moment when the pin-headed birds seem to organize their song into some acute and knowledgeable recognition of the storm's approach. Then there was a fine noise of rushing water from the crown of an oak at his back, as if a spigot there had been turned. Then the noise of fountains came from the crowns of all the tall trees. Why did he love storms, what was the meaning of his excitement when the door sprang open and the rain wind fled rudely up the stairs, why had the simple task of shutting the windows of an old house seemed fitting and urgent, why did the first watery notes of a storm wind have for him the unmistakable sound of good news, cheer, glad tidings? Then there was an explosion, a smell of cordite, and rain lashed the Japanese lanterns that Mrs. Levy had bought in Kyoto the year before last, or was it the year before that?

He stayed in the Levys' gazebo until the storm had passed. The rain had cooled the air and he shivered. The force of the wind had stripped a maple of its red and yellow leaves and scattered them over the grass and the water. Since it was midsummer the tree must be blighted, and yet he felt a peculiar sadness at this sign of autumn. He braced his shoulders, emptied his glass, and started for the Welchers' pool. This meant crossing the Lindleys' riding ring and he was surprised to find it overgrown with grass and all the jumps dismantled. He wondered if the Lindleys had sold their horses or gone away for the summer and put them out to board. He seemed to remember having heard something about the Lindleys and their horses but the memory was unclear. On he went, barefoot through the wet grass, to the Welchers', where he found their pool was dry.

This breach in his chain of water disappointed him absurdly, and he felt like some explorer who seeks a torrential headwater and finds a dead stream. He was disappointed and mystified. It was common enough to go away for the summer but no one ever drained his pool. The Welchers had definitely gone away. The pool furniture was folded, stacked, and covered with a tarpaulin. The bathhouse was locked. All the windows of the house were shut, and when he went around to the driveway in front he saw a for sale sign nailed to a tree. When had he last heard from the Welchers—when, that is, had he and Lucinda last regretted an invitation to dine with them? It seemed only a week or so ago. Was his memory failing or had he so disciplined it in the repression of unpleasant facts that he had damaged his sense of the truth? Then in the distance he heard the sound of a tennis game. This cheered him, cleared away all his apprehensions and let him regard the overcast sky and the cold air with indifference. This was the day that Neddy Merrill swam across the county. That was the day! He started off then for his most difficult portage.

Had you gone for a Sunday afternoon ride that day you might have seen him, close to naked, standing on the shoulders of Route 424, waiting for a chance to cross. You might have wondered if he was the victim of foul play, had his car broken down, or was he merely a fool. Standing barefoot in the deposits of the highway—beer cans, rags, and blowout patches—exposed to all kinds of ridicule, he seemed pitiful. He had known when he started that this was a part of his journey—it had been on his maps—but confronted with the lines of traffic, worming through the summery light, he found himself unprepared. He was laughed at, jeered at, a beer can was thrown at him, and he had no dignity or humor to bring to the situation. He could have gone back, back to the Westerhazys', where Lucinda would still be sitting in the sun. He had signed nothing, vowed nothing, pledged nothing, not even to himself. Why, believing as he did, that all human obduracy was susceptible to common sense, was he unable to turn back? Why was he determined to complete his journey even if it meant putting his life in danger? At what point had this prank, this joke, this piece of horseplay become serious? He could not go back, he could not even recall with any clearness the green water at the Westerhazys', the sense of inhaling the day's components, the friendly and relaxed voices saying that they had *drunk* too much. In the space of an hour, more or less, he had covered a distance that made his return impossible.

An old man, tooling down the highway at fifteen miles an hour, let him get to the middle of the road, where there was a grass divider. Here he was exposed to the ridicule of the northbound traffic, but after ten or fifteen minutes he was able to cross. From here he had only a short walk to the Recreation Center at the edge of the village of Lancaster, where there were some handball courts and a public pool.

The effect of the water on voices, the illusion of brilliance and suspense, was the same here as it had been at the Bunkers' but the sounds here were louder, harsher, and more shrill, and as soon as he entered the crowded enclosure he was confronted with regimentation. "ALL SWIMMERS MUST TAKE A SHOWER BEFORE USING THE POOL. ALL SWIMMERS MUST USE THE FOOTBATH. ALL SWIMMERS MUST WEAR THEIR IDENTIFICATION DISKS." He took a shower, washed his feet in a cloudy and bitter solution, and made his way to the edge of the water. It stank of chlorine and looked to him like a sink. A pair of life-guards in a pair of towers blew police whistles at what seemed to be regular intervals and abused the swimmers through a public address system. Neddy remembered the sapphire water at the Bunkers' with longing and thought that he might contaminate himself—damage his own prosperousness and charm—by swimming in this murk, but he reminded himself that he was an explorer, a pilgrim, and that this was merely a stagnant bend in the Lucinda River. He dove, scowling with distaste, into the chlorine and had to swim with his head above water to avoid collisions, but even so he was bumped into, splashed, and jostled. When he got to the shallow end both lifeguards were shouting at him: "Hey, you, you without the identification disk, get outa the water." He did, but they had no way of pursuing him and he went through the reek of suntan oil and chlorine out through the hurricane fence and passed the hand-ball courts. By crossing the road he entered the wooded part of the Halloran estate. The woods were not cleared and the footing was treacherous and difficult until he reached the lawn and the clipped beech hedge that encircled their pool.

The Hallorans were friends, an elderly couple of enormous wealth who seemed to bask in the suspicion that they might be Communists. They were zealous reformers but they were not Communists, and yet when they were accused, as they sometimes were, of subversion, it seemed to gratify and excite them. Their beech hedge was yellow and he guessed this had been blighted like the Levys' maple. He called hullo, hullo, to warn the Hallorans of his approach, to palliate his invasion of their privacy. The Hallorans, for reasons that had never been explained to him, did not wear bathing suits. No explanations were in order, really. Their nakedness was a detail in their uncompromising zeal for reform and he stepped politely out of his trunks before he went through the opening in the hedge.

Mrs. Halloran, a stout woman with white hair and a serene face, was reading the *Times*. Mr. Halloran was taking beech leaves out of the water with a scoop. They seemed not surprised or displeased to see him. Their pool was perhaps the oldest in the country, a fieldstone rectangle, fed by a brook. It had no filter or pump and its waters were the opaque gold of the stream.

"I'm swimming across the county," Ned said.

"Why, I didn't know one could," exclaimed Mrs. Halloran.

"Well, I've made it from the Westerhazys'," Ned said. "That must be about four miles."

He left his trunks at the deep end, walked to the shallow end, and swam this stretch. As he was pulling himself out of the water he heard Mrs. Halloran say, "We've been *terribly* sorry to hear about all your misfortunes, Neddy."

"My misfortunes?" Ned asked. "I don't know what you mean."

"Why, we heard that you'd sold the house and that your poor children . . ."

"I don't recall having sold the house," Ned said, "and the girls are at home."

"Yes," Mrs. Halloran sighed. "Yes . . ." Her voice filled the air with an unseasonable melancholy and Ned spoke briskly. "Thank you for the swim."

"Well, have a nice trip," said Mrs. Halloran.

Beyond the hedge he pulled on his trunks and fastened them. They were loose and he wondered if, during the space of an afternoon, he could have lost some weight. He was cold and he was tired and the naked Hallorans and their dark water had depressed him. The swim was too much for his strength but how could he have guessed this, sliding down the banister that morning and sitting in the Westerhazys' sun? His arms were lame. His legs felt rubbery and ached at the joints. The worst of it was the cold in his bones and the feeling that he might never be warm again. Leaves were falling down around him and he smelled wood smoke on the wind. Who would be burning wood at this time of year?

He needed a drink. Whiskey would warm him, pick him up, carry him through the last of his journey, refresh his feeling that it was original and valorous to swim across the county. Channel swimmers took brandy. He needed a stimulant. He crossed the lawn in front of the Hallorans' house and went down a little path to where they had built a house for their only daughter, Helen, and her husband, Eric Sachs. The Sachses' pool was small and he found Helen and her husband there.

"Oh, *Neddy*," Helen said. "Did you lunch at Mother's?"

"Not *really*," Ned said. "I *did* stop to see your parents." This seemed to be explanation enough. "I'm terribly sorry to break in on you like this but I've taken a chill and I wonder if you'd give me a drink."

"Why, I'd *love* to," Helen said, "but there hasn't been anything in this house to drink since Eric's operation. That was three years ago."

Was he losing his memory, had his gift for concealing painful facts let him forget that he had sold his house, that his children were in trouble, and that his friend had been ill? His eyes slipped from Eric's face to his abdomen, where he saw three pale, sutured scars, two of them at least a foot long. Gone was his navel, and what, Neddy thought, would the roving hand, bed-checking one's gifts at 3 A.M., make of a belly with no navel, no link to birth, this breach in the succession?

"I'm sure you can get a drink at the Biswangers'," Helen said. "They're having an enormous do. You can hear it from here. Listen!"

She raised her head and from across the road, the lawns, the gardens, the woods, the fields, he heard again the brilliant noise of voices over water. "Well, I'll get wet," he said, still feeling that he had no freedom of choice about his means of travel. He dove into the Sachses' cold water and, gasping, close to drowning, made his way from one end of the pool to the other. "Lucinda and I want *terribly* to see you," he said over his shoulder, his face set toward the Biswangers'. "We're sorry it's been so long and we'll call you *very* soon."

He crossed some fields to the Biswangers' and the sounds of revelry there. They would be honored to give him a drink, they would be happy to give him a drink. The Biswangers invited him and Lucinda for dinner four times a year, six weeks in advance. They were always rebuffed and yet they continued to send out their invitations, unwilling to comprehend the rigid and undemocratic realities of their society. They were the sort of people who discussed the price of things at cocktails, exchanged market tips during dinner, and after dinner told dirty stories to mixed company. They did not belong to Neddy's set—they were not even on Lucinda's Christmas-card list. He went toward their pool with feelings of indifference, charity, and some unease, since it seemed to be getting dark and these were the longest days of the year. The party when he joined it was noisy and large. Grace Biswanger was the kind of hostess who asked the optometrist, the veterinarian, the real-estate dealer, and the dentist. No one was swimming and the twilight, reflected on the water of the pool, had a wintry gleam. There was a bar and he started for this. When Grace Biswanger saw him she came toward him, not affectionately as he had every right to expect, but bellicosely.

"Why, this party has everything," she said loudly, "including a gate crasher."

She could not deal him a social blow—there was no question about this and he did not flinch. "As a gate crasher," he asked politely, "do I rate a drink?"

"Suit yourself," she said. "You don't seem to pay much attention to invitations."

She turned her back on him and joined some guests, and he went to the bar and ordered a whiskey. The bartender served him but he served him rudely. His was a world in which the caterer's men kept the social score, and to be rebuffed by a part-time barkeep meant that he had suffered some loss of social esteem. Or perhaps the man was new and uninformed. Then he heard Grace at his back say: "They went for broke overnight—nothing but income—and he showed up drunk one Sunday and asked us to loan him five thousand dollars. . . ." She was always talking about money. It was worse than eating your peas off a knife. He dove into the pool, swam its length and went away.

The next pool on his list, the last but two, belonged to his old mistress, Shirley Adams. If he had suffered any injuries at the Biswangers' they would be cured here. Love—sexual roughhouse in fact—was the supreme elixir, the pain killer, the brightly colored pill that would put the spring back into his step, the joy of life in his heart. They had had an affair last week, last month, last year. He couldn't remember. It was he who had broken it off, his was the upper hand, and he stepped through the gate of the wall that surrounded her pool with nothing so considered as self-confidence. It seemed in a way to be his pool, as the lover, particularly the illicit lover, enjoys the possessions of his mistress with an authority unknown to holy matrimony. She was there, her hair the color of brass, but her figure, at the edge of the lighted, cerulean water, excited in him no profound memories. It had been, he thought, a light-hearted affair, although she had wept when he broke it off. She seemed confused to see him and he wondered if she was still wounded. Would she, God forbid, weep again?

"What do you want?" she asked.

"I'm swimming across the county."

"Good Christ. Will you ever grow up?"

"What's the matter?"

"If you've come here for money," she said, "I won't give you another cent."

"You could give me a drink."

"I could but I won't. I'm not alone."

"Well, I'm on my way."

He dove in and swam the pool, but when he tried to haul himself up onto the curb he found that the strength in his arms and shoulders had gone, and he paddled to the ladder and climbed out. Looking over his shoulder he saw, in the lighted bathhouse, a young man. Going out onto the dark lawn he smelled chrysanthemums or marigolds—some stubborn autumnal fragrance—on the night air, strong as gas. Looking overhead he saw that the stars had come out, but why should he seem to see Andromeda, Cepheus, and Cassiopeia? What had become of the constellations of midsummer? He began to cry.

It was probably the first time in his adult life that he had ever cried, certainly the first time in his life that he had ever felt so miserable, cold, tired, and bewildered. He could not understand the rudeness of the caterer's barkeep or the rudeness of a mistress who had come to him on her knees and showered his trousers with tears. He had swum too long, he had been immersed too long, and his nose and his throat were sore from the water. What he needed then was a drink, some company, and some clean, dry clothes, and while he could have cut directly across the road to his home he went on to the Gilmartins' pool. Here, for the first time in his life, he did not dive but went down the steps into the icy water and swam a hobbled sidestroke that he might have learned as a youth. He staggered with fatigue on his way to the Clydes' and paddled the length of their pool, stopping again and again with his hand on the curb to rest. He climbed up the ladder and wondered if he had the strength to get home. He had done what he wanted, he had swum the county, but he was so stupefied with exhaustion that his triumph seemed vague. Stooped, holding on to the gateposts for support, he turned up the driveway of his own house.

The place was dark. Was it so late that they had all gone to bed? Had Lucinda stayed at the Westerhazys' for supper? Had the girls joined her there or gone someplace else? Hadn't they agreed, as they usually did on Sunday, to regret all their invitations and stay at home? He tried the garage doors to see what cars were in but the doors were locked and rust came off the handles onto his hands. Going toward the house, he saw that the force of the thunderstorm had knocked one of the rain gutters loose. It hung down over the front door like an umbrella rib, but it could be fixed in the morning. The house was locked, and he thought that the stupid cook or the stupid maid must have locked the place up until he remembered that it had been some time since they had employed a maid or a cook. He shouted, pounded on the door, tried to force it with his shoulder, and then, looking in at the windows, saw that the place was empty.

1964

Battle Royal

RALPH ELLISON

[1914–1994]

It goes a long way back, some twenty years. All my life I had been looking for something, and everywhere I turned someone tried to tell me what it was. I accepted their answers too, though they were often in contradiction and even self-contradictory. I was naïve. I was looking for myself and asking everyone except myself questions which I, and only I, could answer. It took me a long time and much painful boomeranging of my expectations to achieve a realization everyone else appears to have been born with: That I am nobody but myself. But first I had to discover that I am an invisible man!

And yet I am no freak of nature, nor of history. I was in the cards, other things having been equal (or unequal) eighty-five years ago. I am not ashamed of my grandparents for having been slaves. I am only ashamed of myself for having at one time been ashamed. About eighty-five years ago they were told that they were free, united with others of our country in everything pertaining to the common good, and, in everything social, separate like the fingers of the hand. And they believed it. They exulted in it. They stayed in their place, worked hard, and brought up my father to do the same. But my grandfather is the one. He was an odd old guy, my grandfather, and I am told I take after him. It was he who caused the trouble. On his deathbed he called my father to him and said, "Son, after I'm gone I want you to keep up the good fight. I never told you, but our life is a war and I have been a traitor all my born days, a spy in the enemy's country ever since I give up my gun back in the Reconstruction. Live with your head in the lion's mouth. I want you to overcome 'em with yeses, undermine 'em with grins, agree 'em to death and destruction, let 'em swoller you till they vomit or bust wide open." They thought the old man had gone out of his mind. He had been the meekest of men. The younger children were rushed from the room, the shades drawn, and the flame of the lamp turned so low that it sputtered on the wick like the old man's breathing. "Learn it to the younguns," he whispered fiercely; then he died.

But my folks were more alarmed over his last words than over his dying. It was as though he had not died at all, his words caused so much anxiety. I was warned emphatically to forget what he had said and, indeed, this is the first time it has been mentioned outside the family circle. It had a tremendous effect upon me, however. I could never be sure of what he meant. Grandfather had been a quiet old man who never made any trouble, yet on his deathbed he had called himself a traitor and a spy, and he had spoken of his meekness as a dangerous activity. It became a constant puzzle which lay un-answered in the back of my mind. And whenever things went well for me I remembered my grandfather and felt guilty and uncomfortable. It was as though I was carrying out his advice in spite of myself. And to make it worse, everyone loved me for it. I was praised by the most lily-white men of the town. I was considered an example of desirable conduct—just as my grandfather had been. And what puzzled me was that the old man had defined it as *treachery.* When I was praised for my conduct I felt a guilt that in some way I was doing something that was really against the wishes of the white folks, that if they had understood they would have desired me to act just the opposite, that I should have been sulky and mean, and that that really would have been what they wanted, even though they were fooled and thought they wanted me to act as I did. It made me afraid that some day they would look upon me as a traitor and I would be lost. Still I was more afraid to act any other way because they didn't like that at all. The old man's words were like a curse. On my graduation day I delivered an oration in which I showed that humility was the secret, indeed, the very essence of progress. (Not that I believed this—how could I, remembering my grandfather?—I only believed that it worked.) It was a great success. Everyone praised me and I was invited to give the speech at a gathering of the town's leading white citizens. It was a triumph for our whole community.

It was in the main ballroom of the leading hotel. When I got there I discovered that it was on the occasion of a smoker, and I was told that since I was to be there anyway I might as well take part in the battle royal to be fought by some of my schoolmates as part of the entertainment. The battle royal came first.

All of the town's big shots were there in their tuxedoes, wolfing down the buffet foods, drinking beer and whiskey and smoking black cigars. It was a large room with a high ceiling. Chairs were arranged in neat rows around three sides of a portable boxing ring. The fourth side was clear, revealing a gleaming space of polished floor. I had some misgivings over the battle royal, by the way. Not from a distaste for fighting, but because I didn't care too much for the other fellows who were to take part. They were tough guys who seemed to have no grandfather's curse worrying their minds. No one could mistake their toughness. And besides, I suspected that fighting a battle royal might detract from the dignity of my speech. In those pre-invisible days I visualized myself as a potential Booker T. Washington.[1] But the other fellows didn't care too much for me either, and there were nine of them. I felt superior to them in my way, and I didn't like the manner in which we were all crowded together into the servants' elevator. Nor did they like my being there. In fact, as the warmly lighted floors flashed past the elevator we had words over the fact that I, by taking part in the fight, had knocked one of their friends out of a night's work.

We were led out of the elevator through a rococo hall into an anteroom and told to get into our fighting togs. Each of us was issued a pair of boxing gloves and ushered out into the big mirrored hall, which we entered looking cautiously about us and whispering, lest we might accidentally be heard above the noise of the room. It was foggy with cigar smoke. And already the whiskey was taking effect. I was shocked to see some of the most important men of the town quite tipsy. They were all there—bankers, lawyers, judges, doctors, fire chiefs, teachers, merchants. Even one of the more fashionable pastors. Something we could not see was going on up front. A clarinet was vibrating sensuously and the men were standing up and moving eagerly forward. We were a small tight group, clustered together, our bare upper bodies touching and shining with anticipatory sweat; while up front the big shots were becoming increasingly excited over something we still could not see. Suddenly I heard the school superintendent, who had told me to come, yell, "Bring up the shines, gentlemen! Bring up the little shines!"

[1]Booker T. Washington (1856–1915) was an African American educator, reformer, and political leader. He advocated education in industry and economic security for post-Reconstruction African Americans.

We were rushed up to the front of the ballroom, where it smelled even more strongly of tobacco and whiskey. Then we were pushed into place. I almost wet my pants. A sea of faces, some hostile, some amused, ringed around us, and in the center, facing us, stood a magnificent blonde—stark naked. There was dead silence. I felt a blast of cold air chill me. I tried to back away, but they were behind me and around me. Some of the boys stood with lowered heads, trembling. I felt a wave of irrational guilt and fear. My teeth chattered, my skin turned to goose flesh, my knees knocked. Yet I was strongly attracted and looked in spite of myself. Had the price of looking been blindness, I would have looked. The hair was yellow like that of a circus kewpie doll, the face heavily powdered and rouged, as though to form an abstract mask, the eyes hollow and smeared a cool blue, the color of a baboon's butt. I felt a desire to spit upon her as my eyes brushed slowly over her body. Her breasts were firm and round as the domes of East Indian temples, and I stood so close as to see the fine skin texture and beads of pearly perspiration glistening like dew around the pink and erected buds of her nipples. I wanted at one and the same time to run from the room, to sink through the floor, or go to her and cover her from my eyes and the eyes of the others with my body; to feel the soft thighs, to caress her and destroy her, to love her and murder her, to hide from her, and yet to stroke where below the small American flag tattooed upon her belly her thighs formed a capital V. I had a notion that of all in the room she saw only me with her impersonal eyes.

And then she began to dance, a slow sensuous movement; the smoke of a hundred cigars clinging to her like the thinnest of veils. She seemed like a fair bird-girl girdled in veils calling to me from the angry surface of some gray and threatening sea. I was transported. Then I became aware of the clarinet playing and the big shots yelling at us. Some threatened us if we looked and others if we did not. On my right I saw one boy faint. And now a man grabbed a silver pitcher from a table and stepped close as he dashed ice water upon him and stood him up and forced two of us to support him as his head hung and moans issued from his thick bluish lips. Another boy began to plead to go home. He was the largest of the group, wearing dark red fighting trunks much too small to conceal the erection which projected from him as though in answer to the insinuating low-registered moaning of the clarinet. He tried to hide himself with his boxing gloves.

And all the while the blonde continued dancing, smiling faintly at the big shots who watched her with fascination, and faintly smiling at our fear. I noticed a certain merchant who followed her hungrily, his lips loose and drooling. He was a large man who wore diamond studs in a shirtfront which swelled with the ample paunch underneath, and each time the blonde swayed her undulating hips he ran his hand through the thin hair of his bald head and, with his arms upheld, his posture clumsy like that of an intoxicated panda, wound his belly in a slow and obscene grind. This creature was completely hypnotized. The music had quickened. As the dancer flung herself about with a detached expression on her face, the men began reaching out to touch her. I could see their beefy fingers sink into her soft flesh. Some of the others tried to stop them and she began to move around the floor in graceful circles, as they gave chase, slipping and sliding over the polished floor. It was mad. Chairs went crashing, drinks were spilt, as they ran laughing and howling after her. They caught her just as she reached a door, raised her from the floor, and tossed her as college boys are tossed at a hazing, and above her red fixed-smiling lips I saw the terror and disgust in her eyes, almost like my own terror and that which I saw in some of the other boys. As I watched, they tossed her twice and her soft breasts seemed to flatten against the air and her legs flung wildly as she spun. Some of the more sober ones helped her to escape. And I started off the floor, heading for the anteroom with the rest of the boys.

Some were still crying and in hysteria. But as we tried to leave we were stopped and ordered to get into the ring. There was nothing to do but what we were told. All ten of us climbed under the ropes and allowed ourselves to be blindfolded with broad bands of white cloth. One of the men seemed to feel a bit sympathetic and tried to cheer us up as we stood with our backs against the ropes. Some of us tried to grin. "See that boy over there?" one of the men said. "I want you to run across at the bell and give it to him right in the belly. If you don't get him, I'm going to get you. I don't like his looks." Each of us was told the same. The blindfolds were put on. Yet even then I had been going over my speech. In my mind each word was as bright as flame. I felt the cloth pressed into place, and frowned so that it would be loosened when I relaxed.

But now I felt a sudden fit of blind terror. I was unused to darkness. It was as though I had suddenly found myself in a dark room filled with poisonous cottonmouths. I could hear the bleary voices yelling insistently for the battle royal to begin.

"Get going in there!"

"Let me at that big nigger!"

I strained to pick up the school superintendent's voice, as though to squeeze some security out of that slightly more familiar sound.

"Let me at those black sonsabitches!" someone yelled.

"No, Jackson, no!" another voice yelled. "Here, somebody, help me hold Jack."

"I want to get at that ginger-colored nigger. Tear him limb from limb," the first voice yelled.

I stood against the ropes trembling. For in those days I was what they called ginger-colored, and he sounded as though he might crunch me between his teeth like a crisp ginger cookie.

Quite a struggle was going on. Chairs were being kicked about and I could hear voices grunting as with a terrific effort. I wanted to see, to see more desperately than ever before. But the blindfold was as tight as a thick skin-puckering scab and when I raised my gloved hands to push the layers of white aside a voice yelled, "Oh, no you don't, black bastard! Leave that alone!"

"Ring the bell before Jackson kills him a coon!" someone boomed in the sudden silence. And I heard the bell clang and the sound of the feet scuffling forward.

A glove smacked against my head. I pivoted, striking out stiffly as someone went past, and felt the jar ripple along the length of my arm to my shoulder. Then it seemed as though all nine of the boys had turned upon me at once. Blows pounded me from all sides while I struck out as best I could. So many blows landed upon me that I wondered if I were not the only blindfolded fighter in the ring, or if the man called Jackson hadn't succeeded in getting me after all.

Blindfolded, I could no longer control my motions. I had no dignity. I stumbled about like a baby or a drunken man. The smoke had become thicker and with each new blow it seemed to sear and further restrict my lungs. My saliva became like hot bitter glue. A glove connected with my head, filling my mouth with warm blood. It was everywhere. I could not tell if the moisture I felt upon my body was sweat or blood. A blow landed hard against the nape of my neck. I felt myself going over, my head hitting the floor. Streaks of blue light filled the black world behind the blindfold. I lay prone, pretending that I was knocked out, but felt myself seized by hands and yanked to my feet. "Get going, black boy! Mix it up!" My arms were like lead, my head smarting from blows. I managed to feel my way to the ropes and held on, trying to catch my breath. A glove landed in my midsection and I went over again, feeling as though the smoke had become a knife jabbed into my guts. Pushed this way and that by the legs milling around me, I finally pulled erect and discovered that I could see the black, sweat-washed forms weaving in the smoky-blue atmosphere like drunken dancers weaving to the rapid drum-like thuds of blows.

Everyone fought hysterically. It was complete anarchy. Everybody fought everybody else. No group fought together for long. Two, three, four, fought one, then turned to fight each other, were themselves attacked. Blows landed below the belt and in the kidney, with the gloves open as well as closed, and with my eye partly opened now there was not so much terror. I moved carefully, avoiding blows, although not too many to attract attention, fighting from group to group. The boys groped about like blind, cautious crabs crouching to protect their mid-sections, their heads pulled in short against their shoulders, their arms stretched nervously before them, with their fists testing the smoke-filled air like the knobbed feelers of hypersensitive snails. In one corner I glimpsed a boy violently punching the air and heard him scream in pain as he smashed his hand against a ring post. For a second I saw him bent over holding his hand, then going down as a blow caught his unprotected head. I played one group against the other, slipping in and throwing a punch then stepping out of range while pushing the others into the melee to take the blows blindly aimed at me. The smoke was agonizing and there were no rounds, no bells at three minute intervals to relieve our exhaustion. The room spun round me, a swirl of lights, smoke, sweating bodies surrounded by tense white faces. I bled from both nose and mouth, the blood spattering upon my chest.

The men kept yelling, "Slug him, black boy! Knock his guts out!"

"Uppercut him! Kill him! Kill that big boy!"

Taking a fake fall, I saw a boy going down heavily beside me as though we were felled by a single blow, saw a sneaker-clad foot shoot into his groin as the two who had knocked him down stumbled upon him. I rolled out of range, feeling a twinge of nausea.

The harder we fought the more threatening the men became. And yet, I had begun to worry about my speech again. How would it go? Would they recognize my ability? What would they give me?

I was fighting automatically and suddenly I noticed that one after another of the boys was leaving the ring. I was surprised, filled with panic, as though I had been left alone with an unknown danger. Then I understood. The boys had arranged it among themselves. It was the custom for the two men left in the ring to slug it out for the winner's prize. I discovered this too late. When the bell sounded two men in tuxedoes leaped into the ring and removed the blindfold. I found myself facing Tatlock, the biggest of the gang. I felt sick at my stomach. Hardly had the bell stopped ringing in my ears than it clanged again and I saw him moving swiftly toward me. Thinking of nothing else to do I hit him smash on the nose. He kept coming, bringing the rank sharp violence of stale sweat. His face was a black blank of a face, only his eyes alive—with hate of me and aglow with a feverish terror from what had happened to us all. I became anxious. I wanted to deliver my speech and he came at me as though he meant to beat it out of me. I smashed him again and again, taking his blows as they came. Then on a sudden impulse I struck him lightly and as we clinched, I whispered, "Fake like I knocked you out, you can have the prize."

"I'll break your behind," he whispered hoarsely.

"For *them*?"

"For *me*, sonofabitch!"

They were yelling for us to break it up and Tatlock spun me half around with a blow, and as a joggled camera sweeps in a reeling scene, I saw the howling red faces crouching tense beneath the cloud of blue-gray smoke. For a moment the world wavered, unraveled, flowed, then my head cleared and Tatlock bounced before me. That fluttering shadow before my eyes was his jabbing left hand. Then falling forward, my head against his damp shoulder, I whispered,

"I'll make it five dollars more."

"Go to hell!"

But his muscles relaxed a trifle beneath my pressure and I breathed, "Seven!"

"Give it to your ma," he said, ripping me beneath the heart.

And while I still held him I butted him and moved away. I felt myself bombarded with punches. I fought back with hopeless desperation. I wanted to deliver my speech more than anything else in the world, because I felt that only these men could judge truly my ability, and now this stupid clown was ruining my chances. I began fighting carefully now, moving in to punch him and out again with my greater speed. A lucky blow to his chin and I had him going too—until I heard a loud voice yell, "I got my money on the big boy."

Hearing this, I almost dropped my guard. I was confused: Should I try to win against the voice out there? Would not this go against my speech, and was not this a moment for humility, for nonresistance? A blow to my head as I danced about sent my right eye popping like a jack-in-the-box and settled my dilemma. The room went red as I fell. It was a dream fall, my body languid and fastidious as to where to land, until the floor became impatient and smashed up to meet me. A moment later I came to. An hypnotic voice said FIVE emphatically. And I lay there, hazily watching a dark red spot of my own blood shaping itself into a butterfly, glistening and soaking into the soiled gray world of the canvas.

When the voice drawled TEN I was lifted up and dragged to a chair. I sat dazed. My eye pained and swelled with each throb of my pounding heart and I wondered if now I would be allowed to speak. I was wringing wet, my mouth still bleeding. We were grouped along the wall now. The other boys ignored me as they congratulated Tatlock and speculated as to how much they would be paid. One boy whimpered over his smashed hand. Looking up front, I saw attendants in white jackets rolling the portable ring away and placing a small square rug in the vacant space surrounded by chairs. Perhaps, I thought, I will stand on the rug to deliver my speech.

Then the M.C. called to us, "Come on up here boys and get your money."

We ran forward to where the men laughed and talked in their chairs, waiting. Everyone seemed friendly now.

"There it is on the rug," the man said. I saw the rug covered with coins of all dimensions and a few crumpled bills. But what excited me, scattered here and there, were the gold pieces.

"Boys, it's all yours," the man said. "You get all you grab."

"That's right, Sambo," a blond man said, winking at me confidentially.

I trembled with excitement, forgetting my pain. I would get the gold and the bills, I thought. I would use both hands. I would throw my body against the boys nearest me to block them from the gold.

"Get down around the rug now," the man commanded, "and don't anyone touch it until I give the signal."

"This ought to be good," I heard.

As told, we got around the square rug on our knees. Slowly the man raised his freckled hand as we followed it upward with our eyes.

I heard, "These niggers look like they're about to pray!"

Then, "Ready," the man said. "Go!"

I lunged for a yellow coin lying on the blue design of the carpet, touching it and sending a surprised shriek to join those rising around me. I tried frantically to remove my hand but could not let go. A hot, violent force tore through my body, shaking me like a wet rat. The rug was electrified. The hair bristled up on my head as I shook myself free. My muscles jumped, my nerves jangled, writhed. But I saw that this was not stopping the other boys. Laughing in fear and embarrassment, some were holding back and scooping up the coins knocked off by the painful contortions of the others. The men roared above us as we struggled.

"Pick it up, goddamnit, pick it up!" someone called like a bass-voiced parrot. "Go on, get it!"

I crawled rapidly around the floor, picking up the coins, trying to avoid the coppers and to get greenbacks and the gold. Ignoring the shock by laughing, as I brushed the coins off quickly, I discovered that I could contain the electricity—a contradiction, but it works. Then the men began to push us onto the rug. Laughing embarrassedly, we struggled out of their hands and kept after the coins. We were all wet and slippery and hard to hold. Suddenly I saw a boy lifted into the air, glistening with sweat like a circus seal, and dropped, his wet back landing flush upon the charged rug, heard him yell and saw him literally dance upon his back, his elbows beating a frenzied tattoo upon the floor, his muscles twitching like the flesh of a horse stung by many flies. When he finally rolled off, his face was gray and no one stopped him when he ran from the floor amid booming laughter.

"Get the money," the M.C. called. "That's good hard American cash!"

And we snatched and grabbed, snatched and grabbed. I was careful not to come too close to the rug now, and when I felt the hot whiskey breath descend upon me like a cloud of foul air I reached out and grabbed the leg of a chair. It was occupied and I held on desperately.

"Leggo, nigger! Leggo!"

The huge face wavered down to mine as he tried to push me free. But my body was slippery and he was too drunk. It was Mr. Colcord, who owned a chain of movie houses and "entertainment palaces."

Each time he grabbed me I slipped out of his hands. It became a real struggle. I feared the rug more than I did the drunk, so I held on, surprising myself for a moment by trying to topple *him* upon the rug. It was such an enormous idea that I found myself actually carrying it out. I tried not to be obvious, yet when I grabbed his leg, trying to tumble him out of the chair, he raised up roaring with laughter, and, looking at me with soberness dead in the eye, kicked me viciously in the chest. The chair leg flew out of my hand. I felt myself going and rolled. It was as though I had rolled through a bed of hot coals. It seemed a whole century would pass before I would roll free, a century in which I was seared through the deepest levels of my body to the fearful breath within me and the breath seared and heated to the point of explosion. It'll all be over in a flash, I thought as I rolled clear. It'll all be over in a flash.

But not yet, the men on the other side were waiting, red faces swollen as though from apoplexy as they bent forward in their chairs. Seeing their fingers coming toward me I rolled away as a fumbled football rolls off the receiver's fingertips, back into the coals. That time I luckily sent the rug sliding out of place and heard the coins ringing against the floor and the boys scuffling to pick them up and the M.C. calling, "All right, boys, that's all. Go get dressed and get your money."

I was limp as a dish rag. My back felt as though it had been beaten with wires.

When we had dressed the M.C. came in and gave us each five dollars, except Tatlock, who got ten for being last in the ring. Then he told us to leave. I was not to get a chance to deliver my speech, I thought. I was going out into the dim alley in despair when I was stopped and told to go back. I returned to the ballroom, where the men were pushing back their chairs and gathering in groups to talk.

The M.C. knocked on a table for quiet. "Gentlemen," he said, "we almost forgot an important part of the program. A most serious part, gentlemen. This boy was brought here to deliver a speech which he made at his graduation yesterday. . . ."

"Bravo!"

"I'm told that he is the smartest boy we've got out there in Greenwood. I'm told that he knows more big words than a pocket-sized dictionary."

Much applause and laughter.

"So now, gentlemen, I want you to give him your attention."

There was still laughter as I faced them, my mouth dry, my eye throbbing. I began slowly, but evidently my throat was tense, because they began shouting, "Louder! Louder!"

"We of the younger generation extol the wisdom of that great leader and educator," I shouted, "who first spoke these flaming words of wisdom: 'A ship lost at sea for many days suddenly sighted a friendly vessel. From the mast of the unfortunate vessel was seen a signal: "Water, water; we die of thirst!" The answer from the friendly vessel came back: "Cast down your bucket where you are." The captain of the distressed vessel, at last heeding the injunction, cast down his bucket, and it came up full of fresh sparkling water from the mouth of the Amazon River.' And like him I say, and in his words, 'To those of my race who depend upon bettering their condition in a foreign land, or who underestimate the importance of cultivating friendly relations with the Southern white man, who is his next-door neighbor, I would say: "Cast down your bucket where you are"—cast it down in making friends in every manly way of the people of all races by whom we are surrounded. . . .' "

I spoke automatically and with such fervor that I did not realize that the men were still talking and laughing until my dry mouth, filling up with blood from the cut, almost strangled me. I coughed, wanting to stop and go to one of the tall brass, sand-filled spittoons to relieve myself, but a few of the men, especially the superintendent, were listening and I was afraid. So I gulped it down, blood, saliva, and all, and continued. (What powers of endurance I had during those days! What enthusiasm! What a belief in the rightness of things!) I spoke even louder in spite of the pain. But still they talked and still they laughed, as though deaf with cotton in dirty ears. So I spoke with greater emotional emphasis. I closed my ears and swallowed blood until I was nauseated. The speech seemed a hundred times as long as before, but I could not leave out a single word. All had to be said, each memorized nuance considered, rendered. Nor was that all. Whenever I uttered a word of three or more syllables a group of voices would yell for me to repeat it. I used the phrase "social responsibility" and they yelled:

"What's the word you say, boy?"

"Social responsibility," I said.

"What?"

"Social . . ."

"Louder."

". . . responsibility."

"More!"

"Respon —"

"Repeat!"

"— sibility."

The room filled with the uproar of laughter until, no doubt, distracted by having to gulp down my blood, I made a mistake and yelled a phrase I had often seen denounced in newspaper editorials, heard debated in private.

"Social . . ."

"What?" they yelled.

". . . equality —"

The laughter hung smokelike in the sudden stillness. I opened my eyes, puzzled. Sounds of displeasure filled the room. The M.C. rushed forward. They shouted hostile phrases at me. But I did not understand.

A small dry mustached man in the front row blared out, "Say that slowly, son!"

"What sir?"

"What you just said!"

"Social responsibility, sir," I said.

"You weren't being smart, were you, boy?" he said, not unkindly.

"No, sir!"

"You sure that about 'equality' was a mistake?"

"Oh, yes, sir," I said. "I was swallowing blood."

"Well, you had better speak more slowly so we can understand. We mean to do right by you, but you've got to know your place at all times. All right, now, go on with your speech."

I was afraid. I wanted to leave but I wanted also to speak and I was afraid they'd snatch me down.

"Thank you, sir," I said, beginning where I had left off, and having them ignore me as before.

Yet when I finished there was a thunderous applause. I was surprised to see the superintendent come forth with a package wrapped in white tissue paper, and, gesturing for quiet, address the men.

"Gentlemen, you see that I did not overpraise this boy. He makes a good speech and some day he'll lead his people in the proper paths. And I don't have to tell you that that is important in these days and times. This is a good, smart boy, and so to encourage him in the right direction, in the name of the Board of Education I wish to present him a prize in the form of this . . ."

He paused, removing the tissue paper and revealing a gleaming calfskin brief case.

". . . in the form of this first-class article from Shad Whitmore's shop."

"Boy," he said, addressing me, "take this prize and keep it well. Consider it a badge of office. Prize it. Keep developing as you are and some day it will be filled with important papers that will help shape the destiny of your people."

I was so moved that I could hardly express my thanks. A rope of bloody saliva forming a shape like an undiscovered continent drooled upon the leather and I wiped it quickly away. I felt an importance that I had never dreamed.

"Open it and see what's inside," I was told.

My fingers a-tremble, I complied, smelling the fresh leather and finding an official-looking document inside. It was a scholarship to the state college for Negroes. My eyes filled with tears and I ran awkwardly off the floor.

I was overjoyed; I did not even mind when I discovered that the gold pieces I had scrambled for were brass pocket tokens advertising a certain make of automobile.

When I reached home everyone was excited. Next day the neighbors came to congratulate me. I even felt safe from grandfather, whose deathbed curse usually spoiled my triumphs. I stood beneath his photograph with my brief case in hand and smiled triumphantly into his stolid black peasant's face. It was a face that fascinated me. The eyes seemed to follow everywhere I went.

That night I dreamed I was at a circus with him and that he refused to laugh at the clowns no matter what they did. Then later he told me to open my brief case and read what was inside and I did, finding an official envelope stamped with the state seal; and inside the envelope I found another and another, endlessly, and I thought I would fall of weariness. "Them's years," he said. "Now open that one." And I did and in it I found an engraved document containing a short message in letters of gold. "Read it," my grandfather said. "Out loud."

"To Whom It May Concern," I intoned. "Keep This Nigger-Boy Running."

I awoke with the old man's laughter ringing in my ears.

(It was a dream I was to remember and dream again for many years after. But at the time I had no insight into its meaning. First I had to attend college.)

1952

The Lottery

SHIRLEY JACKSON

[1916–1965]

The morning of June 27th was clear and sunny, with the fresh warmth of a full-summer day; the flowers were blossoming profusely and the grass was richly green. The people of the village began to gather in the square, between the post office and the bank, around ten o'clock; in some towns there were so many people that the lottery took two days and had to be started on June 26th, but in this village, where there were only about three hundred people, the whole lottery took less than two hours, so it could begin at ten o'clock in the morning and still be through in time to allow the villagers to get home for noon dinner.

The children assembled first, of course. School was recently over for the summer, and the feeling of liberty sat uneasily on most of them; they tended to gather together quietly for a while before they broke into boisterous play, and their talk was still of the classroom and teacher, of books and reprimands. Bobby Martin had already stuffed his pockets full of stones, and the other boys soon followed his example, selecting the smoothest and roundest stones; Bobby and Harry Jones and Dickie Delacroix—the villagers pronounced this name "Dellacroy"—eventually made a great pile of stones in one corner of the square and guarded it against the raids of the other boys. The girls stood aside, talking among themselves, looking over their shoulders at the boys, and the very small children rolled in the dust or clung to the hands of their older brothers or sisters.

Soon the men began to gather, surveying their own children, speaking of planting and rain, tractors and taxes. They stood together, away from the pile of stones in the corner, and their jokes were quiet and they smiled rather than laughed. The women, wearing faded house dresses and sweaters, came shortly after their menfolk. They greeted one another and exchanged bits of gossip as they went to join their husbands. Soon the women, standing by their husbands, began to call to their children, and the children came reluctantly, having to be called four or five times. Bobby Martin ducked under his mother's grasping hand and ran, laughing, back to the pile of stones. His father spoke up sharply, and Bobby came quickly and took his place between his father and his oldest brother.

The lottery was conducted—as were the square dances, the teenage club, the Halloween program—by Mr. Summers, who had time and energy to devote to civic activities. He was a round-faced, jovial man and he ran the coal business, and people were sorry for him, because he had no children and his wife was a scold. When he arrived in the square, carrying the black wooden box, there was a murmur of conversation among the villagers, and he waved and called, "Little late today, folks." The postmaster, Mr. Graves, followed him, carrying a three-legged stool, and the stool was put in the center of the square and Mr. Summers set the black box down on it. The villagers kept their distance, leaving a space between themselves and the stool, and when Mr. Summers said, "Some of you fellows want to give me a hand?" there was a hesitation before two men, Mr. Martin and his oldest son, Baxter, came forward to hold the box steady on the stool while Mr. Summers stirred up the papers inside it.

The original paraphernalia for the lottery had been lost long ago, and the black box now resting on the stool had been put into use even before Old Man Warner, the oldest man in town, was born. Mr. Summers spoke frequently to the villagers about making a new box, but no one liked to upset even as much tradition as was represented by the black box. There was a story that the present box had been made with some pieces of the box that had preceded it, the one that had been constructed when the first people settled down to make a village here. Every year, after the lottery, Mr. Summers began talking again about a new box, but every year the subject was allowed to fade off without anything's being done. The black box grew shabbier each year; by now it was no longer completely black but splintered badly along one side to show the original wood color, and in some places faded or stained.

Mr. Martin and his oldest son, Baxter, held the black box securely on the stool until Mr. Summers had stirred the papers thoroughly with his hand. Because so much of the ritual had been forgotten or discarded, Mr. Summers had been successful in having slips of paper substituted for the chips of wood that had been used for generations. Chips of wood, Mr. Summers had argued, had been all very well when the village was tiny, but now that the population was more than three hundred and likely to keep on growing, it was necessary to use something that would fit more easily into the black box. The night before the lottery, Mr. Summers and Mr. Graves made up the slips of paper and put them in the box, and it was then taken to the safe of Mr. Summers's coal company and locked up until Mr. Summers was ready to take it to the square next morning. The rest of the year, the box was put away, sometimes one place, sometimes another; it had spent one year in Mr. Graves's barn and another year underfoot in the post office, and sometimes it was set on a shelf in the Martin grocery and left there.

There was a great deal of fussing to be done before Mr. Summers declared the lottery open. There were the lists to make up—of heads of families, heads of households in each family, members of each household in each family. There was the proper swearing-in of Mr. Summers by the postmaster, as the official of the lottery; at one time, some people remembered, there had been a recital of some sort, performed by the official of the lottery, a perfunctory, tuneless chant that had been rattled off duly each year; some people believed that the official of the lottery used to stand just so when he said or sang it, others believed that he was supposed to walk among the people, but years and years ago this part of the ritual had been allowed to lapse. There had been, also, a ritual salute, which the official of the lottery had had to use in addressing each person who came up to draw from the box, but this also had changed with time, until now it was felt necessary only for the official to speak to each person approaching. Mr. Summers was very good at all this; in his clean white shirt and blue jeans, with one hand resting carelessly on the black box, he seemed very proper and important as he talked interminably to Mr. Graves and the Martins.

Just as Mr. Summers finally left off talking and turned to the assembled villagers, Mrs. Hutchinson came hurriedly along the path to the square, her sweater thrown over her shoulders, and slid into place in the back of the crowd. "Clean forgot what day it was," she said to Mrs. Delacroix, who stood next to her, and they both laughed softly. "Thought my old man was out back stacking wood," Mrs. Hutchinson went on, "and then I looked out the window and the kids was gone, and then I remembered it was the twenty-seventh and came a-running." She dried her hands on her apron, and Mrs. Delacroix said, "You're in time, though. They're still talking away up there."

Mrs. Hutchinson craned her neck to see through the crowd and found her husband and children standing near the front. She tapped Mrs. Delacroix on the arm as a farewell and began to make her way through the crowd. The people separated good-humoredly to let her through; two or three people said, in voices just loud enough to be heard across the crowd, "Here comes your Missus, Hutchinson," and "Bill, she made it after all." Mrs. Hutchinson reached her husband, and Mr. Summers, who had been waiting, said cheerfully, "Thought we were going to have to get on without you, Tessie." Mrs. Hutchinson said, grinning, "Wouldn't have me leave m'dishes in the sink, now, would you, Joe?" and soft laughter ran through the crowd as the people stirred back into position after Mrs. Hutchinson's arrival.

"Well, now," Mr. Summers said soberly, "guess we better get started, get this over with, so's we can go back to work. Anybody ain't here?"

"Dunbar," several people said. "Dunbar, Dunbar."

Mr. Summers consulted his list. "Clyde Dunbar," he said. "That's right. He's broke his leg, hasn't he? Who's drawing for him?"

"Me, I guess," a woman said, and Mr. Summers turned to look at her. "Wife draws for her husband," Mr. Summers said. "Don't you have a grown boy to do it for you, Janey?" Although Mr. Summers and everyone else in the village knew the answer perfectly well, it was the business of the official of the lottery to ask such questions formally. Mr. Summers waited with an expression of polite interest while Mrs. Dunbar answered.

"Horace's not but sixteen yet," Mrs. Dunbar said regretfully. "Guess I gotta fill in for the old man this year."

"Right," Mr. Summers said. He made a note on the list he was holding. Then he asked, "Watson boy drawing this year?"

A tall boy in the crowd raised his hand. "Here," he said. "I'm drawing for m'mother and me." He blinked his eyes nervously and ducked his head as several voices in the crowd said things like "Good fellow, Jack," and "Glad to see your mother's got a man to do it."

"Well," Mr. Summers said, "guess that's everyone. Old Man Warner make it?"

"Here," a voice said, and Mr. Summers nodded.

A sudden hush fell on the crowd as Mr. Summers cleared his throat and looked at the list. "All ready?" he called. "Now, I'll read the names—heads of families first—and the men come up and take a paper out of the box. Keep the paper folded in your hand without looking at it until everyone has had a turn. Everything clear?"

The people had done it so many times that they only half listened to the directions; most of them were quiet, wetting their lips, not looking around. Then Mr. Summers raised one hand high and said, "Adams." A man disengaged himself from the crowd and came forward. "Hi, Steve," Mr. Summers said, and Mr. Adams said, "Hi, Joe." They grinned at one another humorlessly and nervously. Then Mr. Adams reached into the black box and took out a folded paper. He held it firmly by one corner as he turned and went hastily back to his place in the crowd, where he stood a little apart from his family, not looking down at his hand.

"Allen," Mr. Summers said, "Anderson. . . . Bentham."

"Seems like there's no time at all between lotteries any more," Mrs. Delacroix said to Mrs. Graves in the back row. "Seems like we got through with the last one only last week."

"Time sure goes fast," Mrs. Graves said.

"Clark. . . . Delacroix."

"There goes my old man," Mrs. Delacroix said. She held her breath while her husband went forward.

"Dunbar," Mr. Summers said, and Mrs. Dunbar went steadily to the box while one of the women said, "Go on, Janey," and another said, "There she goes."

"We're next," Mrs. Graves said. She watched while Mr. Graves came around from the side of the box, greeted Mr. Summers gravely, and selected a slip of paper from the box. By now, all through the crowd there were men holding the small folded papers in their large hands, turning them over and over nervously. Mrs. Dunbar and her two sons stood together, Mrs. Dunbar holding the slip of paper.

"Harburt. . . . Hutchinson."

"Get up there, Bill," Mrs. Hutchinson said, and the people near her laughed.

"Jones."

"They do say," Mr. Adams said to Old Man Warner, who stood next to him, "that over in the north village they're talking of giving up the lottery."

Old Man Warner snorted. "Pack of crazy fools," he said. "Listening to the young folks, nothing's good enough for *them.* Next thing you know, they'll be wanting to go back to living in caves, nobody work any more, live *that* way for a while. Used to be a saying about 'Lottery in June, corn be heavy soon.' First thing you know, we'd all be eating stewed chickweed and acorns. There's *always* been a lottery," he added petulantly. "Bad enough to see young Joe Summers up there joking with everybody."

"Some places have already quit lotteries," Mrs. Adams said.

"Nothing but trouble in *that,*" Old Man Warner said stoutly. "Pack of young fools."

"Martin." And Bobby Martin watched his father go forward. "Overdyke. . . . Percy."

"I wish they'd hurry," Mrs. Dunbar said to her older son. "I wish they'd hurry."

"They're almost through," her son said.

"You get ready to run tell Dad," Mrs. Dunbar said.

Mr. Summers called his own name and then stepped forward precisely and selected a slip from the box. Then he called, "Warner."

"Seventy-seventh year I been in the lottery," Old Man Warner said as he went through the crowd. "Seventy-seventh time."

"Watson." The tall boy came awkwardly through the crowd. Someone said, "Don't be nervous, Jack," and Mr. Summers said, "Take your time, son."

"Zanini."

After that, there was a long pause, a breathless pause, until Mr. Summers, holding his slip of paper in the air, said, "All right, fellows." For a minute, no one moved, and then all the slips of paper were opened. Suddenly, all the women began to speak at once, saying, "Who is it?" "Who's got it?" "Is it the Dunbars?" "Is it the Watsons?" Then the voices began to say, "It's Hutchinson. It's Bill," "Bill Hutchinson's got it."

"Go tell your father," Mrs. Dunbar said to her older son.

People began to look around to see the Hutchinsons. Bill Hutchinson was standing quiet, staring down at the paper in his hand. Suddenly, Tessie Hutchinson shouted to Mr. Summers, "You didn't give him time enough to take any paper he wanted. I saw you. It wasn't fair!"

"Be a good sport, Tessie," Mrs. Delacroix called, and Mrs. Graves said, "All of us took the same chance."

"Shut up, Tessie," Bill Hutchinson said.

"Well, everyone," Mr. Summers said, "that was done pretty fast, and now we've got to be hurrying a little more to get done in time." He consulted his next list. "Bill," he said, "you draw for the Hutchinson family. You got any other households in the Hutchinsons?"

"There's Don and Eva," Mrs. Hutchinson yelled. "Make *them* take their chance!"

"Daughters drew with their husbands' families, Tessie," Mr. Summers said gently. "You know that as well as anyone else."

"It wasn't *fair*," Tessie said.

"I guess not, Joe," Bill Hutchinson said regretfully. "My daughter draws with her husband's family, that's only fair. And I've got no other family except the kids."

"Then, as far as drawing for families is concerned, it's you," Mr. Summers said in explanation, "and as far as drawing for households is concerned, that's you, too. Right?"

"Right," Bill Hutchinson said.

"How many kids, Bill?" Mr. Summers asked formally.

"Three," Bill Hutchinson said. "There's Bill, Jr., and Nancy, and little Dave. And Tessie and me."

"All right, then," Mr. Summers said. "Harry, you got their tickets back?"

Mr. Graves nodded and held up the slips of paper. "Put them in the box, then," Mr. Summers directed. "Take Bill's and put it in."

"I think we ought to start over," Mrs. Hutchinson said, as quietly as she could. "I tell you it wasn't *fair*. You didn't give him time enough to choose. *Every*body saw that."

Mr. Graves had selected the five slips and put them in the box, and he dropped all the papers but those onto the ground, where the breeze caught them and lifted them off.

"Listen, everybody," Mrs. Hutchinson was saying to the people around her.

"Ready, Bill?" Mr. Summers asked, and Bill Hutchinson, with one quick glance around at his wife and children, nodded.

"Remember," Mr. Summers said, "take the slips and keep them folded until each person has taken one. Harry, you help little Dave." Mr. Graves took the hand of the little boy, who came willingly with him up to the box. "Take a paper out of the box, Davy," Mr. Summers said. Davy put his hand into the box and laughed. "Take just *one* paper," Mr. Summers said. "Harry, you hold it for him." Mr. Graves took the child's hand and removed the folded paper from the tight fist and held it while little Dave stood next to him and looked up at him wonderingly.

"Nancy next," Mr. Summers said. Nancy was twelve, and her school friends breathed heavily as she went forward, switching her skirt, and took a slip daintily from the box. "Bill, Jr.," Mr. Summers said, and Billy, his face red and his feet overlarge, nearly knocked the box over as he got a paper out. "Tessie," Mr. Summers said. She hesitated for a minute, looking around defiantly, and then set her lips and went up to the box. She snatched a paper out and held it behind her.

"Bill," Mr. Summers said, and Bill Hutchinson reached into the box and felt around, bringing his hand out at last with the slip of paper in it.

The crowd was quiet. A girl whispered, "I hope it's not Nancy," and the sound of the whisper reached the edges of the crowd.

"It's not the way it used to be," Old Man Warner said clearly. "People ain't the way they used to be."

"All right," Mr. Summers said. "Open the papers. Harry, you open little Dave's."

Mr. Graves opened the slip of paper and there was a general sigh through the crowd as he held it up and everyone could see that it was blank. Nancy and Bill, Jr., opened theirs at the same time, and both beamed and laughed, turning around to the crowd and holding their slips of paper above their heads.

"Tessie," Mr. Summers said. There was a pause, and then Mr. Summers looked at Bill Hutchinson, and Bill unfolded his paper and showed it. It was blank.

"It's Tessie," Mr. Summers said, and his voice was hushed. "Show us her paper, Bill."

Bill Hutchinson went over to his wife and forced the slip of paper out of her hand. It had a black spot on it, the black spot Mr. Summers had made the night before with the heavy pencil in the coal-company office. Bill Hutchinson held it up and there was a stir in the crowd.

"All right, folks," Mr. Summers said. "Let's finish quickly."

Although the villagers had forgotten the ritual and lost the original black box, they still remembered to use stones. The pile of stones the boys had made earlier was ready; there were stones on the ground with the blowing scraps of paper that had come out of the box. Mrs. Delacroix selected a stone so large she had to pick it up with both hands and turned to Mrs. Dunbar. "Come on," she said. "Hurry up."

Mrs. Dunbar had small stones in both hands, and she said, gasping for breath, "I can't run at all. You'll have to go ahead and I'll catch up with you."

The children had stones already, and someone gave little Davy Hutchinson a few pebbles.

Tessie Hutchinson was in the center of a cleared space by now, and she held her hands out desperately as the villagers moved in on her. “It isn’t fair,” she said. A stone hit her on the side of the head.

Old Man Warner was saying, “Come on, come on, everyone.” Steve Adams was in the front of the crowd of villagers, with Mrs. Graves beside him.

“It isn’t fair, it isn’t right,” Mrs. Hutchinson screamed and then they were upon her.

1948

Sonny's Blues

JAMES BALDWIN
[1924–1987]

I read about it in the paper, in the subway, on my way to work. I read it, and I couldn't believe it, and I read it again. Then perhaps I just stared at it, at the newsprint spelling out his name, spelling out the story. I stared at it in the swinging lights of the subway car, and in the faces and bodies of the people, and in my own face, trapped in the darkness which roared outside.

It was not to be believed and I kept telling myself that, as I walked from the subway station to the high school. And at the same time I couldn't doubt it. I was scared, scared for Sonny. He became real to me again. A great block of ice got settled in my belly and kept melting there slowly all day long, while I taught my classes algebra. It was a special kind of ice. It kept melting, sending trickles of ice water all up and down my veins, but it never got less. Sometimes it hardened and seemed to expand until I felt my guts were going to come spilling out or that I was going to choke or scream. This would always be at a moment when I was remembering some specific thing Sonny had once said or done.

When he was about as old as the boys in my classes his face had been bright and open, there was a lot of copper in it; and he'd had wonderfully direct brown eyes, and great gentleness and privacy. I wondered what he looked like now. He had been picked up, the evening before, in a raid on an apartment downtown, for peddling and using heroin.

I couldn't believe it: but what I mean by that is that I couldn't find any room for it anywhere inside me. I had kept it outside me for a long time. I hadn't wanted to know. I had had suspicions, but I didn't name them, I kept putting them away. I told myself that Sonny was wild, but he wasn't crazy. And he'd always been a good boy, he hadn't ever turned hard or evil or disrespectful, the way kids can, so quick, so quick, especially in Harlem. I didn't want to believe that I'd ever see my brother going down, coming to nothing, all that light in his face gone out, in the condition I'd already seen so many others. Yet it had happened and here I was, talking about algebra to a lot of boys who might, every one of them for all I knew, be popping off needles every time they went to the head. Maybe it did more for them than algebra could.

I was sure that the first time Sonny had ever had horse, he couldn't have been much older than these boys were now. These boys, now, were living as we'd been living then, they were growing up with a rush and their heads bumped abruptly against the low ceiling of their actual possibilities. They were filled with rage. All they really knew were two darknesses, the darkness of their lives, which was now closing in on them, and the darkness of the movies, which had blinded them to that other darkness, and in which they now, vindictively, dreamed, at once more together than they were at any other time, and more alone.

When the last bell rang, the last class ended, I let out my breath. It seemed I'd been holding it for all that time. My clothes were wet—I may have looked as though I'd been sitting in a steam bath, all dressed up, all afternoon. I sat alone in the classroom a long time. I listened to the boys outside, downstairs, shouting and cursing and laughing. Their laughter struck me for perhaps the first time. It was not the joyous laughter which—God knows why—one associates with children. It was mocking and insular, its intent to denigrate. It was disenchanted, and in this, also, lay the authority of their curses. Perhaps I was listening to them because I was thinking about my brother and in them I heard my brother. And myself.

One boy was whistling a tune, at once very complicated and very simple, it seemed to be pouring out of him as though he were a bird, and it sounded very cool and moving through all that harsh, bright air, only just holding its own through all those other sounds.

I stood up and walked over to the window and looked down into the courtyard. It was the beginning of the spring and the sap was rising in the boys. A teacher passed through them every now and again, quickly, as though he or she couldn't wait to get out of that courtyard, to get those boys out of their sight and off their minds. I started collecting my stuff. I thought I'd better get home and talk to Isabel.

The courtyard was almost deserted by the time I got downstairs. I saw this boy standing in the shadow of a doorway, looking just like Sonny. I almost called his name. Then I saw that it wasn't Sonny, but somebody we used to know, a boy from around our block. He'd been Sonny's friend. He'd never been mine, having been too young for me, and, anyway, I'd never liked him. And now, even though he was a grown-up man, he still hung around that block, still spent hours on the street corners, was always high and raggy. I used to run into him from time to time and he'd often work around to asking me for a quarter or fifty cents. He always had some real good excuse, too, and I always gave it to him, I don't know why.

But now, abruptly, I hated him. I couldn't stand the way he looked at me, partly like a dog, partly like a cunning child. I wanted to ask him what the hell he was doing in the school courtyard.

He sort of shuffled over to me, and he said, "I see you got the papers. So you already know about it."

"You mean about Sonny? Yes, I already know about it. How come they didn't get you?"

He grinned. It made him repulsive and it also brought to mind what he'd looked like as a kid. "I wasn't there. I stay away from them people."

"Good for you." I offered him a cigarette and I watched him through the smoke. "You come all the way down here just to tell me about Sonny?"

"That's right." He was sort of shaking his head and his eyes looked strange, as though they were about to cross. The bright sun deadened his damp dark brown skin and it made his eyes look yellow and showed up the dirt in his kinked hair. He smelled funky. I moved a little away from him and I said, "Well, thanks. But I already know about it and I got to get home."

"I'll walk you a little ways," he said. We started walking. There were a couple of kids still loitering in the courtyard and one of them said good-night to me and looked strangely at the boy beside me.

"What're you going to do?" he asked me. "I mean, about Sonny?"

"Look. I haven't seen Sonny for over a year. I'm not sure I'm going to do anything. Anyway, what the hell *can* I do?"

"That's right," he said quickly, "ain't nothing you can do. Can't much help old Sonny no more, I guess."

It was what I was thinking and so it seemed to me he had no right to say it.

"I'm surprised at Sonny, though," he went on—he had a funny way of talking, he looked straight ahead as though he were talking to himself—"I thought Sonny was a smart boy, I thought he was too smart to get hung."

"I guess he thought so too," I said sharply, "and that's how he got hung. And how about you? You're pretty goddamn smart, I bet."

Then he looked directly at me, just for a minute. "I ain't smart," he said. "If I was smart, I'd have reached for a pistol a long time ago."

"Look. Don't tell *me* your sad story, if it was up to me, I'd give you one." Then I felt guilty—guilty, probably, for never having supposed that the poor bastard *had* a story of his own, much less a sad one, and I asked, quickly, "What's going to happen to him now?"

He didn't answer this. He was off by himself some place. "Funny thing," he said, and from his tone we might have been discussing the quickest way to get to Brooklyn, "when I saw the papers this morning, the first thing I asked myself was if I had anything to do with it. I felt sort of responsible."

I began to listen more carefully. The subway station was on the corner, just before us, and I stopped. He stopped, too. We were in front of a bar and he ducked slightly, peering in, but whoever he was looking for didn't seem to be there. The juke box was blasting away with something black and bouncy and I half watched the barmaid as she danced her way from the juke box to her place behind the bar. And I watched her face as she laughingly responded to something someone said to her, still keeping time to the music. When she smiled one saw the little girl, one sensed the doomed, still-struggling woman beneath the battered face of the semi-whore.

"I never *give* Sonny nothing," the boy said finally, "but a long time ago I come to school high and Sonny asked me how it felt." He paused, I couldn't bear to watch him, I watched the barmaid, and I listened to the music which seemed to be causing the pavement to shake. "I told him it felt great." The music stopped, the barmaid paused and watched the juke box until the music began again. "It did."

All this was carrying me some place I didn't want to go. I certainly didn't want to know how it felt. It filled everything, the people, the houses, the music, the dark, quicksilver barmaid, with menace; and this menace was their reality.

"What's going to happen to him now?" I asked again.

"They'll send him away some place and they'll try to cure him." He shook his head. "Maybe he'll even think he's kicked the habit. Then they'll let him loose"—he gestured, throwing his cigarette into the gutter. "That's all."

"What do you mean, that's *all*?"

But I knew what he meant.

"I *mean*, that's *all*." He turned his head and looked at me, pulling down the corners of his mouth. "Don't you know what I mean?" he asked, softly.

"How the hell *would* I know what you mean?" I almost whispered it, I don't know why.

"That's right," he said to the air, "how would *he* know what I mean?" He turned toward me again, patient and calm, and yet I somehow felt him shaking, shaking as though he were going to fall apart. I felt that ice in my guts again, the dread I'd felt all afternoon; and again I watched the barmaid, moving about the bar, washing glasses, and singing. "Listen. They'll let him out and then it'll just start all over again. That's what I mean."

"You mean—they'll let him out. And then he'll just start working his way back in again. You mean he'll never kick the habit. Is that what you mean?"

"That's right," he said, cheerfully. "*You* see what I mean."

"Tell me," I said at last, "why does he want to die? He must want to die, he's killing himself, why does he want to die?"

He looked at me in surprise. He licked his lips. "He don't want to die. He wants to live. Don't nobody want to die, ever."

Then I wanted to ask him—too many things. He could not have answered, or if he had, I could not have borne the answers. I started walking. "Well, I guess it's none of my business."

"It's going to be rough on old Sonny," he said. We reached the subway station. "This is your station?" he asked. I nodded. I took one step down. "Damn!" he said, suddenly. I looked up at him. He grinned again. "Damn it if I didn't leave all my money home. You ain't got a dollar on you, have you? Just for a couple of days, is all."

All at once something inside gave and threatened to come pouring out of me. I didn't hate him any more. I felt that in another moment I'd start crying like a child.

"Sure," I said. "Don't sweat." I looked in my wallet and didn't have a dollar, I only had a five. "Here," I said. "That hold you?"

He didn't look at it—he didn't want to look at it. A terrible closed look came over his face, as though he were keeping the number on the bill a secret from him and me. "Thanks," he said, and now he was dying to see me go. "Don't worry about Sonny. Maybe I'll write him or something."

"Sure," I said. "You do that. So long."

"Be seeing you," he said. I went on down the steps.

And I didn't write Sonny or send him anything for a long time. When I finally did, it was just after my little girl died, he wrote me back a letter which made me feel like a bastard.

Here's what he said:

Dear brother,

You don't know how much I needed to hear from you. I wanted to write you many a time but I dug how much I must have hurt you and so I didn't write. But now I feel like a man who's been trying to climb up out of some deep, real deep and funky hole and just saw the sun up there, outside. I got to get outside.

I can't tell you much about how I got here. I mean I don't know how to tell you. I guess I was afraid of something or I was trying to escape from something and you know I have never been very strong in the head (smile). I'm glad Mama and Daddy are dead and can't see what's happened to their son and I swear if I'd known what I was doing I would never have hurt you so, you and a lot of other fine people who were nice to me and who believed in me.

I don't want you to think it had anything to do with me being a musician. It's more than that. Or maybe less than that. I can't get anything straight in my head down here and I try not to think about what's going to happen to me when I get outside again. Sometime I think I'm going to flip and never get outside and sometime I think I'll come straight back. I tell you one thing, though, I'd rather blow my brains out than go through this again. But that's what they all say, so they tell me. If I tell you when I'm coming to New York and if you could meet me, I sure would appreciate it. Give my love to Isabel and the kids and I was sure sorry to hear about little Gracie. I wish I could be like Mama and say the Lord's will be done, but I don't know it seems to me that trouble is the one thing that never does get stopped and I don't know what good it does to blame it on the Lord. But maybe it does some good if you believe it.

Your brother,
Sonny

Then I kept in constant touch with him and I sent him whatever I could and I went to meet him when he came back to New York.

When I saw him many things I thought I had forgotten came flooding back to me. This was because I had begun, finally, to wonder about Sonny, about the life that Sonny lived inside. This life, whatever it was, had made him older and thinner and it had deepened the distant stillness in which he had always moved. He looked very unlike my baby brother. Yet, when he smiled, when we shook hands, the baby brother I'd never known looked out from the depths of his private life, like an animal waiting to be coaxed into the light.

"How you been keeping?" he asked me.

"All right. And you?"

"Just fine." He was smiling all over his face. "It's good to see you again."

"It's good to see you."

The seven years' difference in our ages lay between us like a chasm: I wondered if these years would ever operate between us as a bridge. I was remembering, and it made it hard to catch my breath, that I had been there when he was born; and I had heard the first words he had ever spoken. When he started to walk, he walked from our mother straight to me. I caught him just before he fell when he took the first steps he ever took in this world.

"How's Isabel?"

"Just fine. She's dying to see you."

"And the boys?"

"They're fine, too. They're anxious to see their uncle."

"Oh, come on. You know they don't remember me."

"Are you kidding? Of course they remember you."

He grinned again. We got into a taxi. We had a lot to say to each other, far too much to know how to begin.

As the taxi began to move, I asked, "You still want to go to India?"

He laughed. "You still remember that. Hell, no. This place is Indian enough for me."

"It used to belong to them," I said.

And he laughed again. "They damn sure knew what they were doing when they got rid of it."

Years ago, when he was around fourteen, he'd been all hipped on the idea of going to India. He read books about people sitting on rocks, naked, in all kinds of weather, but mostly bad, naturally, and walking barefoot through hot coals and arriving at wisdom. I used to say that it sounded to me as though they were getting away from wisdom as fast as they could. I think he sort of looked down on me for that.

"Do you mind," he asked, "if we have the driver drive alongside the park? On the west side—I haven't seen the city in so long."

"Of course not," I said. I was afraid that I might sound as though I were humoring him, but I hoped he wouldn't take it that way.

So we drove along, between the green of the park and the stony, lifeless elegance of hotels and apartment buildings, toward the vivid, killing streets of our childhood. These streets hadn't changed, though housing projects jutted up out of them now like rocks in the middle of a boiling sea. Most of the houses in which we had grown up had vanished, as had the stores from which we had stolen, the basements in which we had first tried sex, the rooftops from which we had hurled tin cans and bricks. But houses exactly like the houses of our past yet dominated the landscape, boys exactly like the boys we once had been found themselves smothering in these houses, came down into the streets for light and air and found themselves encircled by disaster. Some escaped the trap, most didn't. Those who got out always left something of themselves behind, as some animals amputate a leg and leave it in the trap. It might be said, perhaps, that I had escaped, after all, I was a school teacher; or that Sonny had, he hadn't lived in Harlem for years. Yet, as the cab moved uptown through streets which seemed, with a rush, to darken with dark people, and as I covertly studied Sonny's face, it came to me that what we both were seeking through our separate cab windows was that part of ourselves which had been left behind. It's always at the hour of trouble and confrontation that the missing member aches.

We hit 110th Street and started rolling up Lenox Avenue. And I'd known this avenue all my life, but it seemed to me again, as it had seemed on the day I'd first heard about Sonny's trouble, filled with a hidden menace which was its very breath of life.

"We almost there," said Sonny.

"Almost." We were both too nervous to say anything more.

We live in a housing project. It hasn't been up long. A few days after it was up it seemed uninhabitably new, now, of course, it's already run-down. It looks like a parody of the good, clean, faceless life—God knows the people who live in it do their best to make it a parody. The beat-looking grass lying around isn't enough to make their lives green, the hedges will never hold out the streets, and they know it. The big windows fool no one, they aren't big enough to make space out of no space. They don't bother with the windows, they watch the TV screen instead. The playground is most popular with the children who don't play at jacks, or skip rope, or roller skate, or swing, and they can be found in it after dark. We moved in partly because it's not too far from where I teach, and partly for the kids; but it's really just like the houses in which Sonny and I grew up. The same things happen, they'll have the same things to remember. The moment Sonny and I started into the house I had the feeling that I was simply bringing him back into the danger he had almost died trying to escape.

Sonny has never been talkative. So I don't know why I was sure he'd be dying to talk to me when supper was over the first night. Everything went fine, the oldest boy remembered him, and the youngest boy liked him, and Sonny had remembered to bring something for each of them; and Isabel, who is really much nicer than I am, more open and giving, had gone to a lot of trouble about dinner and was genuinely glad to see him. And she's always been able to tease Sonny in a way that I haven't. It was nice to see her face so vivid again and to hear her laugh and watch her make Sonny laugh. She wasn't, or, anyway, she didn't seem to be, at all uneasy or embarrassed. She chatted as though there were no subject which had to be avoided and she got Sonny past his first, faint stiffness. And thank God she was there, for I was filled with that icy dread again. Everything I did seemed awkward to me, and everything I said sounded freighted with hidden meaning. I was trying to remember everything I'd heard about dope addiction and I couldn't help watching Sonny for signs. I wasn't doing it out of malice. I was trying to find out something about my brother. I was dying to hear him tell me he was safe.

"Safe!" my father grunted, whenever Mama suggested trying to move to a neighborhood which might be safer for children. "Safe, hell! Ain't no place safe for kids, nor nobody."

He always went on like this, but he wasn't, ever, really as bad as he sounded, not even on weekends, when he got drunk. As a matter of fact, he was always on the lookout for "something a little better," but he died before he found it. He died suddenly, during a drunken weekend in the middle of the war, when Sonny was fifteen. He and Sonny hadn't ever got on too well. And this was partly because Sonny was the apple of his father's eye. It was because he loved Sonny so much and was frightened for him, that he was always fighting with him. It doesn't do any good to fight with Sonny. Sonny just moves back, inside himself, where he can't be reached. But the principal reason that they never hit it off is that they were so much alike. Daddy was big and rough and loud-talking, just the opposite of Sonny, but they both had—that same privacy.

Mama tried to tell me something about this, just after Daddy died. I was home on leave from the army.

This was the last time I ever saw my mother alive. Just the same, this picture gets all mixed up in my mind with pictures I had of her when she was younger. The way I always see her is the way she used to be on a Sunday afternoon, say, when the old folks were talking after the big Sunday dinner. I always see her wearing pale blue. She'd be sitting on the sofa. And my father would be sitting in the easy chair, not far from her. And the living room would be full of church folks and relatives. There they sit, in chairs all around the living room, and the night is creeping up outside, but nobody knows it yet. You can see the darkness growing against the windowpanes and you hear the street noises every now and again, or maybe the jangling beat of a tambourine from one of the churches close by, but it's real quiet in the room. For a moment nobody's talking, but every face looks darkening, like the sky outside. And my mother rocks a little from the waist, and my father's eyes are closed. Everyone is looking at something a child can't see. For a minute they've forgotten the children. Maybe a kid is lying on the rug, half asleep. Maybe somebody's got a kid in his lap and is absent-mindedly stroking the kid's head. Maybe there's a kid, quiet and big-eyed, curled up in a big chair in the corner. The silence, the darkness coming, and the darkness in the faces frightens the child obscurely. He hopes that the hand which strokes his forehead will never stop—will never die. He hopes that there will never come a time when the old folks won't be sitting around the living room, talking about where they've come from, and what they've seen, and what's happened to them and their kinfolk.

But something deep and watchful in the child knows that this is bound to end, is already ending. In a moment someone will get up and turn on the light. Then the old folks will remember the children and they won't talk any more that day. And when light fills the room, the child is filled with darkness. He knows that every time this happens he's moved just a little closer to that darkness outside. The darkness outside is what the old folks have been talking about. It's what they've come from. It's what they endure. The child knows that they won't talk any more because if he knows too much about what's happened to *them*, he'll know too much too soon, about what's going to happen to *him*.

The last time I talked to my mother, I remember I was restless. I wanted to get out and see Isabel. We weren't married then and we had a lot to straighten out between us.

There Mama sat, in black, by the window. She was humming an old church song, *Lord, you brought me from a long ways off.* Sonny was out somewhere. Mama kept watching the streets.

"I don't know," she said, "if I'll ever see you again, after you go off from here. But I hope you'll remember the things I tried to teach you."

"Don't talk like that," I said, and smiled. "You'll be here a long time yet."

She smiled, too, but she said nothing. She was quiet for a long time. And I said, "Mama, don't you worry about nothing. I'll be writing all the time, and you be getting the checks. . . ."

"I want to talk to you about your brother," she said, suddenly. "If anything happens to me he ain't going to have nobody to look out for him."

"Mama," I said, "ain't nothing going to happen to you *or* Sonny. Sonny's all right. He's a good boy and he's got good sense."

"It ain't a question of his being a good boy," Mama said, "nor of his having good sense. It ain't only the bad ones, nor yet the dumb ones that gets sucked under." She stopped, looking at me. "Your Daddy once had a brother," she said, and she smiled in a way that made me feel she was in pain. "You didn't never know that, did you?"

"No," I said, "I never knew that," and I watched her face.

"Oh, yes," she said, "your Daddy had a brother." She looked out of the window again. "I know you never saw your Daddy cry. But *I* did—many a time, through all these years."

I asked her, "What happened to his brother? How come nobody's ever talked about him?"

This was the first time I ever saw my mother look old.

"His brother got killed," she said, "when he was just a little younger than you are now. I knew him. He was a fine boy. He was maybe a little full of the devil, but he didn't mean nobody no harm."

Then she stopped and the room was silent, exactly as it had sometimes been on those Sunday afternoons. Mama kept looking out into the streets.

"He used to have a job in the mill," she said, "and, like all young folks, he just liked to perform on Saturday nights. Saturday nights, him and your father would drift around to different places, go to dances and things like that, or just sit around with people they knew, and your father's brother would sing, he had a fine voice, and play along with himself on his guitar. Well, this particular Saturday night, him and your father was coming home from some place, and they were both a little drunk and there was a moon that night, it was bright like day. Your father's brother was feeling kind of good, and he was whistling to himself, and he had his guitar slung over his shoulder. They was coming down a hill and beneath them was a road that turned off from the highway. Well, your father's brother, being always kind of frisky, decided to run down this hill, and he did, with that guitar banging and clanging behind him, and he ran across the road, and he was making water behind a tree. And your father was sort of amused at him and he was still coming down the hill, kind of slow. Then he heard a car motor and that same minute his brother stepped from behind the tree, into the road, in the moonlight. And he started to cross the road. And your father started to run down the hill, he says he don't know why. This car was full of white men. They was all drunk, and when they seen your father's brother they let out a great whoop and holler and they aimed the car straight at him. They was having fun, they just wanted to scare him, the way they do sometimes, you know. But they was drunk. And I guess the boy, being drunk, too, and scared, kind of lost his head. By the time he jumped it was too late. Your father says he heard his brother scream when the car rolled over him, and he heard the wood of that guitar when it give, and he heard them strings go flying, and he heard them white men shouting, and the car kept on a-going and it ain't stopped till this day. And, time your father got down the hill, his brother weren't nothing but blood and pulp."

Tears were gleaming on my mother's face. There wasn't anything I could say.

"He never mentioned it," she said, "because I never let him mention it before you children. Your Daddy was like a crazy man that night and for many a night thereafter. He says he never in his life seen anything as dark as that road after the lights of that car had gone away. Weren't nothing, weren't nobody on that road, just your Daddy and his brother and that busted guitar. Oh, yes. Your Daddy never did really get right again. Till the day he died he weren't sure but that every white man he saw was the man that killed his brother."

She stopped and took out her handkerchief and dried her eyes and looked at me.

"I ain't telling you all this," she said, "to make you scared or bitter or to make you hate nobody. I'm telling you this because you got a brother. And the world ain't changed."

I guess I didn't want to believe this. I guess she saw this in my face. She turned away from me, toward the window again, searching those streets.

"But I praise my Redeemer," she said at last, "that He called your Daddy home before me. I ain't saying it to throw no flowers at myself, but, I declare, it keeps me from feeling too cast down to know I helped your father get safely through this world. Your father always acted like he was the roughest, strongest man on earth. And everybody took him to be like that. But if he hadn't had *me* there—to see his tears!"

She was crying again. Still, I couldn't move. I said, "Lord, Lord, Mama, I didn't know it was like that."

"Oh, honey," she said, "there's a lot that you don't know. But you are going to find it out." She stood up from the window and came over to me. "You got to hold on to your brother," she said, "and don't let him fall, no matter what it looks like is happening to him and no matter how evil you gets with him. You going to be evil with him many a time. But don't you forget what I told you, you hear?"

"I won't forget," I said. "Don't you worry, I won't forget. I won't let nothing happen to Sonny."

My mother smiled as though she were amused at something she saw in my face. Then, "You may not be able to stop nothing from happening. But you got to let him know you's *there*."

Two days later I was married, and then I was gone. And I had a lot of things on my mind and I pretty well forgot my promise to Mama until I got shipped home on a special furlough for her funeral.

And, after the funeral, with just Sonny and me alone in the empty kitchen, I tried to find out something about him.

"What do you want to do?" I asked him.

"I'm going to be a musician," he said.

For he had graduated, in the time I had been away, from dancing to the juke box to finding out who was playing what, and what they were doing with it, and he had bought himself a set of drums.

"You mean, you want to be a drummer?" I somehow had the feeling that being a drummer might be all right for other people but not for my brother Sonny.

"I don't think," he said, looking at me very gravely, "that I'll ever be a good drummer. But I think I can play a piano."

I frowned. I'd never played the role of the older brother quite so seriously before, had scarcely ever, in fact, *asked* Sonny a damn thing. I sensed myself in the presence of something I didn't really know how to handle, didn't understand. So I made my frown a little deeper as I asked: "What kind of musician do you want to be?"

He grinned. "How many kinds do you think there are?"

"Be *serious*," I said.

He laughed, throwing his head back, and then looked at me. "I *am* serious."

"Well, then, for Christ's sake, stop kidding around and answer a serious question. I mean, do you want to be a concert pianist, you want to play classical music and all that, or—or what?" Long before I finished he was laughing again. "For Christ's *sake*, Sonny!"

He sobered, but with difficulty. "I'm sorry. But you sound so—*scared*!" and he was off again.

"Well, you may think it's funny now, baby, but it's not going to be so funny when you have to make your living at it, let me tell you *that*." I was furious because I knew he was laughing at me and I didn't know why.

"No," he said, very sober now, and afraid, perhaps, that he'd hurt me, "I don't want to be a classical pianist. That isn't what interests me. I mean"—he paused, looking hard at me, as though his eyes would help me to understand, and then gestured helplessly, as though perhaps his hand would help—"I mean, I'll have a lot of studying to do, and I'll have to study *everything*, but, I mean, I want to play *with*—jazz musicians." He stopped. "I want to play jazz," he said.

Well, the word had never before sounded as heavy, as real, as it sounded that afternoon in Sonny's mouth. I just looked at him and I was probably frowning a real frown by this time. I simply couldn't see why on earth he'd want to spend his time hanging around night-clubs, clowning around on bandstands, while people pushed each other around a dance floor. It seemed—beneath him, somehow. I had never thought about it before, had never been forced to, but I suppose I had always put jazz musicians in a class with what Daddy called "good-time people."

"Are you *serious*?"

"Hell, *yes*, I'm serious."

He looked more helpless than ever, and annoyed, and deeply hurt.

I suggested, helpfully: "You mean—like Louis Armstrong?"

His face closed as though I'd struck him. "No. I'm not talking about none of that old-time, down home crap."

"Well, look, Sonny, I'm sorry, don't get mad. I just don't altogether get it, that's all. Name somebody—you know, a jazz musician you admire."

"Bird."

"Who?"

"Bird! Charlie Parker! Don't they teach you nothing in the goddamn army?"

I lit a cigarette. I was surprised and then a little amused to discover that I was trembling. "I've been out of touch," I said. "You'll have to be patient with me. Now. Who's this Parker character?"

"He's just one of the greatest jazz musicians alive," said Sonny, sullenly, his hands in his pockets, his back to me. "Maybe *the* greatest," he added, bitterly, "that's probably why *you* never heard of him."

"All right," I said, "I'm ignorant. I'm sorry. I'll go out and buy all the cat's records right away, all right?"

"It don't," said Sonny, with dignity, "make any difference to me. I don't care what you listen to. Don't do me no favors."

I was beginning to realize that I'd never seen him so upset before. With another part of my mind I was thinking that this would probably turn out to be one of those things kids go through and that I shouldn't make it seem important by pushing it too hard. Still, I didn't think it would do any harm to ask: "Doesn't all this take a lot of time? Can you make a living at it?"

He turned back to me and half leaned, half sat, on the kitchen table. "Everything takes time," he said, "and—well, yes, sure, I can make a living at it. But what I don't seem to be able to make you understand is that it's the only thing I want to do."

"Well, Sonny," I said, gently, "you know people can't always do exactly what they *want* to do —"

"*No*, I don't know that," said Sonny, surprising me. "I think people *ought* to do what they want to do, what else are they alive for?"

"You getting to be a big boy," I said desperately, "it's time you started thinking about your future."

"I'm thinking about my future," said Sonny, grimly. "I think about it all the time."

I gave up. I decided, if he didn't change his mind, that we could always talk about it later. "In the meantime," I said, "you got to finish school." We had already decided that he'd have to move in with Isabel and her folks. I knew this wasn't the ideal arrangement because Isabel's folks are inclined to be dicty[1] and they hadn't especially wanted Isabel to marry me. But I didn't know what else to do. "And we have to get you fixed up at Isabel's."

There was a long silence. He moved from the kitchen table to the window. "That's a terrible idea. You know it yourself."

"Do you have a *better* idea?"

He just walked up and down the kitchen for a minute. He was as tall as I was. He had started to shave. I suddenly had the feeling that I didn't know him at all.

He stopped at the kitchen table and picked up my cigarettes. Looking at me with a kind of mocking, amused defiance, he put one between his lips. "You mind?"

"You smoking already?"

He lit the cigarette and nodded, watching me through the smoke. "I just wanted to see if I'd have the courage to smoke in front of you." He grinned and blew a great cloud of smoke to the ceiling. "It was easy." He looked at my face. "Come on, now. I bet you was smoking at my age, tell the truth."

I didn't say anything but the truth was on my face, and he laughed. But now there was something very strained in his laugh. "Sure. And I bet that ain't all you was doing."

He was frightening me a little. "Cut the crap," I said. "We already decided that you was going to go and live at Isabel's. Now what's got into you all of a sudden?"

"*You* decided it," he pointed out. "*I* didn't decide nothing." He stopped in front of me, leaning against the stove, arms loosely folded. "Look, brother. I don't want to stay in Harlem no more, I really don't." He was very earnest. He looked at me, then over toward the kitchen window. There was something in his eyes I'd never seen before, some thoughtfulness, some worry all his own. He rubbed the muscle of one arm. "It's time I was getting out of here."

"Where do you want to *go*, Sonny?"

"I want to join the army. Or the navy, I don't care. If I say I'm old enough, they'll believe me."

Then I got mad. It was because I was so scared. "You must be crazy. You goddamn fool, what the hell do you want to go and join the *army* for?"

[1]High-class, snobbish.

"I just told you. To get out of Harlem."

"Sonny, you haven't even finished *school*. And if you really want to be a musician, how do you expect to study if you're in the *army*?"

He looked at me, trapped, and in anguish. "There's ways. I might be able to work out some kind of deal. Anyway, I'll have the G.I. Bill when I come out."

"*If* you come out." We stared at each other. "Sonny, please. Be reasonable. I know the setup is far from perfect. But we got to do the best we can."

"I ain't learning nothing in school," he said. "Even when I go." He turned away from me and opened the window and threw his cigarette out into the narrow alley. I watched his back. "At least, I ain't learning nothing you'd want me to learn." He slammed the window so hard I thought the glass would fly out, and turned back to me. "And I'm sick of the stink of these garbage cans!"

"Sonny," I said, "I know how you feel. But if you don't finish school now, you're going to be sorry later that you didn't." I grabbed him by the shoulders. "And you only got another year. It ain't so bad. And I'll come back and I swear I'll help you do *whatever* you want to do. Just try to put up with it till I come back. Will you please do that? For me?"

He didn't answer and he wouldn't look at me.

"Sonny. You hear me?"

He pulled away. "I hear you. But you never hear anything *I* say."

I didn't know what to say to that. He looked out of the window and then back at me. "OK," he said, and sighed. "I'll try."

Then I said, trying to cheer him up a little, "They got a piano at Isabel's. You can practice on it."

And as a matter of fact, it did cheer him up for a minute. "That's right," he said to himself. "I forgot that." His face relaxed a little. But the worry, the thoughtfulness, played on it still, the way shadows play on a face which is staring into the fire.

But I thought I'd never hear the end of that piano. At first, Isabel would write me, saying how nice it was that Sonny was so serious about his music and how, as soon as he came in from school, or wherever he had been when he was supposed to be at school, he went straight to that piano and stayed there until suppertime. And, after supper, he went back to that piano and stayed there until everybody went to bed. He was at the piano all day Saturday and all day Sunday. Then he bought a record player and started playing records.

He'd play one record over and over again, all day long sometimes, and he'd improvise along with it on the piano. Or he'd play one section of the record, one chord, one change, one progression, then he'd do it on the piano. Then back to the record. Then back to the piano.

Well, I really don't know how they stood it. Isabel finally confessed that it wasn't like living with a person at all, it was like living with sound. And the sound didn't make any sense to her, didn't make any sense to any of them—naturally. They began, in a way, to be afflicted by this presence that was living in their home. It was as though Sonny were some sort of god, or monster. He moved in an atmosphere which wasn't like theirs at all. They fed him and he ate, he washed himself, he walked in and out of their door; he certainly wasn't nasty or unpleasant or rude, Sonny isn't any of those things; but it was as though he were all wrapped up in some cloud, some fire, some vision all his own; and there wasn't any way to reach him.

At the same time, he wasn't really a man yet, he was still a child, and they had to watch out for him in all kinds of ways. They certainly couldn't throw him out. Neither did they dare to make a great scene about that piano because even they dimly sensed, as I sensed, from so many thousands of miles away, that Sonny was at that piano playing for his life.

But he hadn't been going to school. One day a letter came from the school board and Isabel's mother got it—there had, apparently, been other letters but Sonny had torn them up. This day, when Sonny came in, Isabel's mother showed him the letter and asked where he'd been spending his time. And she finally got it out of him that he'd been down in Greenwich Village, with musicians and other characters, in a white girl's apartment. And this scared her and she started to scream at him and what came up, once she began—though she denies it to this day—was what sacrifices they were making to give Sonny a decent home and how little he appreciated it.

Sonny didn't play the piano that day. By evening, Isabel's mother had calmed down but then there was the old man to deal with, and Isabel herself. Isabel says she did her best to be calm but she broke down and started crying. She says she just watched Sonny's face. She could tell, by watching him, what was happening with him. And what was happening was that they penetrated his cloud, they had reached him. Even if their fingers had been a thousand times more gentle than human fingers ever are, he could hardly help feeling that they had stripped him naked and were spitting on that nakedness.

For he also had to see that his presence, that music, which was life or death to him, had been torture for them and that they had endured it, not at all for his sake, but only for mine. And Sonny couldn't take that. He can take it a little better today than he could then but he's still not very good at it and, frankly, I don't know anybody who is.

The silence of the next few days must have been louder than the sound of all the music ever played since time began. One morning, before she went to work, Isabel was in his room for something and she suddenly realized that all of his records were gone. And she knew for certain that he was gone. And he was. He went as far as the navy would carry him. He finally sent me a postcard from some place in Greece and that was the first I knew that Sonny was still alive. I didn't see him any more until we were both back in New York and the war had long been over.

He was a man by then, of course, but I wasn't willing to see it. He came by the house from time to time, but we fought almost every time we met. I didn't like the way he carried himself, loose and dreamlike all the time, and I didn't like his friends, and his music seemed to be merely an excuse for the life he led. It sounded just that weird and disordered.

Then we had a fight, a pretty awful fight, and I didn't see him for months. By and by I looked him up, where he was living, in a furnished room in the Village, and I tried to make it up. But there were lots of people in the room and Sonny just lay on his bed, and he wouldn't come downstairs with me, and he treated these other people as though they were his family and I weren't. So I got mad and then he got mad, and then I told him that he might just as well be dead as live the way he was living. Then he stood up and he told me not to worry about him any more in life, that he *was* dead as far as I was concerned. Then he pushed me to the door and the other people looked on as though nothing were happening, and he slammed the door behind me. I stood in the hallway, staring at the door. I heard somebody laugh in the room and then the tears came to my eyes. I started down the steps, whistling to keep from crying, I kept whistling to myself, *You going to need me, baby, one of these cold, rainy days.*

I read about Sonny's trouble in the spring. Little Grace died in the fall. She was a beautiful little girl. But she only lived a little over two years. She died of polio and she suffered. She had a slight fever for a couple of days, but it didn't seem like anything and we just kept her in bed. And we would certainly have called the doctor, but the fever dropped, she seemed to be all right. So we thought it had just been a cold. Then, one day, she was up, playing, Isabel was in the kitchen fixing lunch for the two boys when they'd come in from school, and she heard Grace fall down in the living room. When you have a lot of children you don't always start running when one of them falls, unless they start screaming or something. And, this time, Grace was quiet. Yet, Isabel says that when she heard that *thump* and then that silence, something happened in her to make her afraid. And she ran to the living room and there was little Grace on the floor, all twisted up, and the reason she hadn't screamed was that she couldn't get her breath. And when she did scream, it was the worst sound, Isabel says, that she'd ever heard in all her life, and she still hears it sometimes in her dreams. Isabel will sometimes wake me up with a low, moaning, strangled sound and I have to be quick to awaken her and hold her to me and where Isabel is weeping against me seems a mortal wound.

I think I may have written Sonny the very day that little Grace was buried. I was sitting in the living room in the dark, by myself, and I suddenly thought of Sonny. My trouble made his real.

One Saturday afternoon, when Sonny had been living with us, or, anyway, been in our house, for nearly two weeks, I found myself wandering aimlessly about the living room, drinking from a can of beer, and trying to work up the courage to search Sonny's room. He was out, he was usually out whenever I was home, and Isabel had taken the children to see their grandparents. Suddenly I was standing still in front of the living room window, watching Seventh Avenue. The idea of searching Sonny's room made me still. I scarcely dared to admit to myself what I'd be searching for. I didn't know what I'd do if I found it. Or if I didn't.

On the sidewalk across from me, near the entrance to a barbecue joint, some people were holding an old-fashioned revival meeting. The barbecue cook, wearing a dirty white apron, his conked hair reddish and metallic in the pale sun, and a cigarette between his lips, stood in the doorway, watching them. Kids and older people paused in their errands and stood there, along with some older men and a couple of very tough-looking women who watched everything that happened on the avenue, as though they owned it, or were maybe owned by it. Well, they were watching this, too. The revival was being carried on by three sisters in black, and a brother. All they had were their voices and their Bibles and a tambourine. The brother was testifying and while he testified two of the sisters stood together, seeming to say, amen, and the third sister walked around with the tambourine outstretched and a couple of people dropped coins into it. Then the brother's testimony ended and the sister who had been taking up the collection dumped the coins into her palm and transferred them to the pocket of her long black robe. Then she raised both hands, striking the tambourine against the air, and then against one hand, and she started to sing. And the two other sisters and the brother joined in.

It was strange, suddenly, to watch, though I had been seeing these street meetings all my life. So, of course, had everybody else down there. Yet, they paused and watched and listened and I stood still at the window. *"Tis the old ship of Zion,"* they sang, and the sister with the tambourine kept a steady, jangling beat, *"it has rescued many a thousand!"* Not a soul under the sound of their voices was hearing this song for the first time, not one of them had been rescued. Nor had they seen much in the way of rescue work being done around them. Neither did they especially believe in the holiness of the three sisters and the brother, they knew too much about them, knew where they lived, and how. The woman with the tambourine, whose voice dominated the air, whose face was bright with joy, was divided by very little from the woman who stood watching her, a cigarette between her heavy, chapped lips, her hair a cuckoo's nest, her face scarred and swollen from many beatings, and her black eyes glittering like coal. Perhaps they both knew this, which was why, when, as rarely, they addressed each other, they addressed each other as Sister. As the singing filled the air the watching, listening faces underwent a change, the eyes focusing on something within; the music seemed to soothe a poison out of them; and time seemed, nearly, to fall away from the sullen, belligerent, battered faces, as though they were fleeing back to their first condition, while dreaming of their last. The barbecue cook half shook his head and smiled, and dropped his cigarette and disappeared into his joint. A man fumbled in his pockets for change and stood holding it in his hand impatiently, as though he had just remembered a pressing appointment further up the avenue. He looked furious. Then I saw Sonny, standing on the edge of the crowd. He was carrying a wide, flat notebook with a green cover, and it made him look, from where I was standing, almost like a schoolboy. The coppery sun brought out the copper in his skin, he was very faintly smiling, standing very still. Then the singing stopped, the tambourine turned into a collection plate again. The furious man dropped in his coins and vanished, so did a couple of the women, and Sonny dropped some change in the plate, looking directly at the woman with a little smile. He started across the avenue, toward the house. He has a slow, loping walk, something like the way Harlem hipsters walk, only he's imposed on this his own half-beat. I had never really noticed it before.

I stayed at the window, both relieved and apprehensive. As Sonny disappeared from my sight, they began singing again. And they were still singing when his key turned in the lock.

"Hey," he said.

"Hey, yourself. You want some beer?"

"No. Well, maybe." But he came up to the window and stood beside me, looking out. "What a warm voice," he said.

They were singing *If I could only hear my mother pray again!*

"Yes," I said, "and she can sure beat that tambourine."

"But what a terrible song," he said, and laughed. He dropped his notebook on the sofa and disappeared into the kitchen. "Where's Isabel and the kids?"

"I think they went to see their grandparents. You hungry?"

"No." He came back into the living room with his can of beer. "You want to come some place with me tonight?"

I sensed, I don't know how, that I couldn't possibly say no. "Sure. Where?"

He sat down on the sofa and picked up his notebook and started leafing through it. "I'm going to sit in with some fellows in a joint in the Village."

"You mean, you're going to play, tonight?"

"That's right." He took a swallow of his beer and moved back to the window. He gave me a sidelong look. "If you can stand it."

"I'll try," I said.

He smiled to himself and we both watched as the meeting across the way broke up. The three sisters and the brother, heads bowed, were singing *God be with you till we meet again.* The faces around them were very quiet. Then the song ended. The small crowd dispersed. We watched the three women and the lone man walk slowly up the avenue.

"When she was singing before," said Sonny, abruptly, "her voice reminded me for a minute of what heroin feels like sometimes—when it's in your veins. It makes you feel sort of warm and cool at the same time. And distant. And—and sure." He sipped his beer, very deliberately not looking at me. I watched his face. "It makes you feel—in control. Sometimes you've got to have that feeling."

"Do you?" I sat down slowly in the easy chair.

"Sometimes." He went to the sofa and picked up his notebook again. "Some people do."

"In order," I asked, "to play?" And my voice was very ugly, full of contempt and anger.

"Well"—he looked at me with great, troubled eyes, as though, in fact, he hoped his eyes would tell me things he could never otherwise say—"they *think* so. And *if* they think so—!"

"And what do *you* think?" I asked.

He sat on the sofa and put his can of beer on the floor. "I don't know," he said, and I couldn't be sure if he were answering my question or pursuing his thoughts. His face didn't tell me. "It's not so much to *play.* It's to *stand* it, to be able to make it at all. On any level." He frowned and smiled: "In order to keep from shaking to pieces."

"But these friends of yours," I said, "they seem to shake themselves to pieces pretty goddamn fast."

"Maybe." He played with the notebook. And something told me that I should curb my tongue, that Sonny was doing his best to talk, that I should listen. "But of course you only know the ones that've gone to pieces. Some don't—or at least they haven't *yet* and that's just about all *any* of us can say." He paused. "And then there are some who just live, really, in hell, and they know it and they see what's happening and they go right on. I don't know." He sighed, dropped the notebook, folded his arms. "Some guys, you can tell from the way they play, they on something *all* the time. And you can see that, well, it makes something real for them. But of course," he picked up his beer from the floor and sipped it and put the can down again, "they *want* to, too, you've got to see that. Even some of them that say they don't—*some,* not all."

"And what about you?" I asked—I couldn't help it. "What about you? Do *you* want to?"

He stood up and walked to the window and remained silent for a long time. Then he sighed. "Me," he said. Then: "While I was downstairs before, on my way here, listening to that woman sing, it struck me all of a sudden how much suffering she must have had to go through—to sing like that. It's *repulsive* to think you have to suffer that much."

I said: "But there's no way not to suffer—is there, Sonny?"

"I believe not," he said and smiled, "but that's never stopped anyone from trying." He looked at me. "Has it?" I realized, with this mocking look, that there stood between us, forever, beyond the power of time or forgiveness, the fact that I had held silence—so long!—when he had needed human speech to help him. He turned back to the window. "No, there's no way not to suffer. But you try all kinds of ways to keep from drowning in it, to keep on top of it, and to make it seem—well, like *you*. Like you did something, all right, and now you're suffering for it. You know?" I said nothing. "Well you know," he said, impatiently, "why *do* people suffer? Maybe it's better to do something to give it a reason, *any* reason."

"But we just agreed," I said, "that there's no way not to suffer. Isn't it better, then, just to—take it?"

"But nobody just takes it," Sonny cried, "that's what I'm telling you! *Everybody* tries not to. You're just hung up on the *way* some people try—it's not *your* way!"

The hair on my face began to itch, my face felt wet. "That's not true," I said, "that's not true. I don't give a damn what other people do, I don't even care how they suffer. I just care how *you* suffer." And he looked at me. "Please believe me," I said, "I don't want to see you—die—trying not to suffer."

"I won't," he said, flatly, "die trying not to suffer. At least, not any faster than anybody else."

"But there's no need," I said, trying to laugh, "is there? in killing yourself."

I wanted to say more, but I couldn't. I wanted to talk about will power and how life could be—well, beautiful. I wanted to say that it was all within; but was it? or, rather, wasn't that exactly the trouble? And I wanted to promise that I would never fail him again. But it would all have sounded—empty words and lies.

So I made the promise to myself and prayed that I would keep it.

"It's terrible sometimes, inside," he said, "that's what's the trouble. You walk these streets, black and funky and cold, and there's not really a living ass to talk to, and there's nothing shaking, and there's no way of getting it out—that storm inside. You can't talk it and you can't make love with it, and when you finally try to get with it and play it, you realize *nobody's* listening. So *you've* got to listen. You got to find a way to listen."

And then he walked away from the window and sat on the sofa again, as though all the wind had suddenly been knocked out of him. "Sometimes you'll do *anything* to play, even cut your mother's throat." He laughed and looked at me. "Or your brother's." Then he sobered. "Or your own." Then: "Don't worry. I'm all right now and I think I'll *be* all right. But I can't forget—where I've been. I don't mean just the physical place I've been, I mean where I've *been.* And *what* I've been."

"What have you been, Sonny?" I asked.

He smiled—but sat sideways on the sofa, his elbow resting on the back, his fingers playing with his mouth and chin, not looking at me. "I've been something I didn't recognize, didn't know I could be. Didn't know anybody could be." He stopped, looking inward, looking helplessly young, looking old. "I'm not talking about it now because I feel *guilty* or anything like that—maybe it would be better if I did, I don't know. Anyway, I can't really talk about it. Not to you, not to anybody," and now he turned and faced me. "Sometimes, you know, and it was actually when I was most *out* of the world, I felt that I was in it, that I was *with* it, really, and I could play or I didn't really have to *play*, it just came out of me, it was there. And I don't know how I played, thinking about it now, but I know I did awful things, those times, sometimes, to people. Or it wasn't that I *did* anything to them—it was that they weren't real." He picked up the beer can; it was empty; he rolled it between his palms: "And other times—well, I needed a fix, I needed to find a place to lean, I needed to clear a space to *listen*—and I couldn't find it, and I—went crazy, I did terrible things to *me*, I was terrible *for* me." He began pressing the beer can between his hands, I watched the metal begin to give. It glittered, as he played with it, like a knife, and I was afraid he would cut himself, but I said nothing. "Oh well. I can never tell you. I was all by myself at the bottom of something, stinking and sweating and crying and shaking, and I smelled it, you know? *my* stink, and I thought I'd die if I couldn't get away from it and yet, all the same, I knew that everything I was doing was just locking me in with it. And I didn't know," he paused, still flattening the beer can, "I didn't know, I still *don't* know, something kept telling me that maybe it was good to smell your own stink, but I didn't think that *that* was what I'd been trying to do—and—who can stand it?" and he abruptly dropped the ruined beer can, looking at me with a small, still smile, and then rose, walking to the window as though it were the lodestone rock. I watched his face, he watched the avenue. "I couldn't tell you when Mama died—but the reason I wanted to leave Harlem so bad was to get away from drugs. And then, when I ran away, that's what I was running from—really. When I came back, nothing had changed, *I* hadn't changed, I was just—older." And he stopped, drumming with his fingers on the windowpane. The sun had vanished, soon darkness would fall. I watched his face. "It can come again," he said, almost as though speaking to himself. Then he turned to me. "It can come again," he repeated. "I just want you to know that."

"All right," I said, at last. "So it can come again, All right."

He smiled, but the smile was sorrowful. "I had to try to tell you," he said.

"Yes," I said. "I understand that."

"You're my brother," he said, looking straight at me, and not smiling at all.

"Yes," I repeated, "yes. I understand that."

He turned back to the window, looking out. "All that hatred down there," he said, "all that hatred and misery and love. It's a wonder it doesn't blow the avenue apart."

We went to the only nightclub on a short, dark street, downtown. We squeezed through the narrow, chattering, jam-packed bar to the entrance of the big room, where the bandstand was. And we stood there for a moment, for the lights were very dim in this room and we couldn't see. Then, "Hello, boy," said a voice and an enormous black man, much older than Sonny or myself, erupted out of all that atmospheric lighting and put an arm around Sonny's shoulder. "I been sitting right here," he said, "waiting for you."

He had a big voice, too, and heads in the darkness turned toward us.

Sonny grinned and pulled a little away, and said, "Creole, this is my brother. I told you about him."

Creole shook my hand. "I'm glad to meet you, son," he said, and it was clear that he was glad to meet me *there*, for Sonny's sake. And he smiled, "You got a real musician in *your* family," and he took his arm from Sonny's shoulder and slapped him, lightly, affectionately, with the back of his hand.

"Well. Now I've heard it all," said a voice behind us. This was another musician, and a friend of Sonny's, a coal-black, cheerful-looking man, built close to the ground. He immediately began confiding to me, at the top of his lungs, the most terrible things about Sonny, his teeth gleaming like a lighthouse and his laugh coming up out of him like the beginning of an earthquake. And it turned out that everyone at the bar knew Sonny, or almost everyone; some were musicians, working there, or nearby, or not working, some were simply hangers-on, and some were there to hear Sonny play. I was introduced to all of them and they were all very polite to me. Yet, it was clear that, for them, I was only Sonny's brother. Here, I was in Sonny's world. Or, rather: his kingdom. Here, it was not even a question that his veins bore royal blood.

They were going to play soon and Creole installed me, by myself, at a table in a dark corner. Then I watched them, Creole, and the little black man, and Sonny, and the others, while they horsed around, standing just below the bandstand. The light from the bandstand spilled just a little short of them and, watching them laughing and gesturing and moving about, I had the feeling that they, nevertheless, were being most careful not to step into that circle of light too suddenly: that if they moved into the light too suddenly, without thinking, they would perish in flame. Then, while I watched, one of them, the small, black man, moved into the light and crossed the bandstand and started fooling around with his drums. Then—being funny and being, also, extremely ceremonious—Creole took Sonny by the arm and led him to the piano. A woman's voice called Sonny's name and a few hands started clapping. And Sonny, also being funny and being ceremonious, and so touched, I think, that he could have cried, but neither hiding it nor showing it, riding it like a man, grinned, and put both hands to his heart and bowed from the waist.

Creole then went to the bass fiddle and a lean, very bright-skinned brown man jumped up on the bandstand and picked up his horn. So there they were, and the atmosphere on the bandstand and in the room began to change and tighten. Someone stepped up to the microphone and announced them. Then there were all kinds of murmurs. Some people at the bar shushed others. The waitress ran around, frantically getting in the last orders, guys and chicks got closer to each other, and the lights on the bandstand, on the quartet, turned to a kind of indigo. Then they all looked different there. Creole looked about him for the last time, as though he were making certain that all his chickens were in the coop, and then he—jumped and struck the fiddle. And there they were.

All I know about music is that not many people ever really hear it. And even then, on the rare occasions when something opens within, and the music enters, what we mainly hear, or hear corroborated, are personal, private, vanishing evocations. But the man who creates the music is hearing something else, is dealing with the roar rising from the void and imposing order on it as it hits the air. What is evoked in him, then, is of another order, more terrible because it has no words, and triumphant, too, for that same reason. And his triumph, when he triumphs, is ours. I just watched Sonny's face. His face was troubled, he was working hard, but he wasn't with it. And I had the feeling that, in a way, everyone on the bandstand was waiting for him, both waiting for him and pushing him along. But as I began to watch Creole, I realized that it was Creole who held them all back. He had them on a short rein. Up there, keeping the beat with his whole body, wailing on the fiddle, with his eyes half closed, he was listening to everything, but he was listening to Sonny. He was having a dialogue with Sonny. He wanted Sonny to leave the shoreline and strike out for the deep water. He was Sonny's witness that deep water and drowning were not the same thing—he had been there, and he knew. And he wanted Sonny to know. He was waiting for Sonny to do the things on the keys which would let Creole know that Sonny was in the water.

And, while Creole listened, Sonny moved, deep within, exactly like someone in torment. I had never before thought of how awful the relationship must be between the musician and his instrument. He has to fill it, this instrument, with the breath of life, his own. He has to make it do what he wants it to do. And a piano is just a piano. It's made out of so much wood and wires and little hammers and big ones, and ivory. While there's only so much you can do with it, the only way to find this out is to try; to try and make it do everything.

And Sonny hadn't been near a piano for over a year. And he wasn't on much better terms with his life, not the life that stretched before him now. He and the piano stammered, started one way, got scared, stopped; started another way, panicked, marked time, started again; then seemed to have found a direction, panicked again, got stuck. And the face I saw on Sonny I'd never seen before. Everything had been burned out of it, and, at the same time, things usually hidden were being burned in, by the fire and fury of the battle which was occurring in him up there.

Yet, watching Creole's face as they neared the end of the first set, I had the feeling that something had happened, something I hadn't heard. Then they finished, there was scattered applause, and then, without an instant's warning, Creole started into something else, it was almost sardonic, it was *Am I Blue*. And, as though he commanded, Sonny began to play. Something began to happen. And Creole let out the reins. The dry, low, black man said something awful on the drums, Creole answered, and the drums talked back. Then the horn insisted, sweet and high, slightly detached perhaps, and Creole listened, commenting now and then, dry, and driving, beautiful and calm and old. Then they all came together again, and Sonny was part of the family again. I could tell this from his face. He seemed to have found, right there beneath his fingers, a damn brand-new piano. It seemed that he couldn't get over it. Then, for awhile, just being happy with Sonny, they seemed to be agreeing with him that brand-new pianos certainly were a gas.

Then Creole stepped forward to remind them that what they were playing was the blues. He hit something in all of them, he hit something in me, myself, and the music tightened and deepened, apprehension began to beat the air. Creole began to tell us what the blues were all about. They were not about anything very new. He and his boys up there were keeping it new, at the risk of ruin, destruction, madness, and death, in order to find new ways to make us listen. For, while the tale of how we suffer, and how we are delighted, and how we may triumph is never new, it always must be heard. There isn't any other tale to tell, it's the only light we've got in all this darkness.

And this tale, according to that face, that body, those strong hands on those strings, has another aspect in every country, and a new depth in every generation. Listen, Creole seemed to be saying, listen. Now these are Sonny's blues. He made the little black man on the drums know it, and the bright, brown man on the horn. Creole wasn't trying any longer to get Sonny in the water. He was wishing him Godspeed. Then he stepped back, very slowly, filling the air with the immense suggestion that Sonny speak for himself.

Then they all gathered around Sonny and Sonny played. Every now and again one of them seemed to say, amen. Sonny's fingers filled the air with life, his life. But that life contained so many others. And Sonny went all the way back, he really began with the spare, flat statement of the opening phrase of the song. Then he began to make it his. It was very beautiful because it wasn't hurried and it was no longer a lament. I seemed to hear with what burning he had made it his, with what burning we had yet to make it ours, how we could cease lamenting. Freedom lurked around us and I understood, at last, that he could help us to be free if we would listen, that he would never be free until we did. Yet, there was no battle in his face now. I heard what he had gone through, and would continue to go through until he came to rest in earth. He had made it his: that long line, of which we knew only Mama and Daddy. And he was giving it back, as everything must be given back, so that, passing through death, it can live forever. I saw my mother's face again, and felt, for the first time, how the stones of the road she had walked on must have bruised her feet. I saw the moonlit road where my father's brother died. And it brought something else back to me, and carried me past it. I saw my little girl again and felt Isabel's tears again, and I felt my own tears begin to rise. And I was yet aware that this was only a moment, that the world waited outside, as hungry as a tiger, and that trouble stretched above us, longer than the sky.

Then it was over. Creole and Sonny let out their breath, both soaking wet, and grinning. There was a lot of applause and some of it was real. In the dark, the girl came by and I asked her to take drinks to the bandstand. There was a long pause, while they talked up there in the indigo light and after awhile I saw the girl put a Scotch and milk on top of the piano for Sonny. He didn't seem to notice it, but just before they started playing again, he sipped from it and looked toward me, and nodded. Then he put it back on top of the piano. For me, then, as they began to play again, it glowed and shook above my brother's head like the very cup of trembling.

1957

A Good Man Is Hard to Find

FLANNERY O'CONNOR

[1925–1964]

The dragon is by the side of the road, watching those who pass. Beware lest he devour you. We go to the Father of Souls, but it is necessary to pass by the dragon.

—St. Cyril of Jerusalem

The grandmother didn't want to go to Florida. She wanted to visit some of her connections in east Tennessee and she was seizing at every chance to change Bailey's mind. Bailey was the son she lived with, her only boy. He was sitting on the edge of his chair at the table, bent over the orange sports section of the *Journal.* "Now look here, Bailey," she said, "see here, read this," and she stood with one hand on her thin hip and the other rattling the newspaper at his bald head. "Here this fellow that calls himself The Misfit is aloose from the Federal Pen and headed toward Florida and you read here what it says he did to these people. Just you read it. I wouldn't take my children in any direction with a criminal like that aloose in it. I couldn't answer to my conscience if I did."

Bailey didn't look up from his reading so she wheeled around then and faced the children's mother, a young woman in slacks, whose face was as broad and innocent as a cabbage and was tied around with a green head-kerchief that had two points on the top like rabbit's ears. She was sitting on the sofa, feeding the baby his apricots out of a jar. "The children have been to Florida before," the old lady said. "You all ought to take them somewhere else for a change so they would see different parts of the world and be broad. They never have been to east Tennessee."

The children's mother didn't seem to hear her but the eight-year-old boy, John Wesley, a stocky child with glasses, said, "If you don't want to go to Florida, why dontcha stay at home?" He and the little girl, June Star, were reading the funny papers on the floor.

"She wouldn't stay at home to be queen for a day," June Star said without raising her yellow head.

"Yes and what would you do if this fellow, The Misfit, caught you?" the grandmother asked.

"I'd smack his face," John Wesley said.

"She wouldn't stay at home for a million bucks," June Star said. "Afraid she'd miss something. She has to go everywhere we go."

"All right, Miss," the grandmother said. "Just remember that the next time you want me to curl your hair."

June Star said her hair was naturally curly.

The next morning the grandmother was the first one in the car, ready to go. She had her big black valise that looked like the head of a hippopotamus in one corner, and underneath it she was hiding a basket with Pitty Sing, the cat, in it. She didn't intend for the cat to be left alone in the house for three days because he would miss her too much and she was afraid he might brush against one of the gas burners and accidentally asphyxiate himself. Her son, Bailey, didn't like to arrive at a motel with a cat.

She sat in the middle of the back seat with John Wesley and June Star on either side of her. Bailey and the children's mother and the baby sat in front and they left Atlanta at eight forty-five with the mileage on the car at 55890. The grandmother wrote this down because she thought it would be interesting to say how many miles they had been when they got back. It took them twenty minutes to reach the outskirts of the city.

The old lady settled herself comfortably, removing her white cotton gloves and putting them up with her purse on the shelf in front of the back window. The children's mother still had on slacks and still had her head tied up in a green kerchief, but the grandmother had on a navy blue straw sailor hat with a bunch of white violets on the brim and a navy blue dress with a small white dot in the print. Her collars and cuffs were white organdy trimmed with lace and at her neckline she had pinned a purple spray of cloth violets containing a sachet. In case of an accident, anyone seeing her dead on the highway would know at once that she was a lady.

She said she thought it was going to be a good day for driving, neither too hot nor too cold, and she cautioned Bailey that the speed limit was fifty-five miles an hour and that the patrolmen hid themselves behind billboards and small clumps of trees and sped out after you before you had a chance to slow down. She pointed out interesting details of the scenery: Stone Mountain; the blue granite that in some places came up to both sides of the highway; the brilliant red clay banks slightly streaked with purple; and the various crops that made rows of green lace-work on the ground. The trees were full of silver-white sunlight and the meanest of them sparkled. The children were reading comic magazines and their mother had gone back to sleep.

"Let's go through Georgia fast so we won't have to look at it much," John Wesley said.

"If I were a little boy," said the grandmother, "I wouldn't talk about my native state that way. Tennessee has the mountains and Georgia has the hills."

"Tennessee is just a hillbilly dumping ground," John Wesley said, "and Georgia is a lousy state too."

"You said it," June Star said.

"In my time," said the grandmother, folding her thin veined fingers, "children were more respectful of their native states and their parents and everything else. People did right then. Oh look at the cute little pickaninny!" she said and pointed to a Negro child standing in the door of a shack. "Wouldn't that make a picture, now?" she asked and they all turned and looked at the little Negro out of the back window. He waved.

"He didn't have any britches on," June Star said.

"He probably didn't have any," the grandmother explained. "Little niggers in the country don't have things like we do. If I could paint, I'd paint that picture," she said.

The children exchanged comic books.

The grandmother offered to hold the baby and the children's mother passed him over the front seat to her. She set him on her knee and bounced him and told him about the things they were passing. She rolled her eyes and screwed up her mouth and stuck her leathery thin face into his smooth bland one. Occasionally he gave her a faraway smile. They passed a large cotton field with five or six graves fenced in the middle of it, like a small island. "Look at the graveyard!" the grandmother said, pointing it out. "That was the old family burying ground. That belonged to the plantation."

"Where's the plantation?" John Wesley asked.

"Gone with the Wind," said the grandmother. "Ha. Ha."

When the children finished all the comic books they had brought, they opened the lunch and ate it. The grandmother ate a peanut butter sandwich and an olive and would not let the children throw the box and the paper napkins out the window. When there was nothing else to do they played a game by choosing a cloud and making the other two guess what shape it suggested. John Wesley took one the shape of a cow and June Star guessed a cow and John Wesley said, no, an automobile, and June Star said he didn't play fair, and they began to slap each other over the grandmother.

The grandmother said she would tell them a story if they would keep quiet. When she told a story, she rolled her eyes and waved her head and was very dramatic. She said once when she was a maiden lady she had been courted by a Mr. Edgar Atkins Teagarden from Jasper, Georgia. She said he was a very good-looking man and a gentleman and that he brought her a watermelon every Saturday afternoon with his initials cut in it, E. A. T. Well, one Saturday, she said, Mr. Teagarden brought the watermelon and there was nobody at home and he left it on the front porch and returned in his buggy to Jasper, but she never got the watermelon, she said, because a nigger boy ate it when he saw the initials, E. A. T.! This story tickled John Wesley's funny bone and he giggled and giggled but June Star didn't think it was any good. She said she wouldn't marry a man that just brought her a watermelon on Saturday. The grandmother said she would have done well to marry Mr. Teagarden because he was a gentleman and had bought Coca-Cola stock when it first came out and that he had died only a few years ago, a very wealthy man.

They stopped at The Tower for barbecued sandwiches. The Tower was a part stucco and part wood filling station and dance hall set in a clearing outside of Timothy. A fat man named Red Sammy Butts ran it and there were signs stuck here and there on the building and for miles up and down the highway saying, TRY RED SAMMY'S FAMOUS BARBECUE. NONE LIKE FAMOUS RED SAMMY'S! RED SAM! THE FAT BOY WITH THE HAPPY LAUGH. A VETERAN! RED SAMMY'S YOUR MAN!

Red Sammy was lying on the bare ground outside The Tower with his head under a truck while a gray monkey about a foot high, chained to a small chinaberry tree, chattered nearby. The monkey sprang back into the tree and got on the highest limb as soon as he saw the children jump out of the car and run toward him.

Inside, The Tower was a long dark room with a counter at one end and tables at the other and dancing space in the middle. They all sat down at a board table next to the nickelodeon and Red Sam's wife, a tall burnt-brown woman with hair and eyes lighter than her skin, came and took their order. The children's mother put a dime in the machine and played "The Tennessee Waltz," and the grandmother said that tune always made her want to dance. She asked Bailey if he would like to dance but he only glared at her. He didn't have a naturally sunny disposition like she did and trips made him nervous. The grandmother's brown eyes were very bright. She swayed her head from side to side and pretended she was dancing in her chair. June Star said play something she could tap to so the children's mother put in another dime and played a fast number and June Star stepped out onto the dance floor and did her tap routine.

"Ain't she cute?" Red Sam's wife said, leaning over the counter. "Would you like to come be my little girl?"

"No I certainly wouldn't," June Star said. "I wouldn't live in a broken-down place like this for a million bucks!" and she ran back to the table.

"Ain't she cute?" the woman repeated, stretching her mouth politely.

"Aren't you ashamed?" hissed the grandmother.

Red Sam came in and told his wife to quit lounging on the counter and hurry up with these people's order. His khaki trousers reached just to his hip bones and his stomach hung over them like a sack of meal swaying under his shirt. He came over and sat down at a table nearby and let out a combination sigh and yodel. "You can't win," he said. "You can't win," and he wiped his sweating red face off with a gray handkerchief. "These days you don't know who to trust," he said. "Ain't that the truth?"

"People are certainly not nice like they used to be," said the grandmother.

"Two fellers come in here last week," Red Sammy said, "driving a Chrysler. It was a old beat-up car but it was a good one and these boys looked all right to me. Said they worked at the mill and you know I let them fellers charge the gas they bought? Now why did I do that?"

"Because you're a good man!" the grandmother said at once.

"Yes'm, I suppose so," Red Sam said as if he were struck with this answer.

His wife brought the orders, carrying the five plates all at once without a tray, two in each hand and one balanced on her arm. "It isn't a soul in this green world of God's that you can trust," she said. "And I don't count nobody out of that, not nobody," she repeated, looking at Red Sammy.

"Did you read about that criminal, The Misfit, that's escaped?" asked the grandmother.

"I wouldn't be a bit surprised if he didn't attack this place right here," said the woman. "If he hears about it being here, I wouldn't be none surprised to see him. If he hears it's two cent in the cash register, I wouldn't be a tall surprised if he . . ."

"That'll do," Red Sam said. "Go bring these people their Co'-Colas," and the woman went off to get the rest of the order.

"A good man is hard to find," Red Sammy said. "Everything is getting terrible. I remember the day you could go off and leave your screen door unlatched. Not no more."

He and the grandmother discussed better times. The old lady said that in her opinion Europe was entirely to blame for the way things were now. She said the way Europe acted you would think we were made of money and Red Sam said it was no use talking about it, she was exactly right. The children ran outside into the white sunlight and looked at the monkey in the lacy chinaberry tree. He was busy catching fleas on himself and biting each one carefully between his teeth as if it were a delicacy.

They drove off again into the hot afternoon. The grandmother took cat naps and woke up every few minutes with her own snoring. Outside of Toombsboro she woke up and recalled an old plantation that she had visited in this neighborhood once when she was a young lady. She said the house had six white columns across the front and that there was an avenue of oaks leading up to it and two little wooden trellis arbors on either side in front where you sat down with your suitor after a stroll in the garden. She recalled exactly which road to turn off to get to it. She knew that Bailey would not be willing to lose any time looking at an old house, but the more she talked about it, the more she wanted to see it once again and find out if the little twin arbors were still standing. "There was a secret panel in this house," she said craftily, not telling the truth but wishing that she were, "and the story went that all the family silver was hidden in it when Sherman came through but it was never found . . ."

"Hey!" John Wesley said. "Let's go see it! We'll find it! We'll poke all the woodwork and find it! Who lives there? Where do you turn off at? Hey Pop, can't we turn off there?"

"We never have seen a house with a secret panel!" June Star shrieked. "Let's go to the house with the secret panel! Hey Pop, can't we go see the house with the secret panel!"

"It's not far from here, I know," the grandmother said. "It wouldn't take over twenty minutes."

Bailey was looking straight ahead. His jaw was as rigid as a horseshoe. "No," he said.

The children began to yell and scream that they wanted to see the house with the secret panel. John Wesley kicked the back of the front seat and June Star hung over her mother's shoulder and whined desperately into her ear that they never had any fun even on their vacation, that they could never do what THEY wanted to do. The baby began to scream and John Wesley kicked the back of the seat so hard that his father could feel the blows in his kidney.

"All right!" he shouted and drew the car to a stop at the side of the road. "Will you all shut up? Will you all just shut up for one second? If you don't shut up, we won't go anywhere."

"It would be very educational for them," the grandmother murmured.

"All right," Bailey said, "but get this: this is the only time we're going to stop for anything like this. This is the one and only time."

"The dirt road that you have to turn down is about a mile back," the grandmother directed. "I marked it when we passed."

"A dirt road," Bailey groaned.

After they had turned around and were headed toward the dirt road, the grandmother recalled other points about the house, the beautiful glass over the front doorway and the candle-lamp in the hall. John Wesley said that the secret panel was probably in the fireplace.

"You can't go inside this house," Bailey said. "You don't know who lives there."

"While you all talk to the people in front, I'll run around behind and get in a window," John Wesley suggested.

"We'll all stay in the car," his mother said.

They turned onto the dirt road and the car raced roughly along in a swirl of pink dust. The grandmother recalled the times when there were no paved roads and thirty miles was a day's journey. The dirt road was hilly and there were sudden washes in it and sharp curves on dangerous embankments. All at once they would be on a hill, looking down over the blue tops of trees for miles around, then the next minute, they would be in a red depression with the dust-coated trees looking down on them.

"This place had better turn up in a minute," Bailey said, "or I'm going to turn around."

The road looked as if no one had traveled on it in months.

"It's not much farther," the grandmother said and just as she said it, a horrible thought came to her. The thought was so embarrassing that she turned red in the face and her eyes dilated and her feet jumped up, upsetting her valise in the corner. The instant the valise moved, the newspaper top she had over the basket under it rose with a snarl and Pitty Sing, the cat, sprang onto Bailey's shoulder.

The children were thrown to the floor and their mother, clutching the baby, was thrown out the door onto the ground; the old lady was thrown into the front seat. The car turned over once and landed right-side-up in a gulch off the side of the road. Bailey remained in the driver's seat with the cat—gray-striped with a broad white face and an orange nose—clinging to his neck like a caterpillar.

As soon as the children saw they could move their arms and legs, they scrambled out of the car, shouting, "We've had an ACCIDENT!" The grandmother was curled up under the dashboard, hoping she was injured so that Bailey's wrath would not come down on her all at once. The horrible thought she had had before the accident was that the house she had remembered so vividly was not in Georgia but in Tennessee.

Bailey removed the cat from his neck with both hands and flung it out the window against the side of a pine tree. Then he got out of the car and started looking for the children's mother. She was sitting against the side of the red gutted ditch, holding the screaming baby, but she only had a cut down her face and a broken shoulder. "We've had an ACCIDENT!" the children screamed in a frenzy of delight.

"But nobody's killed," June Star said with disappointment as the grandmother limped out of the car, her hat still pinned to her head but the broken front brim standing up at a jaunty angle and the violet spray hanging off the side. They all sat down in the ditch, except the children, to recover from the shock. They were all shaking.

"Maybe a car will come along," said the children's mother hoarsely.

"I believe I have injured an organ," said the grandmother, pressing her side, but no one answered her. Bailey's teeth were clattering. He had on a yellow sport shirt with bright blue parrots designed in it and his face was as yellow as the shirt. The grandmother decided that she would not mention that the house was in Tennessee.

The road was about ten feet above and they could only see the tops of the trees on the other side of it. Behind the ditch they were sitting in there were more woods, tall and dark and deep. In a few minutes they saw a car some distance away on top of a hill, coming slowly as if the occupants were watching them. The grandmother stood up and waved both arms dramatically to attract their attention. The car continued to come on slowly, disappeared around a bend and appeared again, moving even slower, on top of the hill they had gone over. It was a big black battered hearse-like automobile. There were three men in it.

It came to a stop just over them and for some minutes, the driver looked down with a steady expressionless gaze to where they were sitting, and didn't speak. Then he turned his head and muttered something to the other two and they got out. One was a fat boy in black trousers and a red sweat shirt with a silver stallion embossed on the front of it. He moved around on the right side of them and stood staring, his mouth partly open in a kind of loose grin. The other had on khaki pants and a blue striped coat and a gray hat pulled very low, hiding most of his face. He came around slowly on the left side. Neither spoke.

The driver got out of the car and stood by the side of it, looking down at them. He was an older man than the other two. His hair was just beginning to gray and he wore silver-rimmed spectacles that gave him a scholarly look. He had a long creased face and didn't have on any shirt or undershirt. He had on blue jeans that were too tight for him and was holding a black hat and a gun. The two boys also had guns.

"We've had an ACCIDENT!" the children screamed.

The grandmother had the peculiar feeling that the bespectacled man was someone she knew. His face was as familiar to her as if she had known him all her life but she could not recall who he was. He moved away from the car and began to come down the embankment, placing his feet carefully so that he wouldn't slip. He had on tan and white shoes and no socks, and his ankles were red and thin. "Good afternoon," he said. "I see you all had you a little spill."

"We turned over twice!" said the grandmother.

"Oncet," he corrected. "We seen it happen. Try their car and see will it run, Hiram," he said quietly to the boy with the gray hat.

"What you got that gun for?" John Wesley asked. "Whatcha gonna do with that gun?"

"Lady," the man said to the children's mother, "would you mind calling them children to sit down by you? Children make me nervous. I want all you all to sit down right together there where you're at."

"What are you telling US what to do for?" June Star asked.

Behind them the line of woods gaped like a dark open mouth. "Come here," said the mother.

"Look here now," Bailey began suddenly, "we're in a predicament! We're in . . ."

The grandmother shrieked. She scrambled to her feet and stood staring. "You're The Misfit!" she said. "I recognized you at once!"

"Yes'm," the man said, smiling slightly as if he were pleased in spite of himself to be known, "but it would have been better for all of you, lady, if you hadn't of reckernized me."

Bailey turned his head sharply and said something to his mother that shocked even the children. The old lady began to cry and The Misfit reddened.

"Lady," he said, "don't you get upset. Sometimes a man says things he don't mean. I don't reckon he meant to talk to you thataway."

"You wouldn't shoot a lady, would you?" the grandmother said and removed a clean handkerchief from her cuff and began to slap at her eyes with it.

The Misfit pointed the toe of his shoe into the ground and made a little hole and then covered it up again. "I would hate to have to," he said.

"Listen," the grandmother almost screamed, "I know you're a good man. You don't look a bit like you have common blood. I know you must come from nice people!"

"Yes mam," he said, "finest people in the world." When he smiled he showed a row of strong white teeth. "God never made a finer woman than my mother and my daddy's heart was pure gold," he said. The boy with the red sweat shirt had come around behind them and was standing with his gun at his hip. The Misfit squatted down on the ground. "Watch them children, Bobby Lee," he said. "You know they make me nervous." He looked at the six of them huddled together in front of him and he seemed to be embarrassed as if he couldn't think of anything to say. "Ain't a cloud in the sky," he remarked, looking up at it. "Don't see no sun but don't see no cloud neither."

"Yes, it's a beautiful day," said the grandmother. "Listen," she said, "you shouldn't call yourself The Misfit because I know you're a good man at heart. I can just look at you and tell."

"Hush!" Bailey yelled. "Hush! Everybody shut up and let me handle this!" He was squatting in the position of a runner about to sprint forward but he didn't move.

"I pre-chate that, lady," The Misfit said and drew a little circle in the ground with the butt of his gun.

"It'll take a half a hour to fix this here car," Hiram called, looking over the raised hood of it.

"Well, first you and Bobby Lee get him and that little boy to step over yonder with you," The Misfit said, pointing to Bailey and John Wesley. "The boys want to ast you something," he said to Bailey. "Would you mind stepping back in them woods there with them?"

"Listen," Bailey began, "we're in a terrible predicament! Nobody realizes what this is," and his voice cracked. His eyes were as blue and intense as the parrots in his shirt and he remained perfectly still.

The grandmother reached up to adjust her hat brim as if she were going to the woods with him but it came off in her hand. She stood staring at it and after a second she let it fall on the ground. Hiram pulled Bailey up by the arm as if he were assisting an old man. John Wesley caught hold of his father's hand and Bobby Lee followed. They went off toward the woods and just as they reached the dark edge, Bailey turned and supporting himself against a gray naked pine trunk, he shouted, "I'll be back in a minute, Mamma, wait on me!"

"Come back this instant!" his mother shrilled but they all disappeared into the woods.

"Bailey Boy!" the grandmother called in a tragic voice but she found she was looking at The Misfit squatting on the ground in front of her. "I just know you're a good man," she said desperately. "You're not a bit common!"

"Nome, I ain't a good man," The Misfit said after a second as if he had considered her statement carefully, "but I ain't the worst in the world neither. My daddy said I was a different breed of dog from my brothers and sisters. 'You know,' Daddy said, 'it's some that can live their whole life out without asking about it and it's others has to know why it is, and this boy is one of the latters. He's going to be into everything!' " He put on his black hat and looked up suddenly and then away deep into the woods as if he were embarrassed again. "I'm sorry I don't have on a shirt before you ladies," he said, hunching his shoulders slightly. "We buried our clothes that we had on when we escaped and we're just making do until we can get better. We borrowed these from some folks we met," he explained.

"That's perfectly all right," the grandmother said. "Maybe Bailey has an extra shirt in his suitcase."

"I'll look and see terrectly," The Misfit said.

"Where are they taking him?" the children's mother screamed.

"Daddy was a card himself," The Misfit said. "You couldn't put anything over on him. He never got in trouble with the Authorities though. Just had the knack of handling them."

"You could be honest too if you'd only try," said the grandmother. "Think how wonderful it would be to settle down and live a comfortable life and not have to think about somebody chasing you all the time."

The Misfit kept scratching in the ground with the butt of his gun as if he were thinking about it. "Yes'm, somebody is always after you," he murmured.

The grandmother noticed how thin his shoulder blades were just behind his hat because she was standing up looking down at him. "Do you ever pray?" she asked.

He shook his head. All she saw was the black hat wiggle between his shoulder blades. "Nome," he said.

There was a pistol shot from the woods, followed closely by another. Then silence. The old lady's head jerked around. She could hear the wind move through the tree tops like a long satisfied insuck of breath. "Bailey Boy!" she called.

"I was a gospel singer for a while," The Misfit said. "I been most everything. Been in the arm service, both land and sea, at home and abroad, been twict married, been an undertaker, been with the railroads, plowed Mother Earth, been in a tornado, seen a man burnt alive oncet," and he looked up at the children's mother and the little girl who were sitting close together, their faces white and their eyes glassy; "I even seen a woman flogged," he said.

"Pray, pray," the grandmother began, "pray, pray . . ."

"I never was a bad boy that I remember of," The Misfit said in an almost dreamy voice, "but somewheres along the line I done something wrong and got sent to the penitentiary. I was buried alive," and he looked up and held her attention to him by a steady stare.

"That's when you should have started to pray," she said. "What did you do to get sent to the penitentiary, that first time?"

"Turn to the right, it was a wall," The Misfit said, looking up again at the cloudless sky. "Turn to the left, it was a wall. Look up it was a ceiling, look down it was a floor. I forgot what I done, lady. I set there and set there, trying to remember what it was I done and I ain't recalled it to this day. Oncet in a while, I would think it was coming to me, but it never come."

"Maybe they put you in by mistake," the old lady said vaguely.

"Nome," he said. "It wasn't no mistake. They had the papers on me."

"You must have stolen something," she said.

The Misfit sneered slightly. "Nobody had nothing I wanted," he said. "It was a head-doctor at the penitentiary said what I had done was kill my daddy but I known that for a lie. My daddy died in nineteen ought nineteen of the epidemic flu and I never had a thing to do with it. He was buried in the Mount Hopewell Baptist churchyard and you can go there and see for yourself."

"If you would pray," the old lady said, "Jesus would help you."

"That's right," The Misfit said.

"Well then, why don't you pray?" she asked trembling with delight suddenly.

"I don't want no hep," he said. "I'm doing all right by myself."

Bobby Lee and Hiram came ambling back from the woods. Bobby Lee was dragging a yellow shirt with bright blue parrots in it.

"Thow me that shirt, Bobby Lee," The Misfit said. The shirt came flying at him and landed on his shoulder and he put it on. The grandmother couldn't name what the shirt reminded her of. "No, lady," The Misfit said while he was buttoning it up, "I found out the crime don't matter. You can do one thing or you can do another, kill a man or take a tire off his car, because sooner or later you're going to forget what it was you done and just be punished for it."

The children's mother had begun to make heaving noises as if she couldn't get her breath. "Lady," he asked, "would you and that little girl like to step off yonder with Bobby Lee and Hiram and join your husband?"

"Yes, thank you," the mother said faintly. Her left arm dangled helplessly and she was holding the baby, who had gone to sleep, in the other. "Hep that lady up, Hiram," The Misfit said as she struggled to climb out of the ditch, "and Bobby Lee, you hold onto that little girl's hand."

"I don't want to hold hands with him," June Star said. "He reminds me of a pig."

The fat boy blushed and laughed and caught her by the arm and pulled her off into the woods after Hiram and her mother.

Alone with The Misfit, the grandmother found that she had lost her voice. There was not a cloud in the sky nor any sun. There was nothing around her but woods. She wanted to tell him that he must pray. She opened and closed her mouth several times before anything came out. Finally she found herself saying, "Jesus. Jesus," meaning, Jesus will help you, but the way she was saying it, it sounded as if she might be cursing.

"Yes'm," The Misfit said as if he agreed. "Jesus thown everything off balance. It was the same case with Him as with me except He hadn't committed any crime and they could prove I had committed one because they had the papers on me. Of course," he said, "they never shown me my papers. That's why I sign myself now. I said long ago, you get you a signature and sign everything you do and keep a copy of it. Then you'll know what you done and you can hold up the crime to the punishment and see do they match and in the end you'll have something to prove you ain't been treated right. I call myself The Misfit," he said, "because I can't make what all I done wrong fit what all I gone through in punishment."

There was a piercing scream from the woods, followed closely by a pistol report. "Does it seem right to you, lady, that one is punished a heap and another ain't punished at all?"

"Jesus!" the old lady cried. "You've got good blood! I know you wouldn't shoot a lady! I know you come from nice people! Pray! Jesus, you ought not to shoot a lady. I'll give you all the money I've got!"

"Lady," The Misfit said, looking beyond her far into the woods, "there never was a body that give the undertaker a tip."

There were two more pistol reports and the grandmother raised her head like a parched old turkey hen crying for water and called, "Bailey Boy, Bailey Boy!" as if her heart would break.

"Jesus was the only One that ever raised the dead," The Misfit continued, "and He shouldn't have done it. He thown everything off balance. If He did what He said, then it's nothing for you to do but thow away everything and follow Him, and if He didn't, then it's nothing for you to do but enjoy the few minutes you got left the best you can—by killing somebody or burning down his house or doing some other meanness to him. No pleasure but meanness," he said and his voice had become almost a snarl.

"Maybe He didn't raise the dead," the old lady mumbled, not knowing what she was saying and feeling so dizzy that she sank down in the ditch with her legs twisted under her.

"I wasn't there so I can't say He didn't," The Misfit said. "I wisht I had of been there," he said, hitting the ground with his fist. "It ain't right I wasn't there because if I had of been there I would of known. Listen lady," he said in a high voice, "if I had of been there I would of known and I wouldn't be like I am now." His voice seemed about to crack and the grandmother's head cleared for an instant. She saw the man's face twisted close to her own as if he were going to cry and she murmured, "Why you're one of my babies. You're one of my own children!" She reached out and touched him on the shoulder. The Misfit sprang back as if a snake had bitten him and shot her three times through the chest. Then he put his gun down on the ground and took off his glasses and began to clean them.

Hiram and Bobby Lee returned from the woods and stood over the ditch, looking down at the grandmother who half sat and half lay in a puddle of blood with her legs crossed under her like a child's and her face smiling up at the cloudless sky.

Without his glasses, The Misfit's eyes were red-rimmed and pale and defenseless-looking. "Take her off and throw her where you thrown the others," he said, picking up the cat that was rubbing itself against his leg.

"She was a talker, wasn't she?" Bobby Lee said, sliding down the ditch with a yodel.

"She would of been a good woman," The Misfit said, "if it had been somebody there to shoot her every minute of her life."

"Some fun!" Bobby Lee said.

"Shut up, Bobby Lee," The Misfit said. "It's no real pleasure in life."

1955

A Very Old Man with Enormous Wings

GABRIEL GARCÍA MÁRQUEZ
[1928–2014]

On the third day of rain they had killed so many crabs inside the house that Pelayo had to cross his drenched courtyard and throw them into the sea, because the newborn child had a temperature all night and they thought it was due to the stench. The world had been sad since Tuesday. Sea and sky were a single ash-gray thing and the sands of the beach, which on March nights glimmered like powdered light, had become a stew of mud and rotten shellfish. The light was so weak at noon that when Pelayo was coming back to the house after throwing away the crabs, it was hard for him to see what it was that was moving and groaning in the rear of the courtyard. He had to go very close to see that it was an old man, a very old man, lying face down in the mud, who, in spite of his tremendous efforts, couldn't get up, impeded by his enormous wings.

Frightened by that nightmare, Pelayo ran to get Elisenda, his wife, who was putting compresses on the sick child, and he took her to the rear of the courtyard. They both looked at the fallen body with mute stupor. He was dressed like a ragpicker. There were only a few faded hairs left on his bald skull and very few teeth in his mouth, and his pitiful condition of a drenched great-grandfather had taken away any sense of grandeur he might have had. His huge buzzard wings, dirty and half-plucked, were forever entangled in the mud. They looked at him so long and so closely that Pelayo and Elisenda very soon overcame their surprise and in the end found him familiar. Then they dared speak to him, and he answered in an incomprehensible dialect with a strong sailor's voice. That was how they skipped over the inconvenience of the wings and quite intelligently

Translated by Gregory Rabassa, 1971.

concluded that he was a lonely castaway from some foreign ship wrecked by the storm. And yet, they called in a neighbor woman who knew everything about life and death to see him, and all she needed was one look to show them their mistake.

"He's an angel," she told them. "He must have been coming for the child, but the poor fellow is so old that the rain knocked him down."

On the following day everyone knew that a flesh-and-blood angel was held captive in Pelayo's house. Against the judgment of the wise neighbor woman, for whom angels in those times were the fugitive survivors of a celestial conspiracy, they did not have the heart to club him to death. Pelayo watched over him all afternoon from the kitchen, armed with his bailiff's club, and before going to bed he dragged him out of the mud and locked him up with the hens in the wire chicken coop. In the middle of the night, when the rain stopped, Pelayo and Elisenda were still killing crabs. A short time afterward the child woke up without a fever and with a desire to eat. Then they felt magnanimous and decided to put the angel on a raft with fresh water and provisions for three days and leave him to his fate on the high seas. But when they went out into the courtyard with the first light of dawn, they found the whole neighborhood in front of the chicken coop having fun with the angel, without the slightest reverence, tossing him things to eat through the openings in the wire as if he weren't a supernatural creature but a circus animal.

Father Gonzaga arrived before seven o'clock, alarmed at the strange news. By that time onlookers less frivolous than those at dawn had already arrived and they were making all kinds of conjectures concerning the captive's future. The simplest among them thought that he should be named mayor of the world. Others of sterner mind felt that he should be promoted to the rank of five-star general in order to win all wars. Some visionaries hoped that he could be put to stud in order to implant on earth a race of winged wise men who could take charge of the universe. But Father Gonzaga, before becoming a priest, had been a robust woodcutter. Standing by the wire, he reviewed his catechism in an instant and asked them to open the door so that he could take a close look at that pitiful man who looked more like a huge decrepit hen among the fascinated chickens. He was lying in a corner drying his open wings in the sunlight among the fruit peels and breakfast leftovers that the early risers had thrown him. Alien to the impertinences of the world, he only lifted his antiquarian eyes and murmured something in his dialect when Father Gonzaga went into the chicken coop and said good morning to him in Latin. The parish priest had his first suspicion of an impostor when he saw that he did not understand the language of God or know how to greet His ministers. Then he noticed that seen close up he was much too human: he had an unbearable smell of the outdoors, the back side of his wings was strewn with parasites and his main feathers had been mistreated by terrestrial winds, and nothing about him measured up to the proud dignity of angels. Then he came out of the chicken coop and in a brief sermon warned the curious against the risks of being ingenuous. He reminded them that the devil had the bad habit of making use of carnival tricks in order to confuse the unwary. He argued that if wings were not the essential element in determining the difference between a hawk and an airplane, they were even less so in the recognition of angels. Nevertheless, he promised to write a letter to his bishop so that the latter would write to his primate so that the latter would write to the Supreme Pontiff in order to get the final verdict from the highest courts.

His prudence fell on sterile hearts. The news of the captive angel spread with such rapidity that after a few hours the courtyard had the bustle of a marketplace and they had to call in troops with fixed bayonets to disperse the mob that was about to knock the house down. Elisenda, her spine all twisted from sweeping up so much marketplace trash, then got the idea of fencing in the yard and charging five cents admission to see the angel.

The curious came from far away. A traveling carnival arrived with a flying acrobat who buzzed over the crowd several times, but no one paid any attention to him because his wings were not those of an angel but, rather, those of a sidereal[1] bat. The most unfortunate invalids on earth came in search of health: a poor woman who since childhood had been counting her heartbeats and had run out of numbers; a Portuguese man who couldn't sleep because the noise of the stars disturbed him; a sleep-walker who got up at night to undo the things he had done while awake; and many others with less serious ailments. In the midst of that shipwreck disorder that made the earth tremble, Pelayo and Elisenda were happy with fatigue, for in less than a week they had crammed their rooms with money and the line of pilgrims waiting their turn to enter still reached beyond the horizon.

[1]Coming from the stars.

The angel was the only one who took no part in his own act. He spent his time trying to get comfortable in his borrowed nest, befuddled by the hellish heat of the oil lamps and sacramental candles that had been placed along the wire. At first they tried to make him eat some mothballs, which, according to the wisdom of the wise neighbor woman, were the food prescribed for angels. But he turned them down, just as he turned down the papal lunches that the penitents brought him, and they never found out whether it was because he was an angel or because he was an old man that in the end he ate nothing but eggplant mush. His only supernatural virtue seemed to be patience. Especially during the first days, when the hens pecked at him, searching for the stellar parasites that proliferated in his wings, and the cripples pulled out feathers to touch their defective parts with, and even the most merciful threw stones at him, trying to get him to rise so they could see him standing. The only time they succeeded in arousing him was when they burned his side with an iron for branding steers, for he had been motionless for so many hours that they thought he was dead. He awoke with a start, ranting in his hermetic language and with tears in his eyes, and he flapped his wings a couple of times, which brought on a whirlwind of chicken dung and lunar dust and a gale of panic that did not seem to be of this world. Although many thought that his reaction had been one not of rage but of pain, from then on they were careful not to annoy him, because the majority understood that his passivity was not that of a hero taking his ease but that of a cataclysm in repose.

Father Gonzaga held back the crowd's frivolity with formulas of maidservant inspiration while awaiting the arrival of a final judgment on the nature of the captive. But the mail from Rome showed no sense of urgency. They spent their time finding out if the prisoner had a navel, if his dialect had any connection with Aramaic, how many times he could fit on the head of a pin, or whether he wasn't just a Norwegian with wings. Those meager letters might have come and gone until the end of time if a providential event had not put an end to the priest's tribulations.

It so happened that during those days, among so many other carnival attractions, there arrived in town the traveling show of the woman who had been changed into a spider for having disobeyed her parents. The admission to see her was not only less than the admission to see the angel, but people were permitted to ask her all manner of questions about her absurd state and to examine her up and down so that no one would ever doubt the truth of her horror. She was a frightful tarantula the size of a ram and with the head of a sad maiden. What was most heart-rending, however, was not her outlandish shape but the sincere affliction with which she recounted the details of her misfortune. While still practically a child she had sneaked out of her parents' house to go to a dance, and while she was coming back through the woods after having danced all night without permission, a fearful thunderclap rent the sky in two and through the crack came the lightning bolt of brimstone that changed her into a spider. Her only nourishment came from the meatballs that charitable souls chose to toss into her mouth. A spectacle like that, full of so much human truth and with such a fearful lesson, was bound to defeat without even trying that of a haughty angel who scarcely deigned to look at mortals. Besides, the few miracles attributed to the angel showed a certain mental disorder, like the blind man who didn't recover his sight but grew three new teeth, or the paralytic who didn't get to walk but almost won the lottery, and the leper whose sores sprouted sunflowers. Those consolation miracles, which were more like mocking fun, had already ruined the angel's reputation when the woman who had been changed into a spider finally crushed him completely. That was how Father Gonzaga was cured forever of his insomnia and Pelayo's courtyard went back to being as empty as during the time it had rained for three days and crabs walked through the bedrooms.

The owners of the house had no reason to lament. With the money they saved they built a two-story mansion with balconies and gardens and high netting so that crabs wouldn't get in during the winter, and with iron bars on the windows so that angels wouldn't get in. Pelayo also set up a rabbit warren close to town and gave up his job as bailiff for good, and Elisenda bought some satin pumps with high heels and many dresses of iridescent silk, the kind worn on Sunday by the most desirable women in those times. The chicken coop was the only thing that didn't receive any attention. If they washed it down with creolin and burned tears of myrrh inside it every so often, it was not in homage to the angel but to drive away the dungheap stench that still hung everywhere like a ghost and was turning the new house into an old one. At first, when the child learned to walk, they were careful that he not get too close to the chicken coop. But then they began to lose their fears and got used to the smell, and before the child got his second teeth he'd gone inside the chicken coop to play, where the wires were falling apart. The angel was no less standoffish with him than with other mortals, but he tolerated the most ingenious infamies with the patience of a dog who had no illusions. They both came down with chicken pox at the same time. The doctor who took care of the child couldn't resist the temptation to listen to the angel's heart, and he found so much whistling in the heart and so many sounds in his kidneys that it seemed impossible for him to be alive. What surprised him most, however, was the logic of his wings. They seemed so natural on that completely human organism that he couldn't understand why other men didn't have them too.

When the child began school it had been some time since the sun and rain had caused the collapse of the chicken coop. The angel went dragging himself about here and there like a stray dying man. They would drive him out of the bedroom with a broom and a moment later find him in the kitchen. He seemed to be in so many places at the same time that they grew to think that he'd been duplicated, that he was reproducing himself all through the house, and the exasperated and unhinged Elisenda shouted that it was awful living in that hell full of angels. He could scarcely eat and his antiquarian eyes had also become so foggy that he went about bumping into posts. All he had left were the bare cannulae[2] of his last feathers. Pelayo threw a blanket over him and extended him the charity of letting him sleep in the shed, and only then did they notice that he had a temperature at night, and was delirious with the tongue twisters of an old Norwegian. That was one of the few times they became alarmed, for they thought he was going to die and not even the wise neighbor woman had been able to tell them what to do with dead angels.

And yet he not only survived his worst winter, but seemed improved with the first sunny days. He remained motionless for several days in the farthest corner of the courtyard, where no one would see him, and at the beginning of December some large, stiff feathers began to grow on his wings, the feathers of a scarecrow, which looked more like another misfortune of decrepitude. But he must have known the reason for those changes, for he was quite careful that no one should notice them, that no one should hear the sea chanteys that he sometimes sang under the stars. One morning Elisenda was cutting some bunches of onions for lunch when a wind that seemed to

[2]The tubular pieces by which feathers are attached to a body.

come from the high seas blew into the kitchen. Then she went to the window and caught the angel in his first attempts at flight. They were so clumsy that his fingernails opened a furrow in the vegetable patch and he was on the point of knocking the shed down with the ungainly flapping that slipped on the light and couldn't get a grip on the air. But he did manage to gain altitude. Elisenda let out a sigh of relief, for herself and for him, when she saw him pass over the last houses, holding himself up in some way with the risky flapping of a senile vulture. She kept watching him even when she was through cutting the onions and she kept on watching until it was no longer possible for her to see him, because then he was no longer an annoyance in her life but an imaginary dot on the horizon of the sea.

1955

Cathedral

RAYMOND CARVER

[1938–1988]

This blind man, an old friend of my wife's, he was on his way to spend the night. His wife had died. So he was visiting the dead wife's relatives in Connecticut. He called my wife from his in-laws'. Arrangements were made. He would come by train, a five-hour trip, and my wife would meet him at the station. She hadn't seen him since she worked for him one summer in Seattle ten years ago. But she and the blind man had kept in touch. They made tapes and mailed them back and forth. I wasn't enthusiastic about his visit. He was no one I knew. And his being blind bothered me. My idea of blindness came from the movies. In the movies, the blind moved slowly and never laughed. Sometimes they were led by seeing-eye dogs. A blind man in my house was not something I looked forward to.

That summer in Seattle she had needed a job. She didn't have any money. The man she was going to marry at the end of the summer was in officers' training school. He didn't have any money, either. But she was in love with the guy, and he was in love with her, etc. She'd seen something in the paper: HELP WANTED—*Reading to Blind Man*, and a telephone number. She phoned and went over, was hired on the spot. She'd worked with this blind man all summer. She read stuff to him, case studies, reports, that sort of thing. She helped him organize his little office in the county social-service department. They'd become good friends, my wife and the blind man. How do I know these things? She told me. And she told me something else. On her last day in the office, the blind man asked if he could touch her face. She agreed to this. She told me he touched his fingers to every part of her face, her nose—even her neck! She never forgot it. She even tried to write a poem about it. She was always trying to write a poem. She wrote a poem or two every year, usually after something really important had happened to her.

When we first started going out together, she showed me the poem. In the poem, she recalled his fingers and the way they had moved around over her face. In the poem, she talked about what she had felt at the time, about what went through her mind when the blind man touched her nose and lips. I can remember I didn't think much of the poem. Of course, I didn't tell her that. Maybe I just don't understand poetry. I admit it's not the first thing I reach for when I pick up something to read.

Anyway, this man who'd first enjoyed her favors, the officer-to-be, he'd been her childhood sweetheart. So okay. I'm saying that at the end of the summer she let the blind man run his hands over her face, said good-bye to him, married her childhood etc., who was now a commissioned officer, and she moved away from Seattle. But they'd kept in touch, she and the blind man. She made the first contact after a year or so. She called him up one night from an Air Force base in Alabama. She wanted to talk. They talked. He asked her to send him a tape and tell him about her life. She did this. She sent the tape. On the tape, she told the blind man about her husband and about their life together in the military. She told the blind man she loved her husband but she didn't like it where they lived and she didn't like it that he was part of the military-industrial thing. She told the blind man she'd written a poem and he was in it. She told him that she was writing a poem about what it was like to be an Air Force officer's wife. The poem wasn't finished yet. She was still writing it. The blind man made a tape. He sent her the tape. She made a tape. This went on for years. My wife's officer was posted to one base and then another. She sent tapes from Moody AFB, McGuire, McConnell, and finally Travis, near Sacramento, where one night she got to feeling lonely and cut off from the people she kept losing in that moving-around life. She got to feeling she couldn't go it another step. She went in and swallowed all the pills and capsules in the medicine chest and washed them down with a bottle of gin. Then she got into a hot bath and passed out.

But instead of dying, she got sick. She threw up. Her officer—why should he have a name? he was the childhood sweetheart, and what more does he want?—came home from somewhere, found her, and called the ambulance. In time, she put it all on a tape and sent the tape to the blind man. Over the years, she put all kinds of stuff on tapes and sent the tapes off lickety-split. Next to writing a poem every year, I think it was her chief means of recreation. On one tape, she told the blind man she'd decided to live away from her officer for a time. On another tape, she told him about her divorce. She and I began going out, and of course she told her blind man about it. She told him everything, or so it seemed to me. Once she asked me if I'd like to hear the latest tape from the blind man. This was a year ago. I was on the tape, she said. So I said okay, I'd listen to it. I got us drinks and we settled down in the living room. We made ready to listen. First she inserted the tape into the player and adjusted a couple of dials. Then she pushed a lever. The tape squeaked and someone began to talk in this loud voice. She lowered the volume. After a few minutes of harmless chitchat, I heard my own name in the mouth of this stranger, this blind man I didn't even know! And then this: "From all you've said about him, I can only conclude —" But we were interrupted, a knock at the door, something, and we didn't ever get back to the tape. Maybe it was just as well. I'd heard all I wanted to.

Now this same blind man was coming to sleep in my house.

"Maybe I could take him bowling," I said to my wife. She was at the draining board doing scalloped potatoes. She put down the knife she was using and turned around.

"If you love me," she said, "you can do this for me. If you don't love me, okay. But if you had a friend, any friend, and the friend came to visit, I'd make him feel comfortable." She wiped her hands with the dish towel.

"I don't have any blind friends," I said.

"You don't have *any* friends," she said. "Period. Besides," she said, "goddamn it, his wife's just died! Don't you understand that? The man's lost his wife!"

I didn't answer. She'd told me a little about the blind man's wife. Her name was Beulah. Beulah! That's a name for a colored woman.

"Was his wife a Negro?" I asked.

"Are you crazy?" my wife said. "Have you just flipped or something?" She picked up a potato. I saw it hit the floor, then roll under the stove. "What's wrong with you?" she said. "Are you drunk?"

"I'm just asking," I said.

Right then my wife filled me in with more detail than I cared to know. I made a drink and sat at the kitchen table to listen. Pieces of the story began to fall into place.

Beulah had gone to work for the blind man the summer after my wife had stopped working for him. Pretty soon Beulah and the blind man had themselves a church wedding. It was a little wedding—who'd want to go to such a wedding in the first place?—just the two of them, plus the minister and the minister's wife. But it was a church wedding just the same. It was what Beulah had wanted, he'd said. But even then Beulah must have been carrying the cancer in her glands. After they had been inseparable for eight years—my wife's word, *inseparable*—Beulah's health went into a rapid decline. She died in a Seattle hospital room, the blind man sitting beside the bed and holding on to her hand. They'd married, lived and worked together, slept together—had sex, sure—and then the blind man had to bury her. All this without his having ever seen what the goddamned woman looked like. It was beyond my understanding. Hearing this, I felt sorry for the blind man for a little bit. And then I found myself thinking what a pitiful life this woman must have led. Imagine a woman who could never see herself as she was seen in the eyes of her loved one. A woman who could go on day after day and never receive the smallest compliment from her beloved. A woman whose husband could never read the expression on her face, be it misery or something better. Someone who could wear makeup or not—what difference to him? She could, if she wanted, wear green eye-shadow around one eye, a straight pin in her nostril, yellow slacks and purple shoes, no matter. And then to slip off into death, the blind man's hand on her hand, his blind eyes streaming tears—I'm imagining now—her last thought maybe this: that he never even knew what she looked like, and she on an express to the grave. Robert was left with a small insurance policy and half of a twenty-peso Mexican coin. The other half of the coin went into the box with her. Pathetic.

So when the time rolled around, my wife went to the depot to pick him up. With nothing to do but wait—sure, I blamed him for that—I was having a drink and watching the TV when I heard the car pull into the drive. I got up from the sofa with my drink and went to the window to have a look.

I saw my wife laughing as she parked the car. I saw her get out of the car and shut the door. She was still wearing a smile. Just amazing. She went around to the other side of the car to where the blind man was already starting to get out. This blind man, feature this, he was wearing a full beard! A beard on a blind man! Too much, I say. The blind man reached into the back seat and dragged out a suitcase. My wife took his arm, shut the car door, and, talking all the way, moved him down the drive and then up the steps to the front porch. I turned off the TV. I finished my drink, rinsed the glass, dried my hands. Then I went to the door.

My wife said, "I want you to meet Robert. Robert, this is my husband. I've told you all about him." She was beaming. She had this blind man by his coat sleeve.

The blind man let go of his suitcase and up came his hand.

I took it. He squeezed hard, held my hand, and then he let it go.

"I feel like we've already met," he boomed.

"Likewise," I said. I didn't know what else to say. Then I said, "Welcome. I've heard a lot about you." We began to move then, a little group, from the porch into the living room, my wife guiding him by the arm. The blind man was carrying his suitcase in his other hand. My wife said things like, "To your left here, Robert. That's right. Now watch it, there's a chair. That's it. Sit down right here. This is the sofa. We just bought this sofa two weeks ago."

I started to say something about the old sofa. I'd liked that old sofa. But I didn't say anything. Then I wanted to say something else, small-talk, about the scenic ride along the Hudson. How going *to* New York, you should sit on the right-hand side of the train, and coming *from* New York, the left-hand side.

"Did you have a good train ride?" I said. "Which side of the train did you sit on, by the way?"

"What a question, which side!" my wife said. "What's it matter which side?" she said.

"I just asked," I said.

"Right side," the blind man said. "I hadn't been on a train in nearly forty years. Not since I was a kid. With my folks. That's been a long time. I'd nearly forgotten the sensation. I have winter in my beard now," he said. "So I've been told, anyway. Do I look distinguished, my dear?" the blind man said to my wife.

"You look distinguished, Robert," she said. "Robert," she said. "Robert, it's just so good to see you."

My wife finally took her eyes off the blind man and looked at me. I had the feeling she didn't like what she saw. I shrugged.

I've never met, or personally known, anyone who was blind. This blind man was late forties, a heavy-set, balding man with stooped shoulders, as if he carried a great weight there. He wore brown slacks, brown shoes, a light-brown shirt, a tie, a sports coat. Spiffy. He also had this full beard. But he didn't use a cane and he didn't wear dark glasses. I'd always thought dark glasses were a must for the blind. Fact was, I wished he had a pair. At first glance, his eyes looked like anyone else's eyes. But if you looked close, there was something different about them. Too much white in the iris, for one thing, and the pupils seemed to move around in the sockets without his knowing it or being able to stop it. Creepy. As I stared at his face, I saw the left pupil turn in toward his nose while the other made an effort to keep in one place. But it was only an effort, for that eye was on the roam without his knowing it or wanting it to be.

I said, "Let me get you a drink. What's your pleasure? We have a little of everything. It's one of our pastimes."

"Bub, I'm a Scotch man myself," he said fast enough in this big voice.

"Right," I said. Bub! "Sure you are. I knew it."

He let his fingers touch his suitcase, which was sitting alongside the sofa. He was taking his bearings. I didn't blame him for that.

"I'll move that up to your room," my wife said.

"No, that's fine," the blind man said loudly. "It can go up when I go up."

"A little water with the Scotch?" I said.

"Very little," he said.

"I knew it," I said.

He said, "Just a tad. The Irish actor, Barry Fitzgerald? I'm like that fellow. When I drink water, Fitzgerald said, I drink water. When I drink whiskey, I drink whiskey." My wife laughed. The blind man brought his hand up under his beard. He lifted his beard slowly and let it drop.

I did the drinks, three big glasses of Scotch with a splash of water in each. Then we made ourselves comfortable and talked about Robert's travels. First the long flight from the West Coast to Connecticut, we covered that. Then from Connecticut up here by train. We had another drink concerning that leg of the trip.

I remembered having read somewhere that the blind didn't smoke because, as speculation had it, they couldn't see the smoke they exhaled. I thought I knew that much and that much only about blind people. But this blind man smoked his cigarette down to the nubbin and then lit another one. This blind man filled his ashtray and my wife emptied it.

When we sat down at the table for dinner, we had another drink. My wife heaped Robert's plate with cube steak, scalloped potatoes, green beans. I buttered him up two slices of bread. I said, "Here's bread and butter for you." I swallowed some of my drink. "Now let us pray," I said, and the blind man lowered his head. My wife looked at me, her mouth agape. "Pray the phone won't ring and the food doesn't get cold," I said.

We dug in. We ate everything there was to eat on the table. We ate like there was no tomorrow. We didn't talk. We ate. We scarfed. We grazed that table. We were into serious eating. The blind man had right away located his foods, he knew just where everything was on his plate. I watched with admiration as he used his knife and fork on the meat. He'd cut two pieces of meat, fork the meat into his mouth, and then go all out for the scalloped potatoes, the beans next, and then he'd tear off a hunk of buttered bread and eat that. He'd follow this up with a big drink of milk. It didn't seem to bother him to use his fingers once in a while, either.

We finished everything, including half a strawberry pie. For a few moments, we sat as if stunned. Sweat beaded on our faces. Finally, we got up from the table and left the dirty plates. We didn't look back. We took ourselves into the living room and sank into our places again. Robert and my wife sat on the sofa. I took the big chair. We had us two or three more drinks while they talked about the major things that had come to pass for them in the past ten years. For the most part, I just listened. Now and then I joined in. I didn't want him to think I'd left the room, and I didn't want her to think I was feeling left out. They talked of things that had happened to them—to them!—these past ten years. I waited in vain to hear my name on my wife's sweet lips: "And then my dear husband came into my life"—something like that. But I heard nothing of the sort. More talk of Robert. Robert had done a little of everything, it seemed, a regular blind jack-of-all-trades. But most recently he and his wife had had an Amway distributorship, from which, I gathered, they'd earned their living, such as it was. The blind man was also a ham radio operator. He talked in his loud voice about conversations he'd had with fellow operators in Guam, in the Philippines, in Alaska, and even in Tahiti. He said he'd have a lot of friends there if he ever wanted to go visit those places. From time to time, he'd turn his blind face toward me, put his hand under his beard, ask me something. How long had I been in my present position? (Three years.) Did I like my work? (I didn't.) Was I going to stay with it? (What were the options?) Finally, when I thought he was beginning to run down, I got up and turned on the TV.

My wife looked at me with irritation. She was heading toward a boil. Then she looked at the blind man and said, "Robert, do you have a TV?"

The blind man said, "My dear, I have two TVs. I have a color set and a black-and-white thing, an old relic. It's funny, but if I turn the TV on, and I'm always turning it on, I turn on the color set. It's funny, don't you think?"

I didn't know what to say to that. I had absolutely nothing to say to that. No opinion. So I watched the news program and tried to listen to what the announcer was saying.

"This is a color TV," the blind man said. "Don't ask me how, but I can tell."

"We traded up a while ago," I said.

The blind man had another taste of his drink. He lifted his beard, sniffed it, and let it fall. He leaned forward on the sofa. He positioned his ashtray on the coffee table, then put the lighter to his cigarette. He leaned back on the sofa and crossed his legs at the ankles.

My wife covered her mouth, and then she yawned. She stretched. She said, "I think I'll go upstairs and put on my robe. I think I'll change into something else. Robert, you make yourself comfortable," she said.

"I'm comfortable," the blind man said.

"I want you to feel comfortable in this house," she said.

"I am comfortable," the blind man said.

After she'd left the room, he and I listened to the weather report and then to the sports roundup. By that time, she'd been gone so long I didn't know if she was going to come back. I thought she might have gone to bed. I wished she'd come back downstairs. I didn't want to be left alone with a blind man. I asked him if he wanted another drink, and he said sure. Then I asked if he wanted to smoke some dope with me. I said I'd just rolled a number. I hadn't, but I planned to do so in about two shakes.

"I'll try some with you," he said.

"Damn right," I said. "That's the stuff."

I got our drinks and sat down on the sofa with him. Then I rolled us two fat numbers. I lit one and passed it. I brought it to his fingers. He took it and inhaled.

"Hold it as long as you can," I said. I could tell he didn't know the first thing.

My wife came back downstairs wearing her pink robe and her pink slippers.

"What do I smell?" she said.

"We thought we'd have us some cannabis," I said.

My wife gave me a savage look. Then she looked at the blind man and said, "Robert, I didn't know you smoked."

He said, "I do now, my dear. There's a first time for everything. But I don't feel anything yet."

"This stuff is pretty mellow," I said. "This stuff is mild. It's dope you can reason with," I said. "It doesn't mess you up."

"Not much it doesn't, bub," he said, and laughed.

My wife sat on the sofa between the blind man and me. I passed her the number. She took it and toked and then passed it back to me. "Which way is this going?" she said. Then she said, "I shouldn't be smoking this. I can hardly keep my eyes open as it is. That dinner did me in. I shouldn't have eaten so much."

"It was the strawberry pie," the blind man said. "That's what did it," he said, and he laughed his big laugh. Then he shook his head.

"There's more strawberry pie," I said.

"Do you want some more, Robert?" my wife said.

"Maybe in a little while," he said.

We gave our attention to the TV. My wife yawned again. She said, "Your bed is made up when you feel like going to bed, Robert. I know you must have had a long day. When you're ready to go to bed, say so." She pulled his arm. "Robert?"

He came to and said, "I've had a real nice time. This beats tapes, doesn't it?"

I said, "Coming at you," and I put the number between his fingers. He inhaled, held the smoke, and then let it go. It was like he'd been doing it since he was nine years old.

"Thanks, bub," he said. "But I think this is all for me. I think I'm beginning to feel it," he said. He held the burning roach out for my wife.

"Same here," she said. "Ditto. Me, too." She took the roach and passed it to me. "I may just sit here for a while between you two guys with my eyes closed. But don't let me bother you, okay? Either one of you. If it bothers you, say so. Otherwise, I may just sit here with my eyes closed until you're ready to go to bed," she said. "Your bed's made up, Robert, when you're ready. It's right next to our room at the top of the stairs. We'll show you up when you're ready. You wake me up now, you guys, if I fall asleep." She said that and then she closed her eyes and went to sleep.

The news program ended. I got up and changed the channel. I sat back down on the sofa. I wished my wife hadn't pooped out. Her head lay across the back of the sofa, her mouth open. She'd turned so that her robe slipped away from her legs, exposing a juicy thigh. I reached to draw her robe back over her, and it was then that I glanced at the blind man. What the hell! I flipped the robe open again.

"You say when you want some strawberry pie," I said.

"I will," he said.

I said, "Are you tired? Do you want me to take you up to your bed? Are you ready to hit the hay?"

"Not yet," he said. "No, I'll stay up with you, bub. If that's all right. I'll stay up until you're ready to turn in. We haven't had a chance to talk. Know what I mean? I feel like me and her monopolized the evening." He lifted his beard and he let it fall. He picked up his cigarettes and his lighter.

"That's all right," I said. Then I said, "I'm glad for the company."

And I guess I was. Every night I smoked dope and stayed up as long as I could before I fell asleep. My wife and I hardly ever went to bed at the same time. When I did go to sleep, I had these dreams. Sometimes I'd wake up from one of them, my heart going crazy.

Something about the church and the Middle Ages was on the TV. Not your run-of-the-mill TV fare. I wanted to watch something else. I turned to the other channels. But there was nothing on them, either. So I turned back to the first channel and apologized.

"Bub, it's all right," the blind man said. "It's fine with me. Whatever you want to watch is okay. I'm always learning something. Learning never ends. It won't hurt me to learn something tonight. I got ears," he said.

We didn't say anything for a time. He was leaning forward with his head turned at me, his right ear aimed in the direction of the set. Very disconcerting. Now and then his eyelids drooped and then they snapped open again. Now and then he put his fingers into his beard and tugged, like he was thinking about something he was hearing on the television.

On the screen, a group of men wearing cowls was being set upon and tormented by men dressed in skeleton costumes and men dressed as devils. The men dressed as devils wore devil masks, horns, and long tails. This pageant was part of a procession. The Englishman who was narrating the thing said it took place in Spain once a year. I tried to explain to the blind man what was happening.

"Skeletons," he said. "I know about skeletons," he said, and he nodded.

The TV showed this one cathedral. Then there was a long, slow look at another one. Finally, the picture switched to the famous one in Paris, with its flying buttresses and its spires reaching up to the clouds. The camera pulled away to show the whole of the cathedral rising above the skyline.

There were times when the Englishman who was telling the thing would shut up, would simply let the camera move around over the cathedrals. Or else the camera would tour the countryside, men in fields walking behind oxen. I waited as long as I could. Then I felt I had to say something. I said, "They're showing the outside of this cathedral now. Gargoyles. Little statues carved to look like monsters. Now I guess they're in Italy. Yeah, they're in Italy. There's paintings on the walls of this one church."

"Are those fresco paintings, bub?" he asked, and he sipped from his drink.

I reached for my glass. But it was empty. I tried to remember what I could remember. "You're asking me are those frescoes?" I said. "That's a good question. I don't know."

The camera moved to a cathedral outside Lisbon. The differences in the Portuguese cathedral compared with the French and Italian were not that great. But they were there. Mostly the interior stuff. Then something occurred to me, and I said, "Something has occurred to me. Do you have any idea what a cathedral is? What they look like, that is? Do you follow me? If somebody says cathedral to you, do you have any notion what they're talking about? Do you know the difference between that and a Baptist church, say?"

He let the smoke dribble from his mouth. "I know they took hundreds of workers fifty or a hundred years to build," he said. "I just heard the man say that, of course. I know generations of the same families worked on a cathedral. I heard him say that, too. The men who began their life's work on them, they never lived to see the completion of their work. In that wise, bub, they're no different from the rest of us, right?" He laughed. Then his eyelids drooped again. His head nodded. He seemed to be snoozing. Maybe he was imagining himself in Portugal. The TV was showing another cathedral now. This one was in Germany. The Englishman's voice droned on. "Cathedrals," the blind man said. He sat up and rolled his head back and forth. "If you want the truth, bub, that's about all I know. What I just said. What I heard him say. But maybe you could describe one to me? I wish you'd do it. I'd like that. If you want to know, I really don't have a good idea."

I stared hard at the shot of the cathedral on the TV. How could I even begin to describe it? But say my life depended on it. Say my life was being threatened by an insane guy who said I had to do it or else.

I stared some more at the cathedral before the picture flipped off into the countryside. There was no use. I turned to the blind man and said, "To begin with, they're very tall." I was looking around the room for clues. "They reach way up. Up and up. Toward the sky. They're so big, some of them, they have to have these supports. To help hold them up, so to speak. These supports are called buttresses. They remind me of viaducts, for some reason. But maybe you don't know viaducts, either? Sometimes the cathedrals have devils and such carved into the front. Sometimes lords and ladies. Don't ask me why this is," I said.

He was nodding. The whole upper part of his body seemed to be moving back and forth.

"I'm not doing so good, am I?" I said.

He stopped nodding and leaned forward on the edge of the sofa. As he listened to me, he was running his fingers through his beard. I wasn't getting through to him, I could see that. But he waited for me to go on just the same. He nodded, like he was trying to encourage me. I tried to think what else to say. "They're really big," I said. "They're massive. They're built of stone. Marble, too, sometimes. In those olden days, when they built cathedrals, men wanted to be close to God. In those olden days, God was an important part of everyone's life. You could tell this from their cathedral-building. I'm sorry," I said, "but it looks like that's the best I can do for you. I'm just no good at it."

"That's all right, bub," the blind man said. "Hey, listen. I hope you don't mind my asking you. Can I ask you something? Let me ask you a simple question, yes or no. I'm just curious and there's no offense. You're my host. But let me ask if you are in any way religious? You don't mind my asking?"

I shook my head. He couldn't see that, though. A wink is the same as a nod to a blind man. "I guess I don't believe in it. In anything. Sometimes it's hard. You know what I'm saying?"

"Sure, I do," he said.

"Right," I said.

The Englishman was still holding forth. My wife sighed in her sleep. She drew a long breath and went on with her sleeping.

"You'll have to forgive me," I said. "But I can't tell you what a cathedral looks like. It just isn't in me to do it. I can't do any more than I've done."

The blind man sat very still, his head down, as he listened to me.

I said, "The truth is, cathedrals don't mean anything special to me. Nothing. Cathedrals. They're something to look at on late-night TV. That's all they are."

It was then that the blind man cleared his throat. He brought something up. He took a handkerchief from his back pocket. Then he said, "I get it, bub. It's okay. It happens. Don't worry about it," he said. "Hey, listen to me. Will you do me a favor? I got an idea. Why don't you find us some heavy paper? And a pen. We'll do something. We'll draw one together. Get us a pen and some heavy paper. Go on, bub, get the stuff," he said.

So I went upstairs. My legs felt like they didn't have any strength in them. They felt like they did after I'd done some running. In my wife's room, I looked around. I found some ballpoints in a little basket on her table. And then I tried to think where to look for the kind of paper he was talking about.

Downstairs, in the kitchen, I found a shopping bag with onion skins in the bottom of the bag. I emptied the bag and shook it. I brought it into the living room and sat down with it near his legs. I moved some things, smoothed the wrinkles from the bag, spread it out on the coffee table.

The blind man got down from the sofa and sat next to me on the carpet.

He ran his fingers over the paper. He went up and down the sides of the paper. The edges, even the edges. He fingered the corners.

"All right," he said. "All right, let's do her."

He found my hand, the hand with the pen. He closed his hand over my hand. "Go ahead, bub, draw," he said. "Draw. You'll see. I'll follow along with you. It'll be okay. Just begin now like I'm telling you. You'll see. Draw," the blind man said.

So I began. First I drew a box that looked like a house. It could have been the house I lived in. Then I put a roof on it. At either end of the roof, I drew spires. Crazy.

"Swell," he said. "Terrific. You're doing fine," he said. "Never thought anything like this could happen in your lifetime, did you, bub? Well, it's a strange life, we all know that. Go on now. Keep it up."

I put in windows with arches. I drew flying buttresses. I hung great doors. I couldn't stop. The TV station went off the air. I put down the pen and closed and opened my fingers. The blind man felt around over the paper. He moved the tips of his fingers over the paper, all over what I had drawn, and he nodded.

"Doing fine," the blind man said.

I took up the pen again, and he found my hand. I kept at it. I'm no artist. But I kept drawing just the same.

My wife opened up her eyes and gazed at us. She sat up on the sofa, her robe hanging open. She said, "What are you doing? Tell me, I want to know."

I didn't answer her.

The blind man said, "We're drawing a cathedral. Me and him are working on it. Press hard," he said to me. "That's right. That's good," he said. "Sure. You got it, bub. I can tell. You didn't think you could. But you can, can't you? You're cooking with gas now. You know what I'm saying? We're going to really have us something here in a minute. How's the old arm?" he said. "Put some people in there now. What's a cathedral without people?"

My wife said, "What's going on? Robert, what are you doing? What's going on?"

"It's all right," he said to her. "Close your eyes now," the blind man said to me.

I did it. I closed them just like he said.

"Are they closed?" he said. "Don't fudge."

"They're closed," I said.

"Keep them that way," he said. He said, "Don't stop now. Draw."

So we kept on with it. His fingers rode my fingers as my hand went over the paper. It was like nothing else in my life up to now.

Then he said, "I think that's it. I think you got it," he said. "Take a look. What do you think?"

But I had my eyes closed. I thought I'd keep them that way for a little longer. I thought it was something I ought to do.

"Well?" he said. "Are you looking?"

My eyes were still closed. I was in my house. I knew that. But I didn't feel like I was inside anything.

"It's really something," I said.

1981

Where Are You Going, Where Have You Been?

JOYCE CAROL OATES
[b. 1938]

For Bob Dylan

Her name was Connie. She was fifteen and she had a quick nervous giggling habit of craning her neck to glance into mirrors, or checking other people's faces to make sure her own was all right. Her mother, who noticed everything and knew everything and who hadn't much reason any longer to look at her own face, always scolded Connie about it. "Stop gawking at yourself, who are you? You think you're so pretty?" she would say. Connie would raise her eyebrows at these familiar complaints and look right through her mother, into a shadowy vision of herself as she was right at that moment: she knew she was pretty and that was everything. Her mother had been pretty once too, if you could believe those old snapshots in the album, but now her looks were gone and that was why she was always after Connie.

"Why don't you keep your room clean like your sister? How've you got your hair fixed—what the hell stinks? Hair spray? You don't see your sister using that junk."

Her sister June was twenty-four and still lived at home. She was a secretary in the high school Connie attended, and if that wasn't bad enough—with her in the same building—she was so plain and chunky and steady that Connie had to hear her praised all the time by her mother and her mother's sisters. June did this, June did that, she saved money and helped clean the house and cooked and Connie couldn't do a thing, her mind was all filled with trashy daydreams. Their father was away at work most of the time and when he came home he wanted supper and he read the newspaper at supper and after supper he went to bed. He didn't bother talking much to them, but around his bent head Connie's mother kept picking at her until Connie wished her mother was dead and she herself was dead and it was all over. "She makes me want to throw up sometimes," she complained to her friends. She had a high, breathless, amused voice which made everything she said a little forced, whether it was sincere or not.

There was one good thing: June went places with girl friends of hers, girls who were just as plain and steady as she, and so when Connie wanted to do that her mother had no objections. The father of Connie's best girl friend drove the girls the three miles to town and left them off at a shopping plaza, so that they could walk through the stores or go to a movie, and when he came to pick them up again at eleven he never bothered to ask what they had done.

They must have been familiar sights, walking around that shopping plaza in their shorts and flat ballerina slippers that always scuffed the sidewalk, with charm bracelets jingling on their thin wrists; they would lean together to whisper and laugh secretly if someone passed by who amused or interested them. Connie had long dark blond hair that drew anyone's eye to it, and she wore part of it pulled up on her head and puffed out and the rest of it she let fall down her back. She wore a pullover jersey blouse that looked one way when she was at home and another way when she was away from home. Everything about her had two sides to it, one for home and one for anywhere that was not home: her walk that could be childlike and bobbing, or languid enough to make anyone think she was hearing music in her head, her mouth which was pale and smirking most of the time, but bright and pink on these evenings out, her laugh which was cynical and drawling at home—"Ha, ha, very funny"—but high-pitched and nervous anywhere else, like the jingling of the charms on her bracelet.

Sometimes they did go shopping or to a movie, but sometimes they went across the highway, ducking fast across the busy road, to a drive-in restaurant where older kids hung out. The restaurant was shaped like a big bottle, though squatter than a real bottle, and on its cap was a revolving figure of a grinning boy who held a hamburger aloft. One night in midsummer they ran across, breathless with daring, and right away someone leaned out a car window and invited them over, but it was just a boy from high school they didn't like. It made them feel good to be able to ignore him. They went up through the maze of parked and cruising cars to the bright-lit, fly-infested restaurant, their faces pleased and expectant as if they were entering a sacred building that loomed out of the night to give them what haven and what blessing they yearned for. They sat at the counter and crossed their legs at the ankles, their thin shoulders rigid with excitement, and listened to the music that made everything so good: the music was always in the background like music at a church service, it was something to depend upon.

A boy named Eddie came in to talk with them. He sat backwards on his stool, turning himself jerkily around in semi-circles and then stopping and turning again, and after a while he asked Connie if she would like something to eat. She said she did and so she tapped her friend's arm on her way out—her friend pulled her face up into a brave droll look—and Connie said she would meet her at eleven, across the way. "I just hate to leave her like that," Connie said earnestly, but the boy said that she wouldn't be alone for long. So they went out to his car and on the way Connie couldn't help but let her eyes wander over the windshields and faces all around her, her face gleaming with the joy that had nothing to do with Eddie or even this place; it might have been the music. She drew her shoulders up and sucked in her breath with the pure pleasure of being alive, and just at that moment she happened to glance at a face just a few feet from hers. It was a boy with shaggy black hair, in a convertible jalopy painted gold. He stared at her and then his lips widened into a grin. Connie slit her eyes at him and turned away, but she couldn't help glancing back and there he was still watching her. He wagged a finger and laughed and said, "Gonna get you, baby," and Connie turned away again without Eddie noticing anything.

She spent three hours with him, at the restaurant where they ate hamburgers and drank Cokes in wax cups that were always sweating, and then down an alley a mile or so away, and when he left her off at five to eleven only the movie house was still open at the plaza. Her girl friend was there, talking with a boy. When Connie came up the two girls smiled at each other and Connie said, "How was the movie?" and the girl said, "*You* should know." They rode off with the girl's father, sleepy and pleased, and Connie couldn't help but look at the darkened shopping plaza with its big empty parking lot and its signs that were faded and ghostly now, and over at the drive-in restaurant where cars were still circling tirelessly. She couldn't hear the music at this distance.

Next morning June asked her how the movie was and Connie said, "So-so."

She and that girl and occasionally another girl went out several times a week that way, and the rest of the time Connie spent around the house—it was summer vacation—getting in her mother's way and thinking, dreaming, about the boys she met. But all the boys fell back and dissolved into a single face that was not even a face, but an idea, a feeling, mixed up with the urgent insistent pounding of the music and the humid night air of July. Connie's mother kept dragging her back to the daylight by finding things for her to do or saying suddenly, "What's this about the Pettinger girl?"

And Connie would say nervously, "Oh, her. That dope." She always drew thick clear lines between herself and such girls, and her mother was simple and kindly enough to believe her. Her mother was so simple, Connie thought, that it was maybe cruel to fool her so much. Her mother went scuffling around the house in old bedroom slippers and complained over the telephone to one sister about the other, then the other called up and the two of them complained about the third one. If June's name was mentioned her mother's tone was approving, and if Connie's name was mentioned it was disapproving. This did not really mean she disliked Connie and actually Connie thought that her mother preferred her to June because she was prettier, but the two of them kept up a pretense of exasperation, a sense that they were tugging and struggling over something of little value to either of them. Sometimes, over coffee, they were almost friends, but something would come up—some vexation that was like a fly buzzing suddenly around their heads—and their faces went hard with contempt.

One Sunday Connie got up at eleven—none of them bothered with church—and washed her hair so that it could dry all day long, in the sun. Her parents and sister were going to a barbecue at an aunt's house and Connie said no, she wasn't interested, rolling her eyes, to let mother know just what she thought of it. "Stay home alone then," her mother said sharply. Connie sat out back in a lawn chair and watched them drive away, her father quiet and bald, hunched around so that he could back the car out, her mother with a look that was still angry and not at all softened through the windshield, and in the back seat poor old June all dressed up as if she didn't know what a barbecue was, with all the running yelling kids and the flies. Connie sat with her eyes closed in the sun, dreaming and dazed with the warmth about her as if this were a kind of love, the caresses of love, and her mind slipped over onto thoughts of the boy she had been with the night before and how nice he had been, how sweet it always was, not the way someone like June would suppose but sweet, gentle, the way it was in movies and promised in songs; and when she opened her eyes she hardly knew where she was, the back yard ran off into weeds and a fenceline of trees and behind it the sky was perfectly blue and still. The asbestos "ranch house" that was now three years old startled her—it looked small. She shook her head as if to get awake.

It was too hot. She went inside the house and turned on the radio to drown out the quiet. She sat on the edge of her bed, barefoot, and listened for an hour and a half to a program called XYZ Sunday Jamboree, record after record of hard, fast, shrieking songs she sang along with, interspersed by exclamations from "Bobby King": "An' look here you girls at Napoleon's—Son and Charley want you to pay real close attention to this song coming up!"

And Connie paid close attention herself, bathed in a glow of slow-pulsed joy that seemed to rise mysteriously out of the music itself and lay languidly about the airless little room, breathed in and breathed out with each gentle rise and fall of her chest.

After a while she heard a car coming up the drive. She sat up at once, startled, because it couldn't be her father so soon. The gravel kept crunching all the way in from the road—the driveway was long—and Connie ran to the window. It was a car she didn't know. It was an open jalopy, painted a bright gold that caught the sun opaquely. Her heart began to pound and her fingers snatched at her hair, checking it, and she whispered "Christ. Christ," wondering how bad she looked. The car came to a stop at the side door and the horn sounded four short taps as if this were a signal Connie knew.

She went into the kitchen and approached the door slowly, then hung out the screen door, her bare toes curling down off the step. There were two boys in the car and now she recognized the driver: he had shaggy, shabby black hair that looked crazy as a wig and he was grinning at her.

"I ain't late, am I?" he said.

"Who the hell do you think you are?" Connie said.

"Toldja I'd be out, didn't I?"

"I don't even know who you are."

She spoke sullenly, careful to show no interest or pleasure, and he spoke in a fast bright monotone. Connie looked past him to the other boy, taking her time. He had fair brown hair, with a lock that fell onto his forehead. His sideburns gave him a fierce, embarrassed look, but so far he hadn't even bothered to glance at her. Both boys wore sunglasses. The driver's glasses were metallic and mirrored everything in miniature.

"You wanta come for a ride?" he said.

Connie smirked and let her hair fall loose over one shoulder.

"Don'tcha like my car? New paint job," he said. "Hey."

"What?"

"You're cute."

She pretended to fidget, chasing flies away from the door.

"Don'tcha believe me, or what?" he said.

"Look, I don't even know who you are," Connie said in disgust.

"Hey, Ellie's got a radio, see. Mine's broke down." He lifted his friend's arm and showed her the little transistor the boy was holding, and now Connie began to hear the music. It was the same program that was playing inside the house.

"Bobby King?" she said.

"I listen to him all the time. I think he's great."

"He's kind of great," Connie said reluctantly.

"Listen, that guy's *great*. He knows where the action is."

Connie blushed a little, because the glasses made it impossible for her to see just what this boy was looking at. She couldn't decide if she liked him or if he was just a jerk, and so she dawdled in the doorway and wouldn't come down or go back inside. She said, "What's all that stuff painted on your car?"

"Can'tcha read it?" He opened the door very carefully, as if he was afraid it might fall off. He slid out just as carefully, planting his feet firmly on the ground, the tiny metallic world in his glasses slowing down like gelatine hardening and in the midst of it Connie's bright green blouse. "This here is my name, to begin with," he said. ARNOLD FRIEND was written in tar-like black letters on the side, with a drawing of a round grinning face that reminded Connie of a pumpkin, except it wore sunglasses. "I wanta introduce myself, I'm Arnold Friend and that's my real name and I'm gonna be your friend, honey, and inside the car's Ellie Oscar, he's kinda shy." Ellie brought his transistor up to his shoulder and balanced it there. "Now these numbers are a secret code, honey," Arnold Friend explained. He read off the numbers 33, 19, 17 and raised his eyebrows at her to see what she thought of that, but she didn't think much of it. The left rear fender had been smashed and around it was written, on the gleaming gold background: DONE BY CRAZY WOMAN DRIVER. Connie had to laugh at that. Arnold Friend was pleased at her laughter and looked up at her. "Around the other side's a lot more—you wanta come and see them?"

"No."

"Why not?"

"Why should I?"

"Don'tcha wanta see what's on the car? Don'tcha wanta go for a ride?"

"I don't know."

"Why not?"

"I got things to do."

"Like what?"

"Things."

He laughed as if she had said something funny. He slapped his thighs. He was standing in a strange way, leaning back against the car as if he were balancing himself. He wasn't tall, only an inch or so taller than she would be if she came down to him. Connie liked the way he was dressed, which was the way all of them dressed: tight faded jeans stuffed into black, scuffed boots, a belt that pulled his waist in and showed how lean he was, and a white pull-over shirt that was a little soiled and showed the hard small muscles of his arms and shoulders. He looked as if he probably did hard work, lifting and carrying things. Even his neck looked muscular. And his face was a familiar face, somehow: the jaw and chin and cheeks slightly darkened, because he hadn't shaved for a day or two, and the nose long and hawk-like, sniffing as if she were a treat he was going to gobble up and it was all a joke.

"Connie, you ain't telling the truth. This is your day set aside for a ride with me and you know it," he said, still laughing. The way he straightened and recovered from his fit of laughing showed that it had been all fake.

"How do you know what my name is?" she said suspiciously.

"It's Connie."

"Maybe and maybe not."

"I know my Connie," he said, wagging his finger. Now she remembered him even better, back at the restaurant, and her cheeks warmed at the thought of how she sucked in her breath just at the moment she passed him—how she must have looked to him. And he had remembered her. "Ellie and I come out here especially for you," he said. "Ellie can sit in back. How about it?"

"Where?"

"Where what?"

"Where're we going?"

He looked at her. He took off the sunglasses and she saw how pale the skin around his eyes was, like holes that were not in shadow but instead in light. His eyes were like chips of broken glass that catch the light in an amiable way. He smiled. It was as if the idea of going for a ride somewhere, to some place, was a new idea to him.

"Just for a ride, Connie sweetheart."

"I never said my name was Connie," she said.

"But I know what it is. I know your name and all about you, lots of things," Arnold Friend said. He had not moved yet but stood still leaning back against the side of his jalopy. "I took a special interest in you, such a pretty girl, and found out all about you like I know your parents and sister are gone somewheres and I know where and how long they're going to be gone, and I know who you were with last night, and your best friend's name is Betty. Right?"

He spoke in a simple lilting voice, exactly as if he were reciting the words to a song. His smile assured her that everything was fine. In the car Ellie turned up the volume on his radio and did not bother to look around at them.

"Ellie can sit in the back seat," Arnold Friend said. He indicated his friend with a casual jerk of his chin, as if Ellie did not count and she could not bother with him.

"How'd you find out all that stuff?" Connie said.

"Listen: Betty Schultz and Tony Fitch and Jimmy Pettinger and Nancy Pettinger," he said, in a chant. "Raymond Stanley and Bob Hutter —"

"Do you know all those kids?"

"I know everybody."

"Look, you're kidding. You're not from around here."

"Sure."

"But—how come we never saw you before?"

"Sure you saw me before," he said. He looked down at his boots, as if he were a little offended. "You just don't remember."

"I guess I'd remember you," Connie said.

"Yeah?" He looked up at this, beaming. He was pleased. He began to mark time with the music from Ellie's radio, tapping his fists lightly together. Connie looked away from his smile to the car, which was painted so bright it almost hurt her eyes to look at it.

She looked at that name, ARNOLD FRIEND. And up at the front fender was an expression that was familiar—MAN THE FLYING SAUCERS. It was an expression kids had used the year before, but didn't use this year. She looked at it for a while as if the words meant something to her that she did not yet know.

"What're you thinking about? Huh?" Arnold Friend demanded. "Not worried about your hair blowing around in the car, are you?"

"No."

"Think I maybe can't drive good?"

"How do I know?"

"You're a hard girl to handle. How come?" he said. "Don't you know I'm your friend? Didn't you see me put my sign in the air when you walked by?"

"What sign?"

"My sign." And he drew an X in the air, leaning out toward her. They were maybe ten feet apart. After his hand fell back to his side the X was still in the air, almost visible. Connie let the screen door close and stood perfectly still inside it, listening to the music from her radio and the boy's blend together. She stared at Arnold Friend. He stood there so stiffly relaxed, pretending to be relaxed, with one hand idly on the door handle as if he were keeping himself up that way and had no intention of ever moving again. She recognized most things about him, the tight jeans that showed his thighs and buttocks and the greasy leather boots and the tight shirt, and even that slippery friendly smile of his, that sleepy dreamy smile that all the boys used to get across ideas they didn't want to put into words. She recognized all this and also the singsong way he talked, slightly mocking, kidding, but serious and a little melancholy, and she recognized the way he tapped one fist against the other in homage to the perpetual music behind him. But all these things did not come together.

She said suddenly, "Hey, how old are you?"

His smile faded. She could see then that he wasn't a kid, he was much older—thirty, maybe more. At this knowledge her heart began to pound faster.

"That's a crazy thing to ask. Can'tcha see I'm your own age?"

"Like hell you are."

"Or maybe a coupla years older, I'm eighteen."

"Eighteen?" she said doubtfully.

He grinned to reassure her and lines appeared at the corners of his mouth. His teeth were big and white. He grinned so broadly his eyes became slits and she saw how thick the lashes were, thick and black as if painted with a black tar-like material. Then he seemed to become embarrassed, abruptly, and looked over his shoulder at Ellie. "*Him*, he's crazy," he said. "Ain't he a riot, he's a nut, a real character." Ellie was still listening to the music. His sunglasses told nothing about what he was thinking. He wore a bright orange shirt unbuttoned halfway to show his chest, which was a pale, bluish chest and not muscular like Arnold Friend's. His shirt collar was turned up all around and the very tips of the collar pointed out past his chin as if they were protecting him. He was pressing the transistor radio up against his ear and sat there in a kind of daze, right in the sun.

"He's kinda strange," Connie said.

"Hey, she says you're kinda strange! Kinda strange!" Arnold Friend cried. He pounded on the car to get Ellie's attention. Ellie turned for the first time and Connie saw with shock that he wasn't a kid either—he had a fair, hairless face, cheeks reddened slightly as if the veins grew too close to the surface of his skin, the face of a forty-year-old baby. Connie felt a wave of dizziness rise in her at this sight and she stared at him as if waiting for something to change the shock of the moment, make it all right again. Ellie's lips kept shaping words, mumbling along with the words blasting his ear.

"Maybe you two better go away," Connie said faintly.

"What? How come?" Arnold Friend cried. "We come out here to take you for a ride. It's Sunday." He had the voice of the man on the radio now. It was the same voice, Connie thought. "Don'tcha know it's Sunday all day and honey, no matter who you were with last night today you're with Arnold Friend and don't you forget it!—Maybe you better step out here," he said, and this last was in a different voice. It was a little flatter, as if the heat was finally getting to him.

"No. I got things to do."

"Hey."

"You two better leave."

"We ain't leaving until you come with us."

"Like hell I am —"

"Connie, don't fool around with me. I mean—I mean, don't fool *around*," he said, shaking his head. He laughed incredulously. He placed his sunglasses on top of his head, carefully, as if he were indeed wearing a wig, and brought the stems down behind his ears. Connie stared at him, another wave of dizziness and fear rising in her so that for a moment he wasn't even in focus but was just a blur, standing there against his gold car, and she had the idea that he had driven up the driveway all right but had come from nowhere before that and belonged nowhere and that everything about him and even the music that was so familiar to her was only half real.

"If my father comes and sees you —"

"He ain't coming. He's at a barbecue."

"How do you know that?"

"Aunt Tillie's. Right now they're—uh—they're drinking. Sitting around," he said vaguely, squinting as if he were staring all the way to town and over to Aunt Tillie's back yard. Then the vision seemed to clear and he nodded energetically. "Yeah. Sitting around. There's your sister in a blue dress, huh? And high heels, the poor sad bitch—nothing like you, sweetheart! And your mother's helping some fat woman with the corn, they're cleaning the corn—husking the corn —"

"What fat woman?" Connie cried.

"How do I know what fat woman. I don't know every goddamn fat woman in the world!" Arnold Friend laughed.

"Oh, that's Mrs. Hornby. . . . Who invited her?" Connie said. She felt a little light-headed. Her breath was coming quickly.

"She's too fat. I don't like them fat. I like them the way you are, honey," he said, smiling sleepily at her. They stared at each other for a while, through the screen door. He said softly, "Now what you're going to do is this: you're going to come out that door. You're going to sit up front with me and Ellie's going to sit in the back, the hell with Ellie, right? This isn't Ellie's date. You're my date. I'm your lover, honey."

"What? You're crazy —"

"Yes, I'm your lover. You don't know what that is but you will," he said. "I know that too. I know all about you. But look: it's real nice and you couldn't ask for nobody better than me, or more polite. I always keep my word. I'll tell you how it is, I'm always nice at first, the first time. I'll hold you so tight you won't think you have to try to get away or pretend anything because you'll know you can't. And I'll come inside you where it's all secret and you'll give in to me and you'll love me —"

"Shut up! You're crazy!" Connie said. She backed away from the door. She put her hands against her ears as if she'd heard something terrible, something not meant for her. "People don't talk like that, you're crazy," she muttered. Her heart was almost too big now for her chest and its pumping made sweat break out all over her. She looked out to see Arnold Friend pause and then take a step toward the porch lurching. He almost fell. But, like a clever drunken man, he managed to catch his balance. He wobbled in his high boots and grabbed hold of one of the porch posts.

"Honey?" he said. "You still listening?"

"Get the hell out of here!"

"Be nice, honey. Listen."

"I'm going to call the police —"

He wobbled again and out of the side of his mouth came a fast spat curse, an aside not meant for her to hear. But even this "Christ!" sounded forced. Then he began to smile again. She watched this smile come, awkward as if he were smiling from inside a mask. His whole face was a mask, she thought wildly, tanned down onto his throat but then running out as if he had plastered make-up on his face but had forgotten about his throat.

"Honey—? Listen, here's how it is. I always tell the truth and I promise you this: I ain't coming in that house after you."

"You better not! I'm going to call the police if you—if you don't —"

"Honey," he said, talking right through her voice, "honey, I'm not coming in there but you are coming out here. You know why?"

She was panting. The kitchen looked like a place she had never seen before, some room she had run inside but which wasn't good enough, wasn't going to help her. The kitchen window had never had a curtain, after three years, and there were dishes in the sink for her to do—probably—and if you ran your hand across the table you'd probably feel something sticky there.

"You listening, honey? Hey?"

"— going to call the police —"

"Soon as you touch the phone I don't need to keep my promise and can come inside. You won't want that."

She rushed forward and tried to lock the door. Her fingers were shaking. "But why lock it," Arnold Friend said gently, talking right into her face. "It's just a screen door. It's just nothing." One of his boots was at a strange angle, as if his foot wasn't in it. It pointed out to the left, bent at the ankle. "I mean, anybody can break through a screen door and glass and wood and iron or anything else if he needs to, anybody at all and specially Arnold Friend. If the place got lit up with a fire, honey, you'd come runnin' out into my arms, right into my arms an' safe at home—like you knew I was your lover and'd stopped fooling around, I don't mind a nice shy girl but I don't like no fooling around." Part of those words were spoken with a slight rhythmic lilt, and Connie somehow recognized them—the echo of a song from last year, about a girl rushing into her boy friend's arms and coming home again —

Connie stood barefoot on the linoleum floor, staring at him. "What do you want?" she whispered.

"I want you," he said.

"What?"

"Seen you that night and thought, that's the one, yes sir. I never needed to look any more."

"But my father's coming back. He's coming to get me. I had to wash my hair first —" She spoke in a dry, rapid voice, hardly raising it for him to hear.

"No, your daddy is not coming and yes, you had to wash your hair and you washed it for me. It's nice and shining and all for me. I thank you, sweetheart," he said, with a mock bow, but again he almost lost his balance. He had to bend and adjust his boots. Evidently his feet did not go all the way down; the boots must have been stuffed with something so that he would seem taller. Connie stared out at him and behind him at Ellie in the car, who seemed to be looking off toward Connie's right, into nothing. Then Ellie said, pulling the words out of the air one after another as if he were just discovering them, "You want me to pull out the phone?"

"Shut your mouth and keep it shut," Arnold Friend said, his face red from bending over or maybe from embarrassment because Connie had seen his boots. "This ain't none of your business."

"What—what are you doing? What do you want?" Connie said. "If I call the police they'll get you, they'll arrest you —"

"Promise was not to come in unless you touch that phone, and I'll keep that promise," he said. He resumed his erect position and tried to force his shoulders back. He sounded like a hero in a movie, declaring something important. He spoke too loudly and it was as if he were speaking to someone behind Connie. "I ain't made plans for coming in that house where I don't belong but just for you to come out to me, the way you should. Don't you know who I am?"

"You're crazy," she whispered. She backed away from the door but did not want to go into another part of the house, as if this would give him permission to come through the door. "What do you . . . You're crazy, you. . . ."

"Huh? What're you saying, honey?"

Her eyes darted everywhere in the kitchen. She could not remember what it was, this room.

"This is how it is, honey: you come out and we'll drive away, have a nice ride. But if you don't come out we're gonna wait till your people come home and then they're all going to get it."

"You want that telephone pulled out?" Ellie said. He held the radio away from his ear and grimaced, as if without the radio the air was too much for him.

"I toldja shut up, Ellie," Arnold Friend said, "you're deaf, get a hearing aid, right? Fix yourself up. This little girl's no trouble and's gonna be nice to me, so Ellie keep to yourself, this ain't your date—right? Don't hem in on me, don't hog, don't crush, don't bird dog, don't trail me," he said in a rapid, meaningless voice, as if he were running through all the expressions he'd learned but was no longer sure which one of them was in style, then rushing on to new ones, making them up with his eyes closed. "Don't crawl under my fence, don't squeeze in my chipmunk hole, don't sniff my glue, suck my popsicle, keep your own greasy fingers on yourself!" He shaded his eyes and peered in at Connie, who was backed against the kitchen table. "Don't mind him, honey, he's just a creep. He's a dope. Right? I'm the boy for you and like I said, you come out here nice like a lady and give me your hand, and nobody else gets hurt, I mean, your nice old bald-headed daddy and your mummy and your sister in her high heels. Because listen: why bring them in this?"

"Leave me alone," Connie whispered.

"Hey, you know that old woman down the road, the one with the chickens and stuff—you know her?"

"She's dead!"

"Dead? What? You know her?" Arnold Friend said.

"She's dead —"

"Don't you like her?"

"She's dead—she's—she isn't here any more —"

"But don't you like her, I mean, you got something against her? Some grudge or something?" Then his voice dipped as if he were conscious of rudeness. He touched the sunglasses on top of his head as if to make sure they were still there. "Now you be a good girl."

"What are you going to do?"

"Just two things, or maybe three," Arnold Friend said. "But I promise it won't last long and you'll like me that way you get to like people you're close to. You will. It's all over for you here, so come on out. You don't want your people in any trouble, do you?"

She turned and bumped against a chair or something, hurting her leg, but she ran into the back room and picked up the telephone. Something roared in her ear, a tiny roaring, and she was so sick with fear that she could do nothing but listen to it—the telephone was clammy and very heavy and her fingers groped down to the dial but were too weak to touch it. She began to scream into the phone, into the roaring. She cried out, she cried for her mother, she felt her breath start jerking back and forth in her lungs as if it were something Arnold Friend was stabbing her with again and again with no tenderness. A noisy sorrowful wailing rose all about her and she was locked inside it the way she was locked inside this house.

After a while she could hear again. She was sitting on the floor, with her wet back against the wall.

Arnold Friend was saying from the door, "That's a good girl. Put the phone back."

She kicked the phone away from her.

"No, honey. Pick it up. Put it back right."

She picked it up and put it back. The dial tone stopped.

"That's a good girl. Now you come outside."

She was hollow with what had been fear but what was now just an emptiness. All that screaming had blasted it out of her. She sat, one leg cramped under her, and deep inside her brain was something like a pinpoint of light that kept going and would not let her relax. She thought, I'm not going to see my mother again. She thought, I'm not going to sleep in my bed again. Her bright green blouse was all wet.

Arnold Friend said, in a gentle-loud voice that was like a stage voice, "The place where you came from ain't there any more, and where you had in mind to go is cancelled out. This place you are now—inside your daddy's house—is nothing but a cardboard box I can knock down any time. You know that and always did know it. You hear me?"

She thought, I have got to think. I have got to know what to do.

"We'll go out to a nice field, out in the country here where it smells so nice and it's sunny," Arnold Friend said. "I'll have my arms tight around you so you won't need to try to get away and I'll show you what love is like, what it does. The hell with this house! It looks solid all right," he said. He ran a fingernail down the screen and the noise did not make Connie shiver, as it would have the day before. "Now put your hand on your heart, honey. Feel that? That feels solid too but we know better. Be nice to me, be sweet like you can because what else is there for a girl like you but to be sweet and pretty and give in?—and get away before her people get back?"

She felt her pounding heart. Her hand seemed to enclose it. She thought for the first time in her life that it was nothing that was hers, that belonged to her, but just a pounding, living thing inside this body that wasn't really hers either.

"You don't want them to get hurt," Arnold Friend went on. "Now get up, honey. Get up all by yourself."

She stood.

"Now turn this way. That's right. Come over to me—Ellie, put that away, didn't I tell you? You dope. You miserable creepy dope," Arnold Friend said. His words were not angry but only part of an incantation. The incantation was kindly. "Now come out through the kitchen to me honey and let's see a smile, try it, you're a brave sweet little girl and now they're eating corn and hotdogs cooked to bursting over an outdoor fire, and they don't know one thing about you and never did and honey you're better than them because not a one of them would have done this for you."

Connie felt the linoleum under her feet; it was cool. She brushed her hair back out of her eyes. Arnold Friend let go of the post tentatively and opened his arms for her, his elbows pointing in toward each other and his wrists limp, to show that this was an embarrassed embrace and a little mocking, he didn't want to make her self-conscious.

She put out her hand against the screen. She watched herself push the door slowly open as if she were back safe somewhere in the other doorway, watching this body and this head of long hair moving out into the sunlight where Arnold Friend waited.

"My sweet little blue-eyed girl," he said in a half-sung sigh that had nothing to do with her brown eyes but was taken up just the same by the vast sunlit reaches of the land behind him and on all sides of him—so much land that Connie had never seen before and did not recognize except to know that she was going to it.

1966

The Lesson

TONI CADE BAMBARA

[1939–1995]

Back in the days when everyone was old and stupid or young and foolish and me and Sugar were the only ones just right, this lady moved on our block with nappy hair and proper speech and no makeup. And quite naturally we laughed at her, laughed the way we did at the junk man who went about his business like he was some big-time president and his sorry-ass horse his secretary. And we kinda hated her too, hated the way we did the winos who cluttered up our parks and pissed on our handball walls and stank up our hallways and stairs so you couldn't halfway play hide-and-seek without a goddamn gas mask. Miss Moore was her name. The only woman on the block with no first name. And she was black as hell, cept for her feet, which were fish-white and spooky. And she was always planning these boring-ass things for us to do, us being my cousin, mostly, who lived on the block cause we all moved North the same time and to the same apartment then spread out gradual to breathe. And our parents would yank our heads into some kinda shape and crisp up our clothes so we'd be presentable for travel with Miss Moore, who always looked like she was going to church, though she never did. Which is just one of the things the grownups talked about when they talked behind her back like a dog. But when she came calling with some sachet she'd sewed up or some gingerbread she'd made or some book, why then they'd all be too embarrassed to turn her down and we'd get handed over all spruced up. She'd been to college and said it was only right that she should take responsibility for the young ones' education, and she not even related by marriage or blood. So they'd go for it. Specially Aunt Gretchen. She was the main gofer in the family. You got some ole dumb shit foolishness you want somebody to go for, you send for Aunt Gretchen. She been screwed into the go-along for so long, it's a blood-deep natural thing with her. Which is how she got saddled with me and Sugar and Junior in the first place while our mothers were in a la-de-da apartment up the block having a good ole time.

So this one day, Miss Moore rounds us all up at the mailbox and it's pure-dee hot and she's knockin herself out about arithmetic. And school suppose to let up in summer I heard, but she don't never let up. And the starch in my pinafore scratching the shit outta me and I'm really hating this nappy-head bitch and her goddamn college degree. I'd much rather go to the pool or to the show where it's cool. So me and Sugar leaning on the mailbox being surly, which is a Miss Moore word. And Flyboy checking out what everybody brought for lunch. And Fat Butt already wasting his peanut-butter-and-jelly sandwich like the pig he is. And Junebug punchin on Q.T.'s arm for potato chips. And Rosie Giraffe shifting from one hip to the other waiting for somebody to step on her foot or ask her if she from Georgia so she can kick ass, preferably Mercedes'. And Miss Moore asking us do we know what money is, like we a bunch of retards. I mean real money, she say, like it's only poker chips or monopoly papers we lay on the grocer. So right away I'm tired of this and say so. And would much rather snatch Sugar and go to the Sunset and terrorize the West Indian kids and take their hair ribbons and their money too. And Miss Moore files that remark away for next week's lesson on brotherhood, I can tell. And finally I say we oughta get to the subway cause it's cooler and besides we might meet some cute boys. Sugar done swiped her mama's lipstick, so we ready.

So we heading down the street and she's boring us silly about what things cost and what our parents make and how much goes for rent and how money ain't divided up right in this country. And then she gets to the part about we all poor and live in the slums, which I don't feature. And I'm ready to speak on that, but she steps out in the street and hails two cabs just like that. Then she hustles half the crew in with her and hands me a five-dollar bill and tells me to calculate 10 percent tip for the driver. And we're off. Me and Sugar and Junebug and Flyboy hangin out the window and hollering to everybody, putting lipstick on each other cause Flyboy a faggot anyway, and making farts with our sweaty armpits. But I'm mostly trying to figure how to spend this money. But they all fascinated with the meter ticking and Junebug starts laying bets as to how much it'll read when Flyboy can't hold his breath no more. Then Sugar lays bets as to how much it'll be when we get there. So I'm stuck. Don't nobody want to go for my plan, which is to jump out at the next light and run off to the first bar-b-que we can find. Then the driver tells us to get the hell out cause we there already. And the meter reads eighty-five cents. And I'm stalling to figure out the tip and Sugar say give him a dime. And I decide he don't need it bad as I do, so later for him. But then he tries to take off with Junebug foot still in the door so we talk about his mama something ferocious. Then we check out that we on Fifth Avenue and everybody dressed up in stockings. One lady in a fur coat, hot as it is. White folks crazy.

"This is the place," Miss Moore say, presenting it to us in the voice she uses at the museum. "Let's look in the windows before we go in."

"Can we steal?" Sugar asks very serious like she's getting the ground rules squared away before she plays. "I beg your pardon," say Miss Moore, and we fall out. So she leads us around the windows of the toy store and me and Sugar screamin, "This is mine, that's mine, I gotta have that, that was made for me, I was born for that," till Big Butt drowns us out.

"Hey, I'm going to buy that there."

"That there? You don't even know what it is, stupid."

"I do so," he say punchin on Rosie Giraffe. "It's a microscope."

"Whatcha gonna do with a microscope, fool?"

"Look at things."

"Like what, Ronald?" ask Miss Moore. And Big Butt ain't got the first notion. So here go Miss Moore gabbing about the thousands of bacteria in a drop of water and the somethinorother in a speck of blood and the million and one living things in the air around us is invisible to the naked eye. And what she say that for? Junebug go to town on that "naked" and we rolling. Then Miss Moore ask what it cost. So we all jam into the window smudgin it up and the price tag say $300. So then she ask how long'd take for Big Butt and Junebug to save up their allowances. "Too long," I say. "Yeh," adds Sugar, "outgrown it by that time." And Miss Moore say no, you never outgrow learning instruments. "Why, even medical students and interns and," blah, blah, blah. And we ready to choke Big Butt for bringing it up in the first damn place.

"This here costs four hundred eighty dollars," say Rosie Giraffe. So we pile up all over her to see what she pointin out. My eyes tell me it's a chunk of glass cracked with something heavy, and different-color inks dripped into the splits, then the whole thing put into a oven or something. But for $480 it don't make sense.

"That's a paperweight made of semi-precious stones fused together under tremendous pressure," she explains slowly, with her hands doing the mining and all the factory work.

"So what's a paperweight?" ask Rosie Giraffe.

"To weigh paper with, dumbbell," say Flyboy, the wise man from the East.

"Not exactly," say Miss Moore, which is what she say when you warm or way off too. "It's to weigh paper down so it won't scatter and make your desk untidy." So right away me and Sugar curtsy to each other and then to Mercedes who is more the tidy type.

"We don't keep paper on top of the desk in my class," say Junebug, figuring Miss Moore crazy or lyin one.

"At home, then," she say. "Don't you have a calendar and a pencil case and a blotter and a letter-opener on your desk at home where you do your homework?" And she know damn well what our homes look like cause she nosys around in them every chance she gets.

"I don't even have a desk," say Junebug. "Do we?"

"No. And I don't get no homework neither," say Big Butt.

"And I don't even have a home," say Flyboy like he do at school to keep the white folks off his back and sorry for him. Send this poor kid to camp posters, is his specialty.

"I do," says Mercedes. "I have a box of stationery on my desk and a picture of my cat. My godmother bought the stationery and the desk. There's a big rose on each sheet and the envelopes smell like roses."

"Who wants to know about your smelly-ass stationery," say Rosie Giraffe fore I can get my two cents in.

"It's important to have a work area all your own so that . . ."

"Will you look at this sailboat, please," say Flyboy, cutting her off and pointin to the thing like it was his. So once again we tumble all over each other to gaze at this magnificent thing in the toy store which is just big enough to maybe sail two kittens across the pond if you strap them to the posts tight. We all start reciting the price tag like we in assembly. "Handcrafted sailboat of fiberglass at one thousand one hundred ninety-five dollars."

"Unbelievable," I hear myself say and am really stunned. I read it again for myself just in case the group recitation put me in a trance. Same thing. For some reason this pisses me off. We look at Miss Moore and she lookin at us, waiting for I dunno what.

"Who'd pay all that when you can buy a sailboat set for a quarter at Pop's, a tube of glue for a dime, and a ball of string for eight cents? It must have a motor and a whole lot else besides," I say. "My sailboat cost me about fifty cents."

"But will it take water?" say Mercedes with her smart ass.

"Took mine to Alley Pond Park once," say Flyboy. "String broke. Lost it. Pity."

"Sailed mine in Central Park and it keeled over and sank. Had to ask my father for another dollar."

"And you got the strap," laugh Big Butt. "The jerk didn't even have a string on it. My old man wailed on his behind."

Little Q.T. was staring hard at the sailboat and you could see he wanted it bad. But he too little and somebody'd just take it from him. So what the hell. "This boat for kids, Miss Moore?"

"Parents silly to buy something like that just to get all broke up," say Rosie Giraffe.

"That much money it should last forever," I figure.

"My father'd buy it for me if I wanted it."

"Your father, my ass," say Rosie Giraffe getting a chance to finally push Mercedes.

"Must be rich people shop here," say Q.T.

"You are a very bright boy," say Flyboy. "What was your first clue?" And he rap him on the head with the back of his knuckles, since Q.T. the only one he could get away with. Though Q.T. liable to come up behind you years later and get his licks in when you half expect it.

"What I want to know is," I says to Miss Moore though I never talk to her, I wouldn't give the bitch that satisfaction, "is how much a real boat costs? I figure a thousand'd get you a yacht any day."

"Why don't you check that out," she says, "and report back to the group?" Which really pains my ass. If you gonna mess up a perfectly good swim day least you could do is have some answers. "Let's go in," she say like she got something up her sleeve. Only she don't lead the way. So me and Sugar turn the corner to where the entrance is, but when we get there I kinda hang back. Not that I'm scared, what's there to be afraid of, just a toy store. But I feel funny, shame. But what I got to be shamed about? Got as much right to go in as anybody. But somehow I can't seem to get hold of the door, so I step away from Sugar to lead. But she hangs back too. And I look at her and she looks at me and this is ridiculous. I mean, damn, I have never been shy about doing nothing or going nowhere. But then Mercedes steps up and then Rosie Giraffe and Big Butt crowd in behind and shove, and next thing we all stuffed into the doorway with only Mercedes squeezing past us, smoothing out her jumper and walking right down the aisle. Then the rest of us tumble in like a glued-together jigsaw done all wrong. And people lookin at us. And it's like the time me and Sugar crashed into the Catholic church on a dare. But once we got in there and everything so hushed and holy and the candles and the bowin and the handkerchiefs on all the drooping heads, I just couldn't go through with the plan. Which was for me to run up to the altar and do a tap dance while Sugar played the nose flute and messed around in the holy water. And Sugar kept given me the elbow. Then later teased me so bad I tied her up in the shower and turned it on and locked her in. And she'd be there till this day if Aunt Gretchen hadn't finally figured I was lying about the boarder takin a shower.

Same thing in the store. We all walkin on tiptoe and hardly touchin the games and puzzles and things. And I watched Miss Moore who is steady watchin us like she waitin for a sign. Like Mama Drewery watches the sky and sniffs the air and takes note of just how much slant is in the bird formation. Then me and Sugar bump smack into each other, so busy gazing at the toys, 'specially the sailboat. But we don't laugh and go into our fat-lady bump-stomach routine. We just stare at that price tag. Then Sugar run a finger over the whole boat. And I'm jealous and want to hit her. Maybe not her, but I sure want to punch somebody in the mouth.

"Watcha bring us here for, Miss Moore?"

"You sound angry, Sylvia. Are you mad about something?" Givin me one of them grins like she tellin a grown-up joke that never turns out to be funny. And she's lookin very closely at me like maybe she plannin to do my portrait from memory. I'm mad, but I won't give her that satisfaction. So I slouch around the store being very bored and say, "Let's go."

Me and Sugar at the back of the train watchin the tracks whizzin by large then small then getting gobbled up in the dark. I'm thinkin about this tricky toy I saw in the store. A clown that somersaults on a bar then does chin-ups just cause you yank lightly at his leg. Cost $35. I could see me askin my mother for a $35 birthday clown. "You wanna who that costs what?" she'd say, cocking her head to the side to get a better view of the hole in my head. Thirty-five dollars could buy new bunk beds for Junior and Gretchen's boy. Thirty-five dollars and the whole household could go visit Grand-daddy Nelson in the country. Thirty-five dollars would pay for the rent and the piano bill too. Who are these people that spend that much for performing clowns and $1000 for toy sailboats? What kinda work they do and how they live and how come we ain't in on it? Where we are is who we are, Miss Moore always pointin out. But it don't necessarily have to be that way, she always adds then waits for somebody to say that poor people have to wake up and demand their share of the pie and don't none of us know what kind of pie she talking about in the first damn place. But she ain't so smart cause I still got her four dollars from the taxi and she sure ain't gettin it. Messin up my day with this shit. Sugar nudges me in my pocket and winks.

Miss Moore lines us up in front of the mailbox where we started from, seem like years ago, and I got a headache for thinkin so hard. And we lean all over each other so we can hold up under the draggy-ass lecture she always finishes us off with at the end before we thank her for borin us to tears. But she just looks at us like she readin tea leaves. Finally she say, "Well, what did you think of F.A.O. Schwarz?"

Rosie Giraffe mumbles, "White folks crazy."

"I'd like to go there again when I get my birthday money," says Mercedes, and we shove her out the pack so she has to lean on the mailbox by herself.

"I'd like a shower. Tiring day," say Flyboy.

Then Sugar surprises me by sayin, "You know, Miss Moore, I don't think all of us here put together eat in a year what that sailboat costs." And Miss Moore lights up like somebody goosed her. "And?" she say, urging Sugar on. Only I'm standin on her foot so she don't continue.

"Imagine for a minute what kind of society it is in which some people can spend on a toy what it would cost to feed a family of six or seven. What do you think?"

"I think," say Sugar pushing me off her feet like she never done before, cause I whip her ass in a minute, "that this is not much of a democracy if you ask me. Equal chance to pursue happiness means an equal crack at the dough, don't it?" Miss Moore is besides herself and I am disgusted with Sugar's treachery. So I stand on her foot one more time to see if she'll shove me. She shuts up, and Miss Moore looks at me, sorrowfully I'm thinkin. And somethin weird is goin on, I can feel it in my chest.

"Anybody else learn anything today?" lookin dead at me. I walk away and Sugar has to run to catch up and don't even seem to notice when I shrug her arm off my shoulder.

"Well, we got four dollars anyway," she says.

"Uh, hunh."

"We could go to Hascombs and get half a chocolate layer and then go to the Sunset and still have plenty money for potato chips and ice cream sodas."

"Uh, hunh."

"Race you to Hascombs," she say.

We start down the block and she gets ahead which is O.K. by me cause I'm going to the West End and then over to the Drive to think this day through. She can run if she want to and even run faster. But ain't nobody gonna beat me at nuthin.

1972

Happy Endings

MARGARET ATWOOD
[b. 1939]

John and Mary meet.
What happens next?
If you want a happy ending, try A.

A. John and Mary fall in love and get married. They both have worthwhile and remunerative jobs which they find stimulating and challenging. They buy a charming house. Real estate values go up. Eventually, when they can afford live-in help, they have two children, to whom they are devoted. The children turn out well. John and Mary have a stimulating and challenging sex life and worthwhile friends. They go on fun vacations together. They retire. They both have hobbies which they find stimulating and challenging. Eventually they die. This is the end of the story.

B. Mary falls in love with John but John doesn't fall in love with Mary. He merely uses her body for selfish pleasure and ego gratification of a tepid kind. He comes to her apartment twice a week and she cooks him dinner, you'll notice that he doesn't even consider her worth the price of a dinner out, and after he's eaten the dinner he fucks her and after that he falls asleep, while she does the dishes so he won't think she's untidy, having all those dirty dishes lying around, and puts on fresh lipstick so she'll look good when he wakes up, but when he wakes up he doesn't even notice, he puts on his socks and his shorts and his pants and his shirt and his tie and his shoes, the reverse order from the one in which he took them off. He doesn't take off Mary's clothes, she takes them off herself, she acts as if she's dying for it every time, not because she likes sex exactly, she doesn't, but she wants John to think she does because if they do it often enough surely he'll get used to her, he'll come to depend on her and they will get married, but John goes out the door with hardly so much as a goodnight and three days later he turns up at six o'clock and they do the whole thing over again.

Mary gets run-down. Crying is bad for your face, everyone knows that and so does Mary but she can't stop. People at work notice. Her friends tell her John is a rat, a pig, a dog, he isn't good enough for her, but she can't believe it. Inside John, she thinks, is another John, who is much nicer. This other John will emerge like a butterfly from a cocoon, a Jack from a box, a pit from a prune, if the first John is only squeezed enough.

One evening John complains about the food. He has never complained about the food before. Mary is hurt.

Her friends tell her they've seen him in a restaurant with another woman, whose name is Madge. It's not even Madge that finally gets to Mary: it's the restaurant. John has never taken Mary to a restaurant. Mary collects all the sleeping pills and aspirins she can find, and takes them and a half a bottle of sherry. You can see what kind of a woman she is by the fact that it's not even whiskey. She leaves a note for John. She hopes he'll discover her and get her to the hospital in time and repent and then they can get married, but this fails to happen and she dies.

John marries Madge and everything continues as in A.

C. John, who is an older man, falls in love with Mary, and Mary, who is only twenty-two, feels sorry for him because he's worried about his hair falling out. She sleeps with him even though she's not in love with him. She met him at work. She's in love with someone called James, who is twenty-two also and not yet ready to settle down.

John on the contrary settled down long ago: this is what is bothering him. John has a steady, respectable job and is getting ahead in his field, but Mary isn't impressed by him, she's impressed by James, who has a motorcycle and a fabulous record collection. But James is often away on his motorcycle, being free. Freedom isn't the same for girls, so in the meantime Mary spends Thursday evenings with John. Thursdays are the only days John can get away.

John is married to a woman called Madge and they have two children, a charming house which they bought just before the real estate values went up, and hobbies which they find stimulating and challenging, when they have the time. John tells Mary how important she is to him, but of course he can't leave his wife because a commitment is a commitment. He goes on about this more than is necessary and Mary finds it boring, but older men can keep it up longer so on the whole she has a fairly good time.

One day James breezes in on his motorcycle with some top-grade California hybrid and James and Mary get higher than you'd believe possible and they climb into bed. Everything becomes very underwater, but along comes John, who has a key to Mary's apartment. He finds them stoned and entwined. He's hardly in any position to be jealous, considering Madge, but nevertheless he's overcome with despair. Finally he's middle-aged, in two years he'll be bald as an egg and he can't stand it. He purchases a handgun, saying he needs it for target practice—this is the thin part of the plot, but it can be dealt with later—and shoots the two of them and himself.

Madge, after a suitable period of mourning, marries an understanding man called Fred and everything continues as in A, but under different names.

D. Fred and Madge have no problems. They get along exceptionally well and are good at working out any little difficulties that may arise. But their charming house is by the seashore and one day a giant tidal wave approaches. Real estate values go down. The rest of the story is about what caused the tidal wave and how they escape from it. They do, though thousands drown, but Fred and Madge are virtuous and lucky. Finally on high ground they clasp each other, wet and dripping and grateful, and continue as in A.

E. Yes, but Fred has a bad heart. The rest of the story is about how kind and understanding they both are until Fred dies. Then Madge devotes herself to charity work until the end of A. If you like, it can be "Madge," "cancer," "guilty and confused," and "bird watching."

F. If you think this is all too bourgeois, make John a revolutionary and Mary a counterespionage agent and see how far that gets you. Remember, this is Canada. You'll still end up with A, though in between you may get a lustful brawling saga of passionate involvement, a chronicle of our times, sort of.

You'll have to face it, the endings are the same however you slice it. Don't be deluded by any other endings, they're all fake, either deliberately fake, with malicious intent to deceive, or just motivated by excessive optimism if not by downright sentimentality.

The only authentic ending is the one provided here:

John and Mary die. John and Mary die. John and Mary die.

So much for endings. Beginnings are always more fun. True connoisseurs, however, are known to favor the stretch in between, since it's the hardest to do anything with.

That's about all that can be said for plots, which anyway are just one thing after another, a what and a what and a what.

Now try How and Why.

1983

Everyday Use

ALICE WALKER

[b. 1944]

For Your Grandmama

I will wait for her in the yard that Maggie and I made so clean and wavy yesterday afternoon. A yard like this is more comfortable than most people know. It is not just a yard. It is like an extended living room. When the hard clay is swept clean as a floor and the fine sand around the edges lined with tiny, irregular grooves, anyone can come and sit and look up into the elm tree and wait for the breezes that never come inside the house.

Maggie will be nervous until after her sister goes: she will stand hopelessly in corners, homely and ashamed of the burn scars down her arms and legs, eying her sister with a mixture of envy and awe. She thinks her sister has held life always in the palm of one hand, that "no" is a word the world never learned to say to her.

You've no doubt seen those TV shows where the child who has "made it" is confronted, as a surprise, by her own mother and father, tottering in weakly from backstage. (A pleasant surprise, of course: What would they do if parent and child came on the show only to curse out and insult each other?) On TV mother and child embrace and smile into each other's faces. Sometimes the mother and father weep, the child wraps them in her arms and leans across the table to tell how she would not have made it without their help. I have seen these programs.

Sometimes I dream a dream in which Dee and I are suddenly brought together on a TV program of this sort. Out of a dark and soft-seated limousine I am ushered into a bright room filled with many people. There I meet a smiling, gray, sporty man like Johnny

Carson[1] who shakes my hand and tells me what a fine girl I have. Then we are on the stage and Dee is embracing me with tears in her eyes. She pins on my dress a large orchid, even though she has told me once that she thinks orchids are tacky flowers.

In real life I am a large, big-boned woman with rough, man-working hands. In the winter I wear flannel nightgowns to bed and overalls during the day. I can kill and clean a hog as mercilessly as a man. My fat keeps me hot in zero weather. I can work outside all day, breaking ice to get water for washing; I can eat pork liver cooked over the open fire minutes after it comes steaming from the hog. One winter I knocked a bull calf straight in the brain between the eyes with a sledge hammer and had the meat hung up to chill before nightfall. But of course all this does not show on television. I am the way my daughter would want me to be: a hundred pounds lighter, my skin like an uncooked barley pancake. My hair glistens in the hot bright lights. Johnny Carson has much to do to keep up with my quick and witty tongue.

But that is a mistake. I know even before I wake up. Who ever knew a Johnson with a quick tongue? Who can even imagine me looking a strange white man in the eye? It seems to me I have talked to them always with one foot raised in flight, with my head turned in whichever way is farthest from them. Dee, though. She would always look anyone in the eye. Hesitation was no part of her nature.

"How do I look, Mama?" Maggie says, showing just enough of her thin body enveloped in pink skirt and red blouse for me to know she's there, almost hidden by the door.

"Come out into the yard," I say.

Have you ever seen a lame animal, perhaps a dog run over by some careless person rich enough to own a car, sidle up to someone who is ignorant enough to be kind to him? That is the way my Maggie walks. She has been like this, chin on chest, eyes on ground, feet in shuffle, ever since the fire that burned the other house to the ground.

Dee is lighter than Maggie, with nicer hair and a fuller figure. She's a woman now, though sometimes I forget. How long ago was it that the other house burned? Ten, twelve years? Sometimes I can still hear the flames and feel Maggie's arms sticking to me, her hair

[1]Johnny Carson (1925–2005) was a late-night talk-show host and comedian. *The Tonight Show* starring Carson was on the air from 1962 to 1992.

smoking and her dress falling off her in little black papery flakes. Her eyes seemed stretched open, blazed open by the flames reflected in them. And Dee. I see her standing off under the sweet gum tree she used to dig gum out of; a look of concentration on her face as she watched the last dingy gray board of the house fall in toward the red-hot brick chimney. Why don't you do a dance around the ashes? I'd want to ask her. She had hated the house that much.

I used to think she hated Maggie, too. But that was before we raised the money, the church and me, to send her to Augusta to school. She used to read to us without pity; forcing words, lies, other folks' habits, whole lives upon us two, sitting trapped and ignorant underneath her voice. She washed us in a river of make-believe, burned us with a lot of knowledge we didn't necessarily need to know. Pressed us to her with the serious way she read, to shove us away at just the moment, like dimwits, we seemed about to understand.

Dee wanted nice things. A yellow organdy dress to wear to her graduation from high school; black pumps to match a green suit she'd made from an old suit somebody gave me. She was determined to stare down any disaster in her efforts. Her eyelids would not flicker for minutes at a time. Often I fought off the temptation to shake her. At sixteen she had a style of her own: and knew what style was.

I never had an education myself. After second grade the school was closed down. Don't ask me why: in 1927 colored asked fewer questions than they do now. Sometimes Maggie reads to me. She stumbles along good-naturedly but can't see well. She knows she is not bright. Like good looks and money, quickness passed her by. She will marry John Thomas (who has mossy teeth in an earnest face) and then I'll be free to sit here and I guess just sing church songs to myself. Although I never was a good singer. Never could carry a tune. I was always better at a man's job. I used to love to milk till I was hooked in the side in '49. Cows are soothing and slow and don't bother you, unless you try to milk them the wrong way.

I have deliberately turned my back on the house. It is three rooms, just like the one that burned, except the roof is tin; they don't make shingle roofs any more. There are no real windows, just some holes cut in the sides, like the portholes in a ship, but not round and not square, with rawhide holding the shutters up on the outside. This house is in a pasture, too, like the other one. No doubt when Dee sees it she will want to tear it down. She wrote me once that no matter where we "choose" to live, she will manage to come see us. But she will never bring her friends. Maggie and I thought about this and Maggie asked me, "Mama, when did Dee ever *have* any friends?"

She had a few. Furtive boys in pink shirts hanging about on washday after school. Nervous girls who never laughed. Impressed with her they worshipped the well-turned phrase, the cute shape, the scalding humor that erupted like bubbles in lye. She read to them.

When she was courting Jimmy T she didn't have much time to pay to us, but turned all her faultfinding power on him. He *flew* to marry a cheap city girl from a family of ignorant flashy people. She hardly had time to recompose herself.

When she comes I will meet—but there they are!

Maggie attempts to make a dash for the house, in her shuffling way, but I stay her with my hand. "Come back here," I say. And she stops and tries to dig a well in the sand with her toe.

It is hard to see them clearly through the strong sun. But even the first glimpse of leg out of the car tells me it is Dee. Her feet were always neat-looking, as if God himself had shaped them with a certain style. From the other side of the car comes a short, stocky man. Hair is all over his head a foot long and hanging from his chin like a kinky mule tail. I hear Maggie suck in her breath. "Uhnnnh," is what it sounds like. Like when you see the wriggling end of a snake just in front of your foot on the road. "Uhnnnh."

Dee next. A dress down to the ground, in this hot weather. A dress so loud it hurts my eyes. There are yellows and oranges enough to throw back the light of the sun. I feel my whole face warming from the heat waves it throws out. Earrings gold, too, and hanging down to her shoulders. Bracelets dangling and making noises when she moves her arm up to shake the folds of the dress out of her armpits. The dress is loose and flows, and as she walks closer, I like it. I hear Maggie go "Uhnnnh" again. It is her sister's hair. It stands straight up like the wool on a sheep. It is black as night and around the edges are two long pigtails that rope about like small lizards disappearing behind her ears.

"Wa-su-zo-Tean-o!" she says, coming on in that gliding way the dress makes her move. The short stocky fellow with the hair to his navel is all grinning and he follows up with "Asalamalakim, my mother and sister!" He moves to hug Maggie but she falls back, right up against the back of my chair. I feel her trembling there and when I look up I see the perspiration falling off her chin.

"Don't get up," says Dee. Since I am stout it takes something of a push. You can see me trying to move a second or two before I make it. She turns, showing white heels through her sandals, and goes back to the car. Out she peeks next with a Polaroid. She stoops down quickly and lines up picture after picture of me sitting there in front of the house with Maggie cowering behind me. She never takes a shot without making sure the house is included. When a cow comes nibbling around the edge of the yard she snaps it and me and Maggie *and* the house. Then she puts the Polaroid in the back seat of the car, and comes up and kisses me on the forehead.

Meanwhile Asalamalakim is going through motions with Maggie's hand. Maggie's hand is as limp as a fish, and probably as cold, despite the sweat, and she keeps trying to pull it back. It looks like Asalamalakim wants to shake hands but wants to do it fancy. Or maybe he don't know how people shake hands. Anyhow, he soon gives up on Maggie.

"Well," I say. "Dee."

"No, Mama," she says. "Not 'Dee,' Wangero Leewanika Kemanjo!"

"What happened to 'Dee'?" I wanted to know.

"She's dead," Wangero said. "I couldn't bear it any longer, being named after the people who oppress me."

"You know as well as me you was named after your aunt Dicie," I said. Dicie is my sister. She named Dee. We called her "Big Dee" after Dee was born.

"But who was *she* named after?" asked Wangero.

"I guess after Grandma Dee," I said.

"And who was she named after?" asked Wangero.

"Her mother," I said, and saw Wangero was getting tired. "That's about as far back as I can trace it," I said. Though, in fact, I probably could have carried it back beyond the Civil War through the branches.

"Well," said Asalamalakim, "there you are."

"Uhnnnh," I heard Maggie say.

"There I was not," I said, "before 'Dicie' cropped up in our family, so why should I try to trace it that far back?"

He just stood there grinning, looking down on me like somebody inspecting a Model A car. Every once in a while he and Wangero sent eye signals over my head.

"How do you pronounce this name?" I asked.

"You don't have to call me by it if you don't want to," said Wangero.

"Why shouldn't I?" I asked. "If that's what you want us to call you, we'll call you."

"I know it might sound awkward at first," said Wangero.

"I'll get used to it," I said. "Ream it out again."

Well, soon we got the name out of the way. Asalamalakim had a name twice as long and three times as hard. After I tripped over it two or three times he told me to just call him Hakim-a-barber. I wanted to ask him was he a barber, but I didn't really think he was, so I didn't ask.

"You must belong to those beef-cattle peoples down the road," I said. They said "Asalamalakim" when they met you, too, but they didn't shake hands. Always too busy: feeding the cattle, fixing the fences, putting up salt-lick shelters, throwing down hay. When the white folks poisoned some of the herd the men stayed up all night with rifles in their hands. I walked a mile and a half just to see the sight.

Hakim-a-barber said, "I accept some of their doctrines, but farming and raising cattle is not my style." (They didn't tell me, and I didn't ask, whether Wangero (Dee) had really gone and married him.)

We sat down to eat and right away he said he didn't eat collards and pork was unclean. Wangero, though, went on through the chitlins and corn bread, the greens and everything else. She talked a blue streak over the sweet potatoes. Everything delighted her. Even the fact that we still used the benches her daddy made for the table when we couldn't afford to buy chairs.

"Oh, Mama!" she cried. Then turned to Hakim-a-barber. "I never knew how lovely these benches are. You can feel the rump prints," she said, running her hands underneath her and along the bench. Then she gave a sigh and her hand closed over Grandma Dee's butter dish. "That's it!" she said. "I knew there was something I wanted to ask you if I could have." She jumped up from the table and went over in the corner where the churn stood, the milk in it clabber by now. She looked at the churn and looked at it.

"This churn top is what I need," she said. "Didn't Uncle Buddy whittle it out of a tree you all used to have?"

"Yes," I said.

"Uh huh," she said happily. "And I want the dasher, too."

"Uncle Buddy whittle that, too?" asked the barber.

Dee (Wangero) looked up at me.

"Aunt Dee's first husband whittled the dash," said Maggie so low you almost couldn't hear her. "His name was Henry, but they called him Stash."

"Maggie's brain is like an elephant's," Wangero said, laughing. "I can use the churn top as a centerpiece for the alcove table," she said, sliding a plate over the churn, "and I'll think of something artistic to do with the dasher."

When she finished wrapping the dasher the handle stuck out. I took it for a moment in my hands. You didn't even have to look close to see where hands pushing the dasher up and down to make butter had left a kind of sink in the wood. In fact, there were a lot of small sinks; you could see where thumbs and fingers had sunk into the wood. It was beautiful light yellow wood, from a tree that grew in the yard where Big Dee and Stash had lived.

After dinner Dee (Wangero) went to the trunk at the foot of my bed and started rifling through it. Maggie hung back in the kitchen over the dishpan. Out came Wangero with two quilts. They had been pieced by Grandma Dee and then Big Dee and me had hung them on the quilt frames on the front porch and quilted them. One was in the Lone Star pattern. The other was Walk Around the Mountain. In both of them were scraps of dresses Grandma Dee had worn fifty and more years ago. Bits and pieces of Grandpa Jarrell's Paisley shirts. And one teeny faded blue piece, about the size of a penny matchbox, that was from Great Grandpa Ezra's uniform that he wore in the Civil War.

"Mama," Wangero said sweet as a bird. "Can I have these old quilts?"

I heard something fall in the kitchen, and a minute later the kitchen door slammed.

"Why don't you take one or two of the others?" I asked. "These old things was just done by me and Big Dee from some tops your grandma pieced before she died."

"No," said Wangero. "I don't want those. They are stitched around the borders by machine."

"That'll make them last better," I said.

"That's not the point," said Wangero. "These are all pieces of dresses Grandma used to wear. She did all this stitching by hand. Imagine!" She held the quilts securely in her arms, stroking them.

"Some of the pieces, like those lavender ones, come from old clothes her mother handed down to her," I said, moving up to touch the quilts. Dee (Wangero) moved back just enough so that I couldn't reach the quilts. They already belonged to her.

"Imagine!" she breathed again, clutching them closely to her bosom.

"The truth is," I said, "I promised to give them quilts to Maggie, for when she marries John Thomas."

She gasped like a bee had stung her.

"Maggie can't appreciate these quilts!" she said. "She'd probably be backward enough to put them to everyday use."

"I reckon she would," I said. "God knows I been saving 'em for long enough with nobody using 'em. I hope she will!" I didn't want to bring up how I had offered Dee (Wangero) a quilt when she went away to college. Then she had told me they were old-fashioned, out of style.

"But they're *priceless*!" she was saying now, furiously; for she has a temper. "Maggie would put them on the bed and in five years they'd be in rags. Less than that!"

"She can always make some more," I said. "Maggie knows how to quilt."

Dee (Wangero) looked at me with hatred. "You just will not understand. The point is these quilts, *these* quilts!"

"Well," I said, stumped. "What would *you* do with them?"

"Hang them," she said. As if that was the only thing you *could* do with quilts.

Maggie by now was standing in the door. I could almost hear the sound her feet made as they scraped over each other.

"She can have them, Mama," she said, like somebody used to never winning anything, or having anything reserved for her. "I can 'member Grandma Dee without the quilts."

I looked at her hard. She had filled her bottom lip with checkerberry snuff and it gave her face a kind of dopey, hangdog look. It was Grandma Dee and Big Dee who taught her how to quilt herself. She stood there with her scarred hands hidden in the folds of her skirt. She looked at her sister with something like fear but she wasn't mad at her. This was Maggie's portion. This was the way she knew God to work.

When I looked at her like that something hit me in the top of my head and ran down to the soles of my feet. Just like when I'm in church and the spirit of God touches me and I get happy and shout. I did something I never had done before: hugged Maggie to me, then dragged her on into the room, snatched the quilts out of

Miss Wangero's hands and dumped them into Maggie's lap. Maggie just sat there on my bed with her mouth open.

"Take one or two of the others," I said to Dee.

But she turned without a word and went out to Hakim-a-barber.

"You just don't understand," she said, as Maggie and I came out to the car.

"What don't I understand?" I wanted to know.

"Your heritage," she said. And then she turned to Maggie, kissed her, and said, "You ought to try to make something of yourself, too, Maggie. It's really a new day for us. But from the way you and Mama still live you'd never know it."

She put on some sunglasses that hid everything above the tip of her nose and her chin.

Maggie smiled; maybe at the sunglasses. But a real smile, not scared. After we watched the car dust settle I asked Maggie to bring me a dip of snuff. And then the two of us sat there just enjoying, until it was time to go in the house and go to bed.

1973

The Things They Carried

TIM O'BRIEN

[b. 1946]

First Lieutenant Jimmy Cross carried letters from a girl named Martha, a junior at Mount Sebastian College in New Jersey. They were not love letters, but Lieutenant Cross was hoping, so he kept them folded in plastic at the bottom of his rucksack. In the late afternoon, after a day's march, he would dig his foxhole, wash his hands under a canteen, unwrap the letters, hold them with the tips of his fingers, and spend the last hour of light pretending. He would imagine romantic camping trips into the White Mountains in New Hampshire. He would sometimes taste the envelope flaps, knowing her tongue had been there. More than anything, he wanted Martha to love him as he loved her, but the letters were mostly chatty, elusive on the matter of love. She was a virgin, he was almost sure. She was an English major at Mount Sebastian, and she wrote beautifully about her professors and roommates and midterm exams, about her respect for Chaucer and her great affection for Virginia Woolf. She often quoted lines of poetry; she never mentioned the war, except to say, Jimmy, take care of yourself. The letters weighed ten ounces. They were signed "Love, Martha," but Lieutenant Cross understood that "Love" was only a way of signing and did not mean what he sometimes pretended it meant. At dusk, he would carefully return the letters to his rucksack. Slowly, a bit distracted, he would get up and move among his men, checking the perimeter, then at full dark he would return to his hole and watch the night and wonder if Martha was a virgin.

The things they carried were largely determined by necessity. Among the necessities or near necessities were P-38 can openers, pocket knives, heat tabs, wrist watches, dog tags, mosquito repellant, chewing gum, candy, cigarettes, salt tablets, packets of Kool-Aid, lighters, matches, sewing kits, Military Payment Certificates,

C rations,[1] and two or three canteens of water. Together, these items weighed between fifteen and twenty pounds, depending upon a man's habits or rate of metabolism. Henry Dobbins, who was a big man, carried extra rations; he was especially fond of canned peaches in heavy syrup over pound cake. Dave Jensen, who practiced field hygiene, carried a toothbrush, dental floss, and several hotel-size bars of soap he'd stolen on R&R in Sydney, Australia. Ted Lavender, who was scared, carried tranquilizers until he was shot in the head outside the village of Than Khe in mid-April. By necessity, and because it was SOP,[2] they all carried steel helmets that weighed five pounds including the liner and camouflage cover. They carried the standard fatigue jackets and trousers. Very few carried underwear. On their feet they carried jungle boots—2.1 pounds—and Dave Jensen carried three pairs of socks and a can of Dr. Scholl's foot powder as a precaution against trench foot. Until he was shot, Ted Lavender carried six or seven ounces of premium dope, which for him was a necessity. Mitchell Sanders, the RTO,[3] carried condoms. Norman Bowker carried a diary. Rat Kiley carried comic books. Kiowa, a devout Baptist, carried an illustrated New Testament that had been presented to him by his father, who taught Sunday school in Oklahoma City, Oklahoma. As a hedge against bad times, however, Kiowa also carried his grandmother's distrust of the white man, his grandfather's old hunting hatchet. Necessity dictated. Because the land was mined and booby-trapped, it was SOP for each man to carry a steel-centered, nylon-covered flak jacket, which weighed 6.7 pounds, but which on hot days seemed much heavier. Because you could die so quickly, each man carried at least one large compress bandage, usually in the helmet band for easy access. Because the nights were cold, and because the monsoons were wet, each carried a green plastic poncho that could be used as a raincoat or ground sheet or makeshift tent. With its quilted liner, the poncho weighed almost two pounds, but it was worth every ounce. In April, for instance, when Ted Lavender was shot, they used his poncho to wrap him up, then to carry him across the paddy, then to lift him into the chopper that took him away.

They were called legs or grunts.

To carry something was to "hump" it, as when Lieutenant Jimmy Cross humped his love for Martha up the hills and through the

[1]Combat rations.
[2]Standard operating procedure.
[3]Radiotelephone operator.

swamps. In its intransitive form, "to hump" meant "to walk," or "to march," but it implied burdens far beyond the intransitive.

Almost everyone humped photographs. In his wallet, Lieutenant Cross carried two photographs of Martha. The first was a Kodachrome snapshot signed "Love," though he knew better. She stood against a brick wall. Her eyes were gray and neutral, her lips slightly open as she stared straight-on at the camera. At night, sometimes, Lieutenant Cross wondered who had taken the picture, because he knew she had boyfriends, because he loved her so much, and because he could see the shadow of the picture taker spreading out against the brick wall. The second photograph had been clipped from the 1968 Mount Sebastian yearbook. It was an action shot—women's volleyball—and Martha was bent horizontal to the floor, reaching, the palms of her hands in sharp focus, the tongue taut, the expression frank and competitive. There was no visible sweat. She wore white gym shorts. Her legs, he thought, were almost certainly the legs of a virgin, dry and without hair, the left knee cocked and carrying her entire weight, which was just over one hundred pounds. Lieutenant Cross remembered touching that left knee. A dark theater, he remembered, and the movie was *Bonnie and Clyde*, and Martha wore a tweed skirt, and during the final scene, when he touched her knee, she turned and looked at him in a sad, sober way that made him pull his hand back, but he would always remember the feel of the tweed skirt and the knee beneath it and the sound of the gunfire that killed Bonnie and Clyde, how embarrassing it was, how slow and oppressive. He remembered kissing her good night at the dorm door. Right then, he thought, he should've done something brave. He should've carried her up the stairs to her room and tied her to the bed and touched that left knee all night long. He should've risked it. Whenever he looked at the photographs, he thought of new things he should've done.

What they carried was partly a function of rank, partly of field specialty.

As a first lieutenant and platoon leader, Jimmy Cross carried a compass, maps, code books, binoculars, and a .45-caliber pistol that weighed 2.9 pounds fully loaded. He carried a strobe light and the responsibility for the lives of his men.

As an RTO, Mitchell Sanders carried the PRC-25 radio, a killer, twenty-six pounds with its battery.

As a medic, Rat Kiley carried a canvas satchel filled with morphine and plasma and malaria tablets and surgical tape and comic books and all the things a medic must carry, including M&M's for especially bad wounds, for a total weight of nearly twenty pounds.

As a big man, therefore a machine gunner, Henry Dobbins carried the M-60, which weighed twenty-three pounds unloaded, but which was almost always loaded. In addition, Dobbins carried between ten and fifteen pounds of ammunition draped in belts across his chest and shoulders.

As PFCs[4] or Spec 4s,[5] most of them were common grunts and carried the standard M-16 gas-operated assault rifle. The weapon weighed 7.5 pounds unloaded, 8.2 pounds with its full twenty-round magazine. Depending on numerous factors, such as topography and psychology, the riflemen carried anywhere from twelve to twenty magazines, usually in cloth bandoliers, adding on another 8.4 pounds at minimum, fourteen pounds at maximum. When it was available, they also carried M-16 maintenance gear—rods and steel brushes and swabs and tubes of LSA oil[6]—all of which weighed about a pound. Among the grunts, some carried the M-79 grenade launcher, 5.9 pounds unloaded, a reasonably light weapon except for the ammunition, which was heavy. A single round weighed ten ounces. The typical load was twenty-five rounds. But Ted Lavender, who was scared, carried thirty-four rounds when he was shot and killed outside Than Khe, and he went down under an exceptional burden, more than twenty pounds of ammunition, plus the flak jacket and helmet and rations and water and toilet paper and tranquilizers and all the rest, plus the unweighed fear. He was dead weight. There was no twitching or flopping. Kiowa, who saw it happen, said it was like watching a rock fall, or a big sandbag or something—just boom, then down—not like the movies where the dead guy rolls around and does fancy spins and goes ass over teakettle—not like that, Kiowa said, the poor bastard just flat-fuck fell. Boom. Down. Nothing else. It was a bright morning in mid-April. Lieutenant Cross felt the pain. He blamed himself. They stripped off Lavender's canteens and ammo, all the heavy things, and Rat Kiley said the obvious, the guy's dead, and Mitchell Sanders used his radio to

[4]Privates first class.
[5]Specialists fourth class, rank equivalent to that of corporal.
[6]Lube-small-arms oil.

report one U.S. KIA[7] and to request a chopper. Then they wrapped Lavender in his poncho. They carried him out to a dry paddy, established security, and sat smoking the dead man's dope until the chopper came. Lieutenant Cross kept to himself. He pictured Martha's smooth young face, thinking he loved her more than anything, more than his men, and now Ted Lavender was dead because he loved her so much and could not stop thinking about her. When the dust-off arrived, they carried Lavender aboard. Afterward they burned Than Khe. They marched until dusk, then dug their holes, and that night Kiowa kept explaining how you had to be there, how fast it was, how the poor guy just dropped like so much concrete. Boom-down, he said. Like cement.

In addition to the three standard weapons—the M-60, M-16, and M-79—they carried whatever presented itself, or whatever seemed appropriate as a means of killing or staying alive. They carried catch-as-catch-can. At various times, in various situations, they carried M-14s and CAR-15s and Swedish Ks and grease guns and captured AK-47s and Chi-Coms and RPGs and Simonov carbines and black-market Uzis and .38-caliber Smith & Wesson handguns and 66 mm LAWs and shotguns and silencers and blackjacks and bayonets and C-4 plastic explosives. Lee Strunk carried a slingshot; a weapon of last resort, he called it. Mitchell Sanders carried brass knuckles. Kiowa carried his grandfather's feathered hatchet. Every third or fourth man carried a Claymore antipersonnel mine—3.5 pounds with its firing device. They all carried fragmentation grenades—fourteen ounces each. They all carried at least one M-18 colored smoke grenade—twenty-four ounces. Some carried CS or tear-gas grenades. Some carried white-phosphorus grenades. They carried all they could bear, and then some, including a silent awe for the terrible power of the things they carried.

In the first week of April, before Lavender died, Lieutenant Jimmy Cross received a good-luck charm from Martha. It was a simple pebble, an ounce at most. Smooth to the touch, it was a milky-white color with flecks of orange and violet, oval-shaped, like a miniature egg. In the accompanying letter, Martha wrote that she had found the pebble on the Jersey shoreline, precisely where the land touched water at high tide, where things came together but also

[7]Killed in action.

separated. It was this separate-but-together quality, she wrote, that had inspired her to pick up the pebble and to carry it in her breast pocket for several days, where it seemed weightless, and then to send it through the mail, by air, as a token of her truest feelings for him. Lieutenant Cross found this romantic. But he wondered what her truest feelings were, exactly, and what she meant by separate-but-together. He wondered how the tides and waves had come into play on that afternoon along the Jersey shoreline when Martha saw the pebble and bent down to rescue it from geology. He imagined bare feet. Martha was a poet, with the poet's sensibilities, and her feet would be brown and bare, the toenails unpainted, the eyes chilly and somber like the ocean in March, and though it was painful, he wondered who had been with her that afternoon. He imagined a pair of shadows moving along the strip of sand where things came together but also separated. It was phantom jealousy, he knew, but he couldn't help himself. He loved her so much. On the march, through the hot days of early April, he carried the pebble in his mouth, turning it with his tongue, tasting sea salts and moisture. His mind wandered. He had difficulty keeping his attention on the war. On occasion he would yell at his men to spread out the column, to keep their eyes open, but then he would slip away into daydreams, just pretending, walking barefoot along the Jersey shore, with Martha, carrying nothing. He would feel himself rising. Sun and waves and gentle winds, all love and lightness.

What they carried varied by mission.

When a mission took them to the mountains, they carried mosquito netting, machetes, canvas tarps, and extra bug juice.

If a mission seemed especially hazardous, or if it involved a place they knew to be bad, they carried everything they could. In certain heavily mined AOs,[8] where the land was dense with Toe Poppers[9] and Bouncing Betties,[10] they took turns humping a twenty-eight-pound mine detector. With its headphones and big sensing plate, the equipment was a stress on the lower back and shoulders, awkward to handle, often useless because of the shrapnel in the earth, but they carried it anyway, partly for safety, partly for the illusion of safety.

[8]Areas of operations.

[9]Viet Cong antipersonnel land mines with small firing pins.

[10]Bounding fragmentation land mines, the deadliest of all land mines.

On ambush, or other night missions, they carried peculiar little odds and ends. Kiowa always took along his New Testament and a pair of moccasins for silence. Dave Jensen carried night-sight vitamins high in carotin. Lee Strunk carried his slingshot; ammo, he claimed, would never be a problem. Rat Kiley carried brandy and M&M's. Until he was shot, Ted Lavender carried the starlight scope, which weighed 6.3 pounds with its aluminum carrying case. Henry Dobbins carried his girlfriend's pantyhose wrapped around his neck as a comforter. They all carried ghosts. When dark came, they would move out single file across the meadows and paddies to their ambush coordinates, where they would quietly set up the Claymores and lie down and spend the night waiting.

Other missions were more complicated and required special equipment. In mid-April, it was their mission to search out and destroy the elaborate tunnel complexes in the Than Khe area south of Chu Lai. To blow the tunnels, they carried one-pound blocks of pentrite high explosives, four blocks to a man, sixty-eight pounds in all. They carried wiring, detonators, and battery-powered clackers. Dave Jensen carried earplugs. Most often, before blowing the tunnels, they were ordered by higher command to search them, which was considered bad news, but by and large they just shrugged and carried out orders. Because he was a big man, Henry Dobbins was excused from tunnel duty. The others would draw numbers. Before Lavender died there were seventeen men in the platoon, and whoever drew the number seventeen would strip off his gear and crawl in head first with a flashlight and Lieutenant Cross's .45-caliber pistol. The rest of them would fan out as security. They would sit down or kneel, not facing the hole, listening to the ground beneath them, imagining cobwebs and ghosts, whatever was down there—the tunnel walls squeezing in—how the flashlight seemed impossibly heavy in the hand and how it was tunnel vision in the very strictest sense, compression in all ways, even time, and how you had to wiggle in—ass and elbows—a swallowed-up feeling—and how you found yourself worrying about odd things—will your flashlight go dead? Do rats carry rabies? If you screamed, how far would the sound carry? Would your buddies hear it? Would they have the courage to drag you out? In some respects, though not many, the waiting was worse than the tunnel itself. Imagination was a killer.

On April 16, when Lee Strunk drew the number seventeen, he laughed and muttered something and went down quickly. The morning was hot and very still. Not good, Kiowa said. He looked at the tunnel opening, then out across a dry paddy toward the village of Than Khe. Nothing moved. No clouds or birds or people. As they waited, the men smoked and drank Kool-Aid, not talking much, feeling sympathy for Lee Strunk but also feeling the luck of the draw. You win some, you lose some, said Mitchell Sanders, and sometimes you settle for a rain check. It was a tired line and no one laughed.

Henry Dobbins ate a tropical chocolate bar. Ted Lavender popped a tranquilizer and went off to pee.

After five minutes, Lieutenant Jimmy Cross moved to the tunnel, leaned down, and examined the darkness. Trouble, he thought—a cave-in maybe. And then suddenly, without willing it, he was thinking about Martha. The stresses and fractures, the quick collapse, the two of them buried alive under all that weight. Dense, crushing love. Kneeling, watching the hole, he tried to concentrate on Lee Strunk and the war, all the dangers, but his love was too much for him, he felt paralyzed, he wanted to sleep inside her lungs and breathe her blood and be smothered. He wanted her to be a virgin and not a virgin, all at once. He wanted to know her. Intimate secrets—why poetry? Why so sad? Why the grayness in her eyes? Why so alone? Not lonely, just alone—riding her bike across campus or sitting off by herself in the cafeteria. Even dancing, she danced alone—and it was the aloneness that filled him with love. He remembered telling her that one evening. How she nodded and looked away. And how, later, when he kissed her, she received the kiss without returning it, her eyes wide open, not afraid, not a virgin's eyes, just flat and uninvolved.

Lieutenant Cross gazed at the tunnel. But he was not there. He was buried with Martha under the white sand at the Jersey shore. They were pressed together, and the pebble in his mouth was her tongue. He was smiling. Vaguely, he was aware of how quiet the day was, the sullen paddies, yet he could not bring himself to worry about matters of security. He was beyond that. He was just a kid at war, in love. He was twenty-two years old. He couldn't help it.

A few moments later Lee Strunk crawled out of the tunnel. He came up grinning, filthy but alive. Lieutenant Cross nodded and closed his eyes while the others clapped Strunk on the back and made jokes about rising from the dead.

Worms, Rat Kiley said. Right out of the grave. Fuckin' zombie.

The men laughed. They all felt great relief.

Spook City, said Mitchell Sanders.

Lee Strunk made a funny ghost sound, a kind of moaning, yet very happy, and right then, when Strunk made that high happy moaning sound, when he went *Ahhooooo*, right then Ted Lavender was shot in the head on his way back from peeing. He lay with his mouth open. The teeth were broken. There was a swollen black bruise under his left eye. The cheekbone was gone. Oh shit, Rat Kiley said, the guy's dead. The guy's dead, he kept saying, which seemed profound—the guy's dead. I mean really.

The things they carried were determined to some extent by superstition. Lieutenant Cross carried his good-luck pebble. Dave Jensen carried a rabbit's foot. Norman Bowker, otherwise a very gentle person, carried a thumb that had been presented to him as a gift by Mitchell Sanders. The thumb was dark brown, rubbery to the touch, and weighed four ounces at most. It had been cut from a VC[11] corpse, a boy of fifteen or sixteen. They'd found him at the bottom of an irrigation ditch, badly burned, flies in his mouth and eyes. The boy wore black shorts and sandals. At the time of his death he had been carrying a pouch of rice, a rifle, and three magazines of ammunition.

You want my opinion, Mitchell Sanders said, there's a definite moral here.

He put his hand on the dead boy's wrist. He was quiet for a time, as if counting a pulse, then he patted the stomach, almost affectionately, and used Kiowa's hunting hatchet to remove the thumb.

Henry Dobbins asked what the moral was.

Moral?

You know. *Moral.*

Sanders wrapped the thumb in toilet paper and handed it across to Norman Bowker. There was no blood. Smiling, he kicked the boy's head, watched the flies scatter, and said, It's like with that old TV show—Paladin. Have gun, will travel.

Henry Dobbins thought about it.

Yeah, well, he finally said. I don't see no moral.

There it *is*, man.

Fuck off.

---

[11]Vietcong, a guerrilla fighter of the Vietnamese Communist movement.

They carried USO stationery and pencils and pens. They carried Sterno, safety pins, trip flares, signal flares, spools of wire, razor blades, chewing tobacco, liberated joss sticks[12] and statuettes of the smiling Buddha, candles, grease pencils, *The Stars and Stripes*, fingernail clippers, Psy Ops[13] leaflets, bush hats, bolos, and much more. Twice a week, when the resupply choppers came in, they carried hot chow in green Mermite cans and large canvas bags filled with iced beer and soda pop. They carried plastic water containers, each with a two-gallon capacity. Mitchell Sanders carried a set of starched tiger fatigues for special occasions. Henry Dobbins carried Black Flag insecticide. Dave Jensen carried empty sandbags that could be filled at night for added protection. Lee Strunk carried tanning lotion. Some things they carried in common. Taking turns, they carried the big PRC-77 scrambler radio, which weighed thirty pounds with its battery. They shared the weight of memory. They took up what others could no longer bear. Often, they carried each other, the wounded or weak. They carried infections. They carried chess sets, basketballs, Vietnamese-English dictionaries, insignia of rank, Bronze Stars and Purple Hearts, plastic cards imprinted with the Code of Conduct. They carried diseases, among them malaria and dysentery. They carried lice and ringworm and leeches and paddy algae and various rots and molds. They carried the land itself—Vietnam, the place, the soil—a powdery orange-red dust that covered their boots and fatigues and faces. They carried the sky. The whole atmosphere, they carried it, the humidity, the monsoons, the stink of fungus and decay, all of it, they carried gravity. They moved like mules. By daylight they took sniper fire, at night they were mortared, but it was not battle, it was just the endless march, village to village, without purpose, nothing won or lost. They marched for the sake of the march. They plodded along slowly, dumbly, leaning forward against the heat, unthinking, all blood and bone, simple grunts, soldiering with their legs, toiling up the hills and down into the paddies and across the rivers and up again and down, just humping, one step and then the next and then another, but no volition, no will, because it was automatic, it was anatomy, and the war was entirely a matter of posture and carriage, the hump was everything, a kind of inertia, a kind of emptiness, a dullness of desire and intellect and

[12]Slender sticks of incense.
[13]Psychological operations.

conscience and hope and human sensibility. Their principles were in their feet. Their calculations were biological. They had no sense of strategy or mission. They searched the villages without knowing what to look for, not caring, kicking over jars of rice, frisking children and old men, blowing tunnels, sometimes setting fires and sometimes not, then forming up and moving on to the next village, then other villages, where it would always be the same. They carried their own lives. The pressures were enormous. In the heat of early afternoon, they would remove their helmets and flak jackets, walking bare, which was dangerous but which helped ease the strain. They would often discard things along the route of march. Purely for comfort, they would throw away rations, blow their Claymores and grenades, no matter, because by nightfall the resupply choppers would arrive with more of the same, then a day or two later still more, fresh watermelons and crates of ammunition and sunglasses and woolen sweaters—the resources were stunning—sparklers for the Fourth of July, colored eggs for Easter. It was the great American war chest—the fruits of science, the smokestacks, the canneries, the arsenals at Hartford, the Minnesota forests, the machine shops, the vast fields of corn and wheat—they carried like freight trains; they carried it on their backs and shoulders—and for all the ambiguities of Vietnam, all the mysteries and unknowns, there was at least the single abiding certainty that they would never be at a loss for things to carry.

After the chopper took Lavender away, Lieutenant Jimmy Cross led his men into the village of Than Khe. They burned everything. They shot chickens and dogs, they trashed the village well, they called in artillery and watched the wreckage, then they marched for several hours through the hot afternoon, and then at dusk, while Kiowa explained how Lavender died, Lieutenant Cross found himself trembling.

He tried not to cry. With his entrenching tool, which weighed five pounds, he began digging a hole in the earth.

He felt shame. He hated himself. He had loved Martha more than his men, and as a consequence Lavender was now dead, and this was something he would have to carry like a stone in his stomach for the rest of the war.

All he could do was dig. He used his entrenching tool like an ax, slashing, feeling both love and hate, and then later, when it was full dark, he sat at the bottom of his foxhole and wept. It went on for a long while. In part, he was grieving for Ted Lavender, but mostly it was for Martha, and for himself, because she belonged to another world, which was not quite real, and because she was a junior at Mount Sebastian College in New Jersey, a poet and a virgin and uninvolved, and because he realized she did not love him and never would.

Like cement, Kiowa whispered in the dark. I swear to God—boom-down. Not a word.

I've heard this, said Norman Bowker.

A pisser, you know? Still zipping himself up. Zapped while zipping.

All right, fine. That's enough.

Yeah, but you had to see it, the guy just—

I *heard*, man. Cement. So why not shut the fuck *up*?

Kiowa shook his head sadly and glanced over at the hole where Lieutenant Jimmy Cross sat watching the night. The air was thick and wet. A warm, dense fog had settled over the paddies and there was the stillness that precedes rain.

After a time Kiowa sighed.

One thing for sure, he said. The Lieutenant's in some deep hurt. I mean that crying jag—the way he was carrying on—it wasn't fake or anything, it was real heavy-duty hurt. The man cares.

Sure, Norman Bowker said.

Say what you want, the man does care.

We all got problems.

Not Lavender.

No, I guess not, Bowker said. Do me a favor, though.

Shut up?

That's a smart Indian. Shut up.

Shrugging, Kiowa pulled off his boots. He wanted to say more, just to lighten up his sleep, but instead he opened his New Testament and arranged it beneath his head as a pillow. The fog made things seem hollow and unattached. He tried not to think about Ted Lavender, but then he was thinking how fast it was, no drama, down and dead, and how it was hard to feel anything except surprise. It seemed un-Christian. He wished he could find some great sadness, or even anger, but the emotion wasn't there and he couldn't make it happen. Mostly he felt pleased to be alive. He liked the smell of the

New Testament under his cheek, the leather and ink and paper and glue, whatever the chemicals were. He liked hearing the sounds of night. Even his fatigue, it felt fine, the stiff muscles and the prickly awareness of his own body, a floating feeling. He enjoyed not being dead. Lying there, Kiowa admired Lieutenant Jimmy Cross's capacity for grief. He wanted to share the man's pain, he wanted to care as Jimmy Cross cared. And yet when he closed his eyes, all he could think was Boom-down, and all he could feel was the pleasure of having his boots off and the fog curling in around him and the damp soil and the Bible smells and the plush comfort of night.

After a moment Norman Bowker sat up in the dark.

What the hell, he said. You want to talk, *talk*. Tell it to me.

Forget it.

No, man, go on. One thing I hate, it's a silent Indian.

For the most part they carried themselves with poise, a kind of dignity. Now and then, however, there were times of panic, when they squealed or wanted to squeal but couldn't, when they twitched and made moaning sounds and covered their heads and said Dear Jesus and flopped around on the earth and fired their weapons blindly and cringed and sobbed and begged for the noise to stop and went wild and made stupid promises to themselves and to God and to their mothers and fathers, hoping not to die. In different ways, it happened to all of them. Afterward, when the firing ended, they would blink and peek up. They would touch their bodies, feeling shame, then quickly hiding it. They would force themselves to stand. As if in slow motion, frame by frame, the world would take on the old logic—absolute silence, then the wind, then sunlight, then voices. It was the burden of being alive. Awkwardly, the men would reassemble themselves, first in private, then in groups, becoming soldiers again. They would repair the leaks in their eyes. They would check for casualties, call in dust-offs, light cigarettes, try to smile, clear their throats and spit and begin cleaning their weapons. After a time someone would shake his head and say, No lie, I almost shit my pants, and someone else would laugh, which meant it was bad, yes, but the guy had obviously not shit his pants, it wasn't that bad, and in any case nobody would ever do such a thing and then go ahead and talk about it. They would squint into the dense, oppressive sunlight. For a few moments, perhaps, they would fall silent, lighting a joint and tracking its passage from man to man, inhaling, holding in the humiliation. Scary stuff, one of them might say. But then someone else would grin or flick his eyebrows and say, Roger-dodger, almost cut me a new asshole, *almost.*

There were numerous such poses. Some carried themselves with a sort of wistful resignation, others with pride or stiff soldierly discipline or good humor or macho zeal. They were afraid of dying but they were even more afraid to show it.

They found jokes to tell.

They used a hard vocabulary to contain the terrible softness. *Greased,* they'd say. *Offed, lit up, zapped while zipping.* It wasn't cruelty, just stage presence. They were actors and the war came at them in 3-D. When someone died, it wasn't quite dying, because in a curious way it seemed scripted, and because they had their lines mostly memorized, irony mixed with tragedy, and because they called it by other names, as if to encyst and destroy the reality of death itself. They kicked corpses. They cut off thumbs. They talked grunt lingo. They told stories about Ted Lavender's supply of tranquilizers, how the poor guy didn't feel a thing, how incredibly tranquil he was.

There's a moral here, said Mitchell Sanders.

They were waiting for Lavender's chopper, smoking the dead man's dope.

The moral's pretty obvious, Sanders said, and winked. Stay away from drugs. No joke, they'll ruin your day every time.

Cute, said Henry Dobbins.

Mind-blower, get it? Talk about wiggy—nothing left, just blood and brains.

They made themselves laugh.

There it is, they'd say, over and over, as if the repetition itself were an act of poise, a balance between crazy and almost crazy, knowing without going. There it is, which meant be cool, let it ride, because oh yeah, man, you can't change what can't be changed, there it is, there it absolutely and positively and fucking well *is.*

They were tough.

They carried all the emotional baggage of men who might die. Grief, terror, love, longing—these were intangibles, but the intangibles had their own mass and specific gravity, they had tangible weight. They carried shameful memories. They carried the common secret of cowardice barely restrained, the instinct to run or freeze or hide, and in many respects this was the heaviest burden of all, for it could never be put down, it required perfect balance and perfect posture.

They carried their reputations. They carried the soldier's greatest fear, which was the fear of blushing. Men killed, and died, because they were embarrassed not to. It was what had brought them to the war in the first place, nothing positive, no dreams of glory or honor, just to avoid the blush of dishonor. They died so as not to die of embarrassment. They crawled into tunnels and walked point and advanced under fire. Each morning, despite the unknowns, they made their legs move. They endured. They kept humping. They did not submit to the obvious alternative, which was simply to close the eyes and fall. So easy, really. Go limp and tumble to the ground and let the muscles unwind and not speak and not budge until your buddies picked you up and lifted you into the chopper that would roar and dip its nose and carry you off to the world. A mere matter of falling, yet no one ever fell. It was not courage, exactly; the object was not valor. Rather, they were too frightened to be cowards.

By and large they carried these things inside, maintaining the masks of composure. They sneered at sick call. They spoke bitterly about guys who had found release by shooting off their own toes or fingers. Pussies, they'd say. Candyasses. It was fierce, mocking talk, with only a trace of envy or awe, but even so, the image played itself out behind their eyes.

They imagined the muzzle against flesh. They imagined the quick, sweet pain, then the evacuation to Japan, then a hospital with warm beds and cute geisha nurses.

They dreamed of freedom birds.

At night, on guard, staring into the dark, they were carried away by jumbo jets. They felt the rush of takeoff. *Gone!* they yelled. And then velocity, wings and engines, a smiling stewardess—but it was more than a plane, it was a real bird, a big sleek silver bird with feathers and talons and high screeching. They were flying. The weights fell off, there was nothing to bear. They laughed and held on tight, feeling the cold slap of wind and altitude, soaring, thinking *It's over, I'm gone!*—they were naked, they were light and free—it was all lightness, bright and fast and buoyant, light as light, a helium buzz in the brain, a giddy bubbling in the lungs as they were taken up over the clouds and the war, beyond duty, beyond gravity and mortification and global entanglements—*Sin loi!*[14] they yelled, *I'm sorry, motherfuckers, but I'm out of it, I'm goofed, I'm on a space*

[14]"Sorry about that!"

cruise, I'm gone!—and it was a restful, disencumbered sensation, just riding the light waves, sailing that big silver freedom bird over the mountains and oceans, over America, over the farms and great sleeping cities and cemeteries and highways and the golden arches of McDonald's. It was flight, a kind of fleeing, a kind of falling, falling higher and higher, spinning off the edge of the earth and beyond the sun and through the vast, silent vacuum where there were no burdens and where everything weighed exactly nothing. *Gone!* they screamed, *I'm sorry but I'm gone!* And so at night, not quite dreaming, they gave themselves over to lightness, they were carried, they were purely borne.

On the morning after Ted Lavender died, First Lieutenant Jimmy Cross crouched at the bottom of his foxhole and burned Martha's letters. Then he burned the two photographs. There was a steady rain falling, which made it difficult, but he used heat tabs and Sterno to build a small fire, screening it with his body, holding the photographs over the tight blue flame with the tips of his fingers.

He realized it was only a gesture. Stupid, he thought. Sentimental, too, but mostly just stupid.

Lavender was dead. You couldn't burn the blame.

Besides, the letters were in his head. And even now, without photographs, Lieutenant Cross could see Martha playing volleyball in her white gym shorts and yellow T-shirt. He could see her moving in the rain.

When the fire died out, Lieutenant Cross pulled his poncho over his shoulders and ate breakfast from a can.

There was no great mystery, he decided.

In those burned letters Martha had never mentioned the war, except to say, Jimmy, take care of yourself. She wasn't involved. She signed the letters "Love," but it wasn't love, and all the fine lines and technicalities did not matter.

The morning came up wet and blurry. Everything seemed part of everything else, the fog and Martha and the deepening rain.

It was a war, after all.

Half smiling, Lieutenant Jimmy Cross took out his maps. He shook his head hard, as if to clear it, then bent forward and began planning the day's march. In ten minutes, or maybe twenty, he would rouse the men and they would pack up and head west, where the maps showed the country to be green and inviting. They would do what they had always done. The rain might add some weight, but otherwise it would be one more day layered upon all the other days.

He was realistic about it. There was that new hardness in his stomach.

No more fantasies, he told himself.

Henceforth, when he thought about Martha, it would be only to think that she belonged elsewhere. He would shut down the daydreams. This was not Mount Sebastian, it was another world, where there were no pretty poems or midterm exams, a place where men died because of carelessness and gross stupidity. Kiowa was right. Boom-down, and you were dead, never partly dead.

Briefly, in the rain, Lieutenant Cross saw Martha's gray eyes gazing back at him.

He understood.

It was very sad, he thought. The things men carried inside. The things men did or felt they had to do.

He almost nodded at her, but didn't.

Instead he went back to his maps. He was now determined to perform his duties firmly and without negligence. It wouldn't help Lavender, he knew that, but from this point on he would comport himself as a soldier. He would dispose of his good-luck pebble. Swallow it, maybe, or use Lee Strunk's slingshot, or just drop it along the trail. On the march he would impose strict field discipline. He would be careful to send out flank security, to prevent straggling or bunching up, to keep his troops moving at the proper pace and at the proper interval. He would insist on clean weapons. He would confiscate the remainder of Lavender's dope. Later in the day, perhaps, he would call the men together and speak to them plainly. He would accept the blame for what had happened to Ted Lavender. He would be a man about it. He would look them in the eyes, keeping his chin level, and he would issue the new SOPs in a calm, impersonal tone of voice, an officer's voice, leaving no room for argument or discussion. Commencing immediately, he'd tell them, they would no longer abandon equipment along the route of march. They would police up their acts. They would get their shit together, and keep it together, and maintain it neatly and in good working order.

He would not tolerate laxity. He would show strength, distancing himself.

Among the men there would be grumbling, of course, and maybe worse, because their days would seem longer and their loads heavier, but Lieutenant Cross reminded himself that his obligation was not to be loved but to lead. He would dispense with love; it was not now a factor. And if anyone quarreled or complained, he would simply tighten his lips and arrange his shoulders in the correct command posture. He might give a curt little nod. Or he might not. He might just shrug and say Carry on, then they would saddle up and form into a column and move out toward the villages of Than Khe.

1986

The Man to Send Rain Clouds

LESLIE MARMON SILKO
[b. 1948]

ONE

They found him under a big cottonwood tree. His Levi jacket and pants were faded light-blue so that he had been easy to find. The big cottonwood tree stood apart from a small grove of winterbare cottonwoods which grew in the wide, sandy arroyo. He had been dead for a day or more, and the sheep had wandered and scattered up and down the arroyo. Leon and his brother-in-law, Ken, gathered the sheep and left them in the pen at the sheep camp before they returned to the cottonwood tree. Leon waited under the tree while Ken drove the truck through the deep sand to the edge of the arroyo. He squinted up at the sun and unzipped his jacket—it sure was hot for this time of year. But high and northwest the blue mountains were still deep in snow. Ken came sliding down the low, crumbling bank about fifty yards down, and he was bringing the red blanket.

Before they wrapped the old man, Leon took a piece of string out of his pocket and tied a small gray feather in the old man's long white hair. Ken gave him the paint. Across the brown wrinkled forehead he drew a streak of white and along the high cheekbones he drew a strip of blue paint. He paused and watched Ken throw pinches of corn meal and pollen into the wind that fluttered the small gray feather. Then Leon painted with yellow under the old man's broad nose, and finally, when he had painted green across the chin, he smiled.

"Send us rain clouds, Grandfather." They laid the bundle in the back of the pickup and covered it with a heavy tarp before they started back to the pueblo.

They turned off the highway onto the sandy pueblo road. Not long after they passed the store and post office they saw Father Paul's car coming toward them. When he recognized their faces he slowed his car and waved for them to stop. The young priest rolled down the car window.

"Did you find old Teofilo?" he asked loudly.

Leon stopped the truck. "Good morning, Father. We were just out to the sheep camp. Everything is O.K. now."

"Thank God for that. Teofilo is a very old man. You really shouldn't allow him to stay at the sheep camp alone."

"No, he won't do that any more now."

"Well, I'm glad you understand. I hope I'll be seeing you at Mass this week—we missed you last Sunday. See if you can get old Teofilo to come with you." The priest smiled and waved at them as they drove away.

TWO

Louise and Teresa were waiting. The table was set for lunch, and the coffee was boiling on the black iron stove. Leon looked at Louise and then at Teresa.

"We found him under a cottonwood tree in the big arroyo near the sheep camp. I guess he sat down to rest in the shade and never got up again." Leon walked toward the old man's bed. The red plaid shawl had been shaken and spread carefully over the bed, and a new brown flannel shirt and pair of stiff new Levis were arranged neatly beside the pillow. Louise held the screen door open while Leon and Ken carried in the red blanket. He looked small and shriveled, and after they dressed him in the new shirt and pants he seemed more shrunken.

It was noontime now because the church bells rang the Angelus.[1] They ate the beans with hot bread, and nobody said anything until after Teresa poured the coffee.

Ken stood up and put on his jacket. "I'll see about the gravediggers. Only the top layer of soil is frozen. I think it can be ready before dark."

Leon nodded his head and finished his coffee. After Ken had been gone for a while, the neighbors and clanspeople came quietly to

[1]A devotional prayer commemorating the Annunciation (the angel Gabriel's announcement of the Incarnation of God in the human form of Jesus).

embrace Teofilo's family and to leave food on the table because the gravediggers would come to eat when they were finished.

THREE

The sky in the west was full of pale-yellow light. Louise stood outside with her hands in the pockets of Leon's green army jacket that was too big for her. The funeral was over, and the old men had taken their candles and medicine bags and were gone. She waited until the body was laid into the pickup before she said anything to Leon. She touched his arm, and he noticed that her hands were still dusty from the corn meal that she had sprinkled around the old man. When she spoke, Leon could not hear her.

"What did you say? I didn't hear you."

"I said that I had been thinking about something."

"About what?"

"About the priest sprinkling holy water for Grandpa. So he won't be thirsty."

Leon stared at the new moccasins that Teofilo had made for the ceremonial dances in the summer. They were nearly hidden by the red blanket. It was getting colder, and the wind pushed gray dust down the narrow pueblo road. The sun was approaching the long mesa where it disappeared during the winter. Louise stood there shivering and watching his face. Then he zipped up his jacket and opened the truck door. "I'll see if he's there."

FOUR

Ken stopped the pickup at the church, and Leon got out; and then Ken drove down the hill to the graveyard where people were waiting. Leon knocked at the old carved door with its symbols of the Lamb. While he waited he looked up at the twin bells from the king of Spain with the last sunlight pouring around them in their tower.

The priest opened the door and smiled when he saw who it was. "Come in! What brings you here this evening?"

The priest walked toward the kitchen, and Leon stood with his cap in his hand, playing with the earflaps and examining the living room—the brown sofa, the green armchair, and the brass lamp that hung down from the ceiling by links of chain. The priest dragged a chair out of the kitchen and offered it to Leon.

"No thank you, Father. I only came to ask you if you would bring your holy water to the graveyard."

The priest turned away from Leon and looked out the window at the patio full of shadows and the dining-room windows of the nuns' cloister across the patio. The curtains were heavy, and the light from within faintly penetrated; it was impossible to see the nuns inside eating supper. "Why didn't you tell me he was dead? I could have brought the Last Rites anyway."

Leon smiled. "It wasn't necessary, Father."

The priest stared down at his scuffed brown loafers and the worn hem of his cassock. "For a Christian burial it was necessary."

His voice was distant, and Leon thought that his blue eyes looked tired.

"It's O.K., Father, we just want him to have plenty of water."

The priest sank down in the green chair and picked up a glossy missionary magazine. He turned the colored pages full of lepers and pagans without looking at them.

"You know I can't do that, Leon. There should have been the Last Rites and a funeral Mass at the very least."

Leon put on his green cap and pulled the flaps down over his ears. "It's getting late, Father. I've got to go."

When Leon opened the door Father Paul stood up and said, "Wait." He left the room and came back wearing a long brown overcoat. He followed Leon out the door and across the dim churchyard to the adobe steps in front of the church. They both stooped to fit through the low adobe entrance. And when they started down the hill to the graveyard only half of the sun was visible above the mesa.

The priest approached the grave slowly, wondering how they had managed to dig into the frozen ground; and then he remembered that this was New Mexico, and saw the pile of cold loose sand beside the hole. The people stood close to each other with little clouds of steam puffing from their faces. The priest looked at them and saw a pile of jackets, gloves, and scarves in the yellow, dry tumbleweeds that grew in the graveyard. He looked at the red blanket, not sure that Teofilo was so small, wondering if it wasn't some perverse Indian trick—something they did in March to ensure a good harvest—wondering if maybe old Teofilo was actually at sheep camp corraling the sheep for the night. But there he was, facing into a cold dry wind and squinting at the last sunlight, ready to bury a red wool blanket while the faces of the parishioners were in shadow with the last warmth of the sun on their backs.

His fingers were stiff, and it took them a long time to twist the lid off the holy water. Drops of water fell on the red blanket and soaked into dark icy spots. He sprinkled the grave and the water disappeared almost before it touched the dim, cold sand; it reminded him of something—he tried to remember what it was, because he thought if he could remember he might understand this. He sprinkled more water; he shook the container until it was empty, and the water fell through the light from sundown like August rain that fell while the sun was still shining, almost evaporating before it touched the wilted squash flowers.

The wind pulled at the priest's brown Franciscan robe and swirled away the corn meal and pollen that had been sprinkled on the blanket. They lowered the bundle into the ground, and they didn't bother to untie the stiff pieces of new rope that were tied around the ends of the blanket. The sun was gone, and over on the highway the eastbound lane was full of headlights. The priest walked away slowly. Leon watched him climb the hill, and when he had disappeared within the tall, thick walls, Leon turned to look up at the high blue mountains in the deep snow that reflected a faint red light from the west. He felt good because it was finished, and he was happy about the sprinkling of the holy water; now the old man could send them big thunderclouds for sure.

1969

Girl

JAMAICA KINCAID

[b. 1949]

Wash the white clothes on Monday and put them on the stone heap; wash the color clothes on Tuesday and put them on the clothesline to dry; don't walk barehead in the hot sun; cook pumpkin fritters in very hot sweet oil; soak your little cloths right after you take them off; when buying cotton to make yourself a nice blouse, be sure that it doesn't have gum on it, because that way it won't hold up well after a wash; soak salt fish overnight before you cook it; is it true that you sing benna[1] in Sunday school?; always eat your food in such a way that it won't turn someone else's stomach; on Sundays try to walk like a lady and not like the slut you are so bent on becoming; don't sing benna in Sunday school; you mustn't speak to wharf-rat boys, not even to give directions; don't eat fruits on the street—flies will follow you; *but I don't sing benna on Sundays at all and never in Sunday school*; this is how to sew on a button; this is how to make a button-hole for the button you have just sewed on; this is how to hem a dress when you see the hem coming down and so to prevent yourself from looking like the slut I know you are so bent on becoming; this is how you iron your father's khaki shirt so that it doesn't have a crease; this is how you iron your father's khaki pants so that they don't have a crease; this is how you grow okra—far from the house, because okra tree harbors red ants; when you are growing dasheen,[2] make sure it gets plenty of water or else it makes your throat itch when you are eating it; this is how you sweep a corner; this is how you sweep a whole house; this is how you sweep a yard; this is how you smile to someone you don't like too much; this is how you smile to someone you don't like at all; this

[1]Calypso music.
[2]Taro, an edible starchy plant.

is how you smile to someone you like completely; this is how you set a table for tea; this is how you set a table for dinner; this is how you set a table for dinner with an important guest; this is how you set a table for lunch; this is how you set a table for breakfast; this is how to behave in the presence of men who don't know you very well, and this way they won't recognize immediately the slut I have warned you against becoming; be sure to wash every day, even if it is with your own spit; don't squat down to play marbles—you are not a boy, you know; don't pick people's flowers—you might catch something; don't throw stones at blackbirds, because it might not be a blackbird at all; this is how to make a bread pudding; this is how to make doukona;[3] this is how to make pepper pot; this is how to make a good medicine for a cold; this is how to make a good medicine to throw away a child before it even becomes a child; this is how to catch a fish; this is how to throw back a fish you don't like, and that way something bad won't fall on you; this is how to bully a man; this is how a man bullies you; this is how to love a man, and if this doesn't work there are other ways, and if they don't work don't feel too bad about giving up; this is how to spit up in the air if you feel like it, and this is how to move quick so that it doesn't fall on you; this is how to make ends meet; always squeeze bread to make sure it's fresh; *but what if the baker won't let me feel the bread?*; you mean to say that after all you are really going to be the kind of woman who the baker won't let near the bread?

1978

[3]A spicy plantain pudding.

The House on Mango Street

SANDRA CISNEROS

[b. 1954]

We didn't always live on Mango Street. Before that we lived on Loomis on the third floor, and before that we lived on Keeler. Before Keeler it was Paulina, and before that I can't remember. But what I remember most is moving a lot. Each time it seemed there'd be one more of us. By the time we got to Mango Street we were six—Mama, Papa, Carlos, Kiki, my sister Nenny, and me.

The house on Mango Street is ours, and we don't have to pay rent to anybody, or share the yard with the people downstairs, or be careful not to make too much noise, and there isn't a landlord banging on the ceiling with a broom. But even so, it's not the house we'd thought we'd get.

We had to leave the flat on Loomis quick. The water pipes broke and the landlord wouldn't fix them because the house was too old. We had to leave fast. We were using the washroom next door and carrying water over in empty milk gallons. That's why Mama and Papa looked for a house, and that's why we moved into the house on Mango Street, far away, on the other side of town.

They always told us that one day we would move into a house, a real house that would be ours for always so we wouldn't have to move each year. And our house would have running water and pipes that worked. And inside it would have real stairs, not hallway stairs, but stairs inside like the houses on T.V. And we'd have a basement and at least three washrooms so when we took a bath we wouldn't have to tell everybody. Our house would be white with trees around it, a great big yard and grass growing without a fence. This was the house Papa talked about when he held a lottery ticket and this was the house Mama dreamed up in the stories she told us before we went to bed.

But the house on Mango Street is not the way they told it at all. It's small and red with tight steps in front and windows so small you'd think they were holding their breath. Bricks are crumbling in places, and the front door is so swollen you have to push hard to get in. There is no front yard, only four little elms the city planted by the curb. Out back is a small garage for the car we don't own yet and a small yard that looks smaller between the two buildings on either side. There are stairs in our house, but they're ordinary hallway stairs, and the house has only one washroom. Everybody has to share a bedroom—Mama and Papa, Carlos and Kiki, me and Nenny.

Once when we were living on Loomis, a nun from my school passed by and saw me playing out front. The laundromat downstairs had been boarded up because it had been robbed two days before and the owner had painted on the wood YES WE'RE OPEN so as not to lose business.

Where do you live? she asked.

There, I said pointing up to the third floor.

You live *there?*

There. I had to look to where she pointed—the third floor, the paint peeling, wooden bars Papa had nailed on the windows so we wouldn't fall out. You live *there?* The way she said it made me feel like nothing. *There.* I lived *there.* I nodded.

I knew then I had to have a house. A real house. One I could point to. But this isn't it. The house on Mango Street isn't it. For the time being, Mama says. Temporary, says Papa. But I know how those things go.

1983

The Red Convertible

LOUISE ERDRICH
[b. 1954]

I was the first one to drive a convertible on my reservation. And of course it was red, a red Olds. I owned that car along with my brother Henry Junior. We owned it together until his boots filled with water on a windy night and he bought out my share. Now Henry owns the whole car, and his younger brother Lyman (that's myself), Lyman walks everywhere he goes.

How did I earn enough money to buy my share in the first place? My own talent was I could always make money. I had a touch for it, unusual in a Chippewa. From the first I was different that way, and everyone recognized it. I was the only kid they let in the American Legion Hall to shine shoes, for example, and one Christmas I sold spiritual bouquets for the mission door to door. The nuns let me keep a percentage. Once I started, it seemed the more money I made the easier the money came. Everyone encouraged it. When I was fifteen I got a job washing dishes at the Joliet Café, and that was where my first big break happened.

It wasn't long before I was promoted to busing tables, and then the short-order cook quit and I was hired to take her place. No sooner than you know it I was managing the Joliet. The rest is history. I went on managing. I soon became part owner, and of course there was no stopping me then. It wasn't long before the whole thing was mine.

After I'd owned the Joliet for one year, it blew over in the worst tornado ever seen around here. The whole operation was smashed to bits. A total loss. The fryalator was up in a tree, the grill torn in half like it was paper. I was only sixteen. I had it all in my mother's name, and I lost it quick, but before I lost it I had every one of my relatives, and their relatives, to dinner, and I also bought that red Olds I mentioned, along with Henry.

The first time we saw it! I'll tell you when we first saw it. We had gotten a ride up to Winnipeg, and both of us had money. Don't ask me why, because we never mentioned a car or anything, we just had all our money. Mine was cash, a big bankroll from the Joliet's insurance. Henry had two checks—a week's extra pay for being laid off, and his regular check from the Jewel Bearing Plant.

We were walking down Portage anyway, seeing the sights, when we saw it. There it was, parked, large as life. Really as if it was alive. I thought of the word *repose*, because the car wasn't simply stopped, parked, or whatever. That car reposed, calm and gleaming, a FOR SALE sign in its left front window. Then, before we had thought it over at all, the car belonged to us and our pockets were empty. We had just enough money for gas back home.

We went places in that car, me and Henry. We took off driving all one whole summer. We started off toward the Little Knife River and Mandaree in Fort Berthold and then we found ourselves down in Wakpala somehow, and then suddenly we were over in Montana on the Rocky Boy, and yet the summer was not even half over. Some people hang on to details when they travel, but we didn't let them bother us and just lived our everyday lives here to there.

I do remember this one place with willows. I remember I laid under those trees and it was comfortable. So comfortable. The branches bent down all around me like a tent or a stable. And quiet, it was quiet, even though there was a powwow close enough so I could see it going on. The air was not too still, not too windy either. When the dust rises up and hangs in the air around the dancers like that, I feel good. Henry was asleep with his arms thrown wide. Later on, he woke up and we started driving again. We were somewhere in Montana, or maybe on the Blood Reserve—it could have been anywhere. Anyway it was where we met the girl.

All her hair was in buns around her ears, that's the first thing I noticed about her. She was posed alongside the road with her arm out, so we stopped. That girl was short, so short her lumber shirt looked comical on her, like a nightgown. She had jeans on and fancy moccasins and she carried a little suitcase.

"Hop on in," says Henry. So she climbs in between us.

"We'll take you home," I says. "Where do you live?"

"Chicken," she says.

"Where the hell's that?" I ask her.

"Alaska."

"Okay," says Henry, and we drive.

We got up there and never wanted to leave. The sun doesn't truly set there in summer, and the night is more a soft dusk. You might doze off, sometimes, but before you know it you're up again, like an animal in nature. You never feel like you have to sleep hard or put away the world. And things would grow up there. One day just dirt or moss, the next day flowers and long grass. The girl's name was Susy. Her family really took to us. They fed us and put us up. We had our own tent to live in by their house, and the kids would be in and out of there all day and night. They couldn't get over me and Henry being brothers, we looked so different. We told them we knew we had the same mother, anyway.

One night Susy came in to visit us. We sat around in the tent talking of this and that. The season was changing. It was getting darker by that time, and the cold was even getting just a little mean. I told her it was time for us to go. She stood up on a chair.

"You never seen my hair," Susy said.

That was true. She was standing on a chair, but still, when she unclipped her buns the hair reached all the way to the ground. Our eyes opened. You couldn't tell how much hair she had when it was rolled up so neatly. Then my brother Henry did something funny. He went up to the chair and said, "Jump on my shoulders." So she did that, and her hair reached down past his waist, and he started twirling, this way and that, so her hair was flung out from side to side.

"I always wondered what it was like to have long pretty hair," Henry says. Well we laughed. It was a funny sight, the way he did it. The next morning we got up and took leave of those people.

On to greener pastures, as they say. It was down through Spokane and across Idaho then Montana and very soon we were racing the weather right along under the Canadian border through Columbus, Des Lacs, and then we were in Bottineau County and soon home. We'd made most of the trip, that summer, without putting up the car hood at all. We got home just in time, it turned out, for the army to remember Henry had signed up to join it.

I don't wonder that the army was so glad to get my brother that they turned him into a Marine. He was built like a brick outhouse anyway. We liked to tease him that they really wanted him for his Indian nose. He had a nose big and sharp as a hatchet, like the nose on Red Tomahawk, the Indian who killed Sitting Bull, whose profile is on signs all along the North Dakota highways. Henry went off to training camp, came home once during Christmas, then the next thing you know we got an overseas letter from him. It was 1970, and he said he was stationed up in the northern hill country. Whereabouts I did not know. He wasn't such a hot letter writer, and only got off two before the enemy caught him. I could never keep it straight, which direction those good Vietnam soldiers were from.

I wrote him back several times, even though I didn't know if those letters would get through. I kept him informed all about the car. Most of the time I had it up on blocks in the yard or half taken apart, because that long trip did a hard job on it under the hood.

I always had good luck with numbers, and never worried about the draft myself. I never even had to think about what my number was. But Henry was never lucky in the same way as me. It was at least three years before Henry came home. By then I guess the whole war was solved in the government's mind, but for him it would keep on going. In those years I'd put his car into almost perfect shape. I always thought of it as his car while he was gone, even though when he left he said, "Now it's yours," and threw me his key.

"Thanks for the extra key," I'd said. "I'll put it up in your drawer just in case I need it." He laughed.

When he came home, though, Henry was very different, and I'll say this: the change was no good. You could hardly expect him to change for the better, I know. But he was quiet, so quiet, and never comfortable sitting still anywhere but always up and moving around. I thought back to times we'd sat still for whole afternoons, never moving a muscle, just shifting our weight along the ground, talking to whoever sat with us, watching things. He'd always had a joke, then, too, and now you couldn't get him to laugh, or when he did it was more the sound of a man choking, a sound that stopped up the throats of other people around him.

They got to leaving him alone most of the time, and I didn't blame them. It was a fact: Henry was jumpy and mean.

I'd bought a color TV set for my mom and the rest of us while Henry was away. Money still came very easy. I was sorry I'd ever bought it though, because of Henry. I was also sorry I'd bought color, because with black-and-white the pictures seem older and farther away. But what are you going to do? He sat in front of it, watching it, and that was the only time he was completely still. But it was the kind of stillness that you see in a rabbit when it freezes and before it will bolt. He was not easy. He sat in his chair gripping the armrests with all his might, as if the chair itself was moving at a high speed and if he let go at all he would rocket forward and maybe crash right through the set.

Once I was in the room watching TV with Henry and I heard his teeth click at something. I looked over, and he'd bitten through his lip. Blood was going down his chin. I tell you right then I wanted to smash that tube to pieces. I went over to it but Henry must have known what I was up to. He rushed from his chair and shoved me out of the way, against the wall. I told myself he didn't know what he was doing.

My mom came in, turned the set off real quiet, and told us she had made something for supper. So we went and sat down. There was still blood going down Henry's chin, but he didn't notice it and no one said anything, even though every time he took a bite of his bread his blood fell onto it until he was eating his own blood mixed in with the food.

While Henry was not around we talked about what was going to happen to him. There were no Indian doctors on the reservation, and my mom was afraid of trusting the old man, Moses Pillager, because he courted her long ago and was jealous of her husband. He might take revenge through her son. We were afraid that if we brought Henry to a regular hospital they would keep him.

"They don't fix them in those places," Mom said; "they just give them drugs."

"We wouldn't get him there in the first place," I agreed, "so let's just forget about it."

Then I thought about the car.

Henry had not even looked at the car since he'd gotten home, though like I said, it was in tip-top condition and ready to drive.

I thought the car might bring the old Henry back somehow. So I bided my time and waited for my chance to interest him in the vehicle.

One night Henry was off somewhere. I took myself a hammer. I went out to that car and I did a number on its underside. Whacked it up. Bent the tail pipe double. Ripped the muffler loose. By the time I was done with the car it looked worse than any typical Indian car that has been driven all its life on reservation roads, which they always say are like government promises—full of holes. It just about hurt me, I'll tell you that! I threw dirt in the carburetor and I ripped all the electric tape off the seats. I made it look just as beat up as I could. Then I sat back and waited for Henry to find it.

Still, it took him over a month. That was all right, because it was just getting warm enough, not melting, but warm enough to work outside.

"Lyman," he says, walking in one day, "that red car looks like shit."

"Well it's old," I says. "You got to expect that."

"No way!" says Henry. "That car's a classic! But you went and ran the piss right out of it, Lyman, and you know it don't deserve that. I kept that car in A-one shape. You don't remember. You're too young. But when I left, that car was running like a watch. Now I don't even know if I can get it to start again, let alone get it anywhere near its old condition."

"Well you try," I said, like I was getting mad, "but I say it's a piece of junk."

Then I walked out before he could realize I knew he'd strung together more than six words at once.

After that I thought he'd freeze himself to death working on that car. He was out there all day, and at night he rigged up a little lamp, ran a cord out the window, and had himself some light to see by while he worked. He was better than he had been before, but that's still not saying much. It was easier for him to do the things the rest of us did. He ate more slowly and didn't jump up and down during the meal to get this or that or look out the window. I put my hand in the back of the TV set, I admit, and fiddled around with it good, so that it was almost impossible now to get a clear picture. He didn't look at it very often anyway. He was always out with that car or going off to get parts for it. By the time it was really melting outside, he had it fixed.

I had been feeling down in the dumps about Henry around this time. We had always been together before. Henry and Lyman. But he was such a loner now that I didn't know how to take it. So I jumped at the chance one day when Henry seemed friendly. It's not that he smiled or anything. He just said, "Let's take that old shitbox for a spin." Just the way he said it made me think he could be coming around.

We went out to the car. It was spring. The sun was shining very bright. My only sister, Bonita, who was just eleven years old, came out and made us stand together for a picture. Henry leaned his elbow on the red car's windshield, and he took his other arm and put it over my shoulder, very carefully, as though it was heavy for him to lift and he didn't want to bring the weight down all at once.

"Smile," Bonita said, and he did.

That picture, I never look at it anymore. A few months ago, I don't know why, I got his picture out and tacked it on the wall. I felt good about Henry at the time, close to him. I felt good having his picture on the wall, until one night when I was looking at television. I was a little drunk and stoned. I looked up at the wall and Henry was staring at me. I don't know what it was, but his smile had changed, or maybe it was gone. All I know is I couldn't stay in the same room with that picture. I was shaking. I got up, closed the door, and went into the kitchen. A little later my friend Ray came over and we both went back into that room. We put the picture in a brown bag, folded the bag over and over tightly, then put it way back in a closet.

I still see that picture now, as if it tugs at me, whenever I pass that closet door. The picture is very clear in my mind. It was so sunny that day Henry had to squint against the glare. Or maybe the camera Bonita held flashed like a mirror, blinding him, before she snapped the picture. My face is right out in the sun, big and round. But he might have drawn back, because the shadows on his face are deep as holes. There are two shadows curved like little hooks around the ends of his smile, as if to frame it and try to keep it there—that one, first smile that looked like it might have hurt his face. He has his field jacket on and the worn-in clothes he'd come back in and kept wearing ever since. After Bonita took the picture, she went into the house and we got into the car. There was a full cooler in the trunk. We started off, east, toward

Pembina and the Red River because Henry said he wanted to see the high water.

The trip over there was beautiful. When everything starts changing, drying up, clearing off, you feel like your whole life is starting. Henry felt it, too. The top was down and the car hummed like a top. He'd really put it back in shape, even the tape on the seats was very carefully put down and glued back in layers. It's not that he smiled again or even joked, but his face looked to me as if it was clear, more peaceful. It looked as though he wasn't thinking of anything in particular except the bare fields and windbreaks and houses we were passing.

The river was high and full of winter trash when we got there. The sun was still out, but it was colder by the river. There were still little clumps of dirty snow here and there on the banks. The water hadn't gone over the banks yet, but it would, you could tell. It was just at its limit, hard swollen glossy like an old gray scar. We made ourselves a fire, and we sat down and watched the current go. As I watched it I felt something squeezing inside me and tightening and trying to let go all at the same time. I knew I was not just feeling it myself; I knew I was feeling what Henry was going through at that moment. Except that I couldn't stand it, the closing and opening. I jumped to my feet. I took Henry by the shoulders and I started shaking him. "Wake up," I says, "wake up, wake up, wake up!" I didn't know what had come over me. I sat down beside him again.

His face was totally white and hard. Then it broke, like stones break all of a sudden when water boils up inside them.

"I know it," he says. "I know it. I can't help it. It's no use."

We start talking. He said he knew what I'd done with the car. It was obvious it had been whacked out of shape and not just neglected. He said he wanted to give the car to me for good now, it was no use. He said he'd fixed it just to give it back and I should take it.

"No way," I says, "I don't want it."

"That's okay," he says, "you take it."

"I don't want it, though," I says back to him, and then to emphasize, just to emphasize, you understand, I touch his shoulder. He slaps my hand off.

"Take that car," he says.

"No," I say. "Make me," I say, and then he grabs my jacket and rips the arm loose. That jacket is a class act, suede with tags and zippers. I push Henry backwards, off the log. He jumps up and bowls me over. We go down in a clinch and come up swinging hard, for all we're worth, with our fists. He socks my jaw so hard I feel like it swings loose. Then I'm at his rib cage and land a good one under his chin so his head snaps back. He's dazzled. He looks at me and I look at him and then his eyes are full of tears and blood and at first I think he's crying. But no, he's laughing. "Ha! Ha!" he says. "Ha! Ha! Take good care of it."

"Okay," I says, "okay, no problem. Ha! Ha!"

I can't help it, and I start laughing, too. My face feels fat and strange, and after a while I get a beer from the cooler in the trunk, and when I hand it to Henry he takes his shirt and wipes my germs off. "Hoof-and-mouth disease," he says. For some reason this cracks me up, and so we're really laughing for a while, and then we drink all the rest of the beers one by one and throw them in the river and see how far, how fast, the current takes them before they fill up and sink.

"You want to go on back?" I ask after a while. "Maybe we could snag a couple nice Kashpaw girls."

He says nothing. But I can tell his mood is turning again.

"They're all crazy, the girls up here, every damn one of them."

"You're crazy too," I say, to jolly him up. "Crazy Lamartine boys!"

He looks as though he will take this wrong at first. His face twists, then clears, and he jumps up on his feet. "That's right!" he says. "Crazier 'n hell. Crazy Indians!"

I think it's the old Henry again. He throws off his jacket and starts swinging his legs out from the knees like a fancy dancer. He's down doing something between a grass dance and a bunny hop, no kind of dance I ever saw before, but neither has anyone else on all this green growing earth. He's wild. He wants to pitch whoopee! He's up and at me and all over. All this time I'm laughing so hard, so hard my belly is getting tied up in a knot.

"Got to cool me off!" he shouts all of a sudden. Then he runs over to the river and jumps in.

There's boards and other things in the current. It's so high. No sound comes from the river after the splash he makes, so I run right over. I look around. It's getting dark. I see he's halfway across the water already, and I know he didn't swim there but the current took him. It's far. I hear his voice, though, very clearly across it.

"My boots are filling," he says.

He says this in a normal voice, like he just noticed and he doesn't know what to think of it. Then he's gone. A branch comes by. Another branch. And I go in.

By the time I get out of the river, off the snag I pulled myself onto, the sun is down. I walk back to the car, turn on the high beams, and drive it up the bank. I put it in first gear and then I take my foot off the clutch. I get out, close the door, and watch it plow softly into the water. The headlights reach in as they go down, searching, still lighted even after the water swirls over the back end. I wait. The wires short out. It is all finally dark. And then there is only the water, the sound of it going and running and going and running and running.

1984

Sticks

GEORGE SAUNDERS
[b. 1958]

Every year Thanksgiving night we flocked out behind Dad as he dragged the Santa suit to the road and draped it over a kind of crucifix he'd built out of metal pole in the yard. Super Bowl week the pole was dressed in a jersey and Rod's helmet and Rod had to clear it with Dad if he wanted to take the helmet off. On Fourth of July the pole was Uncle Sam, on Veterans Day a soldier, on Halloween a ghost. The pole was Dad's one concession to glee. We were allowed a single Crayola from the box at a time. One Christmas Eve he shrieked at Kimmie for wasting an apple slice. He hovered over us as we poured ketchup, saying, Good enough good enough good enough. Birthday parties consisted of cupcakes, no ice cream. The first time I brought a date over she said, What's with your dad and that pole? and I sat there blinking.

We left home, married, had children of our own, found the seeds of meanness blooming also within us. Dad began dressing the pole with more complexity and less discernible logic. He draped some kind of fur over it on Groundhog Day and lugged out a floodlight to ensure a shadow. When an earthquake struck Chile he laid the pole on its side and spray-painted a rift in the earth. Mom died and he dressed the pole as Death and hung from the crossbar photos of Mom as a baby. We'd stop by and find odd talismans from his youth arranged around the base: army medals, theater tickets, old sweatshirts, tubes of Mom's makeup. One autumn he painted the pole bright yellow. He covered it with cotton swabs that winter for warmth and provided offspring by hammering in six crossed sticks around the yard. He ran lengths of string between the pole and the sticks, and taped to the string letters of apology, admissions of error, pleas for understanding, all written in a frantic hand on index cards. He painted a sign saying LOVE and hung it from the pole and another that said FORGIVE? and then he died in the hall with the radio on and we sold the house to a young couple who yanked out the pole and left it by the road on garbage day.

1994

The Great Silence

TED CHIANG

[b. 1967]

The humans use Arecibo[1] to look for extraterrestrial intelligence. Their desire to make a connection is so strong that they've created an ear capable of hearing across the universe.

But I and my fellow parrots are right here. Why aren't they interested in listening to our voices?

We're a nonhuman species capable of communicating with them. Aren't we exactly what humans are looking for?

The universe is so vast that intelligent life must surely have arisen many times. The universe is also so old that even one technological species would have had time to expand and fill the galaxy. Yet there is no sign of life anywhere except on Earth. Humans call this the Fermi paradox.

One proposed solution to the Fermi paradox is that intelligent species actively try to conceal their presence, to avoid being targeted by hostile invaders.

Speaking as a member of a species that has been driven nearly to extinction by humans, I can attest that this is a wise strategy.

It makes sense to remain quiet and avoid attracting attention.

The Fermi paradox is sometimes known as the Great Silence. The universe ought to be a cacophony of voices, but instead it's disconcertingly quiet.

Some humans theorize that intelligent species go extinct before they can expand into outer space. If they're correct, then the hush of the night sky is the silence of a graveyard.

[1]A radio telescope and facility of the National Astronomy and Ionosphere Center located in Arecibo, Puerto Rico.

Hundreds of years ago, my kind was so plentiful that the Río Abajo Forest[2] resounded with our voices. Now we're almost gone. Soon this rainforest may be as silent as the rest of the universe.

There was an African grey parrot named Alex. He was famous for his cognitive abilities. Famous among humans, that is.

A human researcher named Irene Pepperberg spent thirty years studying Alex. She found that not only did Alex know the words for shapes and colors, he actually understood the concepts of shape and color.

Many scientists were skeptical that a bird could grasp abstract concepts. Humans like to think they're unique. But eventually Pepperberg convinced them that Alex wasn't just repeating words, that he understood what he was saying.

Out of all my cousins, Alex was the one who came closest being taken seriously as a communication partner by humans.

Alex died suddenly, when he was still relatively young. The evening before he died, Alex said to Pepperberg, "You be good, I love you."

If humans are looking for a connection with a nonhuman intelligence, what more can they ask for than that?

Every parrot has a unique call that it uses to identify itself; biologists refer to this as the parrot's "contact call."

In 1974, astronomers used Arecibo to broadcast a message into outer space intended to demonstrate human intelligence. That was humanity's contact call.

In the wild, parrots address each other by name. One bird imitates another's contact call to get the other bird's attention.

If humans ever detect the Arecibo message being sent back to Earth, they will know someone is trying to get their attention.

Parrots are vocal learners: we can learn to make new sounds after we've heard them. It's an ability that few animals possess. A dog may understand dozens of commands, but it will never do anything but bark.

Humans are vocal learners too. We have that in common. So humans and parrots share a special relationship with sound. We don't simply cry out. We pronounce. We enunciate.

[2]A forest preserve in Puerto Rico that is home to a critically endangered species of parrot.

Perhaps that's why humans built Arecibo the way they did. A receiver doesn't have to be a transmitter, but Arecibo is both. It's an ear for listening, and a mouth for speaking.

Humans have lived alongside parrots for thousands of years, and only recently have they considered the possibility that we might be intelligent.

I suppose I can't blame them. We parrots used to think humans weren't very bright. It's hard to make sense of behavior that's so different from your own.

But parrots are more similar to humans than any extraterrestrial species will be, and humans can observe us up close; they can look us in the eye. How do they expect to recognize an alien intelligence if all they can do is eavesdrop from a hundred light-years a way?

It's no coincidence that "aspiration" means both hope and the act of breathing.

When we speak, we use the breath in our lungs to give our thoughts a physical form. The sounds we make are simultaneously our intentions and our life force.

I speak, therefore I am. Vocal learners, like parrots and humans, are perhaps the only ones who fully comprehend the truth of this.

There's a pleasure that comes with shaping sounds with your mouth. It's so primal and visceral that throughout their history, humans have considered the activity a pathway to the divine.

Pythagorean mystics believed that vowels represented the music of the spheres, and chanted to draw power from them.

Pentecostal Christians believe that when they speak in tongues, they're speaking the language used by angels in Heaven.

Brahmin Hindus believe that by reciting mantras, they're strengthening the building blocks of reality.

Only a species of vocal learners would ascribe such importance to sound in their mythologies. We parrots can appreciate that.

According to Hindu mythology, the universe was created with a sound: "Om." It's a syllable that contains within it everything that ever was and everything that will be.

When the Arecibo telescope is pointed at the space between stars, it hears a faint hum.

Astronomers call that the "cosmic microwave background." It's the residual radiation of the Big Bang, the explosion that created the universe fourteen billion years ago.

But you can also think of it as a barely audible reverberation of that original "Om." That syllable was so resonant that the night sky will keep vibrating for as long as the universe exists.

When Arecibo is not listening to anything else, it hears the voice of creation.

We Puerto Rican parrots have our own myths. They're simpler than human mythology, but I think humans would take pleasure from them.

Alas, our myths are being lost as my species dies out. I doubt the humans will have deciphered our language before we're gone.

So the extinction of my species doesn't just mean the loss of a group of birds. It's also the disappearance of our language, our rituals, our traditions. It's the silencing of our voice.

Human activity has brought my kind to the brink of extinction, but I don't blame them for it. They didn't do it maliciously. They just weren't paying attention.

And humans create such beautiful myths; what imaginations they have. Perhaps that's why their aspirations are so immense. Look at Arecibo. Any species that can build such a thing must have greatness within it.

My species probably won't be here for much longer; it's likely that we'll die before our time and join the Great Silence. But before we go, we are sending a message to humanity. We just hope the telescope at Arecibo will enable them to hear it.

The message is this:

You be good. I love you.

2015

Brownies

ZZ PACKER
[b. 1973]

By our second day at Camp Crescendo, the girls in my Brownie troop had decided to kick the asses of each and every girl in Brownie Troop 909. Troop 909 was doomed from the first day of camp; they were white girls, their complexions a blend of ice cream: strawberry, vanilla. They turtled out from their bus in pairs, their rolled-up sleeping bags chromatized with Disney characters: Sleeping Beauty, Snow White, Mickey Mouse; or the generic ones cheap parents bought: washed-out rainbows, unicorns, curly-eyelashed frogs. Some clutched Igloo coolers and still others held on to stuffed toys like pacifiers, looking all around them like tourists determined to be dazzled.

Our troop was wending its way past their bus, past the ranger station, past the colorful trail guide drawn like a treasure map, locked behind glass.

"Man, did you smell them?" Arnetta said, giving the girls a slow once-over, "They smell like Chihuahuas. *Wet* Chihuahuas." Their troop was still at the entrance, and though we had passed them by yards, Arnetta raised her nose in the air and grimaced.

Arnetta said this from the very rear of the line, far away from Mrs. Margolin, who always strung our troop behind her like a brood of obedient ducklings. Mrs. Margolin even looked like a mother duck—she had hair cropped close to a small ball of a head, almost no neck, and huge, miraculous breasts. She wore enormous belts that looked like the kind that weightlifters wear, except hers would be cheap metallic gold or rabbit fur or covered with gigantic fake sunflowers, and often these belts would become nature lessons in and of themselves. "See," Mrs. Margolin once said to us, pointing to her belt, "this one's made entirely from the feathers of baby pigeons."

The belt layered with feathers was uncanny enough, but I was more disturbed by the realization that I had never actually *seen* a baby pigeon. I searched weeks for one, in vain—scampering after pigeons whenever I was downtown with my father.

But nature lessons were not Mrs. Margolin's top priority. She saw the position of troop leader as an evangelical post. Back at the A.M.E. church[1] where our Brownie meetings were held, Mrs. Margolin was especially fond of imparting religious aphorisms by means of acrostics—"Satan" was the "Serpent Always Tempting and Noisome"; she'd refer to the "Bible" as "Basic Instructions Before Leaving Earth." Whenever she quizzed us on these, expecting to hear the acrostics parroted back to her, only Arnetta's correct replies soared over our vague mumblings. "Jesus?" Mrs. Margolin might ask expectantly, and Arnetta alone would dutifully answer, "Jehovah's Example, Saving Us Sinners."

Arnetta always made a point of listening to Mrs. Margolin's religious talk and giving her what she wanted to hear. Because of this, Arnetta could have blared through a megaphone that the white girls of Troop 909 were "wet Chihuahuas" without so much as a blink from Mrs. Margolin. Once, Arnetta killed the troop goldfish by feeding it a french fry covered in ketchup, and when Mrs. Margolin demanded that she explain what had happened, claimed the goldfish had been eyeing her meal for *hours*, then the fish—giving in to temptation—had leapt up and snatched a whole golden fry from her fingertips.

"*Serious* Chihuahua," Octavia added, and though neither Arnetta nor Octavia could *spell* "Chihuahua," had ever *seen* a Chihuahua, trisyllabic words had gained a sort of exoticism within our fourth-grade set at Woodrow Wilson Elementary. Arnetta and Octavia would flip through the dictionary, determined to work the vulgar-sounding ones like "Djibouti" and "asinine" into conversation.

"*Caucasian* Chihuahuas," Arnetta said.

That did it. The girls in my troop turned elastic: Drema and Elise doubled up on one another like inextricably entwined kites; Octavia slapped her belly; Janice jumped straight up in the air, then did it again, as if to slam-dunk her own head. They could not stop laughing. No one had laughed so hard since a boy named Martez had

[1]African Methodist Episcopal church.

stuck a pencil in the electric socket and spent the whole day with a strange grin on his face.

"Girls, girls," said our parent helper, Mrs. Hedy. Mrs. Hedy was Octavia's mother, and she wagged her index finger perfunctorily, like a windshield wiper. "Stop it, now. Be good." She said this loud enough to be heard, but lazily, bereft of any feeling of indication that she meant to be obeyed, as though she could say these words again at the exact same pitch if a button somewhere on her were pressed.

But the rest of the girls didn't stop; they only laughed louder. It was the word "Caucasian" that got them all going. One day at school, about a month before the Brownie camping trip, Arnetta turned to a boy wearing impossibly high-ankled floodwater jeans and said, "What are you? *Caucasian?*" The word took off from there, and soon everything was Caucasian. If you ate too fast you ate like a Caucasian, if you ate too slow you ate like a Caucasian. The biggest feat anyone at Woodrow Wilson could do was to jump off the swing in midair, at the highest point in its arc, and if you fell (as I had, more than once) instead of landing on your feet, knees bent Olympic gymnast–style, Arnetta and Octavia were prepared to comment. They'd look at each other with the silence of passengers who'd narrowly escaped an accident, then nod their heads, whispering with solemn horror, *"Caucasian."*

Even the only white kid in our school, Dennis, got in on the Caucasian act. That time when Martez stuck a pencil in the socket, Dennis had pointed and yelled, "That was *so* Caucasian!"

When you lived in the south suburbs of Atlanta, it was easy to forget about whites. Whites were like those baby pigeons: real and existing, but rarely seen or thought about. Everyone had been to Rich's to go clothes shopping, everyone had seen white girls and their mothers coo-cooing over dresses; everyone had gone to the downtown library and seen white businessmen swish by importantly, wrists flexed in front of them to check the time as though they would change from Clark Kent into Superman at any second. But those images were as fleeting as cards shuffled in a deck, whereas the ten white girls behind us—*invaders,* Arnetta would later call them—were instantly real and memorable, with their long, shampoo-commercial hair, straight as spaghetti from the box. This alone was reason for envy and hatred. The only black girl most of us had ever seen with hair that long was Octavia, whose hair hung past her butt like a Hawaiian hula dancer's. The sight of Octavia's mane prompted other girls to listen to her reverentially, as though whatever she had to say would somehow activate their own follicles. For example, when, on the first day of camp, Octavia made as if to speak, and everyone fell silent. "Nobody," Octavia said, "calls us niggers."

At the end of that first day, when half of our troop made their way back to the cabin after tag-team restroom visits, Arnetta said she'd heard one of the Troop 909 girls call Daphne a nigger. The other half of the girls and I were helping Mrs. Margolin clean up the pots and pans from the campfire ravioli dinner. When we made our way to the restrooms to wash up and brush our teeth, we met up with Arnetta midway.

"Man, I completely heard the girl," Arnetta reported. "Right, Daphne?"

Daphne hardly ever spoke, but when she did, her voice was petite and tinkly, the voice one might expect from a shiny new earring. She'd written a poem once, for Langston Hughes Day, a poem brimming with all the teacher-winning ingredients—trees and oceans, sunsets and moons—but what cinched the poem for the grown-ups, snatching the win from Octavia's musical ode to Grandmaster Flash and the Furious Five, were Daphne's last lines:

> You are my father, the veteran
> When you cry in the dark
> It rains and rains and rains in my heart

She'd always worn clean, though faded, jumpers and dresses when Chic jeans were the fashion, but when she went up to the dais to receive her prize journal, pages trimmed in gold, she wore a new dress with a velveteen bodice and a taffeta skirt as wide as an umbrella. All the kids clapped, though none of them understood the poem. I'd read encyclopedias the way others read comics, and I didn't get it. But those last lines pricked me, they were so eerie, and as my father and I ate cereal, I'd whisper over my Froot Loops, like a mantra, "*You are my father, the veteran. You are my father, the veteran, the veteran, the veteran,*" until my father, who acted in plays as Caliban and Othello and was not a veteran, marched me up to my teacher one morning and said, "Can you tell me what's wrong with this kid?"

I thought Daphne and I might become friends, but I think she grew spooked by me whispering those lines to her, begging her to tell me what they meant, and I soon understood that two quiet people like us were better off quiet alone.

"Daphne? Didn't you hear them call you a nigger?" Arnetta asked, giving Daphne a nudge.

The sun was setting behind the trees, and their leafy tops formed a canopy of black lace for the flame of the sun to pass through. Daphne shrugged her shoulders at first, then slowly nodded her head when Arnetta gave her a hard look.

Twenty minutes later, when my restroom group returned to the cabin, Arnetta was still talking about Troop 909. My restroom group had passed by some of the 909 girls. For the most part, they deferred to us, waving us into the restrooms, letting us go even though they'd gotten there first.

We'd seen them, but from afar, never within their orbit enough to see whether their faces were the way all white girls appeared on TV—ponytailed and full of energy, bubbling over with love and money. All I could see was that some of them rapidly fanned their faces with their hands, though the heat of the day had long passed. A few seemed to be lolling their heads in slow circles, half purposefully, as if exercising the muscles of their necks, half ecstatically, like Stevie Wonder.

"We can't let them get away with that," Arnetta said, dropping her voice to a laryngitic whisper. "We can't let them get away with calling us niggers. I say we teach them a lesson." She sat down cross-legged on a sleeping bag, an embittered Buddha, eyes glimmering acrylic-black. "We can't go telling Mrs. Margolin, either. Mrs. Margolin'll say something about doing unto others and the path of righteousness and all. Forget that shit." She let her eyes flutter irreverently till they half closed, as though ignoring an insult not worth returning. We could all hear Mrs. Margolin outside, gathering the last of the metal campware.

Nobody said anything for a while. Usually people were quiet after Arnetta spoke. Her tone had an upholstered confidence that was somehow both regal and vulgar at once. It demanded a few moments of silence in its wake, like the ringing of a church bell or the playing of taps. Sometimes Octavia would ditto or dissent to whatever Arnetta had said, and this was the signal that others could speak. But this time Octavia just swirled a long cord of hair into pretzel shapes.

"*Well?*" Arnetta said. She looked as if she had discerned the hidden severity of the situation and was waiting for the rest of us to catch up. Everyone looked from Arnetta to Daphne. It was, after all, Daphne who had supposedly been called the name, but Daphne sat on the bare cabin floor, flipping through the pages of the Girl Scout handbook, eyebrows arched in mock wonder, as if the handbook were a catalogue full of bright and startling foreign costumes. Janice broke the silence. She clapped her hands to broach her idea of a plan.

"They gone be sleeping," she whispered conspiratorially, "then we gone sneak into they cabin, then we'll put daddy longlegs in they sleeping bags. Then they'll wake up. Then we gone beat 'em up till they're as flat as frying pans!" She jammed her fist into the palm of her hand, then made a sizzling sound.

Janice's country accent was laughable, her looks homely, her jumpy acrobatics embarrassing to behold. Arnetta and Octavia volleyed amused, arrogant smiles whenever Janice opened her mouth, but Janice never caught the hint, spoke whenever she wanted, fluttered around Arnetta and Octavia futilely offering her opinions to their departing backs. Whenever Arnetta and Octavia shooed her away, Janice loitered until the two would finally sigh and ask, "What *is* it, Miss Caucasoid? What do you *want*?"

"Shut up, Janice," Octavia said, letting a fingered loop of hair fall to her waist as though just the sound of Janice's voice had ruined the fun of her hair twisting.

Janice obeyed, her mouth hung open in a loose grin, unflappable, unhurt.

"All right," Arnetta said, standing up. "We're going to have a secret meeting and talk about what we're going to do."

Everyone gravely nodded her head. The word "secret" had a built-in importance, the modifier form of the word carried more clout than the noun. A secret meant nothing; it was like gossip: just a bit of unpleasant knowledge about someone who happened to be someone other than yourself. A secret *meeting*, or a secret *club* was entirely different.

That was when Arnetta turned to me as though she knew that doing so was both a compliment and a charity.

"Snot, you're not going to be a bitch and tell Mrs. Margolin, are you?"

I had been called "Snot" ever since first grade, when I'd sneezed in class and two long ropes of mucus had splattered a nearby girl.

"Hey," I said. "Maybe you didn't hear them right—I mean—"

"Are you gonna tell on us or not?" was all Arnetta wanted to know, and by the time the question was asked, the rest of our Brownie troop looked at me as though they'd already decided their course of action, me being the only impediment.

Camp Crescendo used to double as a high-school-band and field hockey camp until an arcing field hockey ball landed on the clasp of a girl's metal barrette, knifing a skull nerve and paralyzing the right side of her body. The camp closed down for a few years and the girl's teammates built a memorial, filling the spot on which the girl fell with hockey balls, on which they had painted—all in nail polish—get-well tidings, flowers, and hearts. The balls were still stacked there, like a shrine of ostrich eggs embedded in the ground.

On the second day of camp, Troop 909 was dancing around the mound of hockey balls, their limbs jangling awkwardly, their cries like the constant summer squeal of an amusement park. There was a stream that bordered the field hockey lawn, and the girls from my troop settled next to it, scarfing down the last of lunch: sandwiches made from salami and slices of tomato that had gotten waterlogged from the melting ice in the cooler. From the stream bank, Arnetta eyed the Troop 909 girls, scrutinizing their movements to glean inspiration for battle.

"Man," Arnetta said, "we could bumrush them right now if that damn lady would *leave*."

The 909 troop leader was a white woman with the severe pageboy hairdo of an ancient Egyptian. She lay on a picnic blanket, sphinx-like, eating a banana, sometimes holding it out in front of her like a microphone. Beside her sat a girl slowly flapping one hand like a bird with a broken wing. Occasionally, the leader would call out the names of girls who'd attempted leapfrogs and flips, or of girls who yelled too loudly or strayed far from the circle.

"I'm just glad Big Fat Mama's not following us here," Octavia said. "At least we don't have to worry about her." Mrs. Margolin, Octavia assured us, was having her Afternoon Devotional, shrouded in mosquito netting, in a clearing she'd found. Mrs. Hedy was cleaning mud from her espadrilles in the cabin.

"I handled them." Arnetta sucked on her teeth and proudly grinned. "I told her we was going to gather leaves."

"Gather leaves," Octavia said, nodding respectfully. "That's a good one. Especially since they're so mad-crazy about this camping thing." She looked from ground to sky, sky to ground. Her hair hung down her back in two braids like a squaw's. "I mean, I really don't know why it's even called *camping*—all we ever do with Nature is find some twigs and say something like, 'Wow, this fell from a tree.' " She then studied her sandwich. With two disdainful fingers, she picked out a slice of dripping tomato, the sections congealed with red slime. She pitched it into the stream embrowned with dead leaves and the murky effigies of other dead things, but in the opaque water, a group of small silver-brown fish appeared. They surrounded the tomato and nibbled.

"Look!" Janice cried. "Fishes! Fishes?" As she scrambled to the edge of the stream to watch, a covey of insects threw up tantrums from the wheatgrass and nettle, a throng of tiny electric machines, all going at once. Octavia sneaked up behind Janice as if to push her in. Daphne and I exchanged terrified looks. It seemed as though only we knew that Octavia was close enough—and bold enough—to actually push Janice into the stream. Janice turned around quickly, but Octavia was already staring serenely into the still water as though she was gathering some sort of courage from it. "What's so funny?" Janice said, eyeing them all suspiciously.

Elise began humming the tune to "Karma Chameleon," all the girls joining in, their hums light and facile. Janice also began to hum, against everyone else, the high-octane opening chords of "Beat It."

"I love me some Michael Jackson," Janice said when she'd finished humming, smacking her lips as though Michael Jackson were a favorite meal. "I *will* marry Michael Jackson."

Before anyone had a chance to impress upon Janice the impossibility of this, Arnetta suddenly rose, made a sun visor of her hand, and watched Troop 909 leave the field hockey lawn.

"Dammit!" she said, "We've got to get them *alone*."

"They won't ever be alone." I said. All the rest of the girls looked at me, for I usually kept quiet. If I spoke even a word, I could count on someone calling me Snot. Everyone seemed to think that we could beat up these girls; no one entertained the thought that they might fight *back*. "The only time they'll be unsupervised is in the bathroom."

"Oh shut up, Snot," Octavia said.

But Arnetta slowly nodded her head. "The bathroom," she said. "The bathroom," she said, again and again. "The bathroom! The bathroom!"

According to Octavia's watch, it took us five minutes to hike to the restrooms, which were midway between our cabin and Troop 909's. Inside, the mirrors above the sinks returned only the vaguest of reflections, as though someone had taken a scouring pad to their surfaces to obscure the shine. Pine needles, leaves, and dirty, flattened wads of chewing gum covered the floor like a mosaic. Webs of hair matted the drain in the middle of the floor. Above the sinks and below the mirrors, stacks of folded white paper towels lay on a long metal counter. Shaggy white balls of paper towels sat on the sinktops in a line like corsages on display. A thread of floss snaked from a wad of tissues dotted with the faint red-pink of blood. One of those white girls, I thought, had just lost a tooth.

Though the restroom looked almost the same as it had the night before, it somehow seemed stranger now. We hadn't noticed the wooden rafters coming together in great V's. We were, it seemed, inside a whale, viewing the ribs of the roof of its mouth.

"Wow. It's a mess," Elise said.

"You can say that again."

Arnetta leaned against the doorjamb of a restroom stall. "This is where they'll be again," she said. Just seeing the place, just having a plan seemed to satisfy her. "We'll go in and talk to them. You know, 'How you doing? How long'll you be here?' That sort of thing. Then Octavia and I are gonna tell them what happens when they call any one of us a nigger."

"I'm going to say something, too," Janice said.

Arnetta considered this. "Sure," she said. "Of course. Whatever you want."

Janice pointed her finger like a gun at Octavia and rehearsed the line she'd thought up, " 'We're gonna teach you a *lesson*!' That's what I'm going to say." She narrowed her eyes like a TV mobster. " 'We're gonna teach you little girls a lesson!' "

With the back of her hand, Octavia brushed Janice's finger away. "You couldn't teach me to shit in a toilet."

"But," I said, "what if they say, 'We didn't say that? We didn't call anyone an N-I-G-G-E-R.'"

"Snot," Arnetta said, and then sighed. "Don't think. Just fight. If you even know how."

Everyone laughed except Daphne. Arnetta gently laid her hand on Daphne's shoulder. "Daphne. You don't have to fight. We're doing this for you."

Daphne walked to the counter, took a clean paper towel, and carefully unfolded it like a map. With it, she began to pick up the trash all around. Everyone watched.

"C'mon," Arnetta said to everyone. "Let's beat it." We all ambled toward the doorway, where the sunshine made one large white rectangle of light. We were immediately blinded, and we shielded our eyes with our hands and our forearms.

"Daphne?" Arnetta asked. "Are you coming?"

We all looked back at the bending girl, the thin of her back hunched like the back of a custodian sweeping a stage, caught in limelight. Stray strands of her hair were lit near-transparent, thin fiber-optic threads. She did not nod yes to the question, nor did she shake her head no. She abided, bent. Then she began again, picking up leaves, wads of paper, the cotton fluff innards from a torn stuffed toy. She did it so methodically, so exquisitely, so humbly, she must have been trained. I thought of those dresses she wore, faded and old, yet so pressed and clean. I then saw the poverty in them; I then could imagine her mother, cleaning the houses of others, returning home, weary.

"I guess she's not coming."

We left her and headed back to our cabin, over pine needles and leaves, taking the path full of shade.

"What about our secret meeting?" Elise asked.

Arnetta enunciated her words in a way that defied contradiction: "We just had it."

It was nearing our bedtime, but the sun had not yet set.

"Hey, your mama's coming," Arnetta said to Octavia when she saw Mrs. Hedy walk toward the cabin, sniffling. When Octavia's mother wasn't giving bored, parochial orders, she sniffled continuously, mourning an imminent divorce from her husband. She might begin a sentence, "I don't know what Robert will do when Octavia and I are gone. Who'll buy him cigarettes?" and Octavia would hotly whisper, "*Mama*," in a way that meant: Please don't talk about our problems in front of everyone. Please shut up.

But when Mrs. Hedy began talking about her husband, thinking about her husband, seeing clouds shaped like the head of her husband, she couldn't be quiet, and no one could dislodge her from the comfort of her own woe. Only one thing could perk her up—Brownie songs. If the girls were quiet, and Mrs. Hedy was in her dopey, sorrowful mood, she would say, "Y'all know I like those songs, girls. Why don't you sing one?" Everyone would groan, except me and Daphne. I, for one, liked some of the songs.

"C'mon, everybody," Octavia said drearily, "She likes the Brownie song best."

We sang, loud enough to reach Mrs. Hedy:

"I've got something in my pocket;
It belongs across my face.
And I keep it very close at hand
  in a most convenient place.
I'm sure you couldn't guess it
If you guessed a long, long while.
So I'll take it out and put it on—
It's a great big Brownie smile!"

The Brownie song was supposed to be sung cheerfully, as though we were elves in a workshop, singing as we merrily cobbled shoes, but everyone except me hated the song so much that they sang it like a maudlin record, played on the most sluggish of rpms.

"That was good," Mrs. Hedy said, closing the cabin door behind her. "Wasn't that nice, Linda?"

"Praise God," Mrs. Margolin answered without raising her head from the chore of counting out Popsicle sticks for the next day's craft session.

"Sing another one," Mrs. Hedy said. She said it with a sort of joyful aggression, like a drunk I'd once seen who'd refused to leave a Korean grocery.

"God, Mama, get over it," Octavia whispered in a voice meant only for Arnetta, but Mrs. Hedy heard it and started to leave the cabin.

"Don't go," Arnetta said. She ran after Mrs. Hedy and held her by the arm. "We haven't finished singing." She nudged us with a single look. "Let's sing the 'Friends Song.' For Mrs. Hedy."

Although I liked some of the songs, I hated this one:

Make new friends
But keep the o-old,
One is silver
And the other gold.

If most of the girls in the troop could be any type of metal, they'd be bunched-up wads of tinfoil, maybe, or rusty iron nails you had to get tetanus shots for.

"No, no, no," Mrs. Margolin said before anyone could start in on the "Friends Song." "An uplifting song. Something to lift her up and take her mind off all these earthly burdens."

Arnetta and Octavia rolled their eyes. Everyone knew what song Mrs. Margolin was talking about, and no one, no one, wanted to sing it.

"Please, no," a voice called out. "Not 'The Doughnut Song.' "

"Please not 'The Doughnut Song,' " Octavia pleaded.

"I'll brush my teeth two times if I don't have to sing 'The Doughnut—' "

"Sing!" Mrs. Margolin demanded.

We sang:

"Life without Jesus is like a do-ough-nut!
Like a do-ooough-nut!
Like a do-ooough-nut!
Life without Jesus is like a do-ough-nut!
There's a hole in the middle of my soul!"

There were other verses, involving other pastries, but we stopped after the first one and cast glances toward Mrs. Margolin to see if we could gain a reprieve. Mrs. Margolin's eyes fluttered blissfully. She was half asleep.

"Awww," Mrs. Hedy said, as though giant Mrs. Margolin were a cute baby, "Mrs. Margolin's had a long day."

"Yes indeed," Mrs. Margolin answered. "If you don't mind, I might just go to the lodge where the beds are. I haven't been the same since the operation."

I had not heard of this operation, or when it had occurred, since Mrs. Margolin had never missed the once-a-week Brownie meetings, but I could see from Daphne's face that she was concerned, and I could see that the other girls had decided that Mrs. Margolin's operation must have happened long ago in some remote time unconnected to our own. Nevertheless, they put on sad faces. We had all been taught that adulthood was full of sorrow and pain, taxes and bills, dreaded work and dealings with whites, sickness and death. I tried to do what the others did. I tried to look silent.

"Go right ahead, Linda," Mrs. Hedy said, "I'll watch the girls." Mrs. Hedy seemed to forget about divorce for a moment; she looked at us with dewy eyes, as if we were mysterious, furry creatures. Meanwhile, Mrs. Margolin walked through the maze of sleeping bags until she found her own. She gathered a neat stack of clothes and pajamas slowly, as though doing so was almost painful. She took her toothbrush, her toothpaste, her pillow. "All right!" Mrs. Margolin said, addressing us all from the threshold of the cabin. "Be in bed by nine." She said it with a twinkle in her voice, letting us know she was allowing us to be naughty and stay up till nine-fifteen.

"C'mon everybody," Arnetta said after Mrs. Margolin left. "Time for us to wash up."

Everyone watched Mrs. Hedy closely, wondering whether she would insist on coming with us since it was night, making a fight with Troop 909 nearly impossible. Troop 909 would soon be in the bathroom, washing their faces, brushing their teeth—completely unsuspecting of our ambush.

"We won't be long," Arnetta said. "We're old enough to go to the restrooms by ourselves."

Ms. Hedy pursed her lips at this dilemma. "Well, I guess you Brownies are almost Girl Scouts, right?"

"Right!"

"Just one more badge," Drema said.

"And about," Octavia droned, "a million more cookies to sell." Octavia looked at all of us, *Now's our chance,* her face seemed to say, but our chance to do *what,* I didn't exactly know.

Finally, Mrs. Hedy walked to the doorway where Octavia stood dutifully waiting to say goodbye but looking bored doing it. Mrs. Hedy held Octavia's chin. "You'll be good?"

"Yes, Mama."

"And remember to pray for me and your father? If I'm asleep when you get back?"

"Yes, Mama."

When the other girls had finished getting their toothbrushes and washcloths and flashlights for the group restroom trip, I was drawing pictures of tiny birds with too many feathers. Daphne was sitting on her sleeping bag, reading.

"You're not going to come?" Octavia asked.

Daphne shook her head.

"I'm gonna stay, too," I said. "I'll go to the restroom when Daphne and Mrs. Hedy go."

Arnetta leaned down toward me and whispered so that Mrs. Hedy, who'd taken over Mrs. Margolin's task of counting Popsicle sticks, couldn't hear. "No, Snot. If we get in trouble, you're going to get in trouble with the rest of us."

We made our way through the darkness by flashlight. The tree branches that had shaded us just hours earlier, along the same path, now looked like arms sprouting menacing hands. The stars sprinkled the sky like spilled salt. They seemed fastened to the darkness, high up and holy, their places fixed and definite as we stirred beneath them.

Some, like me, were quiet because we were afraid of the dark; others were talking like crazy for the same reason.

"Wow!" Drema said, looking up. "Why are all the stars out here? I never see stars back on Oneida Street."

"It's a camping trip, that's why," Octavia said. "You're supposed to see stars on camping trips."

Janice said, "This place smells like my mother's air freshener."

"These woods are *pine*," Elise said. "Your mother probably uses *pine* air freshener."

Janice mouthed an exaggerated "Oh," nodding her head as though she just then understood one of the world's great secrets.

No one talked about fighting. Everyone was afraid enough just walking through the infinite deep of the woods. Even though I didn't fight to fight, was afraid of fighting, I felt I was part of the rest of the troop; like I was defending something. We trudged against the slight incline of the path, Arnetta leading the way.

"You know," I said, "their leader will be there. Or they won't even be there. It's dark already. Last night the sun was still in the sky. I'm sure they're already finished."

Arnetta acted as if she hadn't heard me. I followed her gaze with my flashlight, and that's when I saw the squares of light in the darkness. The bathroom was just ahead.

But the girls were there. We could hear them before we could see them.

"Octavia and I will go in first so they'll think there's just two of us, then wait till I say, 'We're gonna teach you a lesson,' " Arnetta said. "Then, bust in. That'll surprise them."

"That's what I was supposed to say," Janice said.

Arnetta went inside, Octavia next to her. Janice followed, and the rest of us waited outside.

They were in there for what seemed like whole minutes, but something was wrong. Arnetta hadn't given the signal yet. I was with the girls outside when I heard one of the Troop 909 girls say, "NO. That did NOT happen!"

That was to be expected, that they'd deny the whole thing. What I hadn't expected was *the voice* in which the denial was said. The girl sounded as though her tongue were caught in her mouth. "That's a BAD word!" the girl continued. "We don't say BAD words!"

"Let's go in," Elise said.

"No," Drema said, "I don't want to. What if we get beat up?"

"Snot?" Elise turned to me, her flashlight blinding. It was the first time anyone had asked my opinion, though I knew they were just asking because they were afraid.

"I say we go inside, just to see what's going on."

"But Arnetta didn't give us the signal," Drema said. "She's supposed to say, 'We're gonna teach you a lesson,' and I didn't hear her say it."

"C'mon," I said. "Let's just go in."

We went inside. There we found the white girls—about five girls huddled up next to one big girl. I instantly knew she was the owner of the voice we'd heard. Arnetta and Octavia inched toward us as soon as we entered.

"Where's Janice?" Elise asked, then we heard a flush. "Oh."

"I think," Octavia said, whispering to Elise, "they're retarded."

"We ARE NOT retarded!" the big girl said, though it was obvious that she was. That they all were. The girls around her began to whimper.

"They're just pretending," Arnetta said, trying to convince herself. "I know they are."

Octavia turned to Arnetta. "Arnetta. Let's just leave."

Janice came out of a stall, happy and relieved, then she suddenly remembered her line, pointed to the big girl, and said, "We're gonna teach you a lesson."

"Shut up, Janice," Octavia said, but her heart was not in it. Arnetta's face was set in a lost, deep scowl. Octavia turned to the big girl and said loudly, slowly, as if they were all deaf, "We're going to leave. It was nice meeting you, O.K.? You don't have to tell anyone that we were here. O.K.?"

"Why not?" said the big girl, like a taunt. When she spoke, her lips did not meet, her mouth did not close. Her tongue grazed the roof of her mouth, like a little pink fish. "You'll get in trouble. I know. *I* know."

Arnetta got back her old cunning. "If you said anything, then you'd be a tattletale."

The girl looked sad for a moment, then perked up quickly. A flash of genius crossed her face. "I *like* tattletale."

"It's all right, girls. It's gonna be all right!" the 909 troop leader said. All of Troop 909 burst into tears. It was as though someone had instructed them all to cry at once. The troop leader had girls under her arm, and all the rest of the girls crowded about her. It reminded me of a hog I'd seen on a field trip, where all the little hogs gathered about the mother at feeding time, latching onto her teats. The 909 troop leader had come into the bathroom, shortly after the big girl had threatened to tell. Then the ranger came, then, once the ranger had radioed the station, Mrs. Margolin arrived with Daphne in tow.

The ranger had left the restroom area, but everyone else was huddled just outside, swatting mosquitoes.

"Oh. They *will* apologize," Mrs. Margolin said to the 909 troop leader, but she said this so angrily, I knew she was speaking more to us than to the other troop leader. "When their parents find out, every one a them will be on punishment."

"It's all right, it's all right," the 909 troop leader reassured Mrs. Margolin. Her voice lilted in the same way it had when addressing the girls. She smiled the whole time she talked. She was like one of those TV-cooking-show women who talk and dice onions and smile all at the same time.

"See. It could have happened. I'm not calling your girls fibbers or anything." She shook her head ferociously from side to side, her Egyptian-style pageboy flapping against her cheeks like heavy drapes. "It *could* have happened. See. Our girls are *not* retarded. They are *delayed* learners." She said this in a syrupy instructional voice, as though our troop might be delayed learners as well, "We're from the Decatur Children's Academy. Many of them just have special needs."

"Now we won't be able to walk to the bathroom by ourselves!" the big girl said.

"Yes you will," the troop leader said, "but maybe we'll wait till we get back to Decatur—"

"I don't want to wait!" the girl said. "I want my Independence badge!"

The girls in my troop were entirely speechless. Arnetta looked stoic, as though she were soon to be tortured but was determined not to appear weak. Mrs. Margolin pursed her lips solemnly and said, "Bless them, Lord. Bless them."

In contrast, the Troop 909 leader was full of words and energy. "Some of our girls are echolalic—" She smiled and happily presented one of the girls hanging onto her, but the girl widened her eyes in horror, and violently withdrew herself from the center of attention, sensing she was being sacrificed for the village sins. "Echolalic," the troop leader continued. "That means they will say whatever they hear, like an echo—that's where the word comes from. It comes from 'echo.' " She ducked her head apologetically, "I mean, not all of them have the most *progressive* of parents, so if they heard a bad word, they might have repeated it. But I guarantee it would not have been *intentional*."

Arnetta spoke. "I saw her say the word. I heard her." She pointed to a small girl, smaller than any of us, wearing an oversized T-shirt that read: "Eat Bertha's Mussels."

The troop leader shook her head and smiled, "That's impossible. She doesn't speak. She can, but she doesn't."

Arnetta furrowed her brow. "No. It wasn't her. That's right. It was *her*."

The girl Arnetta pointed to grinned as though she'd been paid a compliment. She was the only one from either troop actually wearing a full uniform: the mocha-colored A-line shift, the orange ascot, the sash covered with badges, though all the same one—the Try-It patch. She took a few steps toward Arnetta and made a grand sweeping gesture toward the sash. "See," she said, full of self-importance, "I'm a Brownie." I had a hard time imagining this girl calling anyone a "nigger"; the girl looked perpetually delighted, as though she would have cuddled up with a grizzly if someone had let her.

On the fourth morning, we boarded the bus to go home.

The previous day had been spent building miniature churches from Popsicle sticks. We hardly left the cabin. Mrs. Margolin and Mrs. Hedy guarded us so closely, almost no one talked for the entire day.

Even on the day of departure from Camp Crescendo, all was serious and silent. The bus ride began quietly enough. Arnetta had to sit beside Mrs. Margolin; Octavia had to sit beside her mother. I sat beside Daphne, who gave me her prize journal without a word of explanation.

"You don't want it?"

She shook her head no. It was empty.

Then Mrs. Hedy began to weep. "Octavia," Mrs. Hedy said to her daughter without looking at her, "I'm going to sit with Mrs.Margolin. All right?"

Arnetta exchanged seats with Mrs. Hedy. With the two women up front, Elise felt it safe to speak. "Hey," she said, then she set her face into a placid, vacant stare, trying to imitate that of a Troop 909 girl. Emboldened, Arnetta made a gesture of mock pride toward an imaginary sash, the way the girl in full uniform had done. Then they all made a game of it, trying to do the most exaggerated imitations of the Troop 909 girls, all without speaking, all without laughing loud enough to catch the women's attention.

Daphne looked down at her shoes, white with sneaker polish. I opened the journal she'd given me. I looked out the window, trying to decide what to write, searching for lines, but nothing could compare with what Daphne had written, *"My father, the veteran,"* my favorite line of all time. It replayed itself in my head, and I gave up trying to write.

By then, it seemed that the rest of the troop had given up making fun of the girls in Troop 909. They were now quietly gossiping about who had passed notes to whom in school. For a moment the gossiping fell off, and all I heard was the hum of the bus as we sped down the road and the muffled sounds of Mrs. Hedy and Mrs. Margolin talking about serious things.

"You know," Octavia whispered, "why did *we* have to be stuck at a camp with retarded girls? You know?"

"*You* know why," Arnetta answered. She narrowed her eyes like a cat. "My mama and I were in the mall in Buckhead, and this white lady just kept looking at us. I mean, like we were foreign or something. Like we were from China."

"What did the woman say?" Elise asked.

"Nothing," Arnetta said. "She didn't say nothing."

A few girls quietly nodded their heads.

"There was this time," I said, "when my father and I were in the mall and—"

"Oh shut up, Snot," Octavia said.

I stared at Octavia, then rolled my eyes from her to the window. As I watched the trees blur, I wanted nothing more than to be through with it all: the bus ride, the troop, school—all of it. But we were going home. I'd see the same girls in school the next day. We were on a bus, and there was nowhere else to go.

"Go on, Laurel," Daphne said to me. It seemed like the first time she'd spoken the whole trip, and she'd said my name. I turned to her and smiled weakly so as not to cry, hoping she'd remember when I'd tried to be her friend, thinking maybe that her gift of the journal was an invitation of friendship. But she didn't smile back. All she said was, "What happened?"

I studied the girls, waiting for Octavia to tell me to shut up again before I even had a chance to utter another word, but everyone was amazed that Daphne had spoken. The bus was silent. I gathered my voice. "Well," I said. "My father and I were in this mall, but *I* was the one doing the staring." I stopped and glanced from face to face. I continued. "There were these white people dressed like Puritans or something, but they weren't Puritans. They were Mennonites.

They're these people who, if you ask them to do a favor, like paint your porch or something, they have to do it. It's in their rules."

"That sucks," someone said.

"C'mon," Arnetta said. "You're lying."

"I am not."

"How do you know that's not just some story someone made up?" Elise asked, her head cocked full of daring. "I mean, who's gonna do whatever you ask?"

"It's not made up. I know because when I was looking at them, my father said, 'See those people? If you ask them to do something, they'll do it. Anything you want.' "

No one would call anyone's father a liar—then they'd have to fight the person. But Drema parsed her words carefully. "How does your *father* know that's not just some story? Huh?"

"Because," I said, "he went up to the man and asked him would he paint our porch, and the man said yes. It's their religion."

"Man, I'm glad I'm a Baptist," Elise said, shaking her head in sympathy for the Mennonites.

"So did the guy do it?" Drema asked, scooting closer to hear if the story got juicy.

"Yeah," I said. "His whole family was with him. My dad drove them to our house. They all painted our porch. The woman and girl were in bonnets and long, long skirts with buttons up to their necks. The guy wore this weird hat and these huge suspenders."

"Why," Arnetta asked archly, as though she didn't believe a word, "would someone pick a *porch*? If they'll do anything, why not make them paint the whole *house*? Why not ask for a hundred bucks?"

I thought about it, and then remembered the words my father had said about them painting our porch, though I had never seemed to think about his words after he'd said them.

"He said," I began, only then understanding the words as they uncoiled from my mouth, "it was the only time he'd have a white man on his knees doing something for a black man for free."

I now understood what he meant, and why he did it, though I didn't like it. When you've been made to feel bad for so long, you jump at the chance to do it to others. I remembered the Mennonites bending the way Daphne had bent when she was cleaning the restroom. I remembered the dark blue of their bonnets, the black of their shoes. They painted the porch as though scrubbing a floor. I was already trembling before Daphne asked quietly, "Did he thank them?"

I looked out the window. I could not tell which were the thoughts and which were the trees. "No," I said, and suddenly knew there was something mean in the world that I could not stop.

Arnetta laughed. "If I asked them to take off their long skirts and bonnets and put on some jeans, would they do it?"

And Daphne's voice, quiet, steady: "Maybe they would. Just to be nice."

1999

ADRIAN TOMINE

(b. 1974)

SOMEONE MOVED INTO THAT APARTMENT ACROSS THE STREET, AND IT LOOKS LIKE THE OLD TENANTS TOOK THE CURTAINS WITH THEM.
YEAH? CAN YOU SEE ANYTHING?
RIGHT NOW I JUST SEE SOME GUY PACING AROUND WITHOUT A SHIRT ON. EW... HE'S WEARING THESE WEIRD RUBBER GLOVES!
WELL, LET ME KNOW IF ANYTHING HAPPENS.
HEY! SOME GIRL JUST SHOWED UP!
ARE YOU SERIOUS?
HOLY SHIT. TURN OUT THE LIGHT, WILL YA?
SURE.
CLICK!
OH MY GOD.
I CAN'T BELIEVE THIS! DO YOU REALIZE HOW LUCKY THIS IS?
WAIT... WHERE'D THEY GO?
LOOK! YOU CAN SEE THEIR SHADOWS ON THE WALL. THEY LIT CANDLES OR SOMETHING.

WHAT? WHAT DID I MISS?
NOTHING. THEY JUST... TURNED OUT THE LIGHTS.
DAMN! REALLY?
I WONDER WHAT...
STAY AWAY FROM THE WINDOW.
WHY? I JUST WANNA...
I TOLD YOU TO STAY AWAY FROM THE WINDOW!
JUST...
DON'T LOOK.
WHAT'S THE MATTER, HONEY?
WHAT'S GOTTEN INTO YOU?
TOMINE 94

1994

Birdsong

CHIMAMANDA NGOZI ADICHIE
[b. 1977]

The woman, a stranger, was looking at me. In the glare of the hot afternoon, in the swirl of motorcycles and hawkers, she was looking down at me from the back seat of her jeep. Her stare was too direct, not sufficiently vacant. She was not merely resting her eyes on the car next to hers, as people often do in Lagos traffic; she was *looking* at me. At first, I glanced away, but then I stared back, at the haughty silkiness of the weave that fell to her shoulders in loose curls, the kind of extension called Brazilian Hair and paid for in dollars at Victoria Island hair salons; at her fair skin, which had the plastic sheen that comes from expensive creams; and at her hand, forefinger bejewelled, which she raised to wave a magazine hawker away, with the ease of a person used to waving people away. She was beautiful, or perhaps she was just so unusual-looking, with wide-set eyes sunk deep in her face, that "beautiful" was the easiest way of describing her. She was the kind of woman I imagined my lover's wife was, a woman for whom things were done.

My lover. It sounds a little melodramatic, but I never knew how to refer to him. "Boyfriend" seemed wrong for an urbane man of forty-five who carefully slipped off his wedding ring before he touched me. Chikwado called him "your man," with a faintly sneering smile, as though we were both in on the joke: he was not, of course, mine. "Ah, you are always rushing to leave because of this your man," she would say, leaning back in her chair and smacking her head with her hand, over and over. Her scalp was itchy beneath her weave, and this was the only way she could come close to scratching it. "Have fun oh, as long as your spirit accepts it, but as for me, I cannot spread my legs for a married man." She said this often, with a clear-eyed moral superiority, as I packed my files and shut down my computer for the day.

We were friends out of necessity, because we had both graduated from Enugu Campus and ended up working for Celnet Telecom, in Lagos, as the only females in the community-relations unit. Otherwise, we would not have been friends. I was irritated by how full of simplified certainties she was, and I knew that she thought I behaved like an irresponsible, vaguely foreign teen-ager: wearing my hair in a natural low-cut, smoking cigarettes right in front of the building, where everyone could see, and refusing to join in the prayer sessions our boss led after Monday meetings. I would not have told her about my lover—I did not tell her about my personal life—but she was there when he first walked into our office, a lean, dark man with a purple tie and a moneyed manner. He was full of the glossy self-regard of men who shrugged off their importance in a way that only emphasized it. Our boss shook his hand with both hands and said, "Welcome, sir, it is good to see you, sir, how are you doing, sir, please come and sit down, sir." Chikwado was there when he looked at me and I looked at him and then he smiled, of all things, a warm, open smile. She heard when he said to our boss, "My family lives in America," a little too loudly, for my benefit, with that generic foreign accent of the worldly Nigerian, which, I would discover later, disappeared when he became truly animated about something. She saw him walk over and give me his business card. She was there, a few days later, when his driver came to deliver a gift bag. Because she had seen, and because I was swamped with emotions that I could not name for a man I knew was wrong for me, I showed her the perfume and the card that said, "I am thinking of you."

"*Na wa!* Look at how your eyes are shining because of a married man. You need deliverance prayers," Chikwado said, half joking. She went to night-vigil services often, at different churches, but all with the theme Finding Your God-Given Mate; she would come to work the next morning sleepy, the whites of her eyes flecked with red, but already planning to attend another service. She was thirty-two and tottering under the weight of her desire: to settle down. It was all she talked about. It was all our female co-workers talked about when we had lunch at the cafeteria. *Yewande is wasting her time with that man—he is not ready to settle down. Please ask him oh, if he does not see marriage in the future then you better look elsewhere; nobody is getting any younger. Ekaete is lucky, just six months and she is already engaged.* While they talked, I would look out the window, high up above Lagos, at the acres of rusted roofs, at the rise and fall of hope in this city full of tarnished angels.

Even my lover spoke of this desire. "You'll want to settle down soon," he said. "I just want you to know I'm not going to stand in your way." We were naked in bed; it was our first time. A feather from the pillow was stuck in his hair, and I had just picked it out and showed it to him. I could not believe, in the aftermath of what had just happened, both of us still flush from each other's warmth, how easily the words rolled out of his mouth. "I'm not like other men, who think they can dominate your life and not let you move forward," he continued, propping himself up on his elbow to look at me. He was telling me that he played the game better than others, while I had not yet conceived of the game itself. From the moment I met him, I had had the sensation of possibility, but for him the path was already closed, had indeed never been open; there was no room for things to sweep in and disrupt.

"You're very thoughtful," I said, with the kind of overdone mockery that masks damage. He nodded, as though he agreed with me. I pulled the covers up to my chin. I should have got dressed, gone back to my flat in Surulere, and deleted his number from my phone. But I stayed. I stayed for thirteen months and eight days, mostly in his house in Victoria Island—a faded-white house, with its quiet grandeur and airy spaces, which was built during British colonial rule and sat in a compound full of fruit trees, the enclosing wall wreathed in creeping bougainvillea. He had told me he was taking me to a Lebanese friend's guesthouse, where he was staying while his home in Ikoyi was being refurbished. When I stepped out of the car, I felt as though I had stumbled into a secret garden. A dense mass of periwinkles, white and pink, bordered the walkway to the house. The air was clean here, even fragrant, and there was something about it all that made me think of renewal. He was watching me; I could sense how much he wanted me to like it.

"This is your house, isn't it?" I said. "It doesn't belong to your Lebanese friend."

He moved closer to me, surprised. "Please don't misunderstand. I was going to tell you. I just didn't want you to think it was some kind of . . ." He paused and took my hand. "I know what other men do, and I am not like that. I don't bring women here. I bought it last year to knock it down and build an apartment block, but it was so beautiful. My friends think I'm mad for keeping it. You know nobody respects old things in this country. I work from here most days now, instead of going to my office."

We were standing by sliding glass doors that led to a veranda, over which a large flame tree spread its branches. Wilted red flowers had fallen on the cane chairs. "I like to sit there and watch birds," he said, pointing.

He liked birds. Birds had always been just birds to me, but with him I became someone else: I became a person who liked birds. The following Sunday morning, on our first weekend together, as we passed sections of *Next* to each other in the quiet of that veranda, he looked up at the sky and said, "There's a magpie. They like shiny things." I imagined putting his wedding ring on the cane table so that the bird would swoop down and carry it away forever.

"I knew you were different!" he said, thrilled, when he noticed that I read the business and sports sections, as though my being different reflected his good taste. And so we talked eagerly about newspapers, and about the newscasts on AIT and CNN, marvelling at how similar our opinions were. We never discussed my staying. It was not safe to drive back to Surulere late, and he kept saying, "Why don't you bring your things tomorrow so you can go to work from here?" until most of my clothes were in the wardrobe and my moisturizers were on the bathroom ledge. He left me money on the table, in brown envelopes on which he wrote "For your fuel," as if I could possibly spend fifty thousand naira on petrol. Sometimes, he asked if I needed privacy to change, as if he had not seen me naked many times.

We did not talk about his wife or his children or my personal life or when I would want to settle down so that he could avoid standing in my way. Perhaps it was all the things we left unsaid that made me watch him. His skin was so dark that I teased him about being from Gambia; if he were a woman, I told him, he would never find a face powder that matched his tone. I watched as he carefully unwrapped scented moist tissues to clean his glasses, or cut the chicken on his plate, or tied his towel round his waist in a knot that seemed too elaborate for a mere towel, just below the embossed scar by his navel. I memorized him, because I did not know him. He was courtly, his life lived in well-oiled sequences, his cufflinks always tasteful.

His three cell phones rang often; I knew when it was his wife, because he would go to the toilet or out to the veranda, and I knew when it was a government official, because he would say afterward, "Why won't these governors leave somebody alone?" But it was clear that he liked the governors' calls, and the restaurant manager who came to our table to say, "We are so happy to see you, sah."

He searched the Sunday-magazine pullouts for pictures of himself, and when he found one he said in a mildly complaining tone, "Look at this, why should they turn businessmen into celebrities?" Yet he would not wear the same suit to two events because of the newspaper photographers. He had a glowing ego, like a globe, round and large and in constant need of polishing. He did things for people. He gave them money, introduced them to contacts, helped their relatives get jobs, and when the gratitude and praise came—he showed me text messages thanking him; I remember one that read "History will immortalize you as a great man"—his eyes would glaze over, and I could almost hear him purr.

One day he told me, while we were watching two kingfishers do a mating dance on a guava tree, that most birds did not have penises. I had never thought about the penises of birds.

"My mother had chickens in the yard when I was growing up, and I used to watch them mating," I said.

"Of course they mate, but not with penises," he said. "Did you ever see a cock with a dick?"

I laughed, and he, only just realizing the joke, laughed, too. It became our endearment. "Cock with a dick," I would whisper, hugging him in greeting, and we would burst out laughing. He sent me texts signed "CwithaD." And each time I turned off the potholed road in Victoria Island and into that compound full of birdsong I felt as though I were home.

The woman was still looking at me. Traffic was at a standstill, unusual this early in the afternoon. A tanker must have fallen across the road—tankers were always falling across the road—or a bus had broken down, or cars had formed a line outside a petrol station, blocking the road. My fuel gauge was close to empty. I switched off the ignition and rolled down the window, wondering if the woman would roll down hers as well and say something to me. I stared back at her, and yet she did not waver, her eyes remaining firm, until I looked away. There were many more hawkers now, holding out magazines, phone cards, plantain chips, newspapers, cans of Coke and Amstel Malta dipped in water to make them look cold. The driver in front of me was buying a phone card. The hawker, a boy in a red Arsenal shirt, scratched the card with his fingernail, and then waited for the driver to enter the numbers in his phone to make sure the card was not fake.

I turned again to look at the woman. I was reminded of what Chikwado had said about my lover the first day that he came to our office: "His face is full of overseas." The woman, too, had a face full of overseas, the face of a person whose life was a blur of comforts. There was something in the set of her lips, which were lined with cocoa lip pencil, that suggested an unsatisfying triumph, as though she had won a battle but hated having had to fight in the first place. Perhaps she was indeed my lover's wife and she had come back to Lagos and just found out about me, and then, as though in a bad farce, ended up next to me in traffic. But his wife could not possibly know; he had been so careful.

"I wish I could," he always said, when I asked him to spend Saturday afternoon with me at Jazz Hole, or when I suggested we go to a play at Terra Kulture on Sunday, or when I asked if we could try dinner at a different restaurant. We only ever went to one on a dark street off Awolowo Road, a place with expensive wines and no sign on the gate. He said "I wish I could" as though some great and ineluctable act of nature made it impossible for him to be seen publicly with me. And impossible for him to keep my text messages. I wanted to ask how he could so efficiently delete my texts as soon as he read them, why he felt no urge to keep them on his phone, even if only for a few hours, even if only for a day. There were reams of questions unasked, gathering like rough pebbles in my throat. It was a strange thing to feel so close to a man—to tell him about my resentment of my parents, to lie supine for him with an abandon that was unfamiliar to me—and yet be unable to ask him questions, bound as I was by insecurity and unnamed longings.

The first time we quarrelled, he said to me accusingly, "You don't cry." I realized that his wife cried, that he could handle tears but not my cold defiance.

The fight was about his driver, Emmanuel, an elderly man who might have looked wise if his features were not so snarled with dissatisfaction. It was a Saturday afternoon. I had been at work that morning. My boss had called an emergency meeting that I thought was unnecessary: we all knew that His Royal Highness, the Oba of the town near the lagoon, was causing trouble, saying that Celnet Telecom had made him look bad in front of his people. He had sent many messages asking how we could build a big base station on his ancestral land and yet donate only a small borehole to his people.

That morning, his guards had blocked off our building site, shoved some of our engineers around, and punctured the tires of their van. My boss was furious, and he slammed his hand on the table as he spoke at the meeting. I, too, slammed my hand on the cane table as I imitated him later, while my lover laughed. "That is the problem with these godless, demon-worshipping traditional rulers," my boss said. "The man is a crook. A common crook! What happened to the one million naira we gave him? Should we also bring bags of rice and beans for all his people before we put up our base station? Does he want a supply of meat pies every day? Nonsense!"

"Meat pies" had made Chikwado and me laugh, even though our boss was not being funny. "Why not something more ordinary, like bread?" Chikwado whispered to me, and then promptly raised her hand when our boss asked for volunteers to go see the Oba right away. I never volunteered. I disliked those visits—villagers watching us with awed eyes, young men asking for free phone cards, even free phones—because it all made me feel helplessly powerful.

"Why meat pies?" my lover asked, still laughing.

"I have no idea."

"Actually, I would like to have a meat pie right now."

"Me, too."

We were laughing, and with the sun shining, the sound of birds above, the slight flutter of the curtains against the sliding door, I was already thinking of future Saturdays that we would spend together, laughing at funny stories about my boss. My lover summoned Emmanuel and asked him to take me to the supermarket to buy the meat pies. When I got into the car, Emmanuel did not greet me. He simply stared straight ahead. It was the first time that he had driven me without my lover. The silence was tense. Perhaps he was thinking that all his children were older than me.

"Well done, Emmanuel!" I said finally, greeting him with forced brightness. "Do you know the supermarket on Kofo Abayomi Street?"

He said nothing and started the car. When we arrived, he stopped at the gate. "Come out here, let me go and park," he said.

"Please drop me at the entrance," I said. Every other driver did that, before looking for a parking space.

"Come out here." He still did not look at me. Rage rose under my skin, making me feel detached and bloodless, suspended in air; I could not sense the ground under my feet as I climbed out. After I had selected some meat pies from the display case, I called my lover and told him that Emmanuel had been rude and that I would be taking a taxi back.

"Emmanuel said the road was bad," my lover said when I got back, his tone conciliatory.

"The man insulted me," I said.

"No, he's not like that. Maybe he didn't understand you."

Emmanuel had shown me the power of my lover's wife; he would not have been so rude if he feared he might be reprimanded. I wanted to fling the bag of meat pies through the window.

"Is this what you do, have your driver remind your girlfriends of their place?" I was shrill and I disliked myself for it. Worse, I was horrified to notice that my eyes were watering. My lover gently wrapped his arms around me, as though I were an irrational child, and asked whether I would give him a meat pie.

"You've brought other women here, haven't you?" I asked, not entirely sure how this had become about other women.

He shook his head. "No, I have not. No more of this talk. Let's eat the meat pies and watch a film."

I let myself be mollified, be held, be caressed. Later, he said, "You know, I have had only two affairs since I got married. I'm not like other men."

"You sound as if you think you deserve a prize," I said.

He was smiling. "Both of them were like you." He paused to search for a word, and when he found it he said it with enjoyment. "Feisty. They were feisty like you."

I looked at him. How could he not see that there were things he should not say to me, and that there were things I longed to have with him? It was a willed blindness; it had to be. He chose not to see. "You are such a bastard," I said.

"What?"

I repeated myself.

He looked as though he had just been stung by an insect. "Get out. Leave this house right now," he said, and then muttered, "This is unacceptable."

I had never before been thrown out of a house. Emmanuel sat in a chair in the shade of the garage and watched stone-faced as I hurried to my car. My lover did not call me for five days, and I did not call him. When he finally called, his first words were "There are two pigeons on the flame tree. I'd like you to see them."

"You are acting as if nothing happened."

"I called *you*," he said, as though the call itself were an apology. Later, he told me that if I had cried instead of calling him a bastard he would have behaved better. I should not have gone back—I knew that even then.

The woman, still staring at me, was talking on her cell phone. Her jeep was black and silver and miraculously free of scratches. How was that possible in this city where okada[1] after okada sped through the narrow slices of space between cars in traffic as though motorcycles could shrink to fit any gap? Perhaps whenever her car was hit a mechanic descended from the sky and made the dent disappear. The car in front of me had a gash on its tail-light; it looked like one of the many cars that dripped oil, turning the roads into a slick sheet when the rains came. My own car was full of wounds. The biggest, a mangled bumper, was from a taxi that rammed into me at a red light on Kingsway Road a month before. The driver had jumped out with his shirt unbuttoned, all sweaty bravado, and screamed at me.

"Stupid girl! You are a common nuisance. Why did you stop like that? Nonsense!"

I stared at him, stunned, until he drove away, and then I began to think of what I could have said, what I could have shouted back.

"If you were wearing a wedding ring, he would not have shouted at you like that," Chikwado said when I told her, as she punched the redial button on her desk phone. At the cafeteria, she told our co-workers about it. *Ah, ah, stupid man! Of course he was shouting because he knew he was wrong—that is the Lagos way. So he thinks he can speak big English. Where did he even learn the word "nuisance"?* They sucked their teeth, telling their own stories about taxi-drivers, and then their outrage fizzled and they began to talk, voices lowered and excited, about a fertility biscuit that the new pastor at Redemption Church was giving women.

"It worked for my sister oh. First she did a dry fast for two days, then the pastor did a special deliverance prayer for her before she ate the biscuit. She had to eat it at exactly midnight. The next month, the very next month, she missed her period, I'm telling you," one of them, a contract staffer who was doing a master's degree part time at Ibadan, said.

[1]Motorcycles used as vehicles for hire in Nigeria.

"Is it an actual biscuit?" another asked.

"Yes now. But they bless the ingredients before they make the biscuits. God can work through anything, *sha*. I heard about a pastor that uses handkerchiefs."

I looked away and wondered what my lover would make of this story. He was visiting his family in America for two weeks. That evening, he sent me a text. "At a concert with my wife. Beautiful music. Will call you in ten minutes and leave phone on so you can listen in. CwithaD." I read it twice and then, even though I had saved all his other texts, I deleted it, as though my doing so would mean that it had never been sent. When he called, I let my phone ring and ring. I imagined them at the concert, his wife reaching out to hold his hand, because I could not bear the thought that it might be he who would reach out. I knew then that he could not possibly see me, the inconvenient reality of me; instead, all he saw was himself in an exciting game.

He came back from his trip wearing shoes I did not recognize, made of rich brown leather and much more tapered than his other shoes, almost comically pointy. He was in high spirits, twirling me around when we hugged, caressing the tightly coiled hair at the nape of my neck and saying, "So soft." He wanted to go out to dinner, he said, because he had a surprise for me, and when he went into the bathroom one of his phones rang. I took it and looked at his text messages. It was something I had never thought of doing before, and yet I suddenly felt compelled to do it. Text after text in his "sent" box were to Baby. The most recent said he had arrived safely. What struck me was not how often he texted his wife, or how short the texts were—"stuck in traffic," "missing you," "almost there"—but that all of them were signed "CwithaD." Inside me, something snagged. He had choreographed a conversation with her, nimbly made the joke about a "cock with a dick" and then found a way to turn it into a shared endearment for the two of them? I thought of the effort it would take to do that. I put the phone down and glanced at the mirror, half expecting to see myself morphing into a slack, stringless marionette.

In the car, he asked, "Is something wrong? Are you feeling well?"

"I can't believe you called me so that I could listen to the music you and your wife were listening to."

"I did that because I missed you so much," he said. "I really wanted to be there with you."

"But you *weren't* there with me."

"You're in a bad mood."

"Don't you see? You weren't there with *me*."

He reached over and took my hand, rubbing his thumb on my palm. I looked out at the dimly lit street. We were on our way to our usual hidden restaurant, where I had eaten everything on the menu a hundred times. A mosquito, now sluggish with my blood, had got in the car. I slapped myself as I tried to hit it.

"Good evening, sah," the waiter said when we were seated. "You are welcome, sah."

"Have you noticed that they never greet me?" I asked my lover.

"Well . . ." he said, and adjusted his glasses.

The waiter came back, a sober-faced man with a gentle demeanor, and I waited until he had opened the bottle of red wine before I asked, "Why don't you greet me?"

The waiter glanced at my lover, as though seeking guidance, and this infuriated me even more. "Am I invisible? I am the one who asked you a question. Why do all of you waiters and gatemen and drivers in this Lagos refuse to greet me? Do you not see me?"

"Come back in ten minutes," my lover said to the waiter in his courteous, deep-voiced way. "You need to calm down," he told me. "Do you want us to go?"

"Why don't they greet me?" I asked, and gulped down half my glass of wine.

"I have a surprise for you. I've bought you a new car."

I looked at him blankly.

"Did you hear me?" he asked.

"I heard you." I was supposed to get up and hug him and tell him that history would remember him as a great man. A new car. I drank more wine.

"Did I tell you about my first bus ride when I arrived in Lagos, six years ago?" I asked. "When I got on the bus, a boy was screaming in shock because a stranger had found his lost wallet and given it back to him. The boy looked like me, a green, eager job seeker, and he, too, must have come from his home town armed with warnings. You know all the things they tell you: don't give to street beggars because they are only pretending to be lame; look through tomato pyramids for the rotten ones the hawkers hide underneath; don't help people whose cars have broken down, because they are really armed robbers. And then somebody found his wallet and gave it back to him."

My lover looked puzzled.

"Rituals of distrust," I said. "That is how we relate to one another here, through rituals of distrust. Do you know how carefully I watch the fuel gauge when I buy petrol just to make sure the attendant hasn't tampered with it? We know the rules and we follow them, and we never make room for things we might not have imagined. We close the door too soon." I felt a little silly, saying things I knew he did not understand and did not want to understand, and also a little cowardly, saying them the way I did. He was resting his elbows on the table, watching me, and I knew that all he wanted was my excitement, my gratitude, my questions about when I could see the new car. I began to cry, and he came around and cradled me against his waist. My nose was running and my eyes itched as I dabbed them with my napkin. I never cried elegantly, and I imagined that his wife did; she was probably one of those women who could just have the tears trail down her cheeks, leaving her makeup intact, her nose dry.

The traffic had started to move a little. I saw an okada in my side mirror, coming too fast, swerving and honking, and I waited to hear the crunch as it hit my car. But it didn't. The driver was wearing a helmet, while his passenger merely held hers over her head—the smelly foam inside would have ruined her hair—close enough so that she could slip it on as soon as she saw a LASTMA official ahead. My lover once called it fatalism. He had given free helmets to all his staff, but most of them still got on an okada without one. The day before, an okada, the driver bareheaded and blindly speeding, had hit me as I turned onto Ogunlana Drive; the driver stuck his finger into his mouth and ran it over the scratch on the side of my car. "Auntie, sorry oh! Nothing happen to the car," he said, and continued his journey.

I laughed. I had not laughed in the three weeks since I had left work at lunchtime and driven to my lover's house. I had packed all my clothes, my books, and my toiletries and gone back to my flat, consumed as I went by how relentlessly unpretty Lagos was, with houses sprouting up unplanned like weeds.

During those three weeks, I had said little at work. Our office was suddenly very uncomfortable, the air-conditioning always too cold. His Royal Highness, the Oba of the town near the lagoon, was asking for more money; his town council had written a letter saying that the borehole was spewing blackish water. My boss was calling too many meetings.

"Let us give thanks," he said after one of the meetings.

"Why should we be praying in the workplace?" I asked. "Why must you assume that we are all Christians?"

He looked startled. He knew that I never joined in, never said "Amen," but I had never been vocal about it.

"It is not by force to participate in thanking the Lord," he said, and then in the same breath continued, "In Jesus' name!"

"Amen!" the others chorused.

I turned to leave the meeting room.

"Don't go," my co-worker Gerald whispered to me. "Akin brought his birthday cake."

I stood outside the meeting room until the prayer ended, and then we sang "Happy Birthday" to Akin. His cake looked like the unpretentious kind I liked, probably from Sweet Sensation, the kind that sometimes had bits of forgotten eggshells in it. Our boss asked him to give me or Chikwado the cake to serve.

"Why do we always have to serve the cake?" I asked. "Every time somebody brings in a cake, it is either Chikwado serves it or I serve it. You, Gerald, serve the cake. Or you, Emeka, since you are the most junior."

They stared at me. Chikwado got up hurriedly and began to slice the cake. "Please, don't mind her," she said to everyone, but her eyes were on our boss. "She is behaving like this because she did not take her madness medicine today."

Later, she said to me, "Why have you been behaving somehow? What's the problem? Did something happen with your man?"

For a moment, I wanted to tell her how I felt: as though bits of my skin had warped and cracked and peeled off, leaving patches of raw flesh so agonizingly painful I did not know what to do. I wanted to tell her how often I stared at my phone, even though he had sent two feeble texts saying he did not understand why I'd left and then nothing else; and how I remembered clearly, too clearly, the scent of the moist tissues he used to clean his glasses. I didn't tell her, because I was sure she would deliver one of her petty wisdoms, like "If you see fire and you put your hand in fire, then fire will burn you." Still, there was a softness in her expression, something like sympathy, when I looked up from my computer screen and saw her watching me while her hand went slap, slap, slap on her head. Her weave was a new style, too long and too wiggy, with reddish highlights that brought to mind the hair of cheap plastic dolls. Yet there was an honesty about it; Chikwado owned it in a way that the woman in the jeep did not own her Brazilian hair.

A young boy approached my car, armed with a spray bottle of soapy water and a rag. I turned on my wipers to discourage him, but he still squirted my windscreen. I increased the wiper speed. The boy glared at me and moved on to the car behind me. I was seized with a sudden urge to step out and slap him. For a moment, my vision blurred. It was really the woman I wanted to slap. I turned to her jeep and, because she had looked away, I pressed my horn. I leaned out of my window.

"What is your problem? Why have you been staring at me? Do I owe you?" I shouted.

The traffic began to move. I thought she would roll down her window, too. She made as if to lean toward it, then turned away, the slightest of smiles on her face, her head held high, and I watched the jeep pick up speed and head to the bridge.

2010

At the Round Earth's Imagined Corners

LAUREN GROFF

[b. 1978]

Jude was born in a cracker-style house at the edge of a swamp that boiled with unnamed species of reptiles.

Few people lived in the center of Florida then. Air conditioning was for the rich, and the rest compensated with high ceilings, sleeping porches, attic fans. Jude's father was a herpetologist at the university, and if snakes hadn't slipped their way into their hot house, his father would have filled it with them anyway. Coils of rattlers sat in formaldehyde on the windowsills. Writhing knots of reptiles lived in the coops out back where his mother had once tried to raise chickens.

At an early age, Jude learned to keep a calm heart when touching fanged things. He was barely walking when his mother came into the kitchen to find a coral snake chasing its red and yellow tail around his wrist. His father was watching from across the room, laughing.

His mother was a Yankee, a Presbyterian. She was always weary; she battled the house's mold and humidity and devilish reek of snakes without help. His father wouldn't allow a black person through his doors, and they didn't have the money to hire a white woman. Jude's mother was afraid of scaly creatures and sang hymns in the attempt to keep them out. When she was pregnant with his sister one August night, she came into the bathroom to take a cool bath and, without her glasses, missed the three-foot albino alligator her husband had stored in the bathtub. The next morning, she was gone. She returned a week later. And after Jude's sister was born dead, a perfect petal of a baby, his mother never stopped singing under her breath.

Noise of the war grew louder. At last, it became impossible to ignore. Jude was two. His mother pressed his father's new khaki suit and then Jude's father's absence filled the house with a kind of cool breeze. He was flying cargo planes in France. Jude thought of scaly creatures flapping great wings midair, his father angrily riding.

While Jude napped the first day they were alone in the house, his mother tossed all of the jars of dead snakes into the swamp and neatly beheaded the living ones with a hoe. She bobbed her hair with gardening shears. Within a week, she had moved them ninety miles to the beach. When she thought he was asleep on the first night in the new house, she went down to the water's edge in the moonlight and screwed her feet into the sand. It seemed that the glossed edge of the ocean was chewing her up to her knees. Jude held his breath, anguished. One big wave rolled past her shoulders, and when it receded, she was whole again.

This was a new world, full of dolphins that slid up the coastline in shining arcs. Jude loved the wedges of pelicans ghosting overhead, the mad dig after periwinkles that disappeared deeper into the wet sand. He kept count in his head when they hunted for them, and when they came home, he told his mother that they had dug up 461. She looked at him unblinking behind her glasses and counted the creatures aloud.

When she finished, she washed her hands for a long time at the sink. "You like numbers," she said at last, turning around.

"Yes," he said. And she smiled and a kind of gentle shine came from her that startled him. He felt it seep into him, settle in his bones. She kissed him on the crown and put him to bed, and when he woke in the middle of the night to find her next to him, he tucked his hand under her chin where it stayed until morning.

He began to sense that the world worked in ways beyond him, that he was only grasping at threads of a far greater fabric. Jude's mother started a bookstore. Because women couldn't buy land in Florida for themselves, his uncle, a roly-poly little man who looked nothing like Jude's father, bought the store with her money and signed the place over to her. His mother began wearing suits that showed her décolletage and taking her glasses off before boarding the streetcars, so that the eyes she turned to the public were soft and somewhat misty. Instead of singing Jude to sleep as she had in the snake house, she read to him. She read Shakespeare, Hopkins, Donne, Rilke, and he fell asleep with their cadences and the sea's slow rhythm entwined in his head.

Jude loved the bookstore; it was a bright place that smelled of new paper. Lonely war brides came with their prams and left with an armful of Modern Library classics, sailors on leave wandered in only to exit, charmed, with sacks of books pressed to their chest. After hours, his mother would turn off the lights and open the back door to the black folks who waited patiently there, the dignified man in his watch cap who loved Galsworthy, the fat woman who worked as a maid and read a novel every day. "Your father would squeal. Well, foo on him," his mother said to Jude, looking so fierce she erased the last traces in his mind of the tremulous woman she'd been.

One morning just before dawn, he was alone on the beach when he saw a vast metallic breaching a hundred yards offshore. The submarine looked at him with its single periscope eye and slipped silently under again. Jude told nobody. He kept this dangerous knowledge inside him where it tightened and squeezed, but where it couldn't menace the greater world.

Jude's mother brought in a black woman named Sandy to help her with housework and to watch Jude while she was at the store. Sandy and his mother became friends, and some nights he would awaken to laughter from the veranda and come out to find his mother and Sandy in the night breeze off the ocean. They drank sloe gin fizzes and ate lemon cake, which Sandy was careful to keep on hand, even though by then sugar was getting scarce. They let him have a slice, and he'd fall asleep on Sandy's broad lap, sweetness souring on his tongue and in his ears the exhalation of the ocean, the sound of women's voices.

At six, he discovered multiplication all by himself, crouched over an anthill in the hot sun. If twelve ants left the anthill per minute, he thought, that meant 720 departures per hour, an immensity of leaving, of return. He ran into the bookstore, wordless with happiness. When he buried his head in his mother's lap, the women chatting with her at the counter mistook his sobbing for sadness. "I'm sure the boy misses his father," one lady said, intending to be kind.

"No," his mother said. She alone understood his bursting heart and scratched his scalp gently. But something shifted in Jude; and he thought with wonder of his father, of whom his mother had spoken so rarely in all these years that the man himself had faded. Jude could barely recall the rasp of scale on scale and the darkness of the cracker house in the swamp, curtains closed to keep out the hot, stinking sun.

But it was as if the well-meaning lady had summoned him, and Jude's father came home. He sat, immense and rough-cheeked, in the middle of the sunroom. Jude's mother sat nervously opposite him on the divan, angling her knees away from his. The boy played quietly with his wooden train on the floor. Sandy came in with fresh cookies, and when she went back into the kitchen, his father said something so softly Jude couldn't catch it. His mother stared at his father for a long time, then got up and went to the kitchen, and the screen door slapped, and the boy never saw Sandy again.

While his mother was gone, Jude's father said, "We're going home." Jude couldn't look at his father. The space in the air where he existed was too heavy and dark. He pushed his train around the ankle of a chair. "Come here," his father said, and slowly the boy stood and went to his father's knee.

A big hand flicked out, and Jude's face burned from ear to mouth. He fell down but didn't cry out. He sucked in blood from his nose and felt it pool behind his throat.

His mother ran in and picked him up. "What happened?" she shouted, and his father said in his cold voice, "Boy's timid. Something's wrong with him."

"He keeps things in. He's shy," said his mother, and carried Jude away. He could feel her trembling as she washed the blood from his face. His father came into the bathroom and she said through her teeth, "Don't you ever touch him again."

He said, "I won't have to."

His mother lay beside Jude until he fell asleep, but he woke to the moon through the automobile's windshield and his parents' jagged profiles staring ahead into the tunnel of the dark road.

The house by the swamp filled with snakes again. The uncle who had helped his mother with the bookstore was no longer welcome, although he was the only family his father had. Jude's mother cooked a steak and potatoes every night but wouldn't eat. She became a bone, a blade. She sat in her housedress on the porch rocker, her hair slick with sweat. He stood near her and spoke the old sonnets into her ear. She pulled him to her side and put her face between his shoulder and neck and when she blinked, her wet eyelashes tickled him, and he knew not to move away.

His father had begun, on the side, selling snakes to zoos and universities. He vanished for two, three nights in a row, and returned with clothes full of smoke and sacks of rattlers and blacksnakes. He'd been gone for two nights when his mother packed her blue cardboard suitcase with Jude's things on one side and hers on the other. She said nothing, but gave herself away with humming. They walked together over the dark roads and sat waiting for the train for a long time. The platform was empty; theirs was the last train before the weekend. She handed him caramels to suck, and he felt her whole body tremble through the thigh he pressed hard against hers.

So much had built up in him while they waited that it was almost a relief when the train came sighing into the station. His mother stood and reached for Jude, and he smiled into her soft answering smile. Then Jude's father stepped into the lights and scooped him up. His body under Jude's was taut.

His mother did not look at her husband or her son. She seemed a statue, thin and pale. At last, when the conductor said "All aboard!" she gave an awful strangled sound and rushed through the train's door. The train hooted and slowly moved off. Though Jude shouted, it vanished his mother into the darkness without stopping.

Then they were alone, Jude's father and he, in the house by the swamp.

Language wilted between them. Jude was the one who took up the sweeping and scrubbing, who made their sandwiches for supper. When his father was gone, he'd open the windows to let out some of the reptile rot. His father ripped up his mother's lilies and roses and planted mandarins and blueberries, saying that fruit brought birds and birds brought snakes. The boy walked three miles to school where he told nobody he already knew numbers better than the teachers. He was small, but nobody messed with him. On his first day, when a big ten-year-old tried to sneer at his clothes, he leapt at him with a viciousness he'd learned from watching rattlesnakes and made the big boy's head bleed. The others avoided him. He was an in-between creature, motherless but not fatherless, stunted and ratty-clothed like a poor boy but a professor's son, always correct with answers when the teachers called on him, but never offering a word on his own. The others kept their distance. Jude played by himself, or with one of the succession of puppies that his father brought home. Inevitably, the dogs would run down to the edge of the swamp, and one of the fourteen- or fifteen-foot alligators would get them.

Jude's loneliness grew, became a living creature that shadowed him and wandered off only when he was in the company of his numbers. More than marbles or tin soldiers, they were his playthings. More than sticks of candy or plums, they made his mouth water. As messy as the world was, the numbers, predictable and polite, brought order.

When he was ten, a short, round man that the boy found vaguely familiar stopped him on the street and pushed a brown-paper package into his arms. The man pressed a finger to his lips, minced away. At home in his room at night, Jude unwrapped the books. One was a collection of Frost's poems. The other was a book of geometry, the world whittled down until it became a series of lines and angles.

He looked up and morning was sunshot through the laurel oaks. More than the feeling that the book had taught him geometry was the feeling that it had showed the boy something that had been living inside him, undetected until now.

There was also a letter. It was addressed to him in his mother's round hand. When he sat in school dividing the hours until he could be free, when he made the supper of tuna sandwiches, when he ate with his father who conducted to Benny Goodman on the radio, when he brushed his teeth and put on pajamas far too small for him, the four perfect right angles of the letter called to him. He put it under his pillow, unopened. For a week, the letter burned under everything, the way the sun on a hot, overcast day was hidden but always present.

At last, having squeezed everything to know out of the geometry book, he put the still-sealed envelope inside and taped up the covers and hid it between his mattress and box springs. He checked it every night after saying his prayers and was comforted into sleep. When, one night, he saw the book was untaped and the letter gone, he knew his father had found it and nothing could be done.

The next time he saw the little round man on the street, he stopped him. "Who are you?" he asked, and the man blinked and said, "Your uncle." When Jude said nothing, the man threw his arms up and said, "Oh, honey!" and made as if to hug him, but Jude had already turned away.

Inexorably, the university grew. It swelled and expanded under a steady supply of air conditioning, swallowing the land between it and the swamp until the university's roads were built snug against his father's land. Dinners, now, were full of his father's invective: did the university not know that his snakes needed a home, that this expanse of sandy acres was one of the richest reptile havens in North America? He would never sell, never. He would kill to keep it. Safe and whole.

While his father spoke, the traitor in Jude dreamed of the sums his father had been offered. So simple, it seemed, to make the money grow. Unlike other kinds of numbers, money was already self-fertilized; it would double and double again until at last it made a roiling mass. If you had enough of it, Jude knew, nobody would ever have to worry again.

When Jude was thirteen, he discovered the university library. One summer day, he looked up from the pile of books where he'd been contentedly digging—trigonometry, statistics, calculus, whatever he could find—to see his father opposite him. Jude didn't know how long he'd been there. It was a humid morning, and even in the library the air was stifling, but his father looked leathered, cool in his sunbeaten shirt and red neckerchief.

"Come on, then," he said. Jude followed, feeling ill. They rode in the pickup for two hours before Jude understood that they were going snaking together. This was his first time. When he was smaller, he'd begged to go, but every time, his father had said no, it was too dangerous, and Jude never argued that letting a boy live for a week alone in a house full of venom and guns and questionable wiring was equally unsafe.

His father pitched the tent and they ate beans from a can in the darkness. They lay side by side in their sleeping bags until his father said, "You're good at math."

Jude said, "I am," though with such understatement that it felt like a lie. Something shifted between them, and they fell asleep to a silence that was softer at its edges.

His father woke Jude before dawn and he stumbled out of the tent to grainy coffee with condensed milk and hot hush puppies. His father was after moccasins, and he gave Jude his waders and himself trudged through the swamp, protected only by jeans and boots. He'd been bitten so often, he said, he no longer brought antivenom. He didn't need it. When he handed his son the stick and gestured at a black slash sunning on a rock, the boy had to imagine the snake as a line in space, only connecting point to point, to be able to grasp it. The snake spun from the number one to the number eight to a defeated three and he deposited it in the sack.

They worked in silence all day, and when Jude climbed back up into the truck at the end of the day, his legs shook from the effort it took him to be brave. "So now you know," his father said in a strange holy voice, and Jude was too tired to take the steps necessary, then, and ever afterward until he was his father's own age, to understand.

His father began storing the fodder mice in Jude's closet, and to avoid the doomed squeaks, Jude joined the high school track team. He found his talent in the two-hundred-meter hurdles. When he came home with a trophy from the State Games, his father held the trophy for a moment, then put it down.

"Different if Negroes were allowed to run," he said.

Jude said nothing, and his father said, "Lord knows I'm no lover of the race, but your average Negro could outrun any white boy I know."

Jude again said nothing but avoided his father and didn't make him an extra steak when he cooked himself dinner. He still wasn't talking to him when his father went on an overnight trip and didn't come back for a week. Jude was used to it and didn't get alarmed until the money ran out and his father still didn't come home.

He alerted the secretary at the university who sent out a group of graduate students to where Jude's father had been seen. They found the old man in his tent, bloated, his tongue protruding from a face turned black; and Jude understood then how even the things you loved most could kill you.

At the funeral, out of a twisted loyalty for his father, he avoided his uncle. He didn't know if his mother knew she'd been widowed; he thought probably not. He told nobody at school that his father had died. He thought of himself as an island in the middle of the ocean, with no hope of seeing another island in the distance, or even a ship passing by.

He lived alone in the house. He let the mice die, then tossed the snakes in high twisting parabolas into the swamp. He scrubbed the house until it gleamed and the stench of reptiles was gone, then applied beeswax, paint, polish until it was a house fit for his mother. He waited. She didn't come.

The day he graduated from high school, he packed his clothes and sealed up the house and took the train to Boston. He'd heard from his uncle that his mother lived there and so he'd applied and been accepted to college in the city. She owned a bookstore on a small, dark street. It took Jude a month of slow passing to gather the courage to go in. She was either in the back, or shelving books, or smiling in conversation with somebody, and he'd have a swim of darkness in his gut and know that it was fate telling him that today was not the day. When he went in, it was only because she was alone at the register, and her face—pouchy, waxy—was so sad in repose that the sight of it washed all thought from his head.

She rose with a wordless cry and flew to him. He held her stoically. She smelled like cats, and her clothes flopped on her as if she'd lost a lot of weight quickly. He told her about his father dying and she nodded and said, "I know. I dreamed it."

She wouldn't let him leave her. She dragged him home with her and made him spaghetti carbonara and put clean sheets on the couch for him. Her three cats yowled under the door to her bedroom until she came in with them. In the middle of the night, he woke to find her in her easy chair, clutching her hands, staring at him with glittering eyes. He closed his own and lay stiffly, almost shouting with the agony of being watched so.

He went to see her once a week but refused all dinner invitations. He couldn't bear the density or lateness of her love. He was in his junior year when her long-percolating illness overcame her and she too left him. Now he was alone.

There was nothing but numbers, then.

Later, there were numbers, the great ravishing machine in the laboratory into which he fed punched slips of paper, the motorcycle Jude rode because it roared like murder. He had been given a class to teach, but it was taken away after a month and he was told that he was better suited for research. In his late twenties, there were drunk and silly girls he could seduce without saying a word, because they felt a kind of danger coiled in him.

He rode his motorcycle too fast over icy roads. He swam at night in bays where great whites had been spotted. He bombed down ski slopes with only a hazy idea of the mechanics of snow. He drank so many beers he woke one morning to discover he'd developed a paunch as big as a pregnant woman's belly. He laughed to shake it, liked its wobble. It felt comforting, a child's pillow clutched to his midsection all day long.

By the time he was thirty, Jude was weary. He became drawn to bridges, their tensile strength, the cold river flowing underneath. A resolution was forming under his thoughts, like a contusion hardening under the skin.

And then he was crossing a road, and he hadn't looked first, and a bread truck, filled with soft dinner rolls so yeasty and warm that they were still expanding in their trays, hit him. He woke with a leg twisted beyond recognition, a mouth absent of teeth on one side, and his head in the lap of a woman who was crying for him, though she was a stranger, and he was bleeding all over her skirt, and there were warm mounds of bread scattered around them. It was the bread that made the pain return to his body, the deep warmth and good smell. He bit the hem of the woman's skirt to keep from screaming.

She rode with him to the hospital and stayed all night to keep him from falling asleep and possibly going into a coma. She was homely, three years older than he, a thick-legged antiques dealer who described her shop down a street so tiny the sun never touched her windows. He thought of her in the silent murky shop, swimming from credenza to credenza like a fish in an aquarium. She fed him rice pudding when she came to visit him in the hospital and carefully brushed his wild hair until it was flat on his crown.

He woke one night with a jerk: the stars were angrily bright in the hospital window and someone in the room was breathing. There was a weight on his chest, and when he looked down, he found the girl's sleeping head. For a moment, he didn't know who she was. By the time he identified her, the feeling of unknowing had burrowed in. He would never know her; knowledge of another person was ungraspable, a cloud. He would never begin to hold another in his mind like an equation, pure and entire. He focused at the part of her thin hair, which in the darkness and closeness looked like inept black stitches in white wax. He stared at the part until the horror faded, until her smell, the bitterness of unwashed hair, the lavender soap she used on her face, rose to him and he put his nose against her warmth and inhaled her.

At dawn, she woke. Her cheek was creased from the folds in his gown. She looked at him wildly and he laughed, and she rubbed the drool from the corner of her mouth and turned away as if disappointed. He married her because, during the night, to not marry her had ceased to be an option.

While he was learning how to walk again, he had a letter from the university down in Florida, making a tremendous offer for his father's land.

And so, instead of the honeymoon trip to the Thousand Islands, pines and cold water and his wife's bikini pressing into the dough of her flesh, they took a sleeping train down to Florida and walked in the heat to the edge of the university campus. Where he remembered vast oak hammocks, there were rectilinear brick buildings. Mossy pools were now parking lots.

Only his father's property, one hundred acres, was overgrown with palmettos and vines. He brushed the redbugs off his wife's sensible travel pants and carried her into his father's house. Termites had chiseled long gouges in the floorboards, but the sturdy cracker house had kept out most of the wilderness. His wife touched the mantel made of heart pine and turned to him gladly. Later, after he came home with a box of groceries and found the kitchen scrubbed clean, he heard three thumps upstairs and ran up to find that she had killed a blacksnake in the bathtub with her bare heel and was laughing at herself in amazement.

How magnificent he found her, a Valkyrie, half-naked and warlike with that dead snake at her feet. In her body, the culmination of all things. He didn't say it, of course; he couldn't. He only reached and put his hands upon her.

In the night, she rolled toward him and took his ankles between her own. "All right," she said. "We can stay."

"I didn't say anything," he said.

And she smiled a little bitterly and said, "Well. You don't."

They moved their things into the house where he was born. They put in air conditioning, renovated the structure, put on large additions. His wife opened a shop on the ground floor of the one building in town over four stories tall, though she had to drive to Miami and Atlanta to stock it with antiques. He sold his father's land, but slowly, in small pieces, at prices that rose dizzyingly with each sale. The numbers lived in him, warmed him, brought him a buzzing kind of joy. Jude made investments so shrewd that when he and his wife were in their midthirties, he opened a bottle of wine and announced that neither of them would ever have to work again. His wife laughed and drank but kept up with the store. When she was almost too old, they had a daughter and named her after his mother.

When he held the baby at home for the first time, he understood he had never been so terrified of anything as he was of this mottled lump of flesh. How easily he could break her without meaning to, she could slip from his hands and crack open on the floor, she could catch pneumonia when he bathed her, he could say a terrible thing in anger and she would shrivel. All the mistakes he could make telescoped before him. His wife saw him turn pale and plucked the baby from his hands just before he crashed down. When he came to, she was livid but calm. He protested, but she put the baby in his hands.

"Try again," she said.

His daughter grew, sturdy and blond like his wife, with no flash of Jude's genius for numbers. They were dry as biscuits in her mouth; she preferred music and English. For this, he was glad. She would love more moderately, more externally. If he didn't cuddle with her the way her mother did, he still thought he was a good father: he never hit her, he never left her alone in the house, he told her how much he loved her by providing her with everything he could imagine she'd like. He was a quiet parent, but he was sure she knew the scope of his heart.

And yet his daughter never grew out of wearing a singularly irritating expression, one taut with competition, which he first saw on her face when she was a very little girl at an Easter egg hunt. She could barely walk in her grass-stained bloomers, but even when the other children rested out of the Florida sunshine in the shade, eating their booty of chocolate, Jude's little girl kept returning with eggs too cunningly hidden in the sago palms to have been found in the first frenzy. She heaped them on his lap until they overflowed and shrieked when he told her firmly that enough was enough.

His fat old uncle came over for dinner once, then once a week, then became a friend. When the uncle died of an aneurysm while feeding his canary, he left Jude his estate of moth-eaten smoking jackets and family photos in ornate frames.

The university grew around Jude's last ten-acre parcel, a protective cushion between the old house and the rest of the world. The more construction around their plot of land, the fewer snakes Jude saw, until he felt no qualms about walking barefoot in the St. Augustine grass to take the garbage to the edge of the drive. He built a fence around his land and laughed at the university's offers, sensing desperation in their inflating numbers. He thought of himself as the virus in the busy cell, latent, patient. The swamp's streams were blocked by the university's construction, and it became a small lake, in which he installed some bubblers to keep the mosquitoes away. There were alligators, sometimes large ones, but he put in an invisible fence and it kept his family's dogs from coming too close to the water's edge and being gobbled up, and the gators only eyed them from the banks.

And then, one day, Jude woke with the feeling that a bell jar had descended over him. He showered with a sense of unease, sat at the edge of the bed for a while. When his wife came in to tell him something, he watched in confusion at the way her mouth opened and closed fishily, without sound.

"I think I've gone deaf," he said, and he didn't so much hear his words as feel them vibrating in the bones of his skull.

At the doctors', he submitted to test after test, but nobody understood what had gone wrong in his brain or in his ears. They gave him a hearing aid that turned conversation into an underwater burble. Mostly he kept it off.

At night, he'd come out into the dark kitchen, longing for curried chicken, raw onion, preserved peaches, tastes sharp and simple to remind himself that he was still there. He'd find his daughter at the island, her lovely mean face lit up by her screen. She'd frown at him and turn the screen to show him what she'd discovered: cochlear implants, audiologic rehabilitation, miracles.

But there was nothing for him. He was condemned. He ate Thanksgiving dinner, wanting to weep into his sweet potatoes. His family was gathered around him, his wife and daughter and their closest friends and their children, and he could see them laughing, but he couldn't hear the jokes. He longed for someone to look up, to see him at the end of the table, to reach out a hand and pat his. But they were too happy. They slotted laden forks into their mouths and brought the tines out clean. They picked the flesh off the turkey, they scooped the pecans out of the pie. After the supper, his arms prickling with hot water from the dishes, they sat together, watching football, and he sat in his chair with his feet propped up, and everyone fell asleep around him and he alone sat in vigil over them, watching them sleep.

The day his daughter went to college in Boston, his wife went with her.

She mouthed very carefully to him, "You'll be all right for four days? You can take care of yourself?"

And he said, "Yes, of course. I am an *adult*, sweetheart," but the way she winced, he knew he'd said it too loudly. He loaded their bags into the car, and his daughter cried in his arms, and he kissed her over and over on the crown of the head. His wife looked at him worriedly, but kissed him also and climbed inside. And then, silently as everything, the car moved off.

The house felt immense around him. He sat in the study, which had been his childhood bedroom, and seemed to see the place as it had been, spare and filled with snakes, layered atop the house as it was, with its marble and bright walls and track lights above his head.

That night, he waited, his hearing aid turned up so loud that it began to make sharp beeping sounds that hurt. He wanted the pain. He fell asleep watching a sitcom that, without sound, was just strange-looking people making huge expressions with their faces and woke up and it was only eight o'clock at night, and he felt as if he'd been alone forever.

He hadn't known he'd miss his wife's heavy body in the bed next to his, the sandwiches she made (too much mayonnaise, but he never told her so), the smell of her body wash in the humid bathroom in the morning.

On the second night, he sat in the black density of the veranda, looking at the lake that used to be a swamp. He wondered what had happened to the reptiles out there; where they had gone. Alone in the darkness, Jude wished he could hear the university in its nighttime boil around them, the students shouting drunkenly, the bass thrumming, the noise of football games out at the stadium that used to make them groan with irritation. But he could have been anywhere, in the middle of hundreds of miles of wasteland, for as quiet as the night was for him. Even the mosquitoes had somehow been eradicated. As a child, he would have been a single itchy blister by now.

Unable to sleep, Jude climbed to the roof to straighten the gutter that had crimped in the middle from a falling oak branch. He crept on his hands and knees across the asbestos shingles, still hot from the day, to fix the flashing on the chimney. From up there, the university coiled around him, and in the streetlights, a file of pledging sorority girls in tight, bright dresses and high heels slowly crawled up the hill like ants.

He came down reluctantly at dawn and took a can of tuna and a cold jug of water down to the lake's edge, where he turned over the aluminum johnboat his wife had bought for him a few years earlier, hoping he'd take up fishing.

"Fishing?" he'd said. "I haven't fished since I was a boy." He thought of those childhood shad and gar and snook, how his father cooked them up with lemons from the tree beside the back door and ate them without a word of praise. He must have made a face because his wife had recoiled.

"I thought it'd be a hobby," she'd said. "If you don't like it, find another hobby. Or *something.*"

He'd thanked her but had never had the time to use either the rod or the boat. It sat there, its bright belly dulling under layers of pollen. Now was the time. He was hungry for something indefinable, something he thought he'd left behind him so long ago. He thought he might find it in the lake, perhaps.

He pushed off and rowed out. There was no wind, and the sun was already searing. The water was hot and thick with algae. A heron stood one-legged among the cypress. Something big jumped and sent rings out toward the boat, rocking it slightly. Jude tried to get comfortable but was sweating, and now the mosquitoes smelled him and swarmed. The silence was eerie because he remembered it as a dense tapestry of sound, the click and whirr of sandhill cranes, the cicadas, the owls, the mysterious subhuman cries too distant to identify. He had wanted to connect with something, something he had lost, but it wasn't here.

He gave up. But when he sat up to row himself back, both oars had slid loose from their locks and floated off. They lay ten feet away, caught in the duckweed.

The water thickly hid its danger, but he knew what was there. There were the alligators, their knobby eyes even now watching him. He'd seen one with his binoculars from the bedroom the other day that was at least fourteen feet long. He felt it somewhere nearby, now. And though this was no longer prairie, there were still a few snakes, cottonmouths, copperheads, pygmies under the leaf-rot at the edge of the lake. There was the water itself, superheated until host to flagellates that enter the nose and infect the brain, an infinity of the minuscule, eating away. There was the burning sun above and the mosquitoes feeding on his blood. There was the silence. He wouldn't swim in this terrifying mess. He stood, agitated, and felt the boat slide a few inches from under him, and sat down hard, clinging to the gunwales. He was a hundred feet offshore on a breathless day. He would not be blown to shore. He would be stuck here forever; his wife would come home in two days to find his corpse floating in its johnboat. He drank some water to calm himself. When he decided to remember algorithms in his head, their savor had stolen away.

For now there were silent birds and sun and mosquitoes; below a world of slinking predators. In the delicate cup of the johnboat, he was alone, floating. He closed his eyes and felt his heart beat in his ears.

He had never had the time to be seized by doubt. Now all he had was time. Hours dripped past. He sweated. He was ill. The sun only grew hotter and there was no respite, no shade.

Jude drifted off to sleep, and when he woke he knew that if he opened his eyes, he would see his father sitting in the bow, glowering. Terrible son, Jude was, to ruin what his father loved best. The ancient fear rose in him, and he swallowed it as well as he could with his dry throat. He would not open his eyes, he wouldn't give the old man the satisfaction.

"Go away," he said. "Leave me be." His voice inside his head was only a rumble.

"I'm not like you, Dad," Jude said later. "I don't prefer snakes to people."

Even later, he said, "You were a mean, unhappy man. And I always hated you."

But this seemed harsh and he said, "I didn't completely mean that."

He thought of this lake. He thought of how his father would see Jude's life. Such a delicate ecosystem, so precisely calibrated, in the end destroyed by Jude's careful parceling of love, of land. Greed; the university's gobble. Those scaled creatures, killed. The awe in his father's voice that day they went out gathering moccasins; the bright, sharp love inside Jude, long ago, when he had loved numbers. Jude's promise was unfulfilled, the choices made not the passionate ones. Jude had been safe.

And here he was. Not unlike his father when he died in that tent. Isolated. Sunbattered. Old.

He thought in despair of diving into the perilous water, and how he probably deserved being bitten. But then the wind picked up and began pushing him back across the lake, toward his house. When he opened his eyes, his father wasn't with him, but the house loomed over the bow, ramshackle, too huge, a crazy person's place. He averted his eyes, unable to bear it now. The sun snuffed itself out. Despite his pain, the skin on his legs and arms blistered with sunburn and great, itching mosquito welts, he later realized he must have fallen asleep because when he opened his eyes again, the stars were out and the johnboat was nosing up against the shore.

He stood, his bones aching, and wobbled to the shore.

And now something white and large was rushing at him, and because he'd sat all day with his father's ghost, he understood this was a ghost too, and looked up at it, calm and ready. The lights from the house shined at its back, and it had a golden glow around it. But the figure stopped just before him, and he saw, with a startle, that it was his wife, that the glow was her frizzy gray hair catching the light, and he knew then that she must have come back early, that she was reaching a hand out to him, putting her soft palm on his cheek, and she was saying something forever lost to him, but he knew by the way she was smiling that she was scolding him. He stepped closer to her and put his head in the crook of her neck. He breathed his inadequacy out there, breathed in her love and the grease of her travels and knew he had been lucky; that he had escaped the hungry darkness, once more.

2013

You Can Find Love Now

RAMONA AUSUBEL

[b. 1979]

You are lonely, but you don't have to be. You have so many great qualities! Just think of all the single ladies out there who are waiting to hear from you. Whether you are looking for lasting love or just a little fun, this is the only guide to online dating you'll ever need. Within the hour, you'll be on your way to eternal happiness!

Let's get started. When creating your username keep in mind that it should be concise and easy to remember. Make it personal. If you're a dancer, maybe try hipdancer21.

Find me at cyclops15. Cyclops 1 through 14 were taken.

Now choose a tagline that will attract the woman you want. Secret: do what no one else is doing.

I'm eight feet tall and I have one giant eye.

What are your interests? Be honest but enticing.

I hand-sew my own shoes using a needle made from the fang of a wolf. I sleep hot. I want nothing more than a sheet on my bed, even in winter, even in a cave.

Know who your target is. Where does she live? What does she look like? What hobbies does she have?

I like fat girls, old girls, tall girls, tired girls. Girls who lack adequate clothing, girls whose best idea for getting my attention is to send a photo of themselves holding suggestive Popsicles, their fists covered in red melt. Girls in wheelchairs, girls who work professionally at the Renaissance Faire.

You could choose other men: men who like to think about feet, men who have thick back hair, men whose greatest pride is the time they flew to a nearby nation and tried to deplete its stores of alcohol and slept on the beach one night—wasn't that so fun?—and when they woke up everything had been stolen or lost and they had to walk back to the pastel-yellow hotel naked in the early heat of another day in paradise. Everyone has had good times. Everyone has a picture of himself in front of a pinkening sunset with a glass of white wine. Choose them if you want to. Choose me if you want someone to hold you above his head in the moonlight, bite your wrist until the first rust comes out.

Tell the ladies a little more about yourself! What's your own unique story?

The first generation of Cyclopes were forgers. The next generation, my generation, was a band of thuggish shepherds living in the grasslands of Sicily. We trapped so-called heroes in our caves, we bit into the warm butter of a human leg, but the only one who got famous for it was my brother. We still live under volcanoes, hacking at iron, trying to revive the old tradition. I left home—too hot, too old—and live in Washington state. I like the fog, I like the rain. My volcano is more famous than any of my brothers' volcanoes. I never hear from them. They're not on email.

I teach online English classes, not to get paid but because I like to feel smarter than someone else. I teach all the classic books, except *The Odyssey.*

My photos are taken in profile. Maybe there's time to get braver, to embrace my own unique beauty. I subscribe to the magazines that tell me we are all beautiful, if only we can learn to tap into our potential; I am me and no one else is me, and that is a miracle. I am a miracle.

The downside: my mother has been dead for some hundreds of years, so you'll never meet her. The upside: my father is the god of the sea, so we can guarantee good weather on our honeymoon cruise. He's shitty at love, my dad. He smells like an overcleaned wound, and he won't quit working. Every day and every night somewhere in one of the world's oceans my father is striking the surface of the abyss with swords of fire.

Do you smoke? Do you drink? How often do you exercise? Do you support charities that help animals? With an unexpected bonus would you (a) donate to a cause you really believe in? (b) save half and spend the rest? (c) celebrate with your friends and margaritas?

If you want me to set a trap, I'll set a trap. A first date picking blueberries in the whitest, cleanest sunlight, tin pails. I'll bring sandwiches and chilled Chardonnay and tell you that we are already the good people we wanted to become. Maybe you'll be generous and keep up the conversation all afternoon. Prettykaren98 was generous, Prettykaren98 looked into my eye when we chatted online and laughed at my jokes. But she never answered my messages after our date even though her status was still marked Single.

Don't mention your previous relationship history! Leave your emotional baggage packed and in the closet. You are on the market because you are awesome!

Sorry. Let's try that again. My actual perfect day? Descending belowground early, full of milk and blood and meat, to forge iron. There is no such thing as day or night in the volcano, and any sense of time comes from watching the metal change shape. From ore to spear. From ore to trident. From ore to thunderbolt. If I am strong that day, the mountains will shake with the strike of my hammer, the heat of my flame.

I can't ski. I should be better at basketball than I am. I don't eat vegetables. But my eye is blue, and it's pale and it's beautiful.

My vision is good, though not great, but understand this: I will never again visit an ophthalmologist or an optometrist or anyone else who claims to be an expert of my organ. I do not fit in the chair, and I wish I could forget lying on my back on the floor of that darkened room while a small man climbed onto my chest with that sharp point of light. I'm not sorry for what I did to him. Now he can see for himself what it's like to have one eye.

You have almost finished creating a magnetic online-dating profile that will attract more women than you ever thought possible! What else do you want the ladies to know? Remember: be yourself!

I do remember the old feeling sometimes. A maiden washes up on my island, tailed or otherwise. The cave is sweating and there are mineral stalks growing from the ceiling. I have no idea what time it is, ever. All my wrist and ankle shackles are homemade, struck from iron I myself dug from the earth. The maidens were not as beautiful as the stories tell you—their hair was salt-stringy and their faces were pruned. Too long in seawater can unmake any loveliness. Yet I meant to love them. I meant to tend to their wounds. When I pounded the shackles with my hammer, the person I imagined chaining was my father. I imagined slipping the cuffs around his watery arms. Not to hurt him, but to keep him. But my father never offered himself up on my rocky beach. I'd see his big hand out there sometimes, swilling the surface of the sea, but he never came close. Maybe he was the one who threw the maidens to me, his dear son, his wifeless boy, wanting an heir.

I will not shackle your slender wrists to the cold walls or gnaw your nails down to the quick with my remaining teeth. I will not leave you hungry while I eat a roast goat at your feet. I've dealt with those issues. Imagine the inverse: I have the softest mattress in the world, made of the combed fur of fawns; choose me and you'll be choosing warm oil on your hands and cold water in your glass, meat on your plate from a lamb that suckled on my pinkie when it was first born.

If I came to your house tonight, where would I find you? The living room? The kitchen? Waiting at the door? I'll call you Aphrodite and smell the sea in your hair and shuck oysters for you from the depths. I'll tell you that I've never seen a real goddess until now. Come with me and be adored, deep below the earth. While you sleep, I will strike a huge sheet of metal until the shape of your body comes into relief. You never have to take me to meet your friends; you never have to take me anywhere. You never even have to see me in the light.

Your grandmother will tell you that all the good men are gone, but then here I am, and I'm ready for you.

2018

Vampires in the Lemon Grove

KAREN RUSSELL
[b. 1981]

In October, the men and women of Sorrento harvest the *primo-fiore*, or "first fruit," the most succulent lemons; in March, the yellow *bianchetti* ripen, followed in June by the green *verdelli*. In every season you can find me sitting at my bench, watching them fall. Only one or two lemons tumble from the branches each hour, but I've been sitting here so long, their falling seems contiguous, close as raindrops. My wife has no patience for this sort of meditation. "Jesus Christ, Clyde," she says. "You need a hobby."

Most people mistake me for a small, kindly Italian grandfather, a *nonno*. I have an old *nonno*'s coloring, the dark walnut stain peculiar to southern Italians, a tan that won't fade until I die (which I never will). I wear a neat periwinkle shirt, a canvas sunhat, black suspenders that sag at my chest. My loafers are battered but always polished. The few visitors to the lemon grove who notice me smile blankly into my raisin face and catch the whiff of some sort of tragedy; they whisper that I am a widower, or an old man who has survived his children. They never guess that I am a vampire.

Santa Francesca's Lemon Grove, where I spend my days and nights, was part of a Jesuit convent in the 1800s. Now it's privately owned by the Alberti family, the prices are excessive, and the locals know to buy their lemons elsewhere. In summers a teenage girl named Fila mans a wooden stall at the back of the grove. She's painfully thin, with heavy, black bangs. I can tell by the careful way she saves the best lemons for me, slyly kicking them under my bench, that she knows I am a monster. Sometimes she'll smile vacantly in my direction, but she never gives me any trouble. And because of her benevolent indifference to me, I feel a swell of love for the girl.

Fila makes the lemonade and monitors the hot dog machine, watching the meat rotate on wire spigots. I'm fascinated by this machine. The Italian name for it translates as "carousel of beef." Who would have guessed at such a device two hundred years ago? Back then we were all preoccupied with visions of apocalypse; Santa Francesca, the foundress of this very grove, gouged out her eyes while dictating premonitions of fire. What a shame, I often think, that she foresaw only the end times, never hot dogs.

A sign posted just outside the grove reads:

CIGARETTE PIE
HEAT DOGS
GRANITE DRINKS
SANTA FRANCESCA'S LIMONATA —
THE MOST REFRISHING DRANK ON THE PLENET!!

Every day, tourists from Wales and Germany and America are ferried over from cruise ships to the base of these cliffs. They ride the funicular up here to visit the grove, to eat "heat dogs" with speckly brown mustard and sip lemon ices. They snap photographs of the Alberti brothers, Benny and Luciano, teenage twins who cling to the trees' wooden supports and make a grudging show of harvesting lemons, who spear each other with trowels and refer to the tourist women as "vaginas" in Italian slang. "*Buona sera*, vaginas!" they cry from the trees. I think the tourists are getting stupider. None of them speak Italian anymore, and these new women seem deaf to aggression. Often I fantasize about flashing my fangs at the brothers, just to keep them in line.

As I said, the tourists usually ignore me; perhaps it's the dominoes. A few years back, I bought a battered red set from Benny, a prop piece, and this makes me invisible, sufficiently banal to be hidden in plain sight. I have no real interest in the game; I mostly stack the pieces into little houses and corrals.

At sunset, the tourists all around begin to shout. "Look! Up there!" It's time for the path of *I Pipistrelli Impazziti*—the descent of the bats.

They flow from cliffs that glow like pale chalk, expelled from caves seemingly in billions. Their drop is steep and vertical, a black hail. Sometimes a change in weather sucks a bat beyond the lemon trees and into the turquoise sea. It's three hundred feet to the lemon grove, six hundred feet to the churning foam of the Tyrrhenian. At the precipice, they soar upward and crash around the green tops of the trees.

"Oh!" the tourists shriek, delighted, ducking their heads.

Up close, the bats' spread wings are an alien membrane—fragile, like something internal flipped out. The waning sun washes their bodies a dusky red. They have wrinkled black faces, these bats, tiny, like gargoyles or angry grandfathers. They have teeth like mine.

Tonight, one of the tourists, a Texan lady with a big strawberry-red updo, has successfully captured a bat in her hair, simultaneously crying real tears and howling: "TAKE THE GODDAMN PICTURE, Sarah!"

I stare ahead at a fixed point above the trees and light a cigarette. My bent spine goes rigid. Mortal terror always trips some old wire that leaves me sad and irritable. It will be whole minutes now before everybody stops screaming.

The moon is a muted shade of orange. Twin discs of light burn in the sky and the sea. I scan the darker indents in the skyline, the cloudless spots that I know to be caves. I check my watch again. It's eight o'clock, and all the bats have disappeared into the interior branches. Where is Magreb? My fangs are throbbing, but I won't start without her.

I once pictured time as a black magnifying glass and myself as a microscopic, flightless insect trapped in that circle of night. But then Magreb came along, and eternity ceased to frighten me. Suddenly each moment followed its antecedent in a neat chain, moments we filled with each other.

I watch a single bat falling from the cliffs, dropping like a stone: headfirst, motionless, dizzying to witness.

Pull up.

I close my eyes. I press my palms flat against the picnic table and tense the muscles of my neck.

Pull UP. I tense up until my temples pulse, until little black and red stars flutter behind my eyelids.

"You can look now."

Magreb is sitting on the bench, blinking her bright pumpkin eyes. "You weren't even *watching*. If you saw me coming down, you'd know you have nothing to worry about." I try to smile at her and find I can't. My own eyes feel like ice cubes.

"It's stupid to go so fast." I don't look at her. "That easterly could knock you over the rocks."

"Don't be ridiculous. I'm an excellent flier."

She's right. Magreb can shape-shift midair, much more smoothly than I ever could. Even back in the 1850s when I used to transmute into a bat two, three times a night, my metamorphosis was a shy, halting process.

"Look!" she says, triumphant, mocking. "You're still trembling!"

I look down at my hands, angry to realize it's true.

Magreb roots through the tall, black blades of grass. "It's late, Clyde; where's my lemon?"

I pluck a soft, round lemon from the grass, a summer moon, and hand it to her. The *verdelli* I have chosen is perfect, flawless. She looks at it with distaste and makes a big show of brushing off a marching ribbon of ants.

"A toast!" I say.

"A toast," Magreb replies, with the rote enthusiasm of a Christian saying grace. We left the lemons and swing them to our faces. We plunge our fangs, piercing the skin, and emit a long, united hiss: *"Aaah!"*

Over the years, Magreb and I have tried everything—fangs in apples, fangs in rubber balls. We have lived everywhere: Tunis, Laos, Cincinnati, Salamanca. We spent our honeymoon hopping continents, haunting liquid chimeras: mint tea in Fez, coconut slurries in Oahu, jet black coffee in Bogotá, jackal's milk in Dakar, cherry Coke floats in rural Alabama, a thousand beverages that purported to have magical quenching properties. We went thirsty in every region of the globe before finding our oasis here, in the blue boot of Italy, at this dead nun's lemonade stand. It's only these lemons that give us any relief.

When we first landed in Sorrento I was skeptical. The pitcher of lemonade we ordered looked cloudy and adulterated. Sugar clumped at the bottom. I took a gulp, and a whole small lemon lodged in my mouth; there is no word sufficiently lovely for the first taste, the first feeling of my fangs in that lemon. It was bracingly sour, with a delicate hint of ocean salt. After an initial prickling—a sort of chemical effervescence along my gums—a soothing blankness traveled from the tip of each fang to my fevered brain. These lemons are a vampire's analgesic. If you have been thirsty for a long time, if you have been suffering, then the absence of those two feelings—however brief—becomes a kind of heaven. I breathed deeply through my nostrils. My throbbing fangs were still.

By daybreak, the numbness had begun to wear off. The lemons relieve our thirst without ending it, like a drink we can hold in our mouths but never swallow. Eventually the original hunger returns. I have tried to be very good, very correct and conscientious about not confusing this original hunger with the thing I feel for Magreb.

I can't joke about my early years on the blood, can't even think about them without guilt and acidic embarrassment. Unlike Magreb, who has never had a sip of the stuff, I listened to the village gossips and believed every rumor, internalized every report of corrupted bodies and boiled blood. Vampires were the favorite undead of the Enlightenment, and as a young boy I aped the diction and mannerisms I read about in books: Vlad the Impaler, Count Heinrich the Despoiler, Goethe's blood-sucking bride of Corinth. I eavesdropped on the terrified prayers of an old woman in a cemetery, begging God to protect her from . . . me. I felt a dislocation then, a spreading numbness, as if I were invisible or already dead. After that, I did only what the stories suggested, beginning with that old woman's blood. I slept in coffins, in black cedar boxes, and woke every night with a fierce headache. I was famished, perennially dizzy. I had unspeakable dreams about the sun.

In practice I was no suave viscount, just a teenager in a red velvet cape, awkward and voracious. I wanted to touch the edges of my life. The same instinct, I think, that inspires young mortals to flip tractors and enlist in foreign wars. One night I skulked into a late Mass with some vague plan to defeat eternity. At the back of the nave, I tossed my mousy curls, rolled my eyes heavenward, and then plunged my entire arm into the bronze pail of holy water. Death would be painful, probably, but I didn't care about pain. I wanted to overturn my sentence. It was working; I could feel the burn beginning to spread. Actually, it was more like an itch, but I was sure the burning would start any second. I slid into a pew, snug in my misery, and waited for my body to turn to ash.

By sunrise, I'd developed a rash between my eyebrows, a little late-flowering acne, but was otherwise fine, and I understood I truly was immortal. At that moment I yielded all discrimination; I bit anyone kind or slow enough to let me get close: men, women, even some older boys and girls. The littlest children I left alone, very proud at the time of this one scruple. I'd read stories about Hungarian *vampirs* who drank the blood of orphan girls and mentioned this to Magreb early on, hoping to impress her with my decency. Not *children*! she wept. She wept for a day and a half.

Our first date was in Cementerio de Colón, if I can call a chance meeting between headstones a date. I had been stalking her, following her swishing hips as she took a shortcut through the cemetery grass. She wore her hair in a low, snaky braid that was coming unraveled. When I was near enough to touch her trailing ribbon, she whipped around. "Are you following me?" she asked, annoyed, not scared. She regarded my face with the contempt of a woman confronting the town drunk. "Oh," she said, "your teeth . . ."

And then she grinned. Magreb was the first and only other vampire I'd ever met. We bared our fangs over a tombstone and recognized each other. There is a loneliness that must be particular to monsters, I think, the feeling that each is the only child of a species. And now that loneliness was over.

Our first date lasted all night. Magreb's talk seemed to lunge forward like a train without a conductor; I suspect even she didn't know what she was saying. I certainly wasn't paying attention, staring dopily at her fangs, and then I heard her ask: "So, when did you figure out that the blood does nothing?"

At the time of this conversation, I was edging on 130. I had never gone a day since early childhood without drinking several pints of blood. *The blood does nothing?* My forehead burned and burned.

"Didn't you think it suspicious that you had a heartbeat?" she asked me. "That you had a reflection in water?"

When I didn't answer, Magreb went on. "Every time I saw my own face in a mirror, I knew I wasn't any of those ridiculous things, a blood-sucker, a *sanguina*. You know?"

"Sure," I said, nodding. For me, mirrors had the opposite effect: I saw a mouth ringed in black blood. I saw the pale son of the villagers' fears.

Those initial days with Magreb nearly undid me. At first my euphoria was sharp and blinding, all my thoughts spooling into a single blue thread of relief—*The blood does nothing! I don't have to drink the blood!*—but when that subsided, I found I had nothing left. If we didn't have to drink the blood, then what on earth were these fangs for?

Sometimes I think she preferred me then: I was like her own child, raw and amazed. We smashed my coffin with an ax and spent the night at a hotel. I lay there wide-eyed in the big bed, my heart thudding like a fishtail against the floor of a boat.

"You're really sure?" I whispered to her. "I don't have to sleep in a coffin? I don't have to sleep through the day?" She had already drifted off.

A few months later, she suggested a picnic.

"But the sun."

Magreb shook her head. "You poor thing, believing all that garbage."

By this time we'd found a dirt cellar in which to live in Western Australia, where the sun burned through the clouds like dining lace. That sun ate lakes, rising out of dead volcanoes at dawn, triple the size of a harvest moon and skull-white, a grass-scorcher. Go ahead, try to walk into that sun when you've been told your bones are tinder.

I stared at the warped planks of the trapdoor above us, the copper ladder that led rung by rung to the bright world beyond. Time fell away from me and I was a child again, afraid, afraid. Magreb rested her hand on the small of my back. "You can do it," she said, nudging me gently. I took a deep breath and hunched my shoulders, my scalp grazing the cellar door, my hair soaked through with sweat. I focused my thoughts to still the tremors, lest my fangs slice the inside of my mouth, and turned my face away from Magreb.

"Go on."

I pushed up and felt the wood give way. Light exploded through the cellar. My pupils shrank to dots.

Outside, the whole world was on fire. Mute explosions rocked the scrubby forest, motes of light burning like silent rockets. The sun fell through the eucalyptus and Australian pines in bright red bars. I pulled myself out onto my belly, balled up in the soil, and screamed for mercy until I'd exhausted myself. Then I opened one watery eye and took a long look around. The sun wasn't fatal! It was just uncomfortable, making my eyes itch and water and inducing a sneezing attack.

After that, and for the whole of our next thirty years together, I watched the auroral colors and waited to feel anything but terror. Fingers of light spread across the gray sea toward me, and I couldn't see these colors as beautiful. The sky I lived under was a hideous, lethal mix of orange and pink, a physical deformity. By the 1950s we were living in a Cincinnati suburb; and as a day's first light hit the kitchen windows, I'd press my face against the linoleum and gibber my terror into the cracks.

"So-o," Magreb would say, "I can tell you're not a morning person." Then she'd sit on the porch swing and rock with me, patting my hand.

"What's wrong, Clyde?"

I shook my head. This was a new sadness, difficult to express. My bloodlust was undiminished but now the blood wouldn't fix it.

"It never fixed it," Magreb reminded me, and I wished she would please stop talking.

That cluster of years was a very confusing period. Mostly I felt grateful, above-ground feelings. I was in love. For a vampire, my life was very normal. Instead of stalking prostitutes, I went on long bicycle rides with Magreb. We visited botanical gardens and rowed in boats. In a short time, my face had gone from lithium white to the color of milky coffee. Yet sometimes, especially at high noon, I'd study Magreb's face with a hot, illogical hatred, each pore opening up to swallow me. *You've ruined my life*, I'd think. To correct for her power over my mind I tried to fantasize about mortal women, their wild eyes and bare swan necks; I couldn't do it, not anymore—an eternity of vague female smiles eclipsed by Magreb's tiny razor fangs. Two gray tabs against her lower lip.

But like I said, I was mostly happy. I was making a kind of progress.

One night, children wearing necklaces of garlic bulbs arrived giggling at our door. It was Halloween; they were vampire hunters. The smell of garlic blasted through the mail slot, along with their voices: "Trick or treat!" In the old days, I would have cowered from these children. I would have run downstairs to barricade myself in my coffin. But that night, I pulled on an undershirt and opened the door. I stood in a square of green light in my boxer shorts hefting a bag of Tootsie Roll Pops, a small victory over the old fear.

"Mister, you okay?"

I blinked down at a little blond child and then saw that my two hands were shaking violently, soundlessly, like old friends wishing not to burden me with their troubles. I dropped the candies into the children's bags, thinking: *You small mortals don't realize the power of your stories*.

We were downing strawberry velvet cocktails on the Seine when something inside me changed. Thirty years. Eleven thousand dawns. That's how long it took for me to believe the sun wouldn't kill me.

"Want to go see a museum or something? We're in Paris, after all."

"Okay."

We walked over a busy pedestrian bridge in a flood of light, and my heart was in my throat. Without any discussion, I understood that Magreb was my wife.

Because I love her, my hunger pangs gradually mellowed into a comfortable despair. Sometimes I think of us as two holes cleaved together, two twin hungers. Our bellies growl at each other like companionable dogs. I love the sound, assuring me we're equals in our thirst. We bump our fangs and feel like we're coming up against the same hard truth.

Human marriages amuse me: the brevity of the commitment and all the ceremony that surrounds it, the calla lilies, the veiled mother-in-laws like lilac spiders, the tears and earnest toasts. Till death do us part! Easy. These mortal couples need only keep each other in sight for fifty, sixty years.

Often I wonder to what extent a mortal's love grows from the bedrock of his or her foreknowledge of death, love coiling like a green stem out of that blankness in a way I'll never quite understand. And lately I've been having a terrible thought: *Our love affair will end before the world does*.

One day, without any preamble, Magreb flew up to the caves. She called over her furry, muscled shoulder that she just wanted to sleep for a while.

"What? Wait! What's wrong?"

I'd caught her midshift, halfway between a wife and a bat.

"Don't be so sensitive, Clyde! I'm just tired of this century, so very tired, maybe it's the heat? I think I need a little rest . . ."

I assumed this was an experiment, like my cape, an old habit to which she was returning; and from the clumsy, ambivalent way she crashed around on the wind I understood I was supposed to follow her. Well, too bad. Magreb likes to say she freed me, disabused me of the old stories; but I gave up more than I intended: I can't shudder myself out of this old man's body. I can't fly anymore.

Fila and I are alone. I press my dry lips together and shove dominoes around the table; they buckle like the cars of a tiny train.

"More lemonade, *nonno?*" She smiles. She leans from her waist and boldly touches my right fang, a thin string of hanging drool. "Looks like you're thirsty."

"Please." I gesture at the bench. "Have a seat."

Fila is seventeen now and has known about me for some time. She's toying with the idea of telling her boss, weighing the sentence within her like a bullet in a gun: *There is a vampire in our grove*.

"You don't believe me, signore Alberti?" she'll say, before taking him by the wrist and leading him to this bench, and I'll choose that moment to rise up and bite him in his hog-thick neck. "Right through his stupid tie!" she says with a grin.

But this is just idle fantasy, she assures me. Fila is content to let me alone. "You remind me of my *nonno*," she says approvingly. "You look very Italian."

In fact, she wants to help me hide here. It gives her a warm feeling to do so, like helping her own fierce *nonno* do up the small buttons of his trousers, now too intricate a maneuver for his palsied hands. She worries about me too. And she should: lately I've gotten sloppy, incontinent about my secrets. I've stopped polishing my shoes; I let the tip of one fang hang over my pink lip. "You must be more careful," she reprimands. "There are tourists *everywhere*."

I study her neck as she says this, her head rolling with the natural expressiveness of a girl. She checks to see if I am watching her collarbone, and I let her see that I am. I feel like a threat again.

Last night I went on a rampage. On my seventh lemon I found with a sort of drowsy despair that I couldn't stop. I crawled around on all fours, looking for the last *bianchettis* in the dewy grass: soft with rot, mildewed, sun-shriveled, blackened. Lemon skin bulging with tiny cellophane-green worms. Dirt smells, rain smells, all swirled through with the tart sting of decay.

In the morning, Magreb steps around the wreckage and doesn't say a word.

"I came up with a new name," I say, hoping to distract her. "*Brandolino*. What do you think?"

I have spent the last several years trying to choose an Italian name, and every day that I remain Clyde feels like a defeat. Our names are relics of the places we've been. "Clyde" is a souvenir from the California Gold Rush. I was callow and blood-crazed back then, and I saw my echo in the freckly youths panning along the Sacramento River. I used the name as a kind of bait. It sounded innocuous, like someone a boy might get a malt beer with or follow into the woods.

Magreb chose her name in the Atlas Mountains for its etymology, the root word *ghuroob*, which means "to set" or "to be hidden." "That's what we're looking for," she tells me. "The setting place. Some final answer." She won't change her name until we find it.

She takes a lemon from her mouth, slides it down the length of her fangs, and places its shriveled core on the picnic table. When she finally speaks, her voice is so low, the words are almost unintelligible.

"The lemons aren't working, Clyde."

But the lemons have never worked. At best, they give us eight hours of peace. We aren't talking about the lemons.

"How long?"

"Longer than I've let on. I'm sorry."

"Well, maybe it's this crop. Those Alberti boys haven't been fertilizing properly, maybe the *primofiore* will turn out better."

Magreb fixes me with one fish-bright eye. "Clyde, I think it's time for us to go."

Wind blows the leaves apart. Lemons wink like a firmament of yellow stars, slowly ripening, and I can see the other, truer night behind them.

"Go where?" Our marriage, as I conceive it, is a commitment to starve together.

"We've been resting here for decades. I think it's time . . . what is that thing?"

I have been preparing a present for Magreb, for our anniversary, a "cave" of scavenged materials—newspaper and bottle glass and wooden beams from the lemon tree supports—so that she can sleep down here with me. I've smashed dozens of bottles of fruity beer to make stalactites. Looking at it now, though, I see the cave is very small. It looks like an umbrella mauled by a dog.

"That thing?" I say. "That's nothing. I think it's part of the hot dog machine."

"Jesus. Did it catch on fire?"

"Yes. The girl threw it out yesterday."

"Clyde." Magreb shakes her head. "We never meant to stay here forever, did we? That was never the plan."

"I didn't know we had a plan," I snap. "What if we've outlived our food supply? What if there's nothing left for us to find?"

"You don't really believe that."

"Why can't you just be grateful? Why can't you be happy and admit defeat? Look at what we've found here!" I grab a lemon and wave it in her face.

"Good night, Clyde."

I watch my wife fly up into the watery dawn, and again I feel the awful tension. In the flats of my feet, in my knobbed spine. Love has infected me with a muscular superstition that one body can do the work of another.

I consider taking the funicular, the ultimate degradation—worse than the dominoes, worse than an eternity of sucking cut lemons. All day I watch the cars ascend, and I'm reminded of those American fools who accompany their wives to the beach but refuse to wear bathing suits. I've seen them by the harbor, sulking in their trousers, panting through menthol cigarettes and pacing the dock while the women sea-bathe. They pretend they don't mind when sweat darkens the armpits of their suits. When their wives swim out and leave them. When their wives are just a splash in the distance.

Tickets for the funicular are twenty lire. I sit at the bench and count as the cars go by.

That evening, I take Magreb on a date. I haven't left the lemon grove in upwards of two years, and blood roars in my ears as I stand and clutch at her like an old man. We're going to the Thursday night show, an antique theater in a castle in the center of town. I want her to see that I'm happy to travel with her, so long as our destination is within walking distance.

A teenage usher in a vintage red jacket with puffed sleeves escorts us to our seats, his biceps manacled in clouds, threads loosening from the badge on his chest. I am jealous of the name there: GUGLIELMO.

The movie's title is already scrolling across the black screen: *Something Clandestine Is Happening in the Corn!*

Magreb snorts. "That's a pretty lousy name for a horror movie. It sounds like a student film."

"Here's your ticket," I say. "I didn't make the title up."

It's a vampire movie set in the Dust Bowl. Magreb expects a comedy, but the Dracula actor fills me with the sadness of an old photo album. An Okie has unwittingly fallen in love with the monster, whom she's mistaken for a rich European creditor eager to pay off the mortgage on her family's farm.

"That Okie," says Magreb, "is an idiot."

I turn my head miserably and there's Fila, sitting two rows in front of us with a greasy young man. Benny Alberti. Her white neck is bent to the left, Benny's lips affixed to it as she impassively sips a soda.

"Poor thing," Magreb whispers, indicating the pig-tailed actress. "She thinks he's going to save her."

Dracula shows his fangs, and the Okie flees through a cornfield. Cornstalks smack her face. "Help!" she screams to a sky full of crows. "He's not actually from Europe!"

There is no music, only the girl's breath and the *fwap-fwap-fwap* of the off-screen fan blades. Dracula's mouth hangs wide as a sewer grate. His cape is curiously still.

The movie picture is frozen. The *fwap*ing is emanating from the projection booth; it rises to a grinding *r-r-r*, followed by lyrical Italian cussing and silence and finally a tidal sigh. Magreb shifts in her seat.

"Let's wait," I say, seized with an empathy for these two still figures on the screen, mutely waiting for repair. "They'll fix it."

People begin to file out of the theater, first in twos and threes and then in droves.

"I'm tired, Clyde."

"Don't you want to know what happens?" My voice is more frantic than I intend it to be.

"I already know what happens."

"Don't you leave now, Magreb. I'm telling you, they're going to fix it. If you leave now, that's it for us, I'll never . . ."

Her voice is beautiful, like gravel underfoot: "I'm going to the caves."

I'm alone in the theater. When I turn to exit, the picture is still frozen, the Okie's blue dress floating over windless corn, Dracula's mouth a hole in his white greasepaint.

Outside I see Fila standing in a clot of her friends, lit by the marquee. These kids wear too much makeup, and clothes that move like colored oils. They all looked rained on. I scowl at them and they scowl back; and then Fila crosses to me.

"Hey, you." She grins, breathless, so very close to my face. "Are you stalking somebody?"

My throat tightens.

"Guys!" Her eyes gleam. "Guys, come over and meet the *vampire*."

But the kids are gone.

"Well! Some friends," she says, then winks. "Leaving me alone, defenseless . . ."

"You want the old vampire to bite you, eh?" I hiss. "You want a story for your friends?"

Fila laughs. Her horror is a round, genuine thing, bouncing in both her black eyes. She smells like hard water and glycerin. The hum of her young life all around me makes it difficult to think. A bat filters my thoughts, opens its trembling lampshade wings.

Magreb. She'll want to hear about this. How ridiculous, at my age, to find myself down this alley with a young girl: Fila powdering her neck, doing her hair up with little temptress pins, yanking me behind this Dumpster. "Can you imagine," Magreb will laugh, "a teenager goading you to attack her! You're still a menace, Clyde."

I stare vacantly at a pale mole above the girl's collarbone. *Magreb*, I think again, and I smile; and the smile feels like a muzzle. It seems my hand has tightened on the girl's wrist, and I realize with surprise, as if from a great distance, that she is twisting away.

"Hey, *nonno*, come on now, what are you—"

The girl's head lolls against my shoulder like that of a sleepy child, then swings forward in a rag-doll circle. The starlight is white mercury compared to her blotted-out eyes. There's a dark stain on my periwinkle shirt, and one suspender has snapped. I sit Fila's body against the alley wall, watch it dim and stiffen. Spidery graffiti weaves over the brick behind her, and I scan for some answer contained there: GIOVANNA & FABIANO. VAFFANCULO! VAI IN CULO.

A scabby-furred creature, our only witness, arches its orange back against the Dumpster. If not for the lock I would ease the girl inside. I would climb in with her and let the red stench fill my nostrils, let the flies crawl into the red corners of my eyes. I am a monster again.

I ransack Fila's pockets and find the key to the funicular office, careful not to look at her face. Then I'm walking, running for the lemon grove. I jimmy my way into the control room and turn the silver key, relieved to hear the engine roar to life. Locked, locked, every car is locked, but then I find one with thick tape in *X*'s over a busted door. I dash after it and pull myself onto the cushion, quickly, because the cars are already moving. The box jounces and trembles. The chain pulls me into the heavens link by link.

My lips are soon chapped; I stare through a crack in the glass window. The box swings wildly in the wind. The sky is a deep blue vacuum. I can still smell the girl in the folds of my clothes.

The cave system is vaster than I expected; and with their grandfather faces tucked away, the bats are anonymous as stones. I walk beneath a chandelier of furry bodies, heartbeats wrapped in wings the color of rose petals or corn silk. Breath ripples through each of them, a tiny life in its translucent envelope.

"Magreb?"

Is she up here?

Has she left me?

(I will never find another vampire.)

I double back to the moonlit entrance, the funicular cars. When I find Magreb, I'll beg her to tell me what she dreams up here. I'll tell her my waking dreams in the lemon grove: the mortal men and women floating serenely by in balloons freighted with the ballast of their deaths. Millions of balloons ride over a wide ocean, lives darkening the sky. Death is a dense powder cinched inside tiny sandbags, and in the dream I am given to understand that instead of a sandbag I have Magreb.

I make the bats' descent in a cable car with no wings to spread, knocked around by the wind with a force that feels personal. I struggle to hold the door shut and look for the green speck of our grove.

The box is plunging now, far too quickly. It swings wide, and the igneous surface of the mountain fills the left window. The tufa shines like water, like a black, heat-bubbled river. For a disorienting moment I expect the rock to seep through the glass.

Each swing takes me higher than the last, a grinding pendulum that approaches a full revolution around the cable. I'm on my hands and knees on the car floor, seasick in the high air, pressing my face against the floor grate. I can see stars or boats burning there, and also a ribbon of white, a widening fissure. Air gushes through the cracks in the glass box.

What does Magreb see, if she can see? Is she waking from a nightmare to watch the line snap, the glass box plummet? From her inverted vantage, dangling from the roof of the cave, does the car seem to be sucked upward, rushing not toward the sea but to another sort of sky? To a black mouth open and foaming with stars?

I like to picture my wife like this: Magreb shuts her thin eyelids tighter. She digs her claws into the rock. Little clouds of dust rise around her toes as she swings upside-down. She feels something growing inside her, unstoppable as a dreadful suspicion. It is solid, this new thing, it is the opposite of hunger. She's emerging from a dream of distant thunder, rumbling and loose. Something has happened tonight that she thought impossible. In the morning, she will want to tell me about it.

2007

If You See Me, Don't Say Hi

NEEL PATEL
[b. 1982]

Deepak was my older brother, six years to be exact, which made him sixteen when I was ten. He was dark, the color of the walnut furniture in my parents' bedroom. I was fair. And it was often a joke among our family and friends: how different we were. Like shadow and light, they said. Like milk and coal.

Though I was small for my age, Deepak was very tall, with strong muscles in his shoulders and arms. His armpits smelled sweaty, like the raw onions my mother piled on top of our potato *shaak*.[1] He would pick me up from school in my father's Toyota, blasting rap music from the speakers: Tupac Shakur and the Notorious B.I.G. It was 1994, and he wore oversized T-shirts above his baggy jeans. His thick wavy hair was always tucked under a cap. He wore a twenty-two-karat gold chain around his neck. We would ride around the neighborhood for a while, Deepak reciting every lyric to the song "Juicy." "It was all a dream!" he would say, as trees flickered by.

He was my guard. If a child my age happened to be harassing me at school, Deepak would wait for him on the playground.

"You want me to kick your ass?" he would say, getting right up into the kid's face. "You want me to kick your fucking ass?"

The harassment would stop there, but only for a short while; after all, I was an easy target. At school they called me all sorts of names: Ali Baba, Aladdin, Apu. They asked me about my father's 7-Eleven.

"We don't own a 7-Eleven," I would tell them. "We own a motel."

My teachers were oblivious. Once, after an exam, my fifth-grade teacher asked me to say something to him in Farsi.

"I don't speak Farsi," I said. "I speak Gujarati."

[1]A spiced vegetable dish that is typical in Gujarati cuisine.

He stared at me blankly. "But you're Persian."

"I'm Indian," I said.

"Like a tomahawk?" said Ryan Gillespie, a red-haired boy who'd once pulled my pants down in front of the entire class. "My dad says all Indians are lazy boozers."

Everyone laughed.

I was frightened each morning on my way to school. During the Pledge of Allegiance, I held my breath like I did when we drove by a cemetery, wary of the vague expressions on my classmates' faces. My teachers made us watch movies on slavery and segregation and then told us we were lucky to be living in the greatest nation in the world. It seemed implausible even then.

In school, I learned very quickly what it meant to be brown: it meant that white kids only talked to you if they needed something, black kids only talked to you if no other black kids were around, and the rest of us wouldn't talk at all. Not that it mattered. There were only three of us, anyway: a Persian named Farzad, a Mexican named Flora, and me.

Every now and then, a classmate would tap me on my shoulder and ask me to say something to them in "Indian." I was tempted to say *"ben-chod,"* which, when translated, means "sister-fucker." I taught them *"namaste"* instead.

"Namaste," they would say, folding their hands in prayer.

I never said it back.

I was too busy trying to shrink myself. My parents would blast holy *bhajans*[2] from our back porch on Sundays and I would crawl into my bedroom and shove a pillow over my head. According to my father, Indian people were the source of everything: music, mathematics, and dance. I remember watching TV with my parents once when a Britney Spears video came on. I was embarrassed to be in their presence, watching her swing her hips around, but my father was enthralled.

"Look at this," he said. "Indians dance with their hips and now even the whites are dancing with hips."

"The whites don't have hips," my mother said, laughing.

And I, remembering to record the video so that I could masturbate to it in my room, said nothing at all.

[2]Devotional songs.

I wasn't like Deepak. He had a way with girls—of looking at them, talking to them—that I never possessed. During the holiday of Navratri,[3] my family would join other families at a rec center or a high school gym, where we danced around in a circle, wearing bright-colored clothes, and offered prayers to the goddess Durga.[4] Invariably the children got away, to play basketball on the courts outside, or listen to music in their parents' cars, or drink beer purchased by some older cousin or friend. Deepak would disappear, returning later with a lazy smile on his face, his shirt unbuttoned, his hair tousled or flat. Once, he waved his finger in the air.

"Smell this," he said.

"Why?"

"Just do it."

Afraid that it was a prank, that he had stuck his finger in dog shit or his own ass, I ran away. But later, when he explained to me what he had done, that he had fingered a girl named Deepika behind a Dumpster, and that she had moaned and writhed on his hand, I wished I hadn't.

By the time he was a junior in college, Deepak had screwed half the Indian girls in our town—we lived in Bloomington, Illinois, in a small community surrounded by cornfields and a mall. Meanwhile, I harbored unrequited crushes on white girls. Girls with light brown hair, sparkling blue eyes, and long tanned legs in the summertime, who played tennis and swam laps at the country club and, unlike my cousin Monali, didn't have to bleach their arm hair or wax their upper lips. They were girls who seemed to know their place in the world without ever questioning it, who tromped down the hallways with swinging ponytails and fragrant perfumes, and who teased the athletes with a flick of their smile. They were the kind of girls who would never look at me, not even once, not then at least. Not yet.

There was one other way in which Deepak and I were different: it was that he, unlike me, was an idiot. Halfway into his junior year at a marginally ranked college, Deepak flunked out. My parents were aghast. They treated it like a death in the family, which it was, in many ways: the death of a future, the death of an education, the

[3]A Hindu festival lasting nine nights celebrated every autumn.
[4]The principal form of the Hindu Goddess, Durga is a protector, symbolizing feminine and positive energy.

death of their dreams of raising a doctor. I remember the gloomy day when Deepak returned to us with his suitcases full of unused textbooks and clothes, piling them into his room, locking his bedroom door. He remained there all night, and didn't come out until late the next evening, pulling up a seat at the table and refusing the *daar, baath, rotli*[5] and *shaak* my mother was offering, pouring a bowl of cereal instead. Over the next few days, he sat around the house watching music videos on MTV, staring into his computer screen, flipping through magazines. He started eating voraciously: whole packages of doughnuts and the chocolates my parents had brought back from a trip to London, fried chicken from KFC. He wore sweatpants and collegiate T-shirts he'd purchased from the campus bookstore during his first week at school. In the afternoons, I would come home from school and find him in the same position I'd seen him in when I left, which was with his legs splayed over the couch, his hands in his pants. He got fat—very fat. So fat I wondered how he even bathed. He started to smell like the homeless people who lingered outside our parents' Best Western motel, drinking dark liquor or Colt 45. Sometimes he and my father would get into screaming matches, and my mother and I would exchange nervous glances in front of the TV. Once, Deepak didn't come out of his room for three whole days. When he finally did, he was wearing a rumpled white dress shirt over a pair of faded black slacks.

"I'm going to get a job," he said, triumphantly.

"Where?" my father asked.

"At a car dealership. They're hiring over at Ford."

My father snorted. "What car dealership? What nonsense." He was eating fried puris[6] and dipping them in yogurt. A piece of puri hung from his chin. "Car dealership," he said, shaking his head. "I am buying cars and you are selling them."

But he never sold a single car, because he didn't get the job, and after three weeks of frustration, after arguing late into the night, my parents came to a decision: Deepak would join them in the family business. It was up to me now, their one and only hope, to realize their dreams.

---

[5]Lentil soup, rice, and flatbread, all staple (along with *shaak*) Gujarati dishes.
[6]Unleavened fried bread.

As it turned out, I was well on my way. By then I was a sophomore in high school, an honor student, and a member of the chess club. I had a photographic memory, which meant that I spent the vast majority of my time listening to Warren G albums instead of studying for exams. I still managed to pull straight As. While Deepak went to the motel each morning, to learn about franchising and how to hide small portions of money from the IRS, I went to school, buoyed by the prospect of talking to a girl. And there were many: Cindy and Lisa, Rebecca and Kate. But all of them paled in comparison to Alicia, with her tanned legs, her pendulous breasts. She wore tight shorts and denim tops that practically burst at the seams. She had bright yellow hair that she groomed with a comb. Sometimes I would count the shades of gold in her hair. Once, she caught me staring at her when she turned around to pass back an exam.

"What?" she said, sharply.

I gawked at her. It was like the final moments before hitting a car. You know it's about to happen, you know there's nothing you can do about it, and yet you try, pointlessly, to avoid it.

"Nothing," I said. And then, just as she was about to turn back around, "I like your hair."

"What?"

"Your hair. It smells fresh. There's this Chinese girl who sits in front of me in Trigonometry, and her hair smells like fried food. But yours is clean. I like it."

I thought she would smile at me, the way she had smiled at other guys who paid her court, but she looked at me like I'd just soiled myself. Her nostrils flared as she turned around and twisted the bright silk slash of her hair into a knot, then inched forward in her seat. I told Deepak about this later, in my bedroom, after my parents had gone to sleep.

"You idiot."

He was drinking a beer, one of the many pony-necked bottles he'd taken from a crate in our garage, hiding it under his sweatshirt (even though he was twenty-one). He'd offered me a sip, and, when I'd refused, he'd said I shouldn't be such a pussy all the time.

"These white girls don't even see you," he said, taking a swig of his beer and stretching his legs over my bed. I was on the floor, studying the back pages of a Nas CD insert, memorizing the lyrics so that I could rap them out loud in the shower.

"All they see is what they can get from you."

"What do you mean?"

"Don't you study history?"

I shrugged.

I studied the variations of Alicia's skin tone, how it was mottled and red after gym class, and how it shifted from alabaster to bronze in the summertime. I studied the way her breasts rippled like Jell-O every time she came rushing into the room. I studied, still, the way she mispronounced certain words in Spanish class, never bothering to correct herself—never needing to. I studied the way she glided up and down the stairs with such ease you would have thought the whole school was built in her honor, a monument to her beauty, which, if it were up to me, would have probably been the case.

Deepak finished his beer, belched loudly, and tossed the bottle into my backpack.

"Get rid of it for me."

Then he got up and headed for the door.

"Where are you going?" I asked.

"Out."

"With who?"

"Friends "

I laughed, "You don't have friends."

It was true: the friends who'd once idolized Deepak, who sat around listening to whatever sordid exploits he'd gotten himself into, were all gone. They were in college now, studying to become doctors or pharmacists or dentists. Deepak spent his Friday nights in front of the television, playing video games.

"I have new friends," he said, smiling. And he walked out of the room.

The new friend was sitting on our couch one afternoon when I came home from school, eating popcorn and jiggling her legs up and down. She wore leggings and a pink sweater that hung precariously over one shoulder, revealing the brown slope of her skin.

"Hi there," she said, flashing a set of cherry-red nails.

Her dark hair was highlighted—orange strands over black ones—and her eyes were winged with mascara. She watched me as I dropped my backpack on the floor.

"I'm Deepika," she said. "You must be Deep's brother."

I remembered the night Deepak had walked up to me in the parking lot, raising his finger to my nose. I shook the image from my mind. She told me that Deepak was in the shower; they had gone swimming at my parents' motel after work.

"You work at the motel?" I asked.

She nodded her head. "Just until grad school. I'm studying epidemiology."

"Are you dating my brother?"

She paused, a subtle smile playing across her lips. "Why do you ask?"

"No reason," I said, sitting down beside her. "But if you were dating him, if you two got married, it would be weird."

"Why?"

"Because of your names: Deepak and Deepika. It sounds ridiculous."

She laughed out loud, showing all of her teeth, I didn't think it was that funny, but she dropped her bag of popcorn on the floor and held on to her gut, as if she were in pain. Then she grew still. "I don't know if we're dating," she said, quietly, and I knew, by the way she looked at me, by the way she looked at my brother each day after that, that she hoped they were.

Soon, I was prepping for college, graduating from high school. There was a weird energy in the air. Suddenly, the people who had spent four years tormenting me, calling me names, weren't so bad after all. It was like being trapped on an airplane with a bunch of people who were tired and miserable, and all of a sudden you were landing and everyone was in love. I would see classmates who previously ignored me take a sudden interest in my life. I saw Alicia once at the movie theater and she gave me a hug—she was going to community college that fall; she wanted to be a nurse. The day I left for school, Deepak helped me pack all of my things in milk crates and cardboard boxes and carry them out to my father's van. He slipped a bottle of vodka into my suitcase. He told me not to become an asshole at college. He said that he would visit me sometime, that we would get drunk on campus and that he would buy all my roommates and girlfriends a round of beer. But he never did.

When I came back for Thanksgiving, he was depressed again. My parents had purchased another motel, and Deepak was driving there three times a week to manage it. This time he'd lost weight. His face was slimmer. His waist had thinned out. He said very little at the dinner table before slipping out to a bar. The next morning, my mother sat down with me in the living room, frowning.

"It's that girl," she said.

"Which girl?"

But I remembered her name. "Deepika?"

She nodded her head. Deepak and my father were at work. My mother was in her dressing gown. We were quiet for a while. Then she told me, very discreetly, that two weeks earlier, Deepak had proposed to Deepika in the honeymoon suite at the motel, and that she had refused. I couldn't help myself. I laughed.

"What's your problem?" my mother said, sharply. "Why are you laughing?"

But I couldn't control it. It rose from my gut, bubbling over my lips. I dropped the remote control and hunched over the living room sofa, laughing and laughing, until tears streamed from my eyes.

"Be sharam,"[7] my mother exclaimed, throwing up her hands. "To laugh at your brother this way."

But later, in my bedroom, it was Deepak who laughed. We were drinking a beer—I'd developed a taste for it by then, along with Bailey's Irish Cream—when he shook his head.

"Don't listen to Mom," he said, pushing one of my baseball caps over his head. "She doesn't know what the fuck she's talking about."

I didn't know whom to believe, but after a few days it didn't seem to matter. As soon as I had arrived it was time to leave again, and I was packing suitcases with the sweaters I'd left behind, thick thermals and jeans, tall boots for the blustery treks to class, I kissed my tearful mother and shook my father's hand, and dodged Deepak's swift punch to my left shoulder. He could still overpower me—I had stopped growing, and, at five foot eight, I was far shorter than he.

This didn't seem to matter at school, where I noticed a budding interest from girls, Indian girls mostly, whom I mostly ignored. I continued to harbor crushes on white girls, only now they weren't so unattainable. At parties, I would touch their breasts or their ass as we navigated a crowd, filling their cups with rum punch, watching their lips turn purple or red. Sometimes I would go home with one of them, fumbling with the zipper of my jeans. I grew bolder, asking for one phone number and then another, taking them out for coffee, sometimes not calling at all. Once, a girl named Aubrey fell in love

[7]Shameless.

with me, showing up at my dorm room at 3 A.M., screaming and crying until the RA had to escort her home. I developed a thick skin, not minding when girls started calling me names, only this time it wasn't "Aladdin" or "Ali Baba" or "Apu"; it was "asshole"; it was "prick"; it was "motherfucker." Instead of asking me where I was from, they asked me how I could be so heartless and cruel. I realized that we weren't so different after all, the girls and I—that, when it came to love, everyone was from a foreign place.

Deepak certainly was. Shortly before spring break, he drove six hours to the University of Michigan and proposed to Deepika right outside her apartment. To everyone's surprise, and her parents' disgust and dismay, she said yes. My parents were thrilled; they threw a big party for Deepak and Deepika over spring break, inviting 150 people, renting long tables and chairs, setting up a tent and catering food from the local Indian restaurant, Mughal King. My father went to Sam's Club and bought ten bottles of Black Label scotch and thirty bottles of white wine. On a bright Saturday afternoon, Deepak and I unfolded chairs and carried bags of ice over our shoulders, dropping spoons into large vats of food: chicken tikka masala, two types of dal, potatoes and eggplant swimming in saffron-tinted oil.

I drank a beer in my bedroom. Deepak joined me. We glanced outside to watch the stream of my parents' friends in their saris the colors of tropical fruit candy. Deepak pulled back the curtain, frowning.

"It's like a circus down there."

I laughed.

"This will be you someday," he said. He chugged his beer and opened another one. I could tell, by his eyes, that he had been drinking somewhere before. He wore dress slacks and a collared white shirt, and he was examining himself in the mirror when he turned around and smiled. "Do you have a girlfriend?"

It was the first time he had expressed an interest in my life. Usually, when I talked about school, Deepak would nod along vacantly—as if he were listening to one of the many stories my parents had told about their childhoods in India, with the vague expression of someone who had never lived there before. But this time he was rapt.

"No," I said, shyly. Though this was a lie. I did have a girlfriend. Her name was Kara, and she had called three times that afternoon—in spite of my instructions not to.

"Why can't I come?" she'd asked. When I'd told her why, when I had explained to her the glaring differences between her world and mine, she had cried and cried until she couldn't breathe anymore, saying it didn't matter, that we were all just people in the end.

Two hours later, Deepak was drunk. I could tell by the way he was dancing. The DJ was playing Panjabi MC, and Deepak was waving his arms around like a rapper. I was talking to a girl I'd had tennis lessons with—Rachana Desai—who was a first-year at Yale. She wore a crushed silk sari. She talked about the Whiffenpoofs. She kept adjusting the straps of her bra. At one point I imagined myself kissing her, taking her up to my room. I imagined what she looked like between her legs, how dark or soft or wet. By then I'd had sex with three different girls—all of them white. All of them had rosy nipples and porcelain skin. All of them stripped off their clothes with a confidence I had never seen before in a girl. I was thinking about this when my cell phone bleated and I saw Kara's name in the window. I excused myself, winding my way through the crowd of uncles and aunties and friends, sneaking a beer from the bar, until I was alone in the house. I went upstairs, where I would be away from prying eyes, and opened the bathroom door.

"Oh, shit," I said; turning my head. "Sorry."

It was Deepika. She was standing in front of the mirror, adjusting the straps of her blouse. Her hair was spun up in a jeweled mound on top of her head. She looked beautiful. Normally she wore leggings and sweatshirts and gym shoes and socks, but here, in her colorful *lengha,*[8] with a bindi between her brows, she looked regal. I had no idea she was crying. I didn't realize it until she turned her head.

"What's wrong?" I said.

"Nothing," she replied.

"I can leave," I said, backing away, ignoring Kara's missed calls. "I'll give you your space. I was just trying to get away."

"No, stay," she said. She took a tissue from the counter and dabbed the skin under her eyes. Then she laughed. "I feel like a cliché."

"The crying bride?"

"Bride-to-be," she said. "I was thinking about something you said to me a while back."

"Something *I* said?"

[8]An ankle-length embroidered skirt.

She nodded. "About Deepak and I, how if we ever got married it would be weird: our names. Deepak and Deepika."

I was surprised that she even remembered it; it had already been two years.

"I guess it is kind of weird," she said, staring at her reflection in the mirror. I remembered the way she had laughed in the living room when I had told her, dropping her bag of popcorn onto the floor. I wanted to ask her if she was okay, if she needed to talk, if my brother had done something wrong, but by then I had learned enough to know that sometimes, when a woman cried, it was best to say nothing at all.

Two years later, Deepak and Deepika got married, in a ceremony that made their engagement look like a small tea party. Kara wasn't invited to that, either, and, three days later, after fighting all night in my room, we broke up. Sometimes I would remember that night of the party and wonder what Deepika had been crying about. A year after their wedding, when Deepak and I had what will forever be referred to as "the fight," the thing that tore us apart, the thing that made us disavow each other and promise to never speak to one another again, I realized I never would.

It started with a girl. Her name was Marissa, and she went to my med school. She asked me for directions to the medical library and I asked her for her phone number. She wasn't like anyone I had dated before. By the time she was twenty-four, Marissa had been to twenty-four different countries, posting pictures on her blog. She had long dark hair the color of red wine. Her eyes were like sapphires, but she was not beautiful in any conventional way. That is to say, it wasn't her looks that drew me to her. It was her voice, the funny things she said, the way her eyes flashed wildly whenever I told her a story about my day. Over time, her beauty revealed itself to me like an undiscovered painting in an unknown wing.

We spent our weekends exploring the city of Chicago, where we went to school—going to restaurants and thrift shops and nightclubs and bars. She had an appetite for new experiences, suggesting foods I had never tried before, that neither Deepak nor my parents would ever deign to eat—Indonesian, Peruvian, Ethiopian. If we happened to go to an Indian restaurant, Marissa would skip past the chicken tikka masala and go straight for the lamb *karahi*.[9] She ate with her fingers, explaining that her best friend in grade school, Sangeeta, was Indian, and that she had taught her this when they were twelve. I was in awe of her. Unlike other white women, who viewed my background as a barrier, Marissa was happy to accept me just as I was. At times she would ask me how to say something in Gujarati, and I was reminded of being a child, in school, teaching my classmates to say *"namaste"* with their hands.

I taught her *"ben-chod"* instead.

"That's awesome," she said, laughing, and later, when a waiter happened to be rude to us at a French restaurant, Marissa got up from the table and said it: *"Arre ben-chod!"*

I knew, then, that I was in love.

I also knew I couldn't keep her from my family. By then, my mother had begun to suggest girls for me, some daughter of a friend who worked in an office or a bank—or, like me, was in med school. "Why have one doctor in the family when you can have two?" she'd say.

It went better than I thought it would; as it turned out, my parents had grown accustomed to the idea of mixed marriages. They brought up the friends whose sons and daughters had also married "whites," who had Hindu-Christian weddings and light-skinned children, and who assigned these children Indo-American names, names like Dillon, which, in Hindi, would have been spelled Dhilan. They had heard that white people loved Indian culture, anyway, and that it wasn't such a big deal after all. They were more than accepting; they were thrilled. I would have been, too, had I been announcing our engagement, but I wasn't. We'd only been dating for a year.

"Bring her home," my mother said, standing in the kitchen, frying a batch of samosas, making double of everything and wrapping it twice. "We want to meet her."

On a cold autumn morning, Marissa and I boarded an Amtrak from Chicago to Bloomington, where my father was waiting for us with his van. He helped load our luggage into the trunk, avoiding eye contact with Marissa as he opened the door for her, behaving more like a driver than a dad. I was instantly annoyed. I was annoyed, further,

[9]A spicy Indian dish prepared in a deep, circular pot similar to a wok.

by the abundance of food on the dining room table. I had told my mother a sandwich would do—it was Thanksgiving weekend, and there was no need to overeat. But of course she didn't listen. She was solicitous, shuttling back and forth between the kitchen and dining room table, piling puris onto our plates, not bothering to ask if we were hungry. She pronounced Marissa's name "Mareesa," and she was overly chatty, telling her mundane facts about our town: about the groceries that were on sale, the two-for-one sweaters at Kohl's. Marissa's parents were both professors at Northwestern, and the one time we had gone to their house, we didn't talk at all, listening to Buddha Bar and drinking red wine.

"Your family is great," she said later, in the bedroom, when we were unpacking our bags. I wondered what she would think of Deepak. She hadn't met him yet. He was at the motel, manning the front desk. I asked my mother where Deepika was and she rolled her eyes.

"She has gone to her cousin's house in Michigan."

"Why?"

"I don't know."

"Why didn't Deepak go?"

She was silent. After a while she folded up the rest of the laundry and walked out in a huff. "I don't know," she said, traipsing up the stairs. "I don't know anything anymore. Nobody tells *me* anything in this house!" And she slammed her door.

That evening, Deepak walked into the living room and punched me on my arm.

"Where is this *gori*[10] girl you're hiding?" he said.

"Her name's Marissa," I said. "And she's in the shower."

He stared at me blankly.

"I'm just kidding, man."

But at dinner, Deepak was quiet, staring down at his plate, responding to Marissa's questions with one-word answers. I was uncomfortably aware of how he towered over us at the table, his long arms folded across his chest. My parents asked Marissa about her house in Evanston, her friends at school, gazing up at her in wonder, absorbing each fact, but not Deepak. When Marissa asked Deepak how he enjoyed working at the motel, if he had any interesting stories to share, he snorted.

[10]A white girl (slang).

"It's a job," he said. "Not everyone can be as lucky as my brother."

"It's not luck," I said. "It's hard work."

No one said a word.

After dinner, I decided to take Marissa on a drive, maybe go for a beer. I asked Deepak if he wanted to join us, but he refused, saying he had work to do. Then, just as we were sliding on our coats, he changed his mind.

"Wait," he said. "I'll come."

He was chatty in our father's car, telling me which way to turn, asking Marissa questions, including her in his jokes. He even complimented her, saying it was nice of her to take time away from her family to spend Thanksgiving with us. I was surprised. I'd never heard Deepak compliment anyone in my life. He was a different person, eagerly suggesting we go to a new bar that had opened up on campus, encouraging Marissa to order whatever she wanted on the menu. When the waitress came by he looked up at her and smiled.

"Is Lauren working tonight?"

I stared at him.

The waitress scanned the room before pointing toward the bar. "She's over there," she said. "In the red top."

My eyes followed Deepak's to a young woman dressed in a red top and skinny jeans. Her stiff hair was frosted, her makeup shiny under the lights. Deepak waved to her and smiled.

"I'll be back," he said.

But he didn't come back, not until it was time to leave. By then, Marissa and I had had our fair share of beers.

"Is that a friend of yours?" I said, as we stepped into the chilly parking lot and approached our father's car. He didn't respond. He drove home in silence. All night he remained in his bedroom, whispering over the phone.

The next morning, Marissa and I woke up early to prepare the turkey and stuffing and sweet potato pie, but Deepak stayed in his room, He didn't come out until the bird had been carved, explaining that he would have to go to the motel: one of the desk clerks had called in sick; it being Thanksgiving and all, he would have to fill in. No one said a word. My mother stared down at her plate. My father pretended not to have noticed. It was I who went after Deepak, following him into the driveway and grabbing him by his arm.

"Hey," I said. "What's going on?"

He looked impatient. It was then that I realized how much time we'd spent apart, how little we spoke. I couldn't remember the last time we had listened to an album together in my room. "Where are you really going?" I said.

He was silent.

"Where, Deepak?"

He turned his head.

"Are you going to see that girl—the one from the bar? Are you having an affair?"

He laughed. "An affair," he said, mockingly. "Only white people have *affairs*. Jesus, man, you already sound like one of them."

"One of whom?"

He didn't say anything.

"Why is Deepika at her family's house?" I said. "Why didn't you go with her?"

"Why are you involving yourself?"

"Because she's my sister-in-law."

He walked away. I caught a flash of Deepika crying in the bathroom. I followed him onto the road.

"You can't treat her this way," I said, shouting now. "You can't do that to people!"

He ignored me.

"You need to think about someone else for a change, Deepak. You need to think about Mom and Dad."

He paused to contemplate the rows of identical brick houses ahead of us, the metallic sky above. Then he shook his head.

"You know," he said, softly. "I like Marissa—I do. But to be honest, I'm a little surprised." He was staring at me now, scratching his head. "I figured that, if one of us ever brought home a white girl—if we ever did that to *Mom and Dad*—she would at least be beautiful."

I don't remember what happened next, only that we were struggling on the ground, shouting. Deepak was surprisingly weak for his size, capitulating to me easily. A neighbor came out of her house and started yelling, "Stop it. Stop it. It's Thanksgiving!" but we didn't listen. I said things that afternoon that I had never said before in my life, that I would spend a lifetime regretting, wishing I could revise: that my brother was a failure—a loser—and that, if it weren't for our family, he would probably be dead. I saw the fight drain from his eyes. I saw his fingers loosen their grip. I saw what was once anger fueled by love turn to indifference fueled by hate. I watched him stand up and brush himself off, heading toward his car, turning around to address me one last time. There were tears in his eyes.

"You're done," he said. "I mean it. Don't talk to me. Don't even look at me. If you see me on the street, don't say hi."

I didn't try to stop him as he slammed the door shut and drove away. I went for a walk. Later, when I came back into the house, my mother shot up from the dining room table and asked what was wrong. But I shook my head. It was then that I realized tears were rolling down my face, collecting at my chin. But I hadn't felt a thing. It was windy outside, I explained to everyone in the room, and something must have got caught in my eyes.

Six weeks later, after New Year's Eve, Marissa and I broke up. I never told her about what happened between Deepak and me in the driveway. I didn't tell anyone. Not even my own parents. The day after Thanksgiving, I made up an excuse about an exam I had to study for, forcing Marissa to play along. For weeks I was impenetrable, remaining silent for hours, avoiding Marissa's exhortations to open up. The more she tried to probe me, the more I pushed her away. I could have told her what Deepak had said; it wouldn't have been a big deal. Probably she would have laughed even, thrown her head back and made some witty remark. She wouldn't have hated him the way I did—that's for sure. Sometimes I think it was this fact alone that made me pull away from her: that she could so easily forgive someone. That I still could not.

Over the years, I dated girls at a distance, diving into my work, graduating from medical school and entering a rigorous orthopedic surgery program out of state. I used this as an excuse to avoid going home. For a while, my parents were oblivious, asking only if I had talked to Deepak recently, if we were in touch, reminding me of his birthday, apprising me of some minor incident—a fender bender, an illness, a problem at the motel—that afflicted his life. But after a while my mother grew suspicious, pressing me for details and, when I made something up, catching me in my lies. She asked me why we hadn't spoken, why he never mentioned me at home, why I never invited him to visit me once in a while. I had no answer. I assumed he and Deepika were fine, because one day I received an email from her inviting me home. It was my parents' anniversary. She was hosting a party. She signed the email, "Love, Deepika Bhabhi." I packed a small suitcase and booked the next flight.

There were thirty people in my parents' backyard when I arrived, drinking and laughing and eating. I saw Deepak in passing, but he didn't look at me. He was drunk, and Deepika was watching him from the kitchen window. She was pregnant. My mother had been waiting to tell me the news: that I was no longer just a brother; I was going to be a *kaka*[11] as well. I was surprised. I spent all night watching Deepika answer questions about the baby, sipping a glass of cider. She had gained some weight in her face and her arms, but she still looked beautiful, just as radiant as she had that night of her engagement party. In fact, she was glowing, pausing to allow someone to touch her belly, take her picture, refusing to sit down when my mother insisted she take a break. Later that evening, I joined her in the kitchen and listened to her complain about my brother while she rinsed dishes in the sink.

"He can drown in his drink,'" she said, sharply. "I should never have married him."

But I knew, by the flicker in her eyes, that it was only a joke. I helped her dry the dishes and stack them in a pile on the counter. I led her to the couch. She wore a blue silk dress. Her belly pushed through it like a drum; she rubbed it with her hand.

"Do you need anything?" I asked, "Juice? Seltzer? Water?"

She shook her head. I was about to go outside to talk to one of the uncles who had just arrived when she called out to me from behind.

"Have you heard what he wants to call the baby?"

I turned around, shaking my head.

"Deep," she said.

I laughed.

Later, when my mother called to tell me it was over—that the baby was dead—I cried: for Deepak, for Deepika, for all of us.

In three years, I said three words to my brother: "I'm very sorry." I said them the moment he came back from the hospital. I said them in a sympathy card. I said them in an email, too. I wanted him back. I was sorry for everything. I broke my silence, crying on the phone with him until I couldn't speak anymore, until my throat

[11]Uncle.

closed up and I could no longer swallow. But he didn't say a word. He made a "Hmm" noise which meant that he acknowledged my apology but had nothing further to say. Then he hung up the phone.

We spent the next few years acknowledging each other from a distance. I congratulated him in person when they finally had a baby girl, Shreya, who weighed six pounds two ounces. She had soft brown eyes and hair as thick as wool. She looked more like Deepika than Deepak—which, I said jokingly, was fortunate. But Deepak said nothing. Sometimes I would ask him a question about work or his health and he would stare at me like I was an interloper. Once, we were in the kitchen reaching for the same beer when our hands locked. It was the first time we had touched each other since that night in the driveway. It was also the first time he had spoken more than two words to me.

"I was going to drink that," he said.

"So was I." I looked in the fridge. "It's the last one—split it?"

"No." He let go of my hand. "You have it."

I was flattered, buoyed by his generosity, but later, when he didn't talk to me for three days, I realized what he'd meant: that he would rather go without a beer than split one with me.

I moved to Los Angeles and drowned out the noise: my mother's complaints, her lengthy diatribes, the articles she would send me about the unexpected tragedies of life. Sometimes I would YouTube old music videos Deepak and I used to watch when we were young, remembering all the times I rode around with him in the car. Once, a girl I was dating paused in front of the mantel above my fireplace, pointing to a picture of Deepak and me in India—in matching black T-shirts, our hair slicked into spikes—asking me who he was.

"My brother," I said, and I was surprised by how quickly it rolled off my tongue, how easily he came to mind, as if I had been waiting for the right moment to mention him. As if I had been hoping she would ask me this all along.

Years ticked by like the hands of a faulty watch—quick, then slow—and finally, in the fall of 2015, forty years after my parents had first landed in America, thirty-three years after I was born, ten years after Deepak and I had stopped talking, my parents made an announcement: they were retiring. On the phone, my mother informed me that they would sell their motels to Deepak and spend six months in India, six months at home. The Indians in our hometown threw them a retirement party; I flew in from Los Angeles to attend it. Instead of having my father pick me up from O'Hare, I rented a car, preferring to drive past the rows of never-ending corn, the advertisements for shopping centers, the all-you-can-eat buffets. I stopped at a convenience store near my house and picked up some beer and a bottle of champagne. The cashier stared at me pointedly.

"Are you Premal Patel?"

"Yes," I said.

She could have been anyone, any blond-haired, blue-eyed girl from my past, but then I stared at her name tag, the swell of her breasts, and suddenly, it was clear.

"Alicia?"

I remembered the way she had looked at me in class that morning when I'd told her I liked her hair. She looked older now, with swollen cheeks and a few lines etched into her skin. Still, I was nervous, remembering all the hours I'd spent obsessing over her. She asked me what I was doing in town and I told her. Then she asked me what I did for a living. I could have told her that, too. I could have told her I was a doctor, a surgeon, that I saved people's lives. I could have made her feel small and insignificant, the way I had felt all those years. But I didn't.

"I work in health care," I said, paying for my items and signing the receipt. "In California."

She smiled.

"Well, it was good seeing you," she said, watching me head out into the bright summer afternoon. "Take care."

My parents' house was exactly the same. It was late summer, and the days were getting shorter. I saw my mother's suitcases piled on top of one another near the landing upstairs. They would be flying to London in a few days, and then to Mumbai, and then to Gujarat, where they would stay in a rented flat. I dropped my bag off in my room and freshened up in the bathroom. Then I took out one of the beers I had purchased and felt its warmth stream down my throat. I thought about the last time Deepak and I had drunk a beer together in my room, the night of his engagement party.

Downstairs, I was too preoccupied with the uncles and aunties who had, over time, become like second parents to Deepak and me, to notice him in the backyard, playing with his kids—by then, they'd had another child named Hiral. I was still single, still childless, still the source of my parents' anxiety. Deepika was drinking wine with me in the kitchen, teasing me about prospective brides, when her expression suddenly changed.

"He talks about you," she said, gravely.

She looked pretty in a sleeveless peach dress, a string of pearls at her throat. Her hair was shorter now, no longer streaked with highlights. "He says things like, Premal used to say this, or Premal used to say that. He asks the kids what they want to be when they're older. He asks them if they want to be a doctor like their Premal Kaka."

I was on my third glass of wine by then, but the news shattered the thin membrane of my buzz. "And what do they say?" I asked.

She laughed, gazing out the window.

"They say they want to be a businessman like their daddy."

I followed her gaze to the grassy knoll where Deepak was running around with a rubber ball, stopping frequently to bounce it over his children's heads. There was a plastic swing set that looked brand new, a tire that hung from a tree. The sun was going to set soon, casting a pinkish hue across the sky. By this time, most of the guests had left, leaving behind paper plates smeared with red chili sauce and half-eaten samosas. My parents had gone for a walk. We were alone in the house. I poured her another glass of wine.

"Oh, god. I think that's my third."

"Who's counting?" I said.

She laughed again, and I was reminded of the time in our living room when I had joked with Deepika about her name, and later, in the bathroom, when I'd seen her cry. She told me she didn't really understand what went on between my brother and me, why we drifted apart, but it didn't matter, anyway, because she was glad I was there.

"I miss you," she said. "I miss your sense of humor. We could use more of it around here."

"I miss being here, too," I said. I poured myself another glass of wine and felt the membrane envelop me again, loosening my tongue, so I asked her.

I asked her what I had been meaning to ask her all these years.

"Do you remember that night of your engagement party?" I said. "Do you remember running into me in the bathroom?"

She was silent.

"You were crying," I said.

She nodded her head. "I remember it."

"Why?"

"Why what?"

"Why were you crying?"

Her eyes clouded. I offered her another glass of wine but she shook her head, moving her glass away. Then she changed her mind, pushing it toward me. I emptied the bottle. She took a sip from it and shrugged.

"I don't know," she said. "I was practically a kid then."

"And?"

"And I didn't want to marry your brother," she said, firmly.

"Oh."

"Of course I love him now. We have a life together. It's all worked out for the best; it always does." She examined her glass before taking another sip. "Anyway, it was a long time ago."

I nodded, satisfied with her answer. Then I shook my head.

"But why?"

"Why what?"

"Why did you marry him? What made you change your mind? Your parents didn't even want you to marry my brother. Everyone knew that."

She laughed.

Then she told me that, just before I had walked in on her in the bathroom, she had been planning to leave. She'd told a friend to drive down from Michigan. They had it all planned out. She couldn't bear the thought of confronting Deepak about it, and my parents had spent all that money on the party, so she was going to run away, disappear, change her phone number, her email address. She spoke rapidly, pausing to laugh at something or to catch her breath, taking a sip of her wine. And then it happened: I watched her lips moving and felt the strange compulsion to kiss them. To feel them. To know, once and for all, what my brother had known all those years.

"But then you stopped me," she said. "I don't know what it was. There was something about the way you were looking at me—this kindness, this innocence—and I thought to myself: there must be some of that in Deepak, too." She smiled. "And there was."

I asked her if Deepak knew about it. She shook her head.

"Are you kidding me? He would flip."

We were silent for a while, drinking the rest of our wine, staring at the pink and purple clouds outside our window, when I reached for her hand. She pulled it away. I reached for it again. I pulled her close to me, forcing myself against her, until finally, she gave in. Instead of kissing her, I wrapped my arms around her and felt the give of her shoulders, the slack of her spine, the warm rush of her tears, dampening my shirt. We'd both had enough wine by then, and I helped her rinse the glasses and dispose of the bottle, too. Then I followed her outside, where Deepak was standing on the patio with a beer in his hand, watching the kids from a distance.

His hair was beginning to gray now, and his midsection had widened, but he still retained the impressive fact of his height, the same span of his shoulders, the same girth of his arms, and I still admired these things from afar, crossing the patio to join him, waiting, as usual, for the Deepak I once knew to return.

Eight months later, he did, after our father died unexpectedly in the middle of the night—he'd had a heart attack. My mother was inconsolable. It was Deepak who came to pick me up from the airport. We didn't talk much on the car ride home, preferring to listen to music on the radio instead, but later, in the kitchen, he told me the news.

"Deepika is leaving."

I was stunned. He said it was over—they had tried to make it work, but somehow, in the end, the trying wasn't enough. I asked him if the divorce was his idea, if it was something that he wanted, and I knew, by the soft, sad look in his eyes, that it was not. So I held him for a while, sitting on our kitchen floor, crying: for Deepika, for my father, for the things we never knew.

2018

A Modern Marriage

GRACE OLUSEYI
[b. 1983]

When the phone rang the night before Anu's wedding, she was packing the last of her boxes for the move across the bridge to her fiancé's two-bedroom apartment in Astoria. She was happy to leave her dirty little studio in the Bronx. James's hipster enclave in Queens seemed like a veritable castle in comparison. Hardwood floors, original paneling. A prewar building, Gatsby era, he told her. A real piece of history.

Anu stumbled a bit before she reached the phone. She should have had the line disconnected days ago but had kept it for the international calls she could not make on her mobile. "Hello?"

"Anu, my darling? *Ba wo ni?*[1]" If the soft, accented voice hadn't given it away, the crackling on the line certainly would have. Her cousin Tobi was in Nigeria and was not able to come for her wedding, but she had been calling Anu all week, teasing her about the wedding night and advising her on creams and lotions that would make her skin soft and supple and asking her if she had received her bridal finery, the woven red and gold *aso oke*[2] wrapper and blouse from Lagos that she would wear for her reception. Tobi was excited about this marriage. She had been praying for years for her cousin to meet someone and was determined that the day should go off without a hitch.

"I am fine," Anu replied, and sat on a sealed box.

"James?"

"Out with the bachelors." They were going, James told her, to a boxing match in Brooklyn, and then out for drinks. Anu swung her legs, eyes flickering over the dingy white walls of her apartment. Just in the corner of her line of vision, a cockroach scurried up

[1]"How are you?" (Yoruba).
[2]Handwoven cloth. In English, "top cloth," indicating high status.

toward one of the cracks in the ceiling. They normally weren't this bold—perhaps they sensed she was moving out.

"Good." Her cousin sounded relieved. "I have to. . . . I wanted to speak to you, it is very important."

"Oh?" God, Tobi could be dramatic. "Go for it."

"I have not even told your mother, not yet. I—well, I wanted you to know first."

"Are you pregnant?" Anu joked, but when Tobi didn't laugh, she sat up straight. "Tob. You're not—?"

"No—hei! *Olorun maje,*[3]" she swore. "No. I'm not."

"Is someone sick?" Or dead? She could see them, trying to hide it from her until after the wedding, not wanting to upset her, but Anu always did better when she knew things, saw them coming. "Or—"

"Anu, *jo,* just listen." Tobi inhaled; she was probably smoking, Anu realized. She tended to do that when she was stressed. She pictured her cousin crossing one dark, plump leg over the other, touching her mouth the way she did when she was nervous about something.

Anu was quiet.

"Are you still there?"

"Yes, Tobi."

Tobi's next words came out in a rush, mixing and tumbling over themselves like grains from a bag of rice, landing in no particular order. Anu managed to piece together bits as she went along. James was married. Wife in Lagos. Two children, a boy and a girl, both in primary school. Married six years ago, before he left Nigeria to go to school in New York. It wasn't a state marriage, not really, but he had paid her dowry and taken her from her father's house. . . .

Anu listened. When Tobi was finished, her voice was both high and breathless.

"Anu? *Anu*? I spoke to his uncle this morning, Anu. He was very, very angry. The boy, he said, is just using you for a visa. His own application was denied. Anu—!"

Anu hung up the phone.

Although she was over thirty, badly dressed, too thin, too broad-shouldered, and still possessed the oily, spotted skin of an afflicted teenager, the tall, broad-shouldered PhD student and lecturer James

[3]"God forbid" (Yoruba).

Adeola Adebisi proposed to Anu a scant six weeks after their first date. It was rather exciting. To her, men were foreign creatures who mostly looked at her with astonishment, or ignored her altogether.

It wasn't that he was attracted to her. On the contrary, Anu knew that the man found her repulsive. She'd seen the flicker in his dark eyes the day she'd been brought to him by the dean of philosophical studies, who introduced her as the new office assistant and a "fellow West African." The dean had been all enthusiasm: Americans love coincidences, and he milked this particular one for all it was worth. He beamed at the two of them; Anu imagined the corners of his mouth meeting in the back of his head. *She mentioned that she is Nigerian in her interview, isn't that something? Perhaps you come from the same area? Do you speak the same language?*

During the interrogation, Professor Adebisi's face resembled that of a martyr who feels in the eleventh hour that sainthood isn't worth all the trouble. Anu was embarrassed for him, for them. The professor parried the dean's questions with diplomatic skill, greeted her politely, showed her where his keys were, and gave her his office hours. He was dressed in trendy scholar-wear: wool trousers slung low on his hips, corduroy jacket, skinny tie, vintage denim shirt, brown loafers from some obscure Italian cobbler, Ray-Ban glasses, no socks. It made Anu self-conscious of the ill-fitting polyester suit she wore that day, although she didn't own anything better, not really. It cost money, looking so effortlessly casual.

In those brief first minutes, the professor managed to convey through both manner and tone that he hoped their arrangement was temporary, that she would barely see him due to his schedule, and that his life's happiness depended on the joyful hour of her departure. Anu minded little; she understood his position. Being reminded that you are different from your colleagues by the existence of decidedly unglamorous office help is unsettling, at the very least.

"I won't bother you at all," she said with her usual simplicity. He looked startled but didn't respond.

Despite their rocky start, Professor Adebisi still asked the typical questions. He fired them off at intervals during their first day together: *Who are your parents? Were you born here or at home? Do you speak Yoruba?*[4] The answers tumbled from her lips with ease, as she'd answered them

[4]One of the most spoken languages in Nigeria.

many times before, and the answers were nothing extraordinary. Her devout Christian parents were a nurse and a taxi driver. She'd been born in the States, and yes, she spoke a little Yoruba, but understood more than she could speak. He grunted as if something had been verified, and they never spoke of their shared ancestry again.

The professor did not initiate conversation again, and Anu felt foolish when she found herself hoping that he would. He slunk past her every day, mumbling with eyes averted, but his unfriendliness was little deterrent to developing a crush, which she did, and quickly. It was hard not to. He moved with a quiet, old-fashioned elegance that suited him, spent hours listening to music, and lit a candle that filled the office with the smell of cedar and sandalwood long after the other PhD students had retired for the night. His body hunched when he read, as if he were trying to force something out that had lodged between his shoulder blades. Older professors, confident in their tenure, called him brilliant. His peers called him pretentious. Anu found him fascinating.

Anu discovered that he listened to William Alwyn while writing papers and John Coltrane while grading them. She downloaded compositions from both to her Android, drawing odd looks in the subway as she squeezed her face, trying to follow the rises and falls of the strings, harps, and horns. When he ordered sushi from a restaurant with an unpronounceable name that delivered in an elegantly folded box cooled by dry ice, she rescued the carton from the recycling and went there on a weekend. She spent forty dollars for a seat in the back and struggled for an hour to navigate chunks of rice and raw fish to her lips with those clumsy wooden sticks. She checked out books he mentioned on his blog, struggling with phrases like "the bourgeois declaration of the rights of the egoistic individual," and "dialectical materialism as a heuristic in biology," and other things that were as indecipherable to her as ancient Aramaic.

They were *his* words, though, and because of that, she read them.

Anu wasn't smart. Not in the way Professor Adebisi was, anyway.

She realized this years ago, when her parents started getting letters from her school. Anu, they said, might have a learning disability. They wanted her tested. There were special classes she could take, special books for her to read.

Her mother blamed the devil, blamed evil spirits back in her father's village that had stolen her daughter's intelligence, taken her stars at birth. "They will not label my daughter!" she snapped, and beat Anu with her hands whenever her report card sported those inevitable Ds and, at best, Cs. She took her for prayer once a week at Faith of Fire Ministries and hovered over her as she struggled with homework until both their eyes were red and darkly circled. Her classmates were oddities, with their cramming and all-night study sessions that somehow left room for sports, boyfriends, and clubs. Anu had church, home, and the gritty little desk under a naked yellow bulb where she propped up her face, elbows aching, as she studied.

Anu graduated high school a year late, accustomed to being a disappointment. If only she had been beautiful, she heard her mother sighing on the phone one day to an auntie in Nigeria. It wouldn't have mattered, then.

"I read your blog," Anu told Professor Adebisi one day, after approaching his desk with a stack of books he'd ordered from the library. Kant, Calvin, Hobbes. He stared at her for a moment before moving a stack of papers. She placed the books carefully, soundlessly.

"And?" he asked after a moment, as if trying to decide whether or not her opinion was worth anything. Curiosity won, however, or a need for flattery.

"It was good." She paused. "It's for people like you, though, I think. Intellectuals would like it."

"Huh," was all he said, then asked her to close the door when she left.

The next day, James saw her in the student commons, where she often sat to eat a sandwich while playing games on her phone. He hesitated, coffee in hand; then he came over to her. Anu looked up and immediately lost her appetite. She simply couldn't keep chewing a ham sandwich dripping with mustard and sweet onion sauce when he was sitting across from her, eyes warily scanning her face.

"You shouldn't have said that yesterday," he said. "Not about. . . . It's supposed to be for everyone, that blog."

Anu lifted her shoulders once. Not speaking, she'd learned over the years, was the only certain way of sounding even remotely intelligent.

"If you wouldn't mind. . . ." He cleared his throat. "I'd like your eye. On the blog. When I post. Tell me what you think."

"OK."

"If you're not doing anything after work—food? My last class ends early tonight."

Anu opened her mouth and spoke calmly, like an actress who's spent weeks practicing for a bit part in an enormous production.

"OK. Thank you."

Surprise flashed across his face, quick as a sleight of hand. "I'm very glad," he said gravely, in that peculiar mix of British and Nigerian accents he'd picked up from years at universities around the globe.

"Where did you go to school?" he—James, as she was now permitted to call him—asked her two weeks later.

It was the fourth time they had been out together. Anu wasn't sure whether this meant they were seeing each other. He hadn't tried to touch her or flirt with her, but he looked a little less wary.

Anu paused before speaking. She was feeling particularly confident today, for once. After Googling for an hour and a half, she managed to uncover a sushi restaurant in the Village that was dirty enough to seem unordinary, and the sleeveless linen top she wore actually seemed right for the venue.

"I didn't," she replied. "I—I went to community college for a year."

James nodded. "Too expensive?"

"Yes," Anu agreed, although it wasn't true. Her parents would have been only too glad to fund school for her, if she had managed to go.

"You can go for free, you know. To our school, since you work full-time." James selected a California roll, ignored the wasabi and soy sauce, and deftly lifted the small bit of cold rice and chopped vegetable to his mouth. "It's our responsibility to make the best of this place, Anu. We're strangers, no matter how many years we're here."

Her stomach tightened, appetite gone. "My father often says the same thing." She could not tell him about the years of sitting up late, copying her textbook chapters onto small white cards, as if direct replication would make the words more decipherable. He would not understand it, the futile struggle to achieve something that most managed without even trying.

"You don't seem lazy," he observed.

"No," she agreed, and he peered at her over the table.

"Are you angry?"

She shook her head.

"What are you thinking, then?"

"About your sushi," Anu said, and the corner of her mouth curved upward, slightly.

"My sushi."

"Yes." She could hardly make up an impressive truth, so why make it a lie? "I was thinking about my grandmother, back home. And how she would be horrified that we would pay to eat raw fish."

James's face relaxed into a smile, despite himself. He had, Anu noticed, the clearest eyes she'd ever seen. They were as dark as hers, but were so liquid that they caught the light, reflected it, making them seem bottomless. She could only look for a few moments before she had to lower her head. It was too much.

"How Marxist of you," he said, and his voice was dry. He lifted his wineglass in her direction.

"What is that?"

He laughed out loud.

That, Anu supposed, was the moment when they moved to properly dating. He asked her to go to church with him the following week—practically a declaration in some Nigerian circles—and kissed her for the first time one misty evening after classes in the little moss-covered bower where upperclassmen smoked pot during finals week. He warned her beforehand that he was going to do it. She nodded, then held very still. It was pleasant. She was more aware of the warmth of his body than she was of his mouth, which surprised her. Films had led her to expect the opposite.

He pulled back, looked almost surprised.

"Haven't you been kissed before?"

She looked at him, and his expression was a mixture of shock and—yes, there it was, for the first time—intrigue. "Jesus."

He made it sound like a virtue. Anu was grateful.

That night he took her to the park to see a play performed live in open air. The language was difficult, but she liked the main character. He made eye contact with the audience, tossed roses indiscriminately, grinned at his fellow actors from under a cap of flaming red hair, as if the whole production was based on a joke only they understood.

When she tried to explain this later, he looked at her, that half-smile still in place, and shook his head. "You're quite the enigma," he told her afterward. "Ignorant, and shamelessly so, but quite profound."

"Is that bad?"

He laughed. He did this quite a bit when they were together. She was beginning to like it. "We'll see."

Anu looked it up on her phone when he wasn't looking: *enigma*. She liked that. It gave her a reason for her long silences when they were together: she was mysterious, exotic, she told herself. It wasn't that she had nothing to say. She wished he would take her to more things like this. He often wrote of them on his blog—the plays, operas, and films with titles in languages she didn't recognize. It was difficult, James having a life she wasn't invited to join because she lacked the right that cleverness would have given her.

That would change, she told herself. *Enigma*.

"You and *her*?"

Anu was in the department office, out of sight on the floor, where she'd been attempting to trace her computer monitor cord back to its socket. The speaker was Tara Elliot, who had just walked into the office and stopped in front of James's door.

"They told me you and her. . . ." She let the sentence dangle suggestively. Tara was a professor in James's department and had been hired two years ago. She was tall, lithe, and tan from yoga and sun, and she questioned everyone in the demanding voice of one who felt that her credentials gave her the right. She claimed to have spent time teaching philosophy in a Gulf country and often mentioned, with smug satisfaction, that textbooks for *her* gender studies classes had been seized and censored by the Ministry of Culture nearly every semester.

There was no sound from James's office. Anu strained to hear. Perhaps, she thought, he was shooting her one of those exquisitely nasty looks he usually reserved for incompetent waiters. Or perhaps his face was blank, a nonverbal indication that she should get out. Or maybe, she thought, throat tightening, he was smiling, nodding, trying to pass off the comment as a joke. He was eager to please Tara. Anu knew this, saw the emails that flew back and forth between them on the office servers, saw how he never disagreed with her on personal things, how he puffed up with pride when she praised him. They went to lectures and concerts together sometimes. Tara was an emblem for the part of his life that Anu would never be a part of.

"She's remarkably intelligent," James said of her, the highest praise he knew to give. And now—well. Tara was laughing at her, words bursting out between giggles.

"I nearly shit myself when I found out, James. Well, well. She's got a great ass. That video-girl wig has got to go, though."

"Get out," James was saying, and she could barely hear his next words, although she could make out the fact that—yes, he was defending her, in sharp, measured words that came together in phrases such as *you have no right* and *your condescension is rather common* and *we're all a joke to you, aren't we?*

Anu almost wished he had laughed it off. She stumbled to her feet, not caring now who saw her, then crashed into a trashcan. Her skin was crawling with the cold-hot prickles that always preceded throwing up, and she bolted for the hall.

When she emerged from the bathroom, eyes calm but red-rimmed, James was there, handkerchief in hand. His jaw was set. She could see bone protruding from under smooth skin.

"She's a fool," he said. His voice was calm with contempt as he handed her the square of white linen. Anu pressed it to her mouth. It smelled like him, something woodsy and light.

"Let's go home, Anu."

Anu shook her head, crossed her arms. The stupid weave she'd installed the week before itched unbearably, like the cheap shiny wig it was. She'd thought it quite fetching when she did it, forking over nearly two hundred dollars for it. She thought she had seen a flicker of something in James's eyes when he saw her that Monday, but now she knew. *Video girl?* Oh, God.

"People might see," she said by way of explanation, and his eyes hardened.

"I don't care."

That night in her tiny apartment, she cried in front of him for the first time. He held her wrists, forced her to look at him, spoke soft desperate words that poured out quickly. It was the first time he'd spoken to her in Yoruba since they met. His words were tender and musical in a way that English simply could not be for him. Her sobs quieted and he whispered, "*Pele,*[5] *pele,* I am sorry," over and over again, kissed her temple, stroked the long silky strands that the hairdresser had so carefully set.

Don't pity me, she wanted to whisper, but he kissed her properly then, with an intensity that made her ache. His warm hands had slid beneath her clothing to touch her bare skin, splaying over her waist and back. She was overwhelmed by his closeness and could not speak. When she finally did, it was a husky *please* as she shifted

[5]"I'm sorry" (Yoruba).

her hips. But he pulled away from her, shook his head. There was shame on his face.

Not until they married, he said, cupping her face in his hands, and he pulled her close to him until she slept.

He must have been really desperate, Anu thought now, resting her aching head in her hands. Not as desperate as she'd been, though. He hadn't defended her to Tara. Not even close. He'd merely stated the facts. He'd been angry. No one wants to be accused of screwing the ugly girl, after all.

The boy, he said, is just using you—!

After a few moments of sitting very still, Anu took the phone, dialed out. The call would use up the last of her precious international minutes, but she didn't care. She would be using James's from now on, after all.

Tobi was relieved when she picked up. "Anu—thank God, I was worried. Are you all right?"

"Tobi," Anu said, and her voice was very calm. "I have to tell you something."

She was astonished by how easily the lie slid out. She knew about his wife, she said. He would be divorcing her in a few months, but there were some logistics that were holding up the process. He'd obtained a green card already, but was keeping it quiet. His visa had nothing to do with her. She thanked Tobi for her concern, but she was fine, really. She knew what she was doing.

"Anyway," she finished. "Even if he was, Tobi. Why would you stay Nigerian if you had a chance not to? It's a useless country now."

"You cannot possibly think this is what God wants for you!"

Anu laughed hollowly and hung up the phone again, this time yanking the cord from the wall and placing the phone in a box. Tobi simply could not understand the way it felt, looking up at the sky from the bottom of a pit you've spent all your energy digging.

Anu and James were married the next day.

It was so hot that tree leaves wilted and insects buzzed lazily, too tired to sting. The ceremony was one that their people would remember as pleasant, if not extraordinary.

Invitations on Japanese rice paper had been printed at the university shop and sent to one hundred fifty people, listing the starting time as 5:00 p.m. One hundred eighty-five Nigerian attendees trickled in around 8:30, joining the few white and Asian guests who hadn't been warned about cultural quirks and had thus been treated to hours of watching the DJ and bridesmaids set up. Sagging and swathed in white and red, the tables groaned under the weight of trays that held seasoned rice, goat meat in red pools of palm oil, and hot pepper soup. Glass plates of sweet fried chin chin[6] and roasted peanuts served as centerpieces. It was incredible, Anu thought. No one had ever made a fuss over her before.

James, resplendent in a sleek black tux, surveyed the chaos with disgust. He'd wanted a quiet ceremony at an upstate chapel that he'd frequented while writing his dissertation, but Anu's parents had overruled him, ecstatic that their only daughter had finally found a husband. He gave in at last, with very bad grace.

"Don't let them pepper the soup too much," he instructed Anu. "I'll be inviting people from campus, you know."

The guests listened as the bride's uncle gave the opening toast and prayer, thanking God for the union, praying against spells, family curses, and any other tool of the Evil One that would prevent theirs from being a fruitful marriage. All the *babas* and *mamas* raised a hearty "Amen!" A woman shouted out that they would be blessed with twins; everyone laughed. Then they all ate sticky fufu[7] and okra and bitter-leaf soup and sighed and put their hands on their tummies and ate the great plates of rice with piles of sweet fried plantain, chasing the last grains with their fingers, heading for more in the coolers hidden under the buffet tables.

In faintly grease-stained voices, they gossiped about how God had answered the prayers of the bride and how many degrees the groom had and criticized the bridesmaids' cherry-colored dresses for being too tight and ordered younger girls out of good seats so that they could be closer to the high tables. Then they danced with the bride and groom, spraying bills in the air like feathers, rolling bodies united as a single teeming organism to undulations that slipped out between lines of music. Everyone sang along: *You dey make my heart do yori yori!* Then: *Shay u won no d koko?*[8]

[6]A popular West African snack made of fried dough.
[7]A staple West African dish made from starchy crops like cassava, yam, or plantains boiled and pounded into a sticky dough.
[8]"Do you want to know the facts?" (Yoruba, slang).

James disliked the music. He told Anu privately that they were all rather silly numbers, beneath his dignity. He would have preferred Motown, jazz piano, '70s African highlife. Still, he drew her close on the dance floor, a smile fixed on his narrow face. The dean, his fat florid face flushed with too much palm wine, kissed them both effusively, bragged about his matchmaking, pointed out his wrapped gift of antique Wedgewood china.

Everyone went home on sore feet and felt partly responsible for making the wedding such a success.

That part had been quite easy, Anu thought ruefully, watching the last of their guests trickle out in the small hours as her husband helped her into the back of their private car. She had been watching him all that evening, as if they were characters on a reality show where she already knew the outcome. He spoke fondly about how they met and looked at her now and again with half-hooded eyes that she supposed were meant to denote affection, one hand tucked into hers or wrapped firmly around her waist, nestling her against his side.

It was hard not to feel anything during the ceremony or reception, harder than she thought to look the bishop in the eye and lie, say the vows they'd decided on via email three nights before, copying lines from various websites. He kissed her twice during the reception, for pictures and such. His mouth was warm, soft, with a hint of scratchiness about the chin.

She was glad, she realized with the violent thrill of a conquest she had no right to make. She was glad she knew about his wife. It would spare her the pressure of being his ideal.

"Good job," he said into her ear when they were settled in the back of the car that would take her to her new life. She nodded, unable to speak through a sudden pressure in her throat. James fell asleep soon after their departure, lulled by the car's gentle rhythm. The heat radiating off his chest made her drowsy, but she did not sleep. Instead, she watched the driver. He'd opened the windows and it was misting outside, a warm faint imitation of rain. The man sang quietly to himself, free hand dangling out the window. Anu wondered idly if the defogger was broken, or if he enjoyed the coolness of the mist on his fingertips and face after a day trapped in the small, hot prison.

2016

The Suitcase

MERON HADERO

On Saba's last day in Addis Ababa, she had just one unchecked to-do left on her long and varied list, which was to explore the neighborhood on her own, even though she'd promised her relatives that she would always take someone with her when she left the house. But she was twenty, a grownup, and wanted to know that on her first-ever trip to this city of her birth, she'd gained at least some degree of independence and assimilation. So it happened that Saba had no one to turn to when she got to the intersection around Meskel Square and realized she had seen only one functioning traffic light in all of Addis Ababa, population four million people by official counts, though no one there seemed to trust official counts, and everyone assumed it was much more crowded, certainly too crowded for just one traffic light. That single, solitary, lonely little traffic light in this mushrooming metropolis was near the old National Theater, not too far from the UN offices, the presidential palace, the former African Union—a known, respected part of the city located an unfortunate mile (a disobliging 1.6 kilometers) away from where Saba stood before a sea of cars, contemplating a difficult crossing.

Small, nimble vehicles, Fiats and VW Bugs, skimmed the periphery of the traffic, then seemed to be flung off centrifugally, almost gleefully, in some random direction. The center was a tangled cluster of cars slowly crawling along paths that might take an automobile backward, forward, sideward. In the middle of this jam was a sometimes visible traffic cop whose tense job seemed to be avoiding getting hit while keeping one hand slightly in the air. He was battered by curses, car horns, diesel exhaust as he nervously shifted his body weight and tried to avoid these assaults. Saba quickly saw she couldn't rely on him to help her get across. She dipped her foot from the curb onto the street, and a car raced by, so she retreated. A man walked up next to her and said in English, "True story, I know a guy who crossed the street halfway and gave up."

Saba looked at the stranger. "Pardon, what was that?"

"He had been abroad for many years and came back expecting too much," the man said, now speaking as slowly as Saba. "That sad man lives on the median at the ring road. I bring him books sometimes," he said slyly, taking one out of his messenger bag and holding it up. "A little local wisdom: don't start what you can't finish." Saba watched the stranger dangle his toes off the curb, lean forward, backward, forward and back, and then, as if becoming one with the flow of the city, lunge into the traffic and disappear from her sight until he reemerged on the opposite sidewalk. "Miraculous," Saba said to herself as he turned, pointed at her, then held up the book again. Saba tried to follow his lead and set her body to the rhythm of the cars, swaying forward and back, but couldn't find the beat.

As she was running through her options, a line of idling taxis became suddenly visible when a city bus turned the corner. She realized that, as impractical as it seemed, she could hail a cab to get her across the busy street. The trip took ten minutes; the fare cost 15 USD, for she was unable to negotiate a better rate, though at least she'd found a way to the other side. She turned back to see the taxi driver leaning out the window talking to a few people, gesturing at her, laughing, and she knew just how badly she'd fumbled yet another attempt to fit in. All month Saba had failed almost every test she'd faced, and though she'd seized one last chance to see if this trip had changed her, had taught her at least a little of how to live in this culture, she'd only ended up proving her relatives right: she wasn't even equipped to go for a walk on her own. What she thought would be a romantic, monumental reunion with her home country had turned out to be a fiasco; she didn't belong here.

She was late getting back to her uncle Fassil's house, where family and friends of family were waiting for her to say goodbye, to chat and eat and see her one last time, departures being even more momentous than arrivals. Twelve chairs had been moved into the cramped living room. Along with the three couches, they transformed the space into a theater packed with guests, each of whom sat with his or her elbows pulled in toward the torso to make space for all. They came, they said, to offer help, but she sensed it was the kind of help that gave—and took.

It was time to go, and she was relieved when Fassil said—in English, for her benefit—"We are running out of time, so we have already started to fill this one for you." He pointed past the suitcase that Saba had packed before her walk and gestured to a second, stuffed with items and emitting the faint scent of a kitchen after mealtime. At her mother's insistence, Saba had brought one suitcase for her own clothes and personal items and a second that for the trip there was full of gifts from America—new and used clothes, old books, magazines, medicine—to give to family she had never met. For her return, it would be full of gifts to bring to America from those same relatives and family friends.

Saba knew this suitcase wasn't just a suitcase. She'd heard there was no DHL here, no UPS. Someone thought there was FedEx, but that was just for extremely wealthy businessmen. People didn't trust the government post. So Saba's suitcase offered coveted prime real estate on a vessel traveling between here and there. Everyone wanted a piece; everyone fought to stake a claim to their own space. If they couldn't secure a little spot in some luggage belonging to a traveling friend, they'd not send their things at all. The only reasonable alternative would be to have the items sent as freight on a cargo ship, and how reasonable was that? The shipping container would sail from Djibouti on the Red Sea (and with all the talk of Somali pirates, this seemed almost as risky as hurling a box into the ocean and waiting for the fickle tides). After the Red Sea, a cargo ship that made it through the Gulf of Aden would go south on the Indian Ocean, around the Cape of Good Hope, across the Atlantic, through the Panama Canal, to the Pacific, up the American coast to Seattle. An empty suitcase opened up a rare direct link between two worlds, so Saba understood why relatives and friends wanted to fill her bag with carefully wrapped food things, gifts, sundry items, making space, taking space, moving and shifting the bulging contents of the bag.

Fassil placed a scale in front of Saba and set to zeroing it. She leaned over the scale as he nudged the dial to the right. The red needle moved ever so slightly, so incredibly slightly that Saba doubted it worked at all, but then Fassil's hand slipped, the needle flew too far, to the other side of zero. He pushed the dial just a hair to the left now, and the red needle swung back by full millimeter. He nudged the dial again; now it stuck.

"Fassil, Saba has to go," Lula said, shaking her hands like she was flicking them dry. "Let's get going. Her flight leaves in three hours, and with the traffic at Meskel Square and Bole Road . . ."

Saba leaned toward that wobbly needle as Fassil used his finger-nail to gently coax the dial a breath closer. A tap, nearly there. A gentle pull.

"Looks good, Fassil," Saba said kindly but impatiently.

"It has to be precise," Fassil replied, then turned to the gathered crowd. "Look what you're making the poor girl carry." He pointed to that second suitcase.

Saba tried to lift it, but it was as heavy as an ox. Fassil rushed over and helped her pick it up, and when he felt its weight, he said, "There's no way they'll let her take this." The crowd was unhappy to hear that, and so was Saba. The room hummed with disapproval, punctuated with *tsks* and clicked tongues. "I can just pay the fee," Saba quickly said, but Lula stood again, put up her hands and boomed, "You will not pay a fee. It's too much money. You are *our* guest, and *our* guest will pay no fee!"

"It's okay," Saba said. "If we must, we must." But now the resistance came from everyone. Saba looked helplessly at Fassil. "Let me pay. I have to go. What else can I do?" she asked, She looked at the others and wondered if this was one of those times when a "No" was supposed to be followed by a "Please, yes!" "No, no." "Really, I insist." "No, we couldn't." "Really, yes, you must." "Okay." "Okay." Was it that kind of conversation? That call and response? Or was it the other kind, the "No, no!" "Really, I insist!" "No, we just couldn't." "Okay, no, then."

"Of course you can't pay. They will never let you," Fassil said, ending Saba's deliberation. He announced, "I'll weigh the suitcase," and there was a general sigh of approval. "But," Fassil continued, "if it's overweight, which it is, we are going to have to make some tough choices." He turned to Saba. "You are going to have to make some tough choices." She nodded and hoped silently that it would come in at weight, please. If she could be granted one earthly wish in this moment, that was what she would wish for. She watched Fassil heave the suitcase onto the scale and winced as the needle that hovered, almost vibrated, above zero shot to the right. Thirty kilos—ten kilos too heavy.

The crowd began to murmur anxiously, and a few shouted out sounds of frustration. Then one by one, the guests began to speak in turns, as if pleading their cases before a judge.

Konjit was the first up. She was old, at least seventy, a verified elder who settled disputes and brokered weddings and divorces, part of that council of respected persons that held a neighborhood together. As Konjit walked toward Saba, Saba bowed a little.

"Norr," Saba said, a sign of respect.

"Bugzer," Konjit replied, acknowledging that the order of things hadn't been completely turned on its head. Konjit lifted the edge of her shawl, flung it around her shoulder, and walked slowly right up to the suitcase and unzipped it. She took out a package of chick-peas and tossed it on the ground, and though someone grumbled at this, Konjit just smoothed her pressed hair behind her ears as if she were calming herself before an important announcement, an orator about to make a speech, an actress set to perform. Konjit held a hand up to the others who sat on the couches and chairs, and waited for total silence. Then she turned to Saba, put her hands on both her hips, which swayed as she stepped closer to Saba, and said in a low voice that filled the small space, "Please, Sabayaye, I haven't seen my grandchildren since they were two years old. How old are you?"

"Twenty," Saba said apologetically.

"Twenty? Ah, in all the time you've been alive in this world I have not seen them. Imagine! I'm old now. Who can even say how old I am? I'm too old to count and getting older. I want to send this bread so they know people here love them."

Most of the others in the room nodded in agreement, but not Rahel. Rahel shook her head as she stood from the couch and walked right up to Konjit, putting a hand on Konjit's arm. "Who can say how old you are, Konjit? Me, I can say how old you are. Not the number of years of course, but I can say for sure that I am older than you. One month, remember."

Rahel brought up that one-month position of seniority often, and Saba had come to expect it. Within just her first week there, Saba learned that Rahel and Konjit had grown up and grown old fighting often about things like which church had the most blessed holy water, Ledeta (Rahel) or Giorgis (Konjit), or whether it was better to use white teff[1] flour (Konjit) or brown teff flour (Rahel), or where you could get the best deals on textiles, Mercato (Konjit) or Sheromeda (Rahel). Without fail, each argument ended with Rahel staking out a win by virtue of being slightly elder.

Rahel bent down and removed one of the three loaves of bread from the suitcase and tried to hand it back to Konjit, who refused to take it. Saba, wanting to hurry things along, reached out for the loaf,

[1]A staple grain of Ethiopian cuisine.

but Rahel placed the bread on the floor by her feet. "You can bake a loaf, Konjit, I give you that, but it takes you three hours to make that bread? Eh? I spent two days—two *days*—making this beautiful doro wat[2] for my nephew. The power kept switching off. I had to go to Bole to freeze it in Sintayu's freezer, and she has all those kids and all those in-laws and hardly any space in her house, let alone her freezer, but still, that's what it took to make this beautiful wat. Then I had to wrap the container so tight that, should any melt in transit, it will stay safe and secure—and with these old old old fingers," she said, putting up her index, middle, and ring fingers. "Can you believe it? These old old fingers," she said, now raising her pinky and thumb. "These fingers a month older than yours, Konjit." She pulled Saba over and put her fanned fingers on Saba's left shoulder, leaning on her. "Just take this beautiful wat for me. It will be no problem, right?"

Before Saba could say that this seemed reasonable, Wurro walked up to Saba, and Saba shifted her attention again. "I may not be the oldest, and my hands don't ache like Rahel's, but please, think about this objectively, Saba," said Wurro, whose utilitarian views led her to make obviously questionable decisions, like employing fifteen workers in her small grocery so that fifteen more paychecks went out each month and fifteen more families would be happy, even if it put her one family on the verge of ruin. Wurro never argued her utilitarian views as forcefully, though, as when they matched her own purposes. She cleared her throat, and Saba waited for what she feared would be another well-argued plea. Wurro began, "If you don't send this bread, Konjit, your family will still eat bread. If you don't send this wat, Rahel, your family will still eat wat." Wurro took Saba's hand and said, "My niece had a difficult pregnancy. You have to take this gunfo[3] because if you don't take it, well, there is no way to get gunfo in America, and who has ever heard of a woman not eating gunfo after labor? If you don't bring it, she won't have it. Milk for the baby, gunfo for the mother. It's natural logic. You can't deny it."

"But American women don't eat gunfo. Do they eat gunfo, Saba?" asked Lula.

[2]Spiced chicken stew.

[3]A thick porridge, traditionally made with barley flour and shaped into a volcano-like bowl which is filled with clarified butter and *berbere*, a spice mixture.

"She's never been pregnant in America, right? How would she know?" asked Wurro.

"She's never been pregnant here. Does she even know gunfo?" Konjit asked.

Saba said, "I know gunfo," and was met with whispered words of approval, so she refrained from adding how hard she had to swallow to get a spoonful down of the thick paste made from (she'd heard) corn, wheat, barley, or banana root, she wasn't even sure. Whatever gunfo was, she'd rather not bring it, if it was up to her, but she wasn't actually sure of that either. Was it up to her?

"Saba is a smart girl," Lula said. "She probably read *at least* ten books in the four weeks she was here." Saba felt guilty then, because it was true that she had declined as many invitations as she accepted, choosing sometimes to read alone at home. "She must know Americans have high-tech things for women after their pregnancies. They don't need gunfo," Lula said, rearranging the contents of the suitcase to make room for her own package. "But you know what they do need in America? Have you ever tasted American butter?"

Lula looked at the others as if this would end the discussion. She stood up, opened her arms. "Have you had American butter?" No one spoke, Saba kept quiet, for of course she had eaten American butter, but what good would it do to mention that now? Besides, few had the courage to challenge strong-willed Lula, even with the truth.

"No one here has ever had American butter, so then that settles it." Lula took out another of Konjit's loaves of bread and a bag of roasted grains. "*I* have eaten American butter. *I* have tasted it with my own tongue. *I* can say with certainty that American butter is only the milk part, no spices, no flavor. It just tastes like fat. Please bring this butter to my best friend for her wedding banquet," Lula said with her hands now pressed over her heart and looking pleadingly at Saba. "Ahwe, her wedding! And what a feat to get that man to the altar. His gambling and staying out late and—"

"Aye aye aye," Konjit interrupted, shaking her head and removing Lula's butter and putting a second loaf back into the suitcase. "You want her to bring butter so your friend can marry a bad man? Have you ever heard such nonsense?" Konjit asked Saba. Saba shrugged, and Konjit said, "See, she has never heard such nonsense," and Saba didn't have the heart to correct her and didn't have the heart not to correct her, and she didn't know which would have helped her bring this to the right resolution, so she just made a vague gesture and let them finish.

"He is not a bad man, just a *man* man," Lula said.

"Well, my son is a *good* man raising *good* grandchildren. Lula, my son brought you the stretchy pants you asked for from America when he visited. Wurro, my son brought you a laptop last time he came. Rahel, he brought you cereal with raisins, the kind you always ask for. Fassil, he brought you books, since you have long gone through everything at every library here, I assume. Saba, one day if you live in Ethiopia, he will bring you something too, anything you ask. Name something you miss here."

"Too much talk, Konjit!" Rahel yelled. "The traffic, she has to go!"

Konjit swatted away Rahel's interruption and gestured to Saba.

Saba tried to think of what to say. She didn't want to offend them by making them believe she had lacked for anything. She remembered how hurt Konjit had been when Saba visited after lunchtime, only to find a full meal waiting for her. When Saba refused, Konjit insisted that the dishes were very clean and the food fresh. That wasn't as bad, though, as sitting down to eat "just a little" and passing on the salad, the water, the cheese, the fruit, eating only the lentils and bread, accepting some coffee but not even the milk. "You have all been so kind to me," Saba said, bowing respectfully, pronouncing all her syllables perfectly, precisely, as quickly as she could. "I have not missed a thing. But it's late, and it's true, the traffic is bad . . ."

Konjit dismissed Saba. "She has learned the Ethiopia way. Good girl. Too polite to say you need anything here," Konjit replied, putting an arm on Saba's shoulder. Konjit continued, "Okay, don't tell us, that's okay. But if you visit again to stay a while, and if you find you are homesick for something you grew accustomed to there in America, my son will bring it. He is a good son. I am asking you to take two loaves of bread. Okay, forget about the third, I don't want to ask too much of you, even though I am an old lady who has not seen her grandchildren in, oh, who knows how long. But these two loaves must stay in the suitcase, two loaves for my three grandchildren so they know I am thinking about them. That I have not forgotten them." Saba could see that Konjit was too proud to say what she really meant: she didn't want her grandchildren to forget about her, a fear she must bear, living so far away for so many years with only limited lines of connection.

Konjit's argument hung there in the air until Fikru stood hesitantly and walked over to the suitcase, finding his bags of spices on the floor beside it. He reached into the suitcase and took out three Amharic-English dictionaries and tossed them onto the coffee table. Hanna shouted out, "Aye! Why, Fikru, would you do that?" She ran over and picked up the books, then threw them back in, but Konjit took them out, for they crushed her bread.

Fikru, who kept opening his mouth to speak but found himself overpowered by the more forceful voices, seized his opportunity like a fourth-chair orchestral musician stealing a flourish at the end of a number. He stood next to an overwhelmed Saba and said, "Everyone here has a relative in Seattle, yes? Then why is it that only my son is going to pick Saba up from the airport?" He turned to the others. "You talk about what so-and-so needs or has done, but my son, without asking for anything, has volunteered to get her. He will be carrying this heavy suitcase to his car. Then he will take her to her dorm and bring this heavy suitcase up the stairs, if there are stairs, or down the hall, should there be a hall. What can it hurt to bring a few items for him?" Fikru showed Saba his items. "Just a few bags of spices: corrorima, grain of paradise, berbere. Please, Saba, a humble parcel for my humble son."

Saba turned to her uncle Fassil and discreetly pointed to her watch. "Okay, you all have something to say," Fassil offered, cutting off the remaining guests who gathered around the suitcase, eager to make their appeals. "But the traffic!"

"Yes, the traffic," said Fikru.

"The traffic," Rahel and Konjit said in unison, and Lula nodded.

Fassil turned to Saba. She asked him, "What do you want to do?"

"What do *you* want to do?" Fassil asked her. Though each person in that room had his or her body turned to the suitcase, all eyes were on Saba, who was trying to figure out how to navigate this scene. They looked her over and imagined she looked so . . . what? Different? Just . . . apart with her woven bag, which intermittently glowed with the light from her iPhone or beeped and pinged and vibrated from the sound of her other gadgetry, her American jeans tucked into tall leather boots, a white button-down shirt and gold earrings, while they wore modest clothes and hand-me-downs, some of which she had brought herself.

She had been in the country one whole month and had tried, they must know, to learn the culture, to reacquaint herself with her first home and fit in. And now, here she stood, on the last moments of her last day, still not sure what to do, while they looked at her lovingly and with curiosity too. Saba felt the weight of choosing what should be taken and what should be left behind. She was looking for a way out and a way in, but she realized there really were no shortcuts here.

"You have all been so kind," Saba said. "Rahel, you took me to listen to the Azmaris sing," she said, omitting that she had been too shy to dance such unfamiliar dances no matter how encouraging Rahel had been. A few days later, Rahel came back to take her to one of the fancy new hotels where an American cover band played to a foreign crowd, and Saba pretended to like being there. She imagined Rahel had pretended too.

"Wurro, you took me to the holiday dinner, and we ate that delicious raw meat," Saba said, of course not mentioning that Fassil had to take her to the clinic the next day to get Cipro for her stomach cramps.

"Fikru, you brought me to Mercato to buy a dress," Saba said. But what she most remembered was spending the trip chasing after him through the labyrinthine alleyways; every so often, when Fikru looked back at her, she would wave and smile, and he'd keep going, losing her twice.

She remembered the man with the messenger bag that morning, the one who had crossed the street, and his warning about starting things you can't finish or giving up too soon. Saba walked to the suitcase she had packed herself, filled with her own things, and in one quick gesture opened it, emptied the contents. Her best clothes fell to the floor: her favorite old jeans, most sophisticated dresses, her one polished blazer, a new pair of rain boots, T-shirts collected from concerts and trips and old relationships. She pushed this empty suitcase to the center of the room.

"Dear friends, neighbors, and relatives," she said in forced Amharic,[4] looking at the confused expressions that confronted her, "please, now there is room for it all."

There were gasps, whispers, whistles, an inexplicable loud thud, but no laughter.

"Are you sure?" Fikru asked.

[4]The official language of Ethiopia.

"This is the least I can do," Saba said slowly. "It is the least I can do."

"What about your belongings?" Fassil asked.

"We'll keep them safe for her in case she returns," Konjit said, her voice commanding the space.

"Until she returns," Rahel corrected.

"Until you return?" Konjit asked, and Saba said yes.

Fassil got a bag, put Saba's things in, and told her he would store it in his own closet. The two suitcases were packed, weighed (the room applauded when both came in just under the limit), and thrown into the trunk of Fassil's car, which sagged a little in the rear. There were three cars in their little caravan that headed to the airport. The ride was slow. The weight of the overfull cars possibly complicated the trip, as did the rocky side streets and, of course, the congestion at the difficult intersections. They pressed on, and they reached the airport with absolutely no time to spare. Saba said quick, heartfelt goodbyes, thank-yous, made fresh promises, then pulled the two big suitcases onto a luggage cart. Her family and friends of family watched from the waiting area as she moved quickly through the line to get her boarding pass. They looked on as the two suitcases were weighed and thrown on the screening belt, and they saw her pass the main checkpoint. Every time she looked back to the lobby, she could catch glimpses of them on tiptoe, waiting to see if they might connect with her one more time.

2015

Reading Short Stories Closely

In front of you, on a page or a screen, is a short story that you intend to read. Maybe a friend has recommended it to you, or, more likely, you've been assigned to read it for a class. But you are distracted. Outside your window, passersby are enjoying a beautiful day. You hear some music or chatter coming from down the hall. Your phone buzzes with an update of some sort. You remember something else that is due tomorrow, or something you promised but forgot to do until just now.

With all these potential distractions, how will you gather your attention to focus on those little words streaming across your page or screen? Close the shades, cover your ears, turn off your phone, and accept that the effort of concentration will be worth it. Your challenge is to get into the reading deeply enough, closely enough, that a partnership is forged between you and the text, a partnership in which you collaborate to create something unique: your very own interpretation of the story. Consider the benefits. First, you, the attentive reader, will be entertained. Second, you may find yourself moved, deeply and unforgettably, by the events of the story. Finally, the characters and their situations will expand your sympathy and understanding of the human condition. For this is the magic of the short story: A dozen or so printed pages spring to life in your mind. Characters become real in your imagination, their conflicts become your conflicts, and the distant times and environments inhabit places in your own mind and heart. These experiences and transformations are often why authors write and publish, and why readers often approach reading a story with anticipation and remember it with intense pleasure.

To become involved in this way, you need to read slowly and carefully and concentrate with an active mind on the language of the story. Close reading is more involved than *reading*; it goes beyond understanding the meanings of the printed words. The method involves identifying and evaluating some of the following: a story's diction or vocabulary; its imagery, sentence structure, point of view, setting, characters, plot, and themes; and the vision of life it expresses. (For help with these and other terms in this section, consult the Glossary of Literary Terms.) To analyze a story, a close reader examines details to consider larger meanings. Close reading is challenging because it involves exploration and discovery of patterns, but with practice it becomes easier as the reader builds an active partnership with the text. Annotating a text, discussed below, and recording your thoughts in a reading journal are tools that strengthen your close reading.

As you read this section, keep in mind three general points: First, close reading is widely believed to be the most effective first step in analyzing a story because the process requires you to "enter" the story, read it carefully, and locate important details about its shape and meaning. Second, close reading can easily be applied to all reading and is useful in courses and fields beyond literature. Third, close reading is a natural preparation for writing about short stories and other texts, as you will find in the later section, "Writing about Short Stories."

ANNOTATING SHORT STORIES

While you are reading, you can annotate the text by underlining important phrases and writing brief marginal notes that help you remember your reactions and trace the patterns in a story. The word *annotate* comes from the Latin *annotare*, which means "to mark." Annotation is a process by which you mark up a story in a way that is meaningful to you. Annotation is a helpful tool for close reading because it organizes your thoughts and makes them easily retrievable in later readings and reflections. Annotation also helps you familiarize yourself with the content and structure of a story and is a way to clarify important details, remember them, and use them in discussion and writing. Deciding how many and what kind of notes you will make is up to you. However, making consistent annotations will help you dig deeper into a story and will strengthen your close-reading practice. There are many ways to annotate. The following recommendations are particularly useful:

1. Underline, circle, or highlight key words, phrases, and sentences in the story. After you have read through the story once or twice, underline, circle, or highlight language that might refer to unusual features of character, plot, setting, themes, and recurring images of the story. For example, in Nathaniel Hawthorne's "Young Goodman Brown," you might mark language that alludes to the devilish nature of Brown's companion. Now is a good time to look up those words that you don't know. You might also look up familiar words and be surprised by the layers of meaning that you find there. Read through the story again to find and mark other key words. This step helps you identify the story's elements and think about the patterns you have found.

2. Note main ideas in the margins. This procedure will draw attention to the patterns you have developed in thinking about the story. For example, in "Young Goodman Brown," the underlined phrase "on his present evil purpose" might be labeled as "evil motive." If you find other places in the margin where you have marked "evil motive," you have discovered a pattern in the story that you may want to explore further.

3. Label phrases that signal important changes in story structure or turns of events. Note phrases that describe the function of the sentence, paragraph, or section you are flagging. These comments will trace the action of the story, so look for and annotate places where important turns of events occur. One such place in "Young Goodman Brown" is when Brown refuses Faith's fearful plea that he not go out on "this night . . . of all nights in the year." Your comment might read as such: "Couple differs; husband will go," or "B. will go, though Faith begs otherwise."

4. Refine your own method of annotation. You should develop a system for keeping track of which types of annotation you are using, so that you can quickly understand the function of each annotation. For example, if you always note main ideas in the right-hand margin, you will know, at a glance, which comments represent main ideas. You may find that techniques such as color-coding or labeling different types of annotations with a symbol, such as a star or an asterisk, are particularly helpful, especially if you use the same colors or symbols when you expand your annotations in your reading journal. Never underestimate the power of annotating your text in longhand. Research has shown that writing down your thoughts, rather than merely typing, will slow you down and help you remember your train of thought.

5. Reflect on your annotations to help you develop your own perspective on the story. Your own words may clarify particular patterns in the story. For example, you may comment here and there about the narrator's annoying tone without knowing why. When reflecting on the content and consistency of your notes, you will often find that the author has established a pattern essential to your understanding of the story. You may also compare and contrast the story with another story or with external ideas and contemporary issues; this practice can generate good writing topics. If you think of annotating as the first step in the writing process, you'll be surprised by how many paper topics will emerge.

6. Keep a reading journal. Because most books do not have large margins for extensive notes, you will have to keep your marginal notes brief. But you can expand on your notes in a reading journal or on your course management system (CMS). Your instructor may require you to keep a journal or post responses on your CMS, but, if not, you can start your own journal. Such a practice can help you further develop your ideas and deepen your reading. In the margins of the book, your annotations might be a few words or a short phrase. In your journal, you can expand these annotations into full sentences or paragraphs. This will help you fully record your thoughts, better preparing you to discuss the work in class or write a paper.

ANNOTATED EXCERPT FROM "YOUNG GOODMAN BROWN"

Nathaniel Hawthorne's "Young Goodman Brown" is a masterpiece in the short-story genre. The first two pages, which provide the foundation for our understanding of the entire story, make an ideal sample for close reading and annotation. In the following example, we predominantly use underlining because it is quick and produces a neater page to work from. These underlines and the comments that accompany them are only some of many interpretations of the story.

Young Goodman Brown

Meaning? Setting: time, place, history?

NATHANIEL HAWTHORNE

[1804–1864]

Mysterious image

Young Goodman Brown came forth at sunset into the street at Salem village; but put his head back, after crossing the threshold, to exchange a parting kiss with his young wife. And Faith as the wife was aptly named, thrust her own pretty head into the street, letting the wind play with the pink ribbons of her cap while she called to Goodman Brown.

Setting — place
Double meaning?

"Dearest heart," whispered she, softly and rather sadly, when her lips were close to his ear, "prithee put off your journey until sunrise and sleep in your own bed to-night. A lone woman is troubled with such dreams and such thoughts that she's afeard of herself sometimes. Pray tarry with me this night, dear husband, of all nights in the year."

"My love and my Faith," replied young Goodman Brown, "of all nights in the year, this one night must I tarry away from thee. My journey, as thou callest it, forth and back again, must needs be done 'twixt now and sunrise. What, my sweet, pretty wife, dost thou doubt me already, and we but three months married?"

Theme, setting, plot

"Then God bless you!" said Faith, with the pink ribbons, "and may you find all well when you come back."

"Amen!" cried Goodman Brown. "Say thy prayers, dear Faith, and go to bed at dusk, and no harm will come to thee."

Double standard, trouble ahead

So they parted; and the young man pursued his way until, being about to turn the corner by the meeting-house, he looked back and saw the head of Faith still peeping after him with a melancholy air, in spite of her pink ribbons.

"Poor little Faith!" thought he, for his heart smote him. "What a wretch am I to leave her on such an errand! She talks of dreams, too. Methought as she spoke there was trouble in her face, as if a dream had warned her what work is to be done to-night. But no, no; 't would kill her to think it. Well, she's a blessed angel on earth, and after this one night I'll cling to her skirts and follow her to heaven."

With this excellent resolve for the future, Goodman Brown felt himself justified in making more haste on his present evil purpose. He had taken a dreary road, darkened by all

Husband's evil motive

the gloomiest trees of the forest, which barely stood aside to let the narrow path creep through, and closed immediately behind. It was all as lonely as could be; and there is this peculiarity in such a solitude, that the traveller knows not who may be concealed by the innumerable trunks and the thick boughs overhead; so that with lonely footsteps he may yet be passing through an unseen multitude.

"There may be a devilish Indian behind every tree," said Goodman Brown to himself; and he glanced fearfully behind him as he added, "What if the devil himself should be at my very elbow!" *Devil image?*

His head being turned back, he passed a crook of the road, and, looking forward again, beheld the figure of a man, in grave and decent attire, seated at the foot of an old tree. He arose at Goodman Brown's approach and walked onward side by side with him.

"You are late, Goodman Brown," said he. "The clock of the Old South was striking as I came through Boston, and that is full fifteen minutes agone." *Setting, time, history*

"Faith kept me back a while," replied the young man, with a tremor in his voice, caused by the sudden appearance of his companion, though not wholly unexpected. *Double meaning, blame*

It was now deep dusk in the forest, and deepest in that part of it where these two were journeying. As nearly as could be discerned, the second traveller was about fifty years old, apparently in the same rank of life as Goodman Brown, and bearing a considerable resemblance to him, though perhaps more in expression than features. Still they might have been taken for father and son. And yet, though the elder person was as simply clad as the younger, and as simple in manner too, he had an indescribable air of one who knew the world, and who would not have felt abashed at the governor's dinner table or in King William's court, were it possible that his affairs should call him thither. But the only thing about him that could be fixed upon as remarkable was his staff, which bore the likeness of a great black snake, so curiously wrought that it might almost be seen to twist and wriggle itself like a living serpent. This, of course, must have been an ocular deception, assisted by the uncertain light. *Setting, time, history* *Satanic imagery*

As a tool of close reading, annotating the first two pages of Hawthorne's story has yielded important material for developing an analysis. We were introduced to two major characters and their differing views of the husband's intention to leave his wife and go out into the woods all night. We learned that his motive is evil. We met a devil-like third character who accompanies Brown on his journey. Our next step would be to expand our annotations in a journal.

"Young Goodman Brown" Reading Journal

Title: "Young": youthful and relatively inexperienced; "Goodman": a type of address used by 17th-century colonial Puritans for men below the rank of gentleman.

Paragraph 1, Salem village: Setting, time and place, history — a small village (now Danvers) north of present-day Salem, MA. Accusations in the original Salem led to the infamous witch trials (1692), presided over by Hawthorne's paternal great-great-grandfather, Justice John Hathorne (1641–1717).

Paragraph 1, Faith: He's leaving his wife (Faith). He and she (Faith) "exchange a parting kiss." Double meaning: He is leaving his faith too.

In the example journal, the note about the setting would have required some research, while the note about the name "Faith" would have come solely from your interpretation of the story's patterns. Your annotations and notes are the perfect place to get ideas for writing papers. A bit of research at this stage will not only deepen your understanding of the story but also help you provide evidence for your thesis. Consult "Writing about Short Stories" to develop and support a thesis.

CHECKLIST FOR READING CLOSELY

- ☐ Have you underlined, circled, or highlighted key words, phrases, and sentences in the story?
- ☐ Have you labeled main ideas in the margins of the story?
- ☐ Have you labeled phrases that signal important changes in structure and events in the story?
- ☐ Have you developed an appropriate, flexible system of annotations that will help you keep track of your thinking?
- ☐ Have you reflected on your annotations to develop a perspective on the story, with ideas for discussion or writing?
- ☐ Have you started a reading journal where you can expand on your annotations to start writing a paper about the story?

Writing about Short Stories

Once you know how to read closely, you're on your way to writing effectively. For writing, as for close reading, you have to minimize distractions and concentrate fully on persuading your readers that what you are saying makes sense and matters. To catch and hold their attention, you declare your argument, the point of your paper, your *thesis statement*. After you've done so in your *introduction*, your task in the *body* and *conclusion* of the paper is to convince readers that your thesis is valid and the evidence you have gathered during your close reading supports your interpretation. By *argument*, we don't mean a squabble or an angry dispute, but rather a composition that persuades readers to see things your way. You show them what you have noticed in the story, suggest what it means, support your assertions with evidence, and indicate why it is worth their attention and assent.

Planning and writing such a paper takes time. If you want to produce an effective paper, you'll avoid doing a last-minute job. You'll need enough time to think your project through, step by step. You'll want to experiment with different possibilities, draft and redraft your paper, and finally *revise and edit* it. To see how this process works, we'll run through the basic elements of a paper, using Nathaniel Hawthorne's "Young Goodman Brown," the first story in this book, for most examples.

DRAFTING YOUR THESIS STATEMENT

The thesis, or central idea, of your paper is the touchstone for every sentence you write. This idea must be sharp and clear enough to guide your writing. To be effective, it needs to be phrased in a statement that makes a focused, compelling, and arguable claim. To simply say, for example, "This paper is about Goodman Brown's decline" is to make a claim too large, obvious, vague, and distant from the details of the story that is of little help to you or of interest to the reader. Designing a good thesis statement is not as difficult as you may expect when you first begin.

Decide which elements or patterns in the story you will explore in your paper. After you have chosen and read a story you want to write about, review the preceding section, "Reading Short Stories Closely," and annotate the story, underlining, circling, or highlighting significant details and commenting on them in the margins. Expand your annotations in your reading journal, paying special attention to how they relate to the elements of fiction: **plot, characters, setting, point of view, style,** and **theme.** By reviewing how each element works, you give yourself a range of ways to approach the story. Consult the Glossary of Literary Terms later in this book for definitions, descriptions, and examples of these elements, and reflect on the nature and function of each element in the story.

Your notes will offer many ideas about how the story's elements tie together, making it easier to choose one to develop for your thesis statement. What do you notice about each element? Do you find yourself making more notes about, say, character rather than setting? Is this because character is more important in the story, or because something particular about the characters interests you? If you find something especially interesting in a story, something you agree or disagree with, something that attracts or repels you, something that excites you, and/or something that puzzles you, you're probably on your way to identifying a central idea for your paper.

Review your notes. What questions do your notes ask? What further questions occur to you as you review them? What might the answers be? Once you start imagining and finding answers to your questions, you are probably on the way to finding what the argument of your paper will be: what you have found in the story, or about the story, that you want to persuade a reader to see as well. Your thesis statement points your readers toward what you want them to see or understand. What follows are some possible thesis statements about each element of fiction.

Thesis statements about plot. As the narrative spine of a story, its line of action, plot is an important element in stories. Because the plot is usually obvious and well known to your reader, you do not need to retell it in detail or focus on it to the exclusion of other elements. (A rule of thumb is to assume that your reader knows the story but has to be reminded about certain specifics and details that bear on the argument you are making in your paper.) Instead, you'll want to analyze how the series of events in a story create a structure that is significant. Consider this thesis statement:

> The series of events in Hawthorne's "Young Goodman Brown" creates a crisis for a narrator who cannot distinguish between what appears to be true about members of his community versus what is true.

While this thesis statement focuses on the story's series of events, it also shows how its plot affects the main character's development. Instead of having to recount the story's series of events, the writer will be able to jump right in to key scenes and provide insightful close readings.

Thesis statements about characters. We get to know characters through what the narrator says about them, through what the characters themselves say and do, and through how others respond to these characters. A thesis statement about characters should make a specific and arguable claim about a character or characters. Here's an example of a thesis that focuses on external forces that affect Young Goodman Brown:

> Goodman Brown's disillusionment with the people he meets has a shattering impact on him because they represent the virtues he was raised to believe in.

This sample thesis statement is effective because it is a specific and arguable claim. All the characters Brown meets on his journey are "pillars of the community," known for their purity and piety. But they are shown to be "two-faced" and hypocritical: his father, or the devil, who carries a serpent-stick and boasts of his evil influence in the church and government; Deacon Gookin, his comrade; Goody Cloyse, who taught Brown his catechism; and the remaining congregation at the black mass. When a pink ribbon flutters to the ground, Goodman Brown presumes that it is his wife's, becomes convinced of her corruption, and loses his faith forever.

Thesis statements about setting. Think of the dark, gloomy forest in late-seventeenth-century Salem, Massachusetts, the setting (time, place, atmosphere) of "Young Goodman Brown," and consider how appropriate this setting is for this story of Brown's disillusionment and despair. Here is a specific and arguable sample thesis statement related to setting:

> The contrast between the village and the forest is analogous to the contrast between the tame and the wild; together they represent the conflicts in Goodman Brown's mind that he never resolves.

This thesis statement is compelling because it clearly connects the setting to Young Goodman Brown's inner turmoil. It also suggests a comparative form for the paper with possibilities in the conclusion for implications.

Thesis statements about point of view. The element of point of view means the perspective or angle of vision from which a narrator tells a story. Point of view has great power over our perceptions of a narrator and the characters in a story. (Sometimes the narrator is a character, as in Edgar Allan Poe's "The Cask of Amontillado.") First-person narration, using *I*, and third-person narration, using *he*, *she*, *it*, and *they*, are the most common points of view used. They create very different effects, however. While a first-person point of view usually feels personal, the third person is usually distant, especially if the narrator is looking backward in time. Hawthorne, a native of Salem and a descendant of the Salem Puritans, actually composed the story about 150 years after he imagines it happening. Hawthorne's narrator is removed from the action of the story by time, which suggests his objectivity. Consider the effectiveness of the following thesis, which foregrounds the cultural context of the story as it relates to point of view:

> Hawthorne's choice of third-person narrative point of view gives "Young Goodman Brown" a more distanced, authoritative tone that broadens the meaning of the story from the experience of one man to that of a culture.

This is a contestable thesis that clearly considers the function of point of view in narration.

Thesis statements about style. Style, meaning "style of language," involves diction (choice of words), imagery (those sensory details that make the reader see, smell, hear, taste, or feel), and syntax (arrangement of those words, as in sentence structure). Every author has a distinct style, and every author bends that style to suit the nature of the story. Hawthorne has his characters speak a quaint, pious New England dialect, while his narrator writes in the comparatively more modern style of over a century later. The imagery used to describe Brown's "fellow-traveller" and the crowd at the bonfire brings the story to life visually. Here is a sample thesis statement that focuses on the stylistic function of dialogue in the story:

> At first, the dialogue in "Young Goodman Brown" might seem archaic, but Hawthorne deliberately uses dialogue to create characters that initially seem quaint and formal, when in fact they are steeped in sin.

This thesis statement focuses on a pertinent element of style around which the writer could structure paragraphs that analyze the meanings and function of the dialogue and its relationship to the psychology of the characters.

Thesis statements about theme. *Theme* has many meanings in literary discussion. It can be a synonym for *essay* or *paper*, or it can mean *thesis statement*, the central idea of an essay. But as an element of fiction, *theme* has a precise and useful meaning. A theme is an abstraction—like "faith," "love," "war," and "growing up"—that is explored as a subject of a story. A thesis statement about a theme calls for analysis of that idea and examination of how the story employs the theme. The following thesis focuses on isolation as part of the cultural landscape of the story:

> In "Young Goodman Brown," isolation is the dominant condition among male and female, young and old, in the seventeenth-century village of Salem, as perceived by Brown himself.

With this thesis statement, you could show the commonality of isolation in a small, presumably tightly knit and interdependent religious community. You would also need to identify the sources of this view of the prevalence of isolation: the relatively objective narrator and the very subjective Goodman Brown. The issue of accuracy or inaccuracy of characterizations of groups of people follows naturally from this topic.

Thesis statements that compare and contrast. Thesis statements that compare and contrast two or more stories often point out their similarities and differences on one issue or one element of plot, character, setting, point of view, style, or theme. So you would never see a thesis statement claiming that there are similarities and differences between two stories. For one thing, writing about all the similarities and differences between two or more works would be an overwhelming task. For another, the assertion is meaningless. Such a statement is obviously true. The thesis statement must be narrowed down and made specific so that an argument can be constructed, and a case made for your position.

Consider the following thesis statement that **compares** "Young Goodman Brown" and Toni Cade Bambara's "The Lesson":

> Though Nathaniel Hawthorne's "Young Goodman Brown" and Toni Cade Bambara's "The Lesson" are written about characters and cultures nearly three centuries apart, and Hawthorne's story focuses on an allegorical journey while Bambara's focuses on a more literal trip to Midtown Manhattan, each character's journey is crucial to their social awakening.

Now consider this thesis statement, which provides a **contrast** between the two stories:

> "Young Goodman Brown" and "The Lesson" both use the journey as a way for the leading characters to come to new and painful knowledge about themselves and their cultures. In the case of "Young Goodman Brown," the protagonist's journey leads to a crisis of faith and sense of futility, while in "The Lesson," Sylvia gains insight into economic injustice, which she ultimately decides to overcome.

Both statements make interesting, arguable claims, and both could yield effective papers if their respective authors really explored the reasons why these claims are accurate. Comparing (the similarities) and contrasting (the differences) requires a close study of both stories to discover their relationship. At first, the obvious similarities and differences stand out, and generally the differences seem more important. With closer study and further thought, however, interesting similarities begin to emerge, as here in these stories, between a modern young woman in Harlem and a late-seventeenth-century Puritan young man in Salem who are both radically changed by an experience that makes them see themselves and their cultures in a new way.

Once you have settled on a thesis statement, you can draft your paper, then edit and revise it.

DRAFTING AN INTRODUCTION

The introduction is critical to the success of your paper, since it determines whether your reader will proceed with interest or read on at all. In short papers, introductions are normally brief, three or four sentences designed to arouse interest in the central idea and the argument for it that will follow.

Consider the following introductory sentences. The sentence on the left is vague, while the sentence on the right is more focused:

A vague sentence	A more focused sentence that presents a problem or site of investigation in the story
"Young Goodman Brown" is an interesting story.	Goodman Brown loses his faith because he loses respect for others.

The sentence on the left is not only too broad, it is also merely descriptive. The sentence on the right, however, presents a thesis that is contestable and can drive the energy of the writer's analysis. Once you've established your thesis, you use the rest of the sentences in your paragraph to prepare your reader for what they will encounter in your essay:

> Goodman Brown loses his faith because he loses respect for others. Everyone he meets, the people he admires in his church for their piety, show a new and opposite side, leading him to conclude that they are corrupt hypocrites. His experience in the woods destroys his naïve innocence. Disrespecting them, he loses faith in what they stand for.

When you have decided on your thesis and written your introduction, you can move on to the body of your paper, which involves organization and evidence, and then on to the conclusion. You can rewrite your introduction any time during the writing of your paper, even when you have completed your draft—which is when you will know your paper best.

DRAFTING THE BODY OF THE ESSAY

When we talk about the body of the essay, we're talking about the progression of paragraphs, how they are organized individually and collectively, sentence by sentence, to advance the argument of your thesis. The *organization* of a paper is its structure, why and how it holds together. Does the paper's organization, large and small, serve the paper's purpose? Does the organization advance the thesis?

Look at the formal or informal outline of the paper you are writing: Does it have an introduction with a thesis, a section of argument or development, and a conclusion?

Look at the paragraphs, most of which resemble mini essays, with a clear central idea and line of development.

- Can you find the paragraph's topic sentence, which should provide a smooth transition from the previous paragraph and in some way reassert the thesis?
- Do the sentences that follow the topic sentence provide context for textual evidence that supports your thesis?
- Does each paragraph provide compelling textual evidence in the form of a paraphrase or direct quote?
- Once you've provided textual evidence, have you provided a close reading that carefully analyzes the passage?
- Are the paragraphs arranged in the best sequence to support your thesis? Does one paragraph lead into the next, with clear and logical connections?

An important way to develop the body of your essay is to use transitions effectively. When you move from sentence to sentence, from paragraph to paragraph, signal the direction of your argument to your reader with transitional words and phrases. For example, if you are adding a new idea, words and phrases like *also*, *further*, *moreover*, *in addition to*, and *similarly* will keep your reader with you. If you are introducing a contrasting idea, words and phrases like *although*, *despite*, *nevertheless*, *rather than*, *by contrast*, and *yet* will alert your reader to a change in direction or your argument or thought. If you are pointing your reader to a logical conclusion, words or phrases such as *consequently*, *as a result*, *thus*, *therefore*, *in sum*, and *finally* will indicate the idea that readers should take away with them as they continue reading.

Organization is one part of developing the body of your essay; the other is *evidence*. With a compelling thesis and strong organization, you will need persuasive evidence to make your case. Sources of your evidence are the text itself, other people's views, and your own ideas. All three can enrich your writing. As we noted in "Reading Short Stories Closely," many writers find that it's good practice to keep a reading journal to record ideas that seem pertinent and otherwise might be forgotten. Of course, the text itself is your essential source. You can return to it again and again to get more and better examples to support the points you are making. Depending on your thesis, you can draw evidence from narrative, descriptive, and conversational passages.

Be sure to make it clear when you are using the author's (or anyone else's) words as evidence when you are building your argument. When you quote directly, you must use quotation marks and attribute the words to the author as part of the regular sentence, in parentheses, or in a footnote. When you use your own words to retell an event or describe a person or scene in the story, you are either paraphrasing or summarizing. A paraphrase is about the same length as the original passage, while a summary condenses a longer passage into your own words. Still, it must be clear to your reader who and what you are paraphrasing and summarizing. There are numerous rules and technicalities about properly quoting, paraphrasing, and summarizing, most of them having to do with giving clear credit to those whose ideas you are using in your essay. Your instructor can provide guidelines for crediting sources or may refer you to a book that includes this information, such as the ninth edition of the *MLA Handbook for Writers of Research Papers*.

WRITING A CONCLUSION

A conclusion is not a summary. It is not a place to declare that you have proven your thesis. What will matter to your readers is that reading your essay will broaden their knowledge, deepen their understanding, and raise new questions about literature and life that they will want to answer. Imagine that you are writing a paper on the thesis "Goodman Brown loses his faith because he loses respect for himself." Your carefully chosen evidence comes from the narrator's comments on Brown's psychological distress, from the reactions of other characters to him and about him, and from Brown's own self-blame. Consider the strengths of the following conclusion, which confirms your thesis argument and speculates on one of the story's implications:

> The troubled Goodman Brown has brought about his own downfall. When he left his wife for his night in the forest, he declined to explain his purpose and refused her pleas to stay home. He told himself that this experience was necessary and would not be repeated. He felt guilty from the moment he left his wife to venture into the forest to the day he died. He saw evil in everyone he encountered. He saw himself and his wife as Adam and Eve, first partners in original sin. He was a man increasingly disturbed by his real and imagined sins. The Puritans believed in total depravity, but they also believed in the possibility of salvation, through Christ's mercy, for the elect. Goodman Brown was so beset by his belief in his own corruption that he could see no good in or outside himself and lost his balance psychologically. Hawthorne may have been identifying the destructive powers of self-absorbed dwelling on sinfulness and endorsing the wisdom of the classical model of moderation. We cannot know for sure in this story, since the self-destructive vision of Goodman Brown is all-pervasive.

In addition to summarizing some of the main points of the argument, this conclusion also speculates about what Hawthorne may be doing in the story ("Hawthorne may have been identifying . . .") and leaves the door open for further interpretations ("We cannot know for sure in this story . . ."). Effective conclusions rarely close down discussion; it is a very rare paper that offers the last word on a topic, or definitively proves a thesis. More open-ended ways to conclude a paper are to suggest why what you have argued should matter to readers, or to hazard a larger point about the author or the text that would be worth further exploration. A work of literature is not a problem to be resolved, but rather an opportunity to open or join an illuminating conversation about it.

REVISING AND EDITING

Whether you have written your paper in sections or all at once, you have a first draft now and are ready to refine it. Before you begin, though, it's helpful to put your writing aside for a day or two, or even overnight, so that you can return to it with critical objectivity. We call this next step a *revision* because we are "seeing it again." Revision has two stages: large-scale and small-scale. In the first stage, you read a clean printout of your paper with "new eyes," as if you were someone else, to see if the thesis, introduction, body (organization and evidence), and conclusion support each other. Be tough. Ask yourself whether your introduction and conclusion do their jobs and whether your paragraphs are relevant to your argument and ordered in the most effective way. Ask if paragraphs transition smoothly from one to the next. See if you need to add more evidence or strengthen your organization to make your case. You may need to move paragraphs around, delete some, or add others.

When you are convinced that the thesis, introduction, body, and conclusion work together effectively, you can proceed to small-scale revision, evaluating sentences, phrases, and words to see if they are doing their job, if they advance your argument by being persuasive on behalf of your thesis. Large- and small-scale revision should be done at least twice, so make sure to leave enough time for it. Experienced writers revise many times to make their work as good as it can be.

The final step, *editing*, examines a paper's language very closely for correctness and appropriateness of word choice, spelling, punctuation, grammar, and usage. Here, you use your close-up lens. Is your language clear, fresh, and direct? Have you avoided clichés? Have you double-checked the spelling of words you aren't sure of? Are your grammar and usage correct?

In some situations, it's possible to do large- and small-scale revising and editing in classroom or workshop formats. Since you are writing to an audience of one or more readers, others' reactions to your work can be very helpful in showing you how your writing is coming across and in identifying aspects of it that are successful and aspects that need strengthening. Conferences with your instructor will clarify the nature of your assignment and assist you in designing a thesis statement, locating sources (if outside sources are to be used), and organizing your paper. In the end, though, you and the short story will determine the outcome. When you have worked hard on your paper in all the ways we've talked about, and produced a piece of writing that is unified, compelling, and persuasive in the ways we have described, you will know that you've taken a major step in understanding and appreciating your abilities and the dynamic complexities of the short story.

CHECKLIST FOR WRITING ABOUT SHORT STORIES

- ☐ Have you reviewed the "Checklist for Reading Closely" and your reading journal?
- ☐ Have you thoughtfully annotated the story and identified interesting elements and patterns of ideas?
- ☐ Have you chosen a particular element or pattern that you will explore in your paper?
- ☐ In your introductory paragraph, have you drafted a compelling thesis statement that sets up the argument that you will develop in your paper?
- ☐ Have you organized your evidence into paragraphs, with each paragraph building on what came before and leading logically into the next paragraph throughout the body of the paper?
- ☐ Does your conclusion do more than summarize your argument?
- ☐ Have you reviewed the whole paper for clarity and strength of argument and language? Have you made your case?
- ☐ After some time away (several days to a week are recommended), did you read your paper closely again and make the changes that you believed necessary? Did you make your case?

A STUDENT ESSAY

In the following student essay, Mya Nunnally analyzes how Young Goodman Brown loses his faith in humanity. As you read her essay, notice how she positions her thesis statement in her first paragraph, uses strong topic sentences to transition from one idea to the next, and uses her body paragraphs to support her thesis with solid textual evidence.

Nunnally 1

Mya Nunnally
Professor Diaz
English 170
1 April 2020

Revelations of Duplicity in "Young Goodman Brown"

From the very first sentence, which establishes the setting in Salem Village, readers of Nathaniel Hawthorne's "Young Goodman Brown" are alerted to the story's supernatural or eerie potential. After all, stories rarely take place in such a notorious setting (home of the Salem Witch Trials) without good reason. But, though some frightening events develop, like a wicked ceremony in the deep woods, the most sinister part of Goodman Brown's journey is the deception he uncovers. It is not just that his townspeople are participating in unholy rituals; it is particularly unsettling to Brown that they appeared so normal and Christian in every way before. In this way, the duplicity of the characters in "Young Goodman Brown" conveys the overall duplicity found in human beings that eventually destroys Goodman Brown's faith in humanity.

Mya announces a strong thesis statement in her first paragraph.

The character who most obviously possesses a duplicitous nature is the man who walks with Brown through the woods. He isn't described in concrete detail, besides that he bears "a considerable resemblance to [Goodman Brown], though perhaps more in expression than features" (Hawthorne 2), meaning that this man begins as a character that Brown himself identifies with in some way. But, in the same paragraph some inklings of a deeper, duplicitous nature begin to come to light: the man's staff has "the likeness of a great black snake, so curiously wrought that it might almost be seen to twist and wriggle itself like a living serpent" (Hawthorne 2). The staff *should* be an inanimate object but instead seems to move like a living thing. Brown, who at the beginning of the story still has faith in the goodness of his fellow neighbors, quickly rationalizes the duality present in the staff: "This, of course, must have been an ocular deception, assisted by the uncertain light," Brown tells himself to ease his confusion (Hawthorne 2).

Mya uses this topic sentence to introduce an important character who illustrates her point.

Nunnally 2

While Brown and the man walk through the woods, they speak about Brown's ancestors, and it's clear that Brown is trying to reassure himself of their goodness. Presenting his knowledge of the moral quality of his family, Brown says his ancestors have "been a race of honest men and good Christians since the days of the martyrs" (Hawthorne 3). But, the old man offers a sobering alternative to Brown's romanticized notion of those who came before him: "I helped your grandfather, the constable, when he lashed the Quaker woman so smartly through the streets of Salem; and it was I that brought your father a pitch-pine knot, kindled at my own hearth, to set fire to an Indian village, in King Philip's war" (Hawthorne 3). Not only does this further break down Goodman Brown's positive view of those he trusted and admired, but it also lends a supernatural quality to the older unnamed man. How could this traveler have known and assisted Brown's grandfather, if the traveler himself is only "about fifty years old" (Hawthorne 2) and therefore only old enough to be the age of Brown's father? Perhaps he isn't a mortal man at all. This, coupled with the man's serpentine staff, makes obvious connections between the traveler and the devil.

Mya uses this topic sentence to build upon what she wrote in her last paragraph and introduce a new one.

When Brown and his companion encounter Brown's old catechism teacher, Goody Cloyse, in the woods, Brown realizes just how little he knows about the members of his community. Despite the fact that Goody Cloyse was responsible for teaching Brown early religious education, she seems to be familiar and even friendly with Brown's companion (the devil). She also speaks of a recipe she is working on that involves witchcraft, one of "the juice of smallage, and cinquefoil, and wolf's bane" (Hawthorne 5). Brown can only look on in distress and confusion and dumbly remark that "that old woman taught me my catechism" (Hawthorne 5). As the narrator remarks, "there was a world of meaning in this simple comment" (Hawthorne 5). Here is yet another revelation that someone Brown thought he knew and trusted is instead involved with nefarious people and practices. This realization is so startling for Brown that he refuses to walk with the devilish traveler any longer and takes a moment to rest.

Mya introduces another character whose behavior supports her thesis statement.

In every paragraph, Mya cites textual evidence to support her claims.

Nunnally 3

However, he soon notices that the town minister and deacon are also in the forest, riding horses toward an unknown destination. They too speak about "deviltry" and become yet another example of corrupted members of the town (Hawthorne 7). Distraught after finding his wife's ribbon, Goodman Brown cries "My Faith is gone! [. . .] There is no good on earth; and sin is but a name. Come, devil; for to thee is this world given" (Hawthorne 8). Not only is Brown yelling for his wife Faith in hopes that she has not been hurt or corrupted by the evil members of Salem, he laments for his own moral faith that is crumbling under the weight of such realizations.

When Brown later reaches the congregation of devil worshippers, the final straw that removes all hope from him is seeing the other member to be inducted into the evil ritual—his wife. Though Brown urges Faith to "look up to heaven, and resist the wicked one" (Hawthorne 12), he never truly finds out what path Faith chooses. It doesn't matter for Brown, however—by then his hope in goodness has been eradicated. When Faith "[burst] into such joy at sight of him" (Hawthorne 12) the next morning, Goodman Brown cannot reciprocate his love. Instead he "looked sternly and sadly into her face, and passed on without a greeting" (Hawthorne 12). From that moment on, Brown loses both Faith his wife and faith in human goodness, forcing him to live as a jaded cynic for the rest of his days, so much so that even "his dying hour was gloom" (Hawthorne 13).

Mya carefully integrates Hawthorne's direct quotes into her own prose.

Nathaniel Hawthorne's "Young Goodman Brown" illustrates that all humans are capable of deception. As shown in the story, it isn't just the disturbing nature of the devil worship that affects Brown so completely. It is also the fact that the sinners in question were people he had trusted, believed he knew, and even admired or loved. Where he once had a grand idea of his father and grandfather's accomplished lives, he now can only see them as cruel individuals. Where he once saw a perfect wife, he is now disturbed by the idea that even she could turn toward the devil at any moment. Faced with the reality that human beings can in fact have a duplicitous nature, Brown cannot live a happy life.

Nunnally 4

How could he, knowing that everyone in his life could be deceiving him, and only masquerading as virtuous? Instead of having faith that some people are good and can resist sin, Brown cannot cope with the idea that even those he thought were good have the capacity for wickedness. Much like the Genesis tale of the fruit from the Tree of Knowledge which forever damned Adam and Eve, Hawthorne's story suggests that sometimes, gaining knowledge is a curse.

Mya ends with a strong conclusion that does not merely summarize but points to what's at stake in her paper, and its larger implications.

Works Cited

Hawthorne, Nathaniel. "Young Goodman Brown." *40 Short Stories*, edited by Beverly Lawn and Joanne Diaz, 6th edition, Bedford/St. Martin's, 2021, pp. 1–13.

Biographical Notes on the Authors

[Arranged Alphabetically]

CHIMAMANDA NGOZI ADICHIE [b. 1977]

Adichie was born in 1977 in Enegu, Nigeria, the fifth of six children. After high school, guided by her father, a university professor, she registered to study medicine at the University of Nigeria. At nineteen, she moved to the United States to continue her education. After studying at Drexel University in Philadelphia, she transferred to Eastern Connecticut State University and graduated in 2001 as a communications and political studies major, *summa cum laude*. By now her plans had crystallized: in 2003 she completed a master's degree in creative writing at Johns Hopkins University and in 2008 a master's in African Studies from Yale University, bringing together her love of writing and her understanding of African cultures in the manner of the famous writer Chinua Achebe, a major influence. Adichie, recognized as an outstanding writer, is the author of the novels *Purple Hibiscus* (2003), *Half of a Yellow Sun* (2006), and *Americanah* (2013), and the highly praised short-story collection *The Thing around Your Neck* (2009). She is also the author of two nonfiction books: *We Should All Be Feminists* (2014) and *Dear Ijeawele, or a Feminist Manifesto in Fifteen Suggestions* (2017).

Among Adichie's many honors include selection to *The New Yorker*'s 2010 Fiction Issue, "20 Under 40." Her short story "Ceiling" was selected in *The Best American Short Stories* (2011). *The New York Times* identified *Americanah* as one of their Ten Best Books of the Year in 2013, the same year Adichie won the National Book Critics Circle Award for Fiction. She is also the recipient of a MacArthur "genius" grant.

MARGARET ATWOOD [b. 1939]

Born in the city of Ottawa, Ontario, Canada, Atwood studied at the University of Toronto, Radcliffe College, and Harvard University. A dominant figure in Canadian literature and winner of many prizes and recipient of many honorary degrees, she is widely known for her concern for the survival of vitality and humane values in a dangerous and exploitive world. Unusually versatile, she has written much poetry and prose nonfiction, as well as numerous novels and short-story collections. Her varied subjects have always related to deep moral concerns. In the early novel *The Handmaid's Tale* (1985) and continuing in works such as *Oryx and Crake* (2003) and *Madd/Addam* (2013), she employs a feminist vision with techniques of science fiction, or what she and literary critics have termed "speculative fiction" and "social science fiction." Other well-known novels by this very prolific writer are *The Edible Woman* (1969), *Surfacing* (1972), and *Cat's Eye* (1988); her recent novels are *Hag-Seed* (2016) and *The Testaments* (2019), which was awarded the prestigious Booker Prize. Familiar volumes of poetry by Atwood include *The Circle Game* (1964), *The Animals in That Country* (1968), *Procedures for Underground* (1970), *Two-Headed Poems* (1978), *Love Song of a Terminator* (1983), *Interlunar* (1984), and two volumes of *Selected Poems* (1976, 1988). Her most recent story collections are *The Tent* (2006), *Moral Disorder* (2006), and *Stone Mattress* (2014).

RAMONA AUSUBEL [b. 1979]

Ramona Ausubel graduated from the MFA program at the University of California, Irvine. While there, she won the Glenn Schaeffer Award in Fiction. Ausubel is the author of two novels: *Sons and Daughters of Ease and Plenty* (2016), which was a San Francisco Chronicle and NPR Best Book of the Year and a *People* magazine Book of the Week, as well as *No One is Here Except All of Us* (2012). Her debut story collection, *A Guide to Being Born*, was published in 2013 and was a *New York Times* Notable Book. Her latest collection of short stories, *Awayland*, was released in 2018. Winner of the PEN Center USA Literary Award for Fiction and the VCU Cabell First Novelist Award, Ausubel has also been a finalist for the New York Public Library Young Lions Fiction Award, and long-listed for the Story Prize, Frank O'Connor International Story Award, and the International Impac Dublin Literary Award. Her work has appeared in *The New Yorker*, *Tin House*, *The New York Times*, *NPR's Selected Shorts*, *One Story*, *Electric Literature*, *Ploughshares*, *The Oxford American*, and collected in *The Best American Fantasy* and online in *The Paris Review*. Currently, Ausubel is a professor of the Low-Residency MFA program at the Institute of American Indian Arts and a visiting professor at Colorado College.

JAMES BALDWIN [1924–1987]

Born in New York City, the son of a revivalist minister, Baldwin was raised in Harlem, where, at fourteen, he became a preacher in the Fireside Pentecostal Church. After graduating from high school, he decided to become a writer, and with the help of the African American expatriate writer Richard Wright, Baldwin won a grant that enabled him to move to Paris, where he lived for most of his remaining years. There he wrote the critically acclaimed *Go Tell It on the Mountain* (1953), a novel about the religious awakening of a fourteen-year-old boy. Subsequent works focusing on the intellectual and spiritual trials of black men in a white racist society include the novels *Giovanni's Room* (1956), *Another Country* (1962)—both famous at the time for their homosexual themes—*Tell Me How Long the Train's Been Gone* (1968), and *Harlem Quartet* (1987); the play *Blues for Mister Charlie* (1964); and the powerful nonfiction commentaries *Notes of a Native Son* (1955), *Nobody Knows My Name* (1961), and *The Fire Next Time* (1963). Baldwin's stories are collected in *Going to Meet the Man* (1965).

TONI CADE BAMBARA [1939–1995]

Born in New York City and raised in Harlem, Bambara began writing as a child and continued writing through her bachelor's degree at Queens College and her master's degree at City College. After the publication of her story collection *Gorilla, My Love* (1972), she felt her sense of herself as an African American writer clarify and deepen. She focused on the experiences of black Americans and employed their dialects to express them authentically. Her employment as a social worker, a recreation director, a film writer and producer, and a college English teacher, as well as her active civil rights work in the 1960s and 1970s, contributed to the reality and power of her characterizations. A second story collection, *The Sea Birds Are Still Alive* (1977); a novel, *The Salt Eaters* (1981), which won an American Book Award; two anthologies she edited; and scripts for film and television are among her major work. *Deep Sightings and Rescue Missions* was published posthumously in 1996.

AMBROSE BIERCE [1842–1914?]

Ambrose Bierce was born in Meigs County, Ohio. He enlisted to fight in the U.S. Civil War, and afterward he found work as an editor, journalist, and short story writer. In his poems, short stories, and newspaper articles, he relayed his war experience in great detail, offering a visceral insight into one of America's most pivotal historical moments. His viewpoint was often satirical, even sardonic, which earned him the nickname "Bitter Bierce." In 1913, Bierce traveled to Mexico, inspired by the Pancho Villa–led revolution. He disappeared sometime in 1914, while he was rumored to be traveling with rebel troops.

RAYMOND CARVER [1938–1988]

Born in Clatskanie, Oregon, Carver lived in Port Angeles, Washington, until his death from lung cancer. Among the many honors accorded this story writer and poet during his lifetime were a 1979 Guggenheim Fellowship, two grants from the National Endowment for the Arts, and election to the American Academy of Arts and Letters. Carver's writing, known for its spare, stark depiction of contemporary existence, has been translated into more than twenty languages. Carver's fame as the forerunner of literary minimalism, a style that seeks to empower a text by paring it down to its bare essentials, has been undermined by a 1980 letter from Carver to his editor, Gordon Lish, to stop publication of *What We Talk About When We Talk About Love* (1981). Lish refused and later claimed that his own radical editing was responsible for Carver's pared-down style from 1981 onward. Carver's other story collections are *Will You Please Be Quiet, Please?* (1976), nominated for a National Book Award; *Furious Seasons* (1977); *Cathedral* (1983), nominated for a Pulitzer Prize; and *Where I'm Calling From* (1988).

JOHN CHEEVER [1912–1982]

John Cheever was born May 27, 1912, in Quincy, Massachusetts. Many of his pieces on life in suburban American appeared in *The New Yorker*, and it is those very pieces that propelled Cheever into literary conversation. Sometimes called the "Chekhov of the suburbs," many of Cheever's works are rooted in a yearning for a vanishing way of life, such as the vanishing sense of community in modern suburban communities. He was known best for his short stories— *The Stories of John Cheever* earned him a Pulitzer Prize in 1978—but he was also quite the accomplished novelist, penning *The Wapshot Chronicle* (1957), *The Wapshot Scandal* (1964), and *Falconer* (1977).

ANTON CHEKHOV [1860–1904]

Born the son of a grocer and grandson of a serf in Taganrog, a seacoast town in southern Russia, Chekhov wrote humorous tales to support himself while studying medicine at Moscow University. In 1884, he received his medical degree and published his first collection of short stories, *Tales of Melpomene*. Besides being a highly respected writer of short stories, Chekhov is probably Russia's leading playwright. The Moscow Art Theatre produced his most famous plays in series: *The Seagull* (1898), *Uncle Vanya* (1899), *The Three Sisters* (1901), and *The Cherry Orchard* (1904). Chekhov, known for his sad and subtle explorations of people's inability to communicate and for his humanitarian activities, died at age forty-four of tuberculosis, which he had contracted in his student days.

TED CHIANG [b. 1967]

Ted Chiang graduated from Brown University with a degree in computer science. Though his fiction is frequently categorized as science fiction, it has a wide appeal and his work has been honored with numerous awards, including the Hugo Award, the Nebula Award, and the World Fantasy Award. His novella "The Story of Your Life" (1998) was adapted into the film *Arrival* in 2016.

KATE CHOPIN [1851–1904]

Katherine O'Flaherty was the daughter of a French Creole mother and a prosperous St. Louis businessman who died when she was four. Raised by her mother and a great-grandmother, she was sent to Catholic school and trained for a place in St. Louis society. At age eighteen, she married Oscar Chopin and moved with him to New Orleans, where he became a cotton broker. When his business failed, the family moved to a plantation in northern Louisiana and opened a general store, which she managed for a year after her husband's death in 1883. She then returned to St. Louis with her six children and began writing realistic fiction. Among her works are the story collections *Bayou Folk* (1894) and *A Night in Arcadie* (1897), and the novel *The Awakening* (1899), shocking at the time for its frank portrayal of adultery, but widely praised today for its sensitive portrayal of a woman's need for independence and sensual fulfillment.

SANDRA CISNEROS [b. 1954]

Born in a Hispanic neighborhood in Chicago, Cisneros spoke Spanish at home with her Mexican father, Chicana mother, and six brothers. At ten, she began writing poetry and soon experimented with other literary forms. In 1977, when she was studying for an MFA at the University of Iowa Writers' Workshop, she came to see herself as a Chicana writer. Cisneros has published three books of poetry; a book of interrelated autobiographical narratives, *The House on Mango Street* (1983, 2005), which won the 1985 Before Columbus American Book Award; a short-fiction collection, *Woman Hollering Creek and Other Stories* (1991); and a novel, *Caramelo* (2002). Among her many other awards are two National Endowment for the Arts Fellowships for fiction and poetry, a Lannan Foundation Literary Award, a

Texas Medal of the Arts, and a John D. and Catherine T. MacArthur Fellowship. To actively encourage and promote young writers, Cisneros founded the Macondo Foundation, which celebrated its twentieth year in 2016.

Following in the style of *The House on Mango Street, A House of My Own: Stories from My Life* (2015) continues to unfold her background in a narrative that includes poems, essays, and stories worked into very short chapters.

RALPH ELLISON [1914–1994]

Born in Oklahoma City, Ellison was three when his father, an ice and coal deliverer, died. His mother worked as a domestic to support herself and her son. After studying music at Tuskegee Institute, Ellison headed for New York City, where, encouraged by the novelist Richard Wright, Ellison joined the Federal Writers' Project. His first novel, *Invisible Man* (1952), received a National Book Award and became a classic in American fiction. Other works include two collections of essays, *Shadow and Act* (1964) and *Going to the Territory* (1986), and three posthumous works prepared by John F. Callahan, literary executor of the Ellison family estate: *The Collected Essays of Ralph Ellison* (1995), *Flying Home and Other Stories* (1996), and *Juneteenth* (1999), a novel shaped and edited by Callahan from manuscripts left unfinished when Ellison died.

LOUISE ERDRICH [b. 1954]

Born to a Chippewa Indian mother and a German American father, Louise Erdrich is well-known for her exploration of Native American themes in her works. Erdrich often visits the North Dakota lands, the meeting place of her ancestors, and she's published three critically acclaimed collections of poetry: *Jacklight* (1984), *Baptism of Desire* (1989), and *Original Fire: New and Selected Poems* (2003). Although Erdrich has had success in writing poetry, she is best known as a novelist, having published seven novels that tell the story of three families living in and around a reservation in the fictional town of Argus, North Dakota. Her multi-voiced and nonchronological storytelling have earned her comparisons to William Faulkner, and her exploration of Native American experiences is like no author's exploration before her. Her most recent work is *The Night Watchman* (2020).

WILLIAM FAULKNER [1897–1962]

Born in New Albany, Mississippi, Faulkner moved as a young boy to Oxford, Mississippi, the town he called home for the rest of his life. He completed two years of high school and a little more than one year at the University of Mississippi. After a brief stint in the Royal Air Force in Canada in World War I, Faulkner worked at various jobs before he became a writer. His first book, *The Marble Faun* (1924), was a poetry collection. Encouraged by the writer Sherwood Anderson, Faulkner wrote his first novel, *Soldier's Pay* (1926); it was favorably reviewed. His third novel, *Sartoris* (1929), was his first set in Yoknapatawpha County, a fictional re-creation of the area around Oxford that appeared throughout his later fiction. In over thirty years, he published nineteen novels, more than forty short stories, collections of poems and essays, and several film scripts. Collections of his short stories include *Go Down, Moses* (1942); *Collected Stories* (1950), which won a National Book Award; and *Big Woods* (1955). Among his best-known novels are *The Sound and the Fury* (1929), *As I Lay Dying* (1930), *Sanctuary* (1931), *Light in August* (1932), and *Absalom! Absalom!* (1936). Faulkner was awarded the Nobel Prize in Literature in 1949. *A Fable* (1954) and *The Reivers* (1962) both won Pulitzer Prizes for fiction.

GABRIEL GARCÍA MÁRQUEZ [1928–2014]

García Márquez was born in the small village of Aracataca, Colombia, one of twelve children in a poor family. He was a good student and attended the University of Bogotá, where he gave up the study of law to become a writer, initially working as a journalist and film critic for *El Espectador,* a Colombian newspaper. A political activist, he moved to Mexico in 1954, to Barcelona, Spain, in 1973, and back to Mexico in the late 1970s. His first novel, *La hojarasca* (1955; tr. *Leaf Storm,* 1972), was followed by *One Hundred Years of Solitude* (1967), his most famous novel. Well-known and more recent novels are *Love in the Time of Cholera* (1985), *The General in His Labyrinth* (1989), *Love and Other Demons* (1994), and *Memories of My Melancholy Whores* (2004). He also published many short stories and several story collections. When García Márquez was awarded the Nobel Prize for Literature in 1982, the selection committee praised him for fiction "in which the fantastic and the realistic are richly combined in a world of imagination, reflecting a continent's life and conflicts." A book of memoirs, *Living to Tell the Tale,* was published in 2003; he also wrote seven books of nonfiction and three screenplays. Late in his life he was afflicted by dementia that curtailed his writing. He died of pneumonia at the age of eighty-seven in Mexico City.

CHARLOTTE PERKINS GILMAN [1860–1935]

Shortly after her birth in Hartford, Connecticut, Gilman's father left the family and gave only small support thereafter. Gilman studied at the Rhode Island School of Design and worked briefly as a commercial artist and teacher. This grandniece of Harriet Beecher Stowe became concerned quite early with issues of social inequality and the circumscribed role of women. In 1888, following the birth of a child and a period of severe depression, Gilman left her husband of four years and moved to California. After a divorce, she married George Gilman; the couple lived together for thirty-five years. In 1935, afflicted by cancer, she took her own life. Gilman wrote many influential books and articles about social problems, including *Women and Economics* (1898). From 1909 to 1917, she published her own journal. *The Yellow Wallpaper,* written about 1890, draws on her experience with paternalism, repression, and mental illness and is highly praised for its insight and boldness.

LAUREN GROFF [b. 1978]

A native of Cooperstown, New York, with a BA from Amherst College and an MFA in fiction from the University of Wisconsin-Madison, Groff has written three novels and two short story collections: *Delicate Edible Birds* (2009) and *Florida* (2018). Many of her stories have appeared in respected anthologies and in eight journals, including *The Atlantic Monthly, Ploughshares,* and *The New Yorker.* Among many honors, her first novel, *The Monsters of Templeton* (2008), was named by Amazon.com and *The San Francisco Chronicle* as one of the Best Books of 2008. Groff's second novel, *Arcadia* (2012), received many positive reviews and was named by *The New York Times, The Washington Post, NPR, Vogue, The Globe and Mail, Christian Science Monitor,* and *Kirkus Reviews* as one of the Best Books of 2012. Her third novel, *Fates and Furies* (2015), was nominated for the 2015 National Book Award in Fiction. In 2018, she was awarded a Guggenheim Fellowship. Groff is interested in imaginative exploration of history. In *The Monsters of Templeton,* for example, she combines elements of historical Cooperstown, which James Fenimore Cooper named Templeton in his novel *The Pioneers,* with voices of historical personalities to construct a creative blend of history and contemporary life.

MERON HADERO

Meron Hadero is an Ethiopian American writer of short stories and creative nonfiction. Born in Addis Ababa, she came to the United States in her childhood. Her short stories appear in several journals including *Best American Short Stories, Selected Shorts on NPR/PRI, McSweeney's Quarterly Concern, Zyzzyva, The Iowa Review,* and *The Missouri Review,* as well as *The New York Times Book Review,* and the anthology *The Displaced: Refugee Writers on Refugee Lives* (2018). Hadero's work has been supported by the International Institute at the University of Michigan, the Elizabeth George

Foundation, and Artist Trust. She has received an NEA award through MacDowell, and has also held fellowships at the World Affairs Council, Yaddo, and Ragdale. In 2018, she appeared in *San Francisco Magazine*'s feature "Making Waves: 100 Artists Putting the East Bay on the Map." She is a member of the San Francisco Writers Grotto and was selected as a 2019–20 Steinbeck Fellow. Also, in 2019, she was shortlisted for the Caine Prize for her story "The Wall" in *McSweeney's Quarterly Concern*.

NATHANIEL HAWTHORNE [1804–1864]

Born in Salem, Massachusetts, to a family descended from the original New England Puritans, Hawthorne graduated from Bowdoin College and spent twelve years reading, reflecting, and observing the New England landscape and people, and writing *Fanshawe* (published anonymously, 1828) and the first series of *Twice-Told Tales* (1837). The second series, published in 1842, was reviewed by Edgar Allan Poe. To support himself, Hawthorne took a job at the Boston customhouse but resigned in 1841 to live at Brook Farm, a utopian community founded by New England Transcendentalists to enable artists to live cooperatively and create freely. The following year, he resigned from Brook Farm and moved with his wife to Concord, Massachusetts, where his neighbors included Ralph Waldo Emerson and Henry David Thoreau. There he wrote the stories collected in *Mosses from an Old Manse* (1846). Returning to Salem, he took a position as a customs inspector and began intensive work on his most celebrated novel, *The Scarlet Letter* (1850), and developed a deep artistic friendship with Herman Melville, who was composing *Moby-Dick* (1852). The novels *The House of the Seven Gables* (1851) and *The Blithedale Romance* (1852), based on his Brook Farm experience, quickly followed. Also, in 1852, he wrote a presidential campaign biography for Franklin Pierce, a former college friend, who, upon his victory, named Hawthorne U.S. consul at Liverpool. Subsequent travels in Europe contributed to *The Marble Faun* (1860), his final major work. Considered a master of American fiction, Hawthorne helped establish the short story as a significant literary form.

ERNEST HEMINGWAY [1899–1961]

Born in Oak Park, Illinois, Hemingway had an active, vigorous childhood, summering in the northern wilds of Michigan with his physician father and playing football and boxing at school. His first job was as a reporter for the *Kansas City Star*. During World War I, he served as an ambulance driver in Italy; he was seriously wounded when he was eighteen and was decorated by the Italian government. Later, while working in Paris for the *Toronto Star*, he became friendly with Gertrude Stein, Ezra Pound, F. Scott Fitzgerald, and other writers and artists who influenced his work. Hemingway's first two books, *Three Stories and Ten Poems* (1923) and *In Our Time* (1924), were followed by a masterpiece about expatriate life during the Spanish Civil War, *The Sun Also Rises* (1925), which made him spokesman for the "Lost Generation." *A Farewell to Arms* (1929) and *For Whom the Bell Tolls* (1930) firmly established his reputation. In World War II, he served as a correspondent and received a Bronze Star. His frequent travels took him to Spain for bullfights, on fishing trips to the Caribbean, and on big-game expeditions to the American West and Africa. In his later years, he suffered from declining physical health and severe depression, which eventually led to his suicide. Among other important fiction and nonfiction works are *Death in the Afternoon* (1932) and *The Green Hills of Africa* (1935); the Pulitzer Prize–winning novel *Old Man and the Sea* (1952), after which he received the 1954 Nobel Prize in Literature; *A Moveable Feast* (1964); and *Islands in the Stream* (1970). The fullest collection of his short stories (the *Finca Vigia* edition) was published in 1991.

SHIRLEY JACKSON [1916–1965]

Born in San Francisco and raised in Burlingame, California, and Rochester, New York, Jackson was educated at the University of Rochester and Syracuse University. At Syracuse she worked on the campus newspaper, met the author and critic Stanley Edgar Hyman, and founded and edited the campus literary magazine. After graduation she married Hyman, and they moved to Vermont, where they raised four children while Hyman taught at Bennington College. Jackson's experiences as wife and mother are recorded in two memoirs: *Life Among the Savages* (1953) and *Raising Demons* (1957). Jackson is best known for stories of gothic horror and the occult. The story that launched her career as a major writer was "The Lottery" (1948), published in *The New Yorker*. This story and her novel *The Haunting of Hill House* (1959) attracted wide audiences and raised controversy with critics and the public alike. Other fiction by Jackson includes *The Road Through the Wall* (1948); *Hangsaman* (1951); *The Sundial* (1958); and the posthumously published *Come Along with Me* (1968) and *Just an Ordinary Day: The Uncollected Stories of Shirley Jackson* (1997). Writing in the tradition of Hawthorne and Poe, Jackson is often cited as a major influence on writers such as Stephen King.

JAMES JOYCE [1882–1941]

Joyce was born in Dublin, Ireland, and educated in Jesuit schools in preparation for the priesthood. He abandoned Catholicism when still young and in 1904 left Dublin for what he felt would be the broader horizons of continental Europe. Over the next twenty-five years, he lived in Paris, Zurich, and Trieste, supporting his family by teaching languages and singing. In 1912, he returned to Dublin briefly, to arrange for publication of his short stories. Because of the printer's fear of censorship and libel suits, the edition was burned, and *Dubliners* did not appear in England until 1914. During World War I, Joyce lived in Zurich, where he wrote *Portrait of the Artist as a Young Man* (1916), a partly autobiographical account of his adolescence that introduced some of the experimental techniques found in his later novels. About this time Joyce developed glaucoma and for the rest of his life suffered periods of intense pain and near blindness. His masterpiece, the novel *Ulysses* (1922), known for its stream-of-consciousness style, was written and published in periodicals between 1914 and 1921. Book publication was delayed because of obscenity charges. *Ulysses* was finally issued by Shakespeare & Company, a Paris bookstore owned and operated by Sylvia Beach, an American expatriate; publication in the United States was banned until 1933. *Finnegans Wake* (1939), an equally experimental novel, took seventeen years to write. Because of the controversy surrounding his work, Joyce earned little in royalties and often relied on friends for support. He died in Zurich after surgery for a perforated ulcer.

FRANZ KAFKA [1883–1924]

Born in Prague, Bohemia (present-day Czech Republic, then part of Austria-Hungary), the son of middle-class German-Jewish parents, Kafka studied law at the German University of Prague. After completing his degree in 1906, he was employed by the workmen's compensation division of the Austrian government. Although he liked to write, he could not earn a living doing so because he wrote very slowly. By the time of his death, he had published little and asked his friend Max Brod to burn the incomplete manuscripts when he did die. Fortunately, Brod ignored the request and arranged posthumous publication of the major long works: *The Trial* (1925), *The Castle* (1926), and *Amerika* (1927), as well as many of his stories. Important stories published while he was living include "The Judgment" (1913), "The Metamorphosis" (1915), and "A Hunger Artist" (1924). Kafka's fiction is known for its gripping portrayals of individual helplessness before political, judicial, and paternal authority and power.

JAMAICA KINCAID [b. 1949]

Born Elaine Potter Richardson in St. John's, the capital of Antigua, British West Indies, Kincaid moved to New York to study photography. She entered college but withdrew to write. Her stories began to appear in notable publications, and she was offered, and took, a staff writer position at *The New Yorker*. Her first book, a story collection entitled *At the Bottom of the River* (1984), won a major award from the American Academy and Institute of Arts and Letters. In 1985, her book *Annie John*, a collection of interrelated stories about a girl growing up in the West Indies, also won wide critical notice. Throughout her career, Kincaid has used her experience of Antigua extensively but carefully, writing under her pen name to protect the privacy of her family and acquaintances. She continues to write about the people and landscape of Antigua in novels such as *Autobiography of My Mother* (1996) and *Jupiter* (2004). She is also the author of three nonfiction books: *My Brother* (1997), *My Garden Book* (2001); and *Among Flowers: A Walk in the Himalaya* (2005). Kincaid's most recent novel is *See Now Then* (2013).

KATHERINE MANSFIELD [1888–1923]

She was born Kathleen Mansfield Beauchamp in Wellington, New Zealand. When she was fifteen, she persuaded her banker and industrialist father to send her to London to study the cello. After a brief visit to New Zealand, she returned to London with a larger allowance and decided, after meeting D. H. Lawrence and Virginia Woolf, that writing, not music, was to be her career. Her first book of stories, *In a German Pension* (1911), was published the same year she met John Middleton Murray, whom she married seven years later. The story collections *Bliss and Other Stories* (1920) and *The Garden-Party* (1922) established her as a writer of importance. In 1918, she came down with tuberculosis and found regular writing difficult. She sought treatment at the Gurdjieff Institute in France but died two months later. At her death, she was just thirty-four, author of eighty-eight finished and fifteen unfinished stories, and, with James Joyce and her model Anton Chekhov, considered a major architect of the modern short story.

JOYCE CAROL OATES [b. 1938]

Born in Lockport, New York, Oates is a graduate of Syracuse University and the University of Wisconsin. Astoundingly prolific, she is the author of numerous novels, books of poetry, and collections of short stories, many of which deal with destructive forces and sudden violence. She is also a literary theorist. Among her early novels is a trilogy partly inspired by a famous Hieronymus Bosch triptych painting: *A Garden of Earthly Delights* (1967), *them* (1969), and *Expensive People* (1972). Later novels that received much attention are *We Were the Mulvaneys* (1996), *Blonde* (2000), *The Tattooed Girl* (2003), and *The Gravedigger's Daughter* (2007). Among her story collections are *The Female of the Species: Tales of Mystery and Suspense* (2006) and *The Museum of Dr. Moses* (2007). Oates is a three-time recipient of the Pulitzer Prize and a winner of the National Book Award and of a PEN/Malamud Award for Excellence in Short Fiction. She is the Roger S. Berland '52 Professor of the Humanities with the Program in Creative Writing at Princeton University. Since 2007, Joyce Carol Oates has written twelve story collections, most recently *Night Gaunts and Other Tales of Suspense* (2018), and twelve novels, most recently *My Life as a Rat* (2019).

TIM O'BRIEN [b. 1946]

Born in Austin, Minnesota, O'Brien studied at Macalester College, where he earned a BA in political science, *summa cum laude*, in 1968. He went on to study government at the graduate level at Harvard University. He then worked as a journalist for the *Washington Post* until he was drafted into the army during the Vietnam War, promoted to the rank of sergeant, and awarded a Purple Heart for wounds suffered at My Lai one year after the massacre. Much of his fiction deals with his experiences during the war, and his style of writing is often compared to the "magic realism" of Gabriel García Márquez. His novels include *Northern Lights* (1975); *Going after Cacciato* (1978), which won the National Book Award; *The Things They Carried* (1990); *In the Lake of the Woods* (1994); *Tom Cat in Love* (1998); and *July, July* (2002).

FLANNERY O'CONNOR [1925–1964]

Born in Savannah, Georgia, and raised on a farm in Milledgeville, Georgia, O'Connor graduated from Georgia State College for Women in 1945 and attended the University of Iowa Writers' Workshop, from which she received a master's degree in 1947. From Iowa she moved to New York City to begin her writing career but, after little more than two years, was forced by illness to return to her mother's Georgia farm. Confined as an invalid by the degenerative disease lupus, O'Connor spent her remaining fourteen years raising peacocks and writing fiction set in rural Georgia. Her works are distinguished by irreverent humor, often grotesque characters, and intense, often mystical affirmation of the passions of religious faith. Her work includes two novels, *Wise Blood* (1952) and *The Violent Bear It Away* (1960); and two short-story collections, *A Good Man Is Hard to Find* (1955) and *Everything*

That Rises Must Converge (1965). After her death at thirty-nine, a selection of occasional prose, *Mystery and Manners* (1969), was edited by her friends Sally and Robert Fitzgerald, and a collection of letters, *The Habit of Being* (1979), was edited by Sally Fitzgerald. O'Connor's *The Complete Stories* (1971) received the National Book Award.

TILLIE OLSEN [1913–2007]

Tillie Olsen was born Tillie Lerner in Omaha, Nebraska, in 1912 or 1913; the author wasn't sure which was her birth date because her birth was unrecorded. The daughter of refugees from Tsarist Russia after the Revolution of 1905, she grew up in a poor, hardworking family. Her father worked as a farmer, a housepainter, and a packer; her mother in a factory; and she at odd jobs as a sixteen-year-old high school dropout during the Depression. She started her first novel, *Yonnondio: From the Thirties* (1974), when she was nineteen, and completed four chapters in four years; at the same time, she married, had a child, and was left by her first husband. Throughout her life, Olsen was an activist for several social causes, including pro-union organizing, antiwar movements, and women's rights. An influential feminist writer, Olsen's work is recognized for its attention to women and lower socioeconomic classes. Her writings include the short-story collection *Tell Me a Riddle* (1961) and the nonfiction book *Silences* (1978).

GRACE OLUSEYI [b. 1983]

Grace Oluseyi is an emerging Nigerian writer best known for her debut short story "A Modern Marriage." Oluseyi is a writer and a book history scholar who divides her time in work and study between London, New York, and the Middle East. "A Modern Marriage" was published in the March/April 2016 issue of *Boston Review*. This story won the 2017 PEN/Robert J. Dau Short Story Prize for Emerging Writers.

ZZ PACKER [b. 1973]

ZZ Packer has earned degrees from Yale University, Johns Hopkins University, and the Iowa Writers Workshop. She is the author of *Drinking Coffee Elsewhere* (2003), which was a *New York Times* Notable Book. She is the recipient of a Guggenheim Fellowship and a Whiting Award, and her work has appeared in the *Best American Short Stories* series. She teaches in the creative writing program at San Francisco State University.

NEEL PATEL [b. 1982]

Neel Patel is a screenwriter and author whose short stories have appeared in *Indiana Review, The Southampton Review, Hyphen Magazine, The American Literary Review,* and on Nerve.com. His story collection *If You See Me, Don't Say Hi* was a *New York Times* Editors' Choice and an NPR Best Book of 2018. He currently resides in Los Angeles, California.

EDGAR ALLAN POE [1809–1849]

Born in Boston, Massachusetts, the son of traveling actors, Poe was abandoned at one year of age by his father; Poe's mother died soon after. The baby became the ward of John Allan of Richmond, Virginia, whose surname became Poe's middle name. When the family's wealth declined, the Allans moved to England, where Poe was educated. On their return to Richmond, Poe attended the new University of Virginia. Although he was an excellent student, Poe drank and gambled heavily, causing Allan to withdraw him from the university. Poe made his way to Boston, enlisted in the army, and, with Allan's help, took an appointment at West Point. After further dissipation ended his military career, Poe tried to support himself by writing. Three volumes of poetry—*Tamerlane and Other Poems* (1827), *Al Aaraaf, Tamerlane and Minor Poems* (1829), and *Poems* (1831)—brought little money. In 1835, Poe took a position as an assistant editor of *The Southern Literary Messenger,* the first of many positions he lost because of heavy drinking. He began to publish short stories. In 1836, he married his thirteen-year-old cousin, Virginia Clemm, and took on the support of her mother, adding to his financial difficulties. They moved to New York City, where Poe published *The Narrative of Arthur Gordon Pym* (1838) and assembled the best stories he had published in magazines in *Tales of the Grotesque and Arabesque* (1840), his first story collection. At that time, he began writing detective stories, virtually inventing the genre. Already respected as a critic, Poe became known as a poet with *The Raven and Other Poems* (1845). In 1847, after Virginia died, Poe became engaged to the poet Sarah Helen Whitman, a wealthy widow six years his senior, who resisted marriage because of his drinking problem. In 1849, he met a childhood sweetheart, Elmira Royster Shelton, now a widow, who agreed to marry him. After celebrating his apparent good fortune with friends in Baltimore, he was found unconscious on the street and died shortly afterwards. Always admired in Europe, Poe's major stories of horror and detection, major poems, and major critical pieces on the craft of writing—especially his review of Hawthorne's *Twice-Told Tales* (1842), "The Philosophy of Composition" (1846), and "The Poetic Principle" (1850)—are considered American classics.

KAREN RUSSELL [b. 1981]

After graduating from Northwestern University with a BA in Spanish in 2003, and from Columbia University with an MFA in 2006, Karen Russell rapidly became a successful novelist and short-story writer. Her work is unusually distinctive, often drawing its characters, settings, and plots from myth and gothic traditions. Her stories have appeared in *The New Yorker* and other prestigious magazines and journals and have been included in the anthologies *Best American Short Stories* and *20 Under 40*. Her first book of short stories, *St. Lucy's Home for Girls Raised by Wolves* (2007), was honored by the National Book Foundation in 2009 as the work of one of "5 Under 35" young writers and by Bard College with a fiction prize in 2011. That same year, *Swamplandia!*, her first novel, was listed by *The New York Times* as one of the "Ten Best Books of 2011." Another banner year for Russell was 2012, when she won the New York Public Library Young Lions Fiction Award and became one of three finalists for the Pulitzer Prize for Fiction. Russell's second collection of short stories, *Vampires in the Lemon Grove* (2013), whose title story is included here, was favorably reviewed and its author made a distinguished visiting professor at Rutgers University. That same year Karen Russell won a 2013 MacArthur Foundation Fellowship. Her most recent short-story collection is *Orange World* (2019).

GEORGE SAUNDERS [b. 1958]

George Saunders is an American writer born in Amarillo, Texas in 1958, and raised in Chicago. After earning a degree in exploration geophysics, Saunders worked in oil fields in Sumatra at a camp that was forty-minutes from the nearest town. After working in Sumatra for a year and a half, Saunders returned to America and worked as a doorman, a roofer, a convenience store clerk, and a slaughterhouse worker. In 1986, Saunders was accepted into the MFA program at Syracuse University. Since 1996, Saunders has worked as a professor in the MFA program at Syracuse. His writing has appeared in *The New Yorker*, *Harper's*, *McSweeney's*, and *GQ*. He also contributed a weekly column, "American Psyche," to the weekend magazine of *The Guardian* between 2006 and 2008. In 2001, Saunders was selected by *Entertainment Weekly* as one of the 100 topmost creative people in entertainment, and in 2002, *The New Yorker* named him one of the best writers 40 and under. In 2006, he was awarded both a Guggenheim Fellowship and a MacArthur Fellowship. In 2009, Saunders received an Academy Award from the American Academy of Arts and Letters.

LESLIE MARMON SILKO [b. 1948]

A Laguna Pueblo Native American, Silko was born and raised in New Mexico. Her mixed ancestral background (Laguna, Mexican, white) presented challenges. She was educated at the Bureau of Indian Affairs school in Laguna, a Catholic school in Albuquerque, and the University of New Mexico, where she received a BA in English in 1969. With teaching experience at several colleges, she was appointed professor of English at the University of Arizona at Tucson. While still in college, Silko published a short story, "The Man to Send Rain Clouds," for which she was awarded a National Endowment for the Humanities Discovery Grant. She published a book of poems, *Laguna Woman*, in 1974. Her first novel, *Ceremony* (1977), sets forth the Native American view of the individual's relationship to the tribe's shared history, with a focus on the powerful role of storytelling. Among her many honors, Silko won a National Endowment for the Arts Fellowship, a Pushcart Prize, and a MacArthur Foundation grant that made it possible for her to write full-time. Other work for which she has been highly praised includes *Storyteller* (1981), *Almanac of the Dead* (1991), *Sacred Water* (1993), *Yellow Woman + the Beauty of Spirit: Essays on Native American Literature* (1996), and *Gardens in the Dunes* (1999). She has also published many articles on literary and social topics. Her most recent book, *The Turquoise Ledge: A Memoir* (2010), is about the beauty and unity of nature as she experiences it on her meditative walks.

ADRIAN TOMINE [b. 1974]

Adrian Tomine is the child of two Japanese American physicians who spent part of their childhoods in the Japanese American Internment camps during World War II. He is the author of a number of graphic novels, including *Summer Blonde* (2002), *Shortcomings* (2007), and *Killing and Dying* (2015). He is a regular contributor to *The New Yorker.*

ALICE WALKER [b. 1944]

Born in Eatonton, Georgia, Alice Malsenior Walker was educated at Spelman College and Sarah Lawrence College, where she published her first poem. After much activity in the civil rights movement, she returned to personal writing while maintaining her political activism on behalf of many causes. In 1967, she married a white civil rights attorney, Melvyn Roseman Leventhal, and two years later had a daughter, Rebecca. In the mid-1990s, Walker was romantically involved with the singer-songwriter Tracy Chapman. Her literary reputation was initially based on her depiction of the lives of Southern blacks. Walker is a versatile writer who has produced books of different types since 1990; she has also been interested in continuity. Two of her best-known novels, *The Temple of My Familiar* (1989) and *Possessing the Secret of Joy* (1992), use characters that were introduced in *The Color Purple* (1982). Among her story collections are *In Love and Trouble: Stories of Black Women* (1973), *You Can't Keep a Good Woman Down* (1981), and *The Complete Stories* (1994); among her eight books of poems are *Once* (1968), *Revolutionary Petunias* (1973), *Good Night, Willie Lee . . .* (1979), and *Horses Make a Landscape Look More Beautiful* (1984). Her novels have also been popular with critics and the public: *The Color Purple* won an American Book Award and a Pulitzer Prize in 1983 and was made into a successful film in 1985 and a Broadway musical in 2005. Walker has also written a biography of Langston Hughes for children and edited many books about race, women, and writing. A writer of novels and short stories, poems, biographies and memoirs, travel writing, children's literature, film, and political and social commentary, Walker's work often focuses on race and womanhood.

VIRGINIA WOOLF [1882–1941]

Virginia Woolf was born into a well-connected and financially comfortable family. Woolf was educated by her parents, who tutored her in languages, literature, and mathematics, and she made frequent use of her father's enormous library. Her childhood summers were spent at a cottage in Cornwall that overlooked the Godrevy Lighthouse, which became the inspiration for *To the Lighthouse* (1927). She was a prolific author whose works include *The Voyage Out* (1915), *Mrs. Dalloway* (1925), *Orlando* (1928), and *A Room of One's Own* (1929). Woolf was a central figure in what became known as the Bloomsbury group, a coterie of artists and intellectuals that included Lytton Strachey, Dora Carrington, Clive Bell, E. M. Forster, Leonard Woolf, and John Maynard Keynes. In 1917, Woolf founded the Hogarth Press with her husband Leonard, and the couple went on to publish Woolf's work as well as works by T. S. Eliot and Vita Sackville-West. Woolf struggled with mental illness through much of her adult life and died by suicide in 1941. One cannot overstate the influence that Woolf has had on feminist theory and literary criticism, especially with her famous essay "A Room of One's Own." In addition, her technical and aesthetic innovations—especially her use of stream-of-consciousness in her writing—were an unparalleled achievement that helped to shape what is now referred to as Modernism.

Glossary of Literary Terms

Abstract language Any language that employs intangible, non-specific concepts. *Love*, *truth*, and *beauty* are abstractions. Abstract language is the opposite of concrete language. Both types have different effects and are important features of an author's style.

Allegory A narrative in which persons, objects, settings, or events represent general concepts, moral qualities, or other abstractions. Many readers find allegorical features in details of the plot, characters, and settings of Hawthorne's "Young Goodman Brown."

Allusion A subtle or obvious reference to historical or legendary people, events, or situations. In "Young Goodman Brown," for reasons central to the story, there are allusions to the devil.

Ambiguity Multiple meanings introduced to increase the complexity of a work. Ambiguity is used frequently by poets and fiction writers, but rarely by reporters and essayists (expository writers), who typically rely on directness and clarity to shape their meanings. Hawthorne keeps Goodman Brown's motivation for his forest journey ambiguous to emphasize Brown's secretive state of mind and to intensify readers' curiosity about Brown's purposes.

Antagonist A character in some fiction, whose motives and actions work against, or are thought to work against, those of the hero, or protagonist. The conflict between these characters shapes the plot of their story.

Antihero, antiheroine A leading character, male or female, without the heroic attributes and status found in classic drama. Sometimes the antihero is used for comic purposes, sometimes to point up the absence of heroism, and at other times to redefine the meaning of *hero* as an idea.

Archetype A term introduced in the 1930s by the psychologist C. G. Jung, who described archetypes as "primordial images" repeated throughout human history. Archetypes, or archetypal patterns, recur in myths, religion, dreams, fantasies, and art and are said to have power because we know them, even if unconsciously. In literature, archetypes appear in character types, plot patterns, and descriptions. Consider what archetypes may be employed in Hawthorne's "Young Goodman Brown" and Oates's "Where Are You Going, Where Have You Been?"

Characterization The development of a character or characters throughout a story. Characterization includes the narrator's description of what characters look like and what they think, say, and do (these are sometimes very dissimilar). Their own actions and views of themselves, and other characters' views of and behavior toward them, are also means of characterization. We learn from the narrator of Tim O'Brien's "The Things They Carried" that First Lieutenant Jimmy Cross is obsessed with the letters that he receives from a girl named Martha, and at first that seems like a romantic detail, but we have to read the entire story to realize what price he pays for his distraction.

Characters One of the elements of fiction, usually the people of a work of literature. Characters may also be animals or some other beings. Characters are those about whom a story is told and sometimes, too, the ones telling the story. Characters may be minor, like Goody Cloyse, or major, like Goodman Brown, in Hawthorne's "Young Goodman Brown." Depending on the depth of characterization, they may be simple or complex, flat or round.

Climax The moment of greatest intensity and conflict in the action of a story. In Hawthorne's "Young Goodman Brown," events reach their climax when the devil welcomes Goodman Brown and his wife, Faith, as his children, commanding them to turn to see his "fiend worshippers"—once respectable townspeople—welcome them too. The devil urges them to drink bloodlike fluid in "the communion of your race," and Brown cries out to his wife, "Faith! Faith! . . . look up to heaven, and resist the wicked one."

Concrete language Any specific, physical language that appeals to one or more of the senses—sight, hearing, taste, smell, or touch. *Stones*, *chairs*, and *hands* are concrete words. Concrete language is the opposite of abstract language. Both types are important features of an author's style.

Conflict Antagonism between characters, ideas, or lines of action; between one character and the outside world; or between aspects of a character's own nature. Conflict is essential in a traditional plot. Montresor and Fortunato are antagonists in conflict in Poe's "The Cask of Amontillado."

Denotation, connotation Terms describing two kinds of reference. A word or phrase's *denotation* is its definitive meaning, what a word or phrase specifically refers to. A word or phrase's *connotations* are its associations and implications. A cherry blossom is a physical flower connoting spring, renewal, and sometimes loss and impermanence, as in the Japanese cultural tradition.

Denouement The falling action of a plot, in which events are brought to a close and issues resolved. In Hawthorne's "Young Goodman Brown," the denouement is when Brown realizes that he does not know whether Faith obeyed his plea to choose heaven rather than the devil, awakens in the village among his neighbors, last night's revelers, and lives out his long life as a dispirited, embittered, isolated man, "borne to his grave a hoary corpse, followed by Faith, an aged woman." In French, the word *denouement* means "unknotting."

Description Language that presents specific features of a character, object, or setting; or the details of an action or event. Meron Hadero provides a vivid description of traffic in Addis Ababa in "The Suitcase" in order to provide the reader with a better sense of that place.

Dialogue Words spoken by characters, often in the form of conversation between two or more. In stories and other forms of prose, dialogue is commonly enclosed between quotation marks. Dialogue is an important element in characterization and plot: much of the characterization in Hemingway's "Hills Like White Elephants" is accomplished through dialogue.

Diction A writer's selection of words. Particular patterns or arrangements of words in sentences and paragraphs constitute prose style. Hemingway's diction is said to be precise, concrete, and economical. Diction also offers clues to characters' inner lives and their social and educational backgrounds. In "The Lesson," Toni Cade Bambara makes skillful use of dialect in order to develop a full portrait of Sylvia and her friends.

Elements of fiction Major elements of fiction are plot, characters, setting, point of view, style, and theme. Skillful employment of these entities is essential in effective novels and stories. From beginning to end, each element is active and relates to the others dynamically.

Empathy Identification with another's situation to experience similar emotions and physical sensations. Empathy is more complete and pervasive than sympathy, which is confined to one experience or situation and limited primarily to grief or joy. Empathy can be seen as the heart of literature, the means by which writers create their characters and stories and by which readers or viewers of plays and films absorb and re-create these characters and stories.

Epiphany In literature, a sudden illumination of the significance or true meaning of a person, place, thing, idea, or situation. Often a word, gesture, or other action reveals the significance. The term was popularized by Joyce, who explained it fully in his autobiographical novel *Stephen Hero* (written in 1914; pub. 1944), and it is demonstrated in Joyce's "Araby."

Episode In a story, an incident, seemingly complete in itself, a "little story." A short story may consist of one main episode and possibly one or two minor ones, or a story may be composed of a string of episodes and thus be episodic in structure.

Fiction Traditionally, a prose narrative whose plot, characters, and settings are constructions of its writer's imagination, which draws on his or her experiences and reflections. Short stories are comparatively short works of fiction, while novels are longer ones.

Figurative language Suggestive, rather than literal, language employing metaphor, simile, or other figures of speech. Figurative language is often employed in poetry, less often in plays and stories. Yet stories and plays often use figurative language powerfully.

First-person narrator In a story told by one person, the *I* who tells the story. Sometimes, as in Faulkner's "A Rose for Emily," the first-person narrator is an objective witness, personally present but emotionally uninvolved. More often he or she is directly or indirectly involved in the story. Montresor is the first-person narrator of, and one of two characters in, Poe's "The Cask of Amontillado." As the narrator, he reveals much about his own emotions and motivations.

Flashback A writer's way of introducing important earlier material. As a narrator tells a story, he or she may stop the flow of events and direct the reader to an earlier time. Sometimes the reader is returned to the present, sometimes kept in the past. Adichie's "Birdsong" is built on the leading character's perceptions of the past history and present circumstances of her love affair with a married man. As she drives through the city traffic, with increasing awareness of the staring woman in the jeep beside her whom she takes to be her lover's wife, the central character flashes back to significant moments in the relationship.

Folktale A short fiction narrative expressing the concerns, beliefs, and experiences of ordinary people (as opposed to scholars and thinkers). The many kinds of folktales, including animal tales, fairy tales, mythical tales, legends, and tall tales, are rooted in the oral tradition.

Foreshadowing Words, gestures, and other actions that suggest future events or outcomes. The opening of Hawthorne's "Young Goodman

Brown" foreshadows serious trouble ahead when Faith, Brown's wife, begs him to stay home with her "this night, dear husband, of all nights in the year."

Frame story A story that contains another story or stories within it. This form can be found as early as the *Arabian Nights* (ninth century B.C.E.) and was used extensively by Boccaccio and Chaucer. Adichie's "Birdsong" is a frame story about a young woman caught in traffic who reconstructs the history of her love affair. Her current perceptions of the traffic and another woman, possibly her lover's wife, who seems to be staring at her, open and close the story.

Genre A type or form of literature. The major literary genres are fiction, drama, poetry, and nonfiction (essay or book-length biography, criticism, history, and so on). Subgenres of fiction are the novel and the short story.

Hero, heroine Loosely, a leading character or protagonist of a play, dramatic or epic poem, novel, or short story. The terms originated with classical poetry and drama, however, and were used as classifications for leading characters of high stature whose destinies affected everyone. In the short story, a modern literary form, leading characters are usually ordinary; yet, when looked at closely, they may become heroic to us. Consider Robert in Raymond Carver's "Cathedral." At first, Robert's visit seems like a fairly ordinary domestic episode; however, Robert's perspective affects the narrator in profound ways.

Image A word or group of words evoking concrete visual, auditory, or tactile associations. An image, sometimes called a *word-picture*, is an important instance of figurative language. In "Young Goodman Brown," Hawthorne creates an image of the forest as a place of evil by describing Brown's path as dark and gloomy, with sudden twists and turns.

Interior monologue An extended speech or narrative, presumed to be thought rather than spoken by a character. Interior monologues are similar to, but different from, stream of consciousness, which describes mental life at the border of consciousness. Interior monologues are typically more consciously controlled and conventionally structured, however private the character's thoughts. While reviewing the background and circumstances of his murder of Fortunato, Montresor, the narrator of Poe's "The Cask of Amontillado," presents a revealing self-portrait.

Irony A way of writing or speaking that asserts the opposite of what the author, reader, and character know to be true. Verbal or rhetorical irony accomplishes these contradictory meanings by direct misstatements. Situational irony is achieved when events in a narrative turn out to be very different from, or even opposite to, what is expected. Hemingway's "Hills Like White Elephants" is a string of ironies, generated by the couple's predicament and their inability to speak about it directly. At the end of the story, the man moves her bags across the tracks to the side where they will catch the train, presumably to where the abortion will take place. He asks her if she feels better. "'I feel fine,' she said. 'There's nothing wrong with me. I feel fine.'"

Literary analysis The practice of examining a work of literature, with a particular purpose or thesis in mind, to discover how its elements (plot, character, setting, point of view, theme, style) contribute to the meaning of the whole. See "Reading Short Stories Closely" and "Writing about Short Stories," both of which are located in this book.

Magic realism A narrative technique developed by many Caribbean and Central and South American writers, including García Márquez, who interweave personal daily life and vivid, often fabulous, landscapes and histories. Writers across the globe now use magic realism. García Márquez's "A Very Old Man with Enormous Wings" is an example of magic realism.

Narrative A narrator's story of characters and events over a period of time. Usually the characters can be analyzed and generally understood; usually the events proceed in a cause-and-effect relation; and usually some unity can be found among a narrative's characters, plot, point of view, style, and theme(s). Novels as well as stories are usually narratives, and journalism commonly employs narrative form.

Narrator The storyteller, usually an observer who is narrating in the third-person point of view, or a participant in the story's action speaking in the first person. Style and tone are important clues to the nature of a narrator and the validity and objectivity of the story itself. Sometimes a narrator who takes part in the action is too emotionally involved to be trusted for objectivity or accuracy. This narrator would be called an *unreliable narrator*. For example, Montresor, narrator of "The Cask of Amontillado," creates his own self-portrait as he presents the flow of events.

Naturalism A literary movement that began in France in the late nineteenth century, spread, moderated, and influenced much twentieth-century literature. The movement, which started in reaction against the antiscientific sentimentality of the period, borrowed from the principles, aims, and methods of such scientific thinkers as Charles Darwin and Herbert Spencer. Early naturalists held that human lives are determined externally by society and internally by drives and instincts and that free will is an illusion. Writers were to proceed in a reporter-like, objective manner. In the objective style and tone of his writing, and often in the predicaments of his characters, Hemingway shows the influence of naturalism.

Novel An extended prose narrative or work of prose fiction, usually published alone. Hawthorne's *The Scarlet Letter* is a fairly short novel; Melville's *Moby-Dick, or, The White Whale* is a very long one. The length of a novel enables its author to develop his or her characters, plot, and settings in greater detail than a short-story writer can. Ellison's story "Battle Royal" is taken from his novel *Invisible Man* (1948).

Novella A work of prose fiction, between the short story and the novel in size and complexity. Sometimes the novella is called a long short story. Baldwin's "Sonny's Blues" is a novella.

Omniscient narrator A narrator who seems to know everything about a story's events and characters, even their inner feelings. Usually an omniscient narrator maintains emotional distance from the characters. The narrator of Jackson's "The Lottery" is omniscient.

Parable A simple story that illustrates a moral point or teaches a lesson. The persons, places, things, and events are connected by the moral question only. The moral position of a parable is developed through the choices of people who believe and act in certain ways and are not abstract personifications, as in allegory, or animal characters, as in folktales.

Parody Usually, a comic or satirical imitation of a serious piece of writing, exaggerating its weaknesses and ignoring its strengths. Its distinctive features are ridiculed through exaggeration and inappropriate placement in the parody.

Plot One of the elements of fiction; the sequence of major events in a story, usually in a cause-effect relation. Plot and character are intimately related, since characters carry out the plot's action. Plots may be described as simple or complex depending on their degree of complication. "Traditional" writers, such as Poe and Chekhov, usually plot their stories tightly; modernist writers such as Joyce employ looser, often ambiguous plots.

Point of view One of the elements of fiction; the perspective, or angle of vision, from which a narrator presents a story. Point of view tells us about the narrator as well as about the characters, setting, and theme of a story. Two common points of view are *first-person narration* and *third-person narration*. If a narrator speaks of himself or herself as *I*, the narration is in the first person; if the narrator's self is not apparent and the story is told about others from some distance, using *he*, *she*, *it*, and *they*, then third-person narration is likely in force. The point of view may be omniscient (all-knowing) or limited, objective or subjective. When determining a story's point of view, it is helpful to decide whether the narrator is reporting events as they are happening or as they happened in the past; is observing or participating in the action; and is or is not emotionally involved. Grace Oluseyi's "A Modern Marriage" is told from the third-person objective point of view, since its narrator observes what the character is doing, thinking, and feeling, yet seems emotionally distant. Poe's "The Cask of Amontillado" and Joyce's "Araby" are told in the first-person subjective and limited point of view, since their narrators are very much involved in the action.

Protagonist The hero or main character of a narrative or drama. The action is the presentation and resolution of the protagonist's conflict, internal or external; if the conflict is with another major character, that character is the antagonist.

Realism Literature that seeks to present life as it is really lived by real people, without didacticism or moral agendas. In the eighteenth and nineteenth centuries, realism was controversial; today it is quite common. Hemingway and ZZ Packer are realists.

Regionalism Literature that is strongly identified with a specific place. Writers like Jamaica Kincaid, who concentrate on one area, are called *regional realists*; writers who do so for several works are said to have strong regional elements in their body of work. Faulkner is an example of the latter.

Rising action The part of a story's action that develops its conflict and leads to its climax. In Hawthorne's "Young Goodman Brown," the rising action builds until the moment when Brown seizes the pink ribbon and knows his "Faith is gone."

Setting One of the elements of fiction; the context for the action: the time, place, culture, and atmosphere in which the action occurs. A work may have several settings; the relation among them may be significant to the meaning of the work. In Hawthorne's "Young Goodman Brown," for example, the larger setting is seventeenth-century Puritan Salem, Massachusetts, but Brown's mysterious journey is set in a forest, and its prelude and melancholy aftermath are set in the village.

Short story A short work of narrative fiction whose plot, characters, settings, point of view, style, and theme reinforce each other, often in subtle ways, creating an overall unity.

Spirit of place A conception of environment as having the power to shape residents, animals, vegetables, minerals, and the course of events.

This mystical, nonscientific idea is ancient, developed by preindustrial, indigenous peoples whose relationship with nature was spiritual as well as physical. The influence of spirit of place on literature can be observed when setting is a major feature. For example, in Hawthorne's "Young Goodman Brown," the forest is believed by the seventeenth-century Salem, Massachusetts, Puritans to be the residence of evil. In Leslie Marmon Silko's story "The Man to Send Rain Clouds," the Pueblo residents transcend the conflict between native and non-native cultures by privately continuing to rely on the spirit of place.

Stream of consciousness A narrative technique based primarily on the works of psychologist-philosophers Sigmund Freud, Henri Bergson, and William James, who originated the phrase in 1890. In fiction, the technique is designed to represent a character's inner thoughts, which flow in a stream without grammatical structure and punctuation or apparent coherence. The novels *Ulysses* and *Finnegans Wake*, both by Joyce, contain the most famous and celebrated use of the technique. Stream of consciousness, which represents the borders of consciousness, may be distinguished from the interior monologue, which is more structured and rational.

Structure The organizational pattern or relation among the parts of a story. Questions to help determine a story's structure may include the following: Is the story told without stop from beginning to end or is it divided into sections? Does the narrator begin at the beginning of a plot or when actions are already under way (*in medias res*, in the middle of things)? Does the narrator begin at the end of the plot and tell the story through a series of flashbacks? Is the story organized by major events or episodes, or by images or moods?

Style One of the elements of fiction; in a literary work, the diction (choice of words), syntax (arrangement of words), and other linguistic features of a work. Just as no two people have identical fingerprints or voices, so no two writers use words in the exact same way. Style distinguishes one writer's language from another's. Faulkner and Hemingway, two major modern writers, had very different styles, as the opening paragraphs of "A Rose for Emily" and "Hills Like White Elephants" show. Two noticeable differences have to do with interior or exterior focus and sentence length. In his second paragraph, Faulkner uses long and complex sentences to represent the architecture, ambience, and sentimental value of Miss Emily's neighborhood. Hemingway's first paragraph, on the other hand, describes the setting and characters in plain, concrete language and generally short sentences, from a more objective and exterior point of view than Faulkner's.

Symbol A reference to a concrete image, object, character, pattern, or action whose associations evoke significant meanings beyond the literal ones. An archetype, or an archetypal symbol, is a symbol whose associations are said to be universal, that is, they extend beyond the locale of a particular nation or culture. Religious symbols, such as the cross, are of this kind. Personal symbols are Faith's ribbons in Hawthorne's "Young Goodman Brown" and the wallpaper in Gilman's "The Yellow Wallpaper." In literature, *symbolism* refers to an author's use of symbols.

Theme One of the elements of fiction, the main idea that is explored in a story. Characters, plot, settings, point of view, and style all contribute to a theme's development. The theme may be complex, often with interrelated subthemes. For example, Ellison's "Battle Royal" is surely about racism and oppression, but it is also about striving to achieve one's potential and subversion through success.

Thesis A literary thesis is a writer's main argument, point, or purpose, the idea that governs an essay or paper. All evidence must support the chosen thesis, which, to be effective, must be limited and specific; without a clear thesis, a paper will be confused and weak. A thesis statement declares the writer's thesis or argument in the first or second paragraph, before the body of the paper begins. See "Writing about Short Stories" in this book.

Third-person narrator The type of narration being used if a storyteller is not identified, does not speak of himself or herself with the pronoun *I*, asserts no connection between the narrator and the characters in the story, and tells the story with some objectivity and distance, using the pronouns *he*, *she*, *it*, and *they*—but not *I*. Hemingway and Hadero chose third-person narration to tell the moving stories of the couple in "Hills Like White Elephants" and Saba in "The Suitcase," respectively, because as writers they wanted distance.

Tone Like tone of voice, literary tone is determined by the attitude of a narrator toward characters in a story and the story's readers. For example, the tone of a work may be impassioned, playful, haughty, grim, or matter-of-fact. Tone is distinct from atmosphere, which refers to the mood of a story and can be analyzed as part of its setting. The tone of Bambara's "The Lesson" is streetwise and tough, like the voice of its first-person narrator.

Acknowledgments *(continued from pg. iv)*

Chimamanda Ngozi Adichie, "Birdsong." Originally published in the *New Yorker.* Copyright © 2010 by Chimamanda Ngozi Adichie. Used by permission of The Wylie Agency LLC.

Margaret Atwood, "Happy Endings," from *Good Bones and Simple Murders* by Margaret Atwood. Copyright © 1983, 1992, 1994 by O. W. Toad, Ltd. Reprinted by permission of Nan A. Talese, an imprint of the Knopf Doubleday Publishing Group, a division of Penguin Random House LLC, and by permission of McClelland & Stewart, a division of Penguin Random House Canada Limited. All rights reserved.

Ramona Ausubel, "You Can Find Love Now," from *Awayland: Stories* by Ramona Ausubel. Copyright © 2018 by Ramona Ausubel. Used by permission of Riverhead, an imprint of Penguin Publishing Group, a division of Penguin Random House LLC. All rights reserved.

James Baldwin, "Sonny's Blues." Copyright © 1957 by James Baldwin. Copyright renewed. Originally published in the *Partisan Review*. Collected in *Going to Meet the Man*, published by Vintage Books. Used by arrangement with the James Baldwin Estate.

Toni Cade Bambara, "The Lesson," from *Gorilla, My Love* by Toni Cade Bambara. Copyright © 1972 by Toni Cade Bambara. Used by permission of Random House, an imprint and division of Penguin Random House LLC. All rights reserved.

Raymond Carver, "Cathedral," from *Cathedral* by Raymond Carver. Copyright © 1981, 1982, 1983 by Tess Gallagher. Used by permission of Alfred A. Knopf, an imprint of the Knopf Doubleday Publishing Group, a division of Penguin Random House LLC. All rights reserved.

John Cheever, "The Swimmer," from *Collected Stories* by John Cheever. Copyright © 1978 by John Cheever. Used by permission of The Wylie Agency LLC.

Ted Chiang, "The Great Silence," from *Exhalation: Stories* by Ted Chiang. Compilation copyright © 2019 by Ted Chiang. Used by permission of Alfred A. Knopf, an imprint of the Knopf Doubleday Publishing Group, a division of Penguin Random House LLC. All rights reserved.

Sandra Cisneros, "The House on Mango Street," from *The House on Mango Street.* Copyright © 1984 by Sandra Cisneros. Published by Vintage Books, a division of Penguin Random House, and in hardcover by Alfred A. Knopf in 1994. Reprinted by permission of Susan Bergholz Literary Services, New York, NY, and Lamy, NM. All rights reserved.

Ralph Ellison, "Chapter 1 [Battle Royal]," from *Invisible Man* by Ralph Ellison. Copyright © 1948 and renewed 1976 by Ralph Ellison. Used by permission of Random House, an imprint and division of Penguin Random House LLC. All rights reserved.

Louise Erdrich, "The Red Convertible," from *The Red Convertible: Selected and New Stories, 1978–2008* by Louise Erdrich. Copyright © 2009 by Louise Erdrich. Used by permission of HarperCollins Publishers.

William Faulkner, "A Rose for Emily," from *Collected Stories of William Faulkner* by William Faulkner. Copyright © 1930 and renewed 1958 by William Faulkner. Used by permission of Random House, an imprint and division of Penguin Random House LLC, and by permission of W. W. Norton & Company, Inc. All rights reserved.

Gabriel García Márquez, "A Very Old Man with Enormous Wings," from *Leaf Storm and Other Stories* by Gabriel García Márquez, translated by Gregory Rabassa. English translation copyright © 1972 by Harper & Row Publishers, Inc. Also: Gabriel García Márquez, "Un señor muy viejo con unas alas enormes," *La increíble y triste historia de la cándida Erendira y de su abuela desalmada.* © Gabriel García Márquez, 1972, y herederos de Gabriel García Márquez. Used by permission of HarperCollins Publishers and Agencia Literaria Carmen Balcells S.A.

Lauren Groff, "At the Round Earth's Imagined Corners." Originally published in *Five Points: A Journal of Literature and Art* 15 (Spring 2013). Copyright © 2013 by Lauren Groff. All rights not specifically granted herein are hereby reserved to the Licensor. Reprinted by permission.

Meron Hadero, "The Suitcase." Originally published in the *Missouri Review* 38.3 (Fall 2015), pp. 96–109. Copyright ©, Meron Hadero. Reprinted by permission of HG Literary.

Ernest Hemingway, "Hills Like White Elephants," from *Men without Women* by Ernest Hemingway. Copyright © 1927 by Charles Scribner's Sons; copyright renewed © 1955 by Ernest Hemingway. Reprinted with the permission of Scribner, a division of Simon & Schuster, Inc. All rights reserved.

Shirley Jackson, "The Lottery," from *The Lottery* by Shirley Jackson. Copyright © 1948, 1949 by Shirley Jackson. Copyright renewed 1976, 1977 by Laurence Hyman, Barry Hyman, Mrs. Sarah Webster, and Mrs. Joanne Schnurer. Reprinted by permission of Farrar, Straus & Giroux, LLC.

Franz Kafka, "A Hunger Artist," translated by Willa and Edwin Muir, from *The Complete Stories* by Franz Kafka, edited by Nahum N. Glatzer. Copyright © 1946, 1947, 1948, 1949, 1954, 1958, 1971 by Penguin Random House LLC. Used by permission of Schocken Books, an imprint of the Knopf Doubleday Publishing Group, a division of Penguin Random House LLC. All rights reserved.

Jamaica Kincaid, "Girl," from *At the Bottom of the River* by Jamaica Kincaid. Copyright © 1983 by Jamaica Kincaid. Reprinted by permission of Farrar, Straus & Giroux, LLC.

Joyce Carol Oates, "Where Are You Going, Where Have You Been?," from *High Lonesome: New and Selected Stories, 1966–2006* by Joyce Carol Oates. Copyright © 2006 by The Ontario Review, Inc. Used by permission of HarperCollins Publishers.

Tim O'Brien, "The Things They Carried," from *The Things They Carried* by Tim O'Brien. Copyright © 1990 by Tim O'Brien. Reprinted by permission of Houghton Mifflin Harcourt Publishing Company. All rights reserved.

Flannery O'Connor, "A Good Man Is Hard to Find," from *A Good Man Is Hard to Find and Other Stories* by Flannery O'Connor. Copyright © 1953 by Flannery O'Connor, renewed 1981 by Regina O'Connor. Reprinted by permission of Houghton Mifflin Harcourt Publishing Company. All rights reserved.

Tillie Olsen, "I Stand Here Ironing," from *Tell Me a Riddle, Requa I, and Other Works* by Tillie Olsen. Copyright © 2013 by the Tillie Olsen Trust. Reprinted by permission of the University of Nebraska Press.

Grace Oluseyi, "A Modern Marriage," *Boston Review*, March/April 2016. Copyright © 2016 by Grace Oluseyi. Reprinted by permission of the author.

ZZ Packer, "Brownies," from *Drinking Coffee Elsewhere* by ZZ Packer. Copyright © 2003 by ZZ Packer. Used by permission of Riverhead, an imprint of Penguin Publishing Group, a division of Penguin Random House LLC. All rights reserved.

Neel Patel, "If You See Me, Don't Say Hi," from *If You See Me, Don't Say Hi: Stories* by Neel Patel. Copyright © 2018 by Neel Patel. Reprinted by permission of Flatiron Books, a division of Macmillan Publishing Group, LLC. All rights reserved.

Karen Russell, "Vampires in the Lemon Grove," from *Vampires in the Lemon Grove: Stories* by Karen Russell. Copyright © 2013 by Karen Russell. Used by permission of Alfred A. Knopf, an imprint of the Knopf Doubleday Publishing Group, a division of Penguin Random House LLC. All rights reserved.

George Saunders, "Sticks," from *Tenth of December: Stories* by George Saunders. Copyright © 2013 by George Saunders. Used by permission of Random House, an imprint and division of Penguin Random House LLC. All rights reserved.

Leslie Marmon Silko, "The Man to Send Rain Clouds," from *Storyteller* by Leslie Marmon Silko. Copyright © 1981, 2012 by Leslie Marmon Silko. Used by permission of Viking Books, an imprint of Penguin Publishing Group, a division of Penguin Random House LLC. All rights reserved.

Adrian Tomine, "Echo Ave.," from *Sleepwalk and Other Stories* by Adrian Tomine. Copyright © 1995, 1996, 1997, 1998, 2004 by Adrian Tomine. Reprinted by permission of Drawn & Quarterly. All rights reserved.

Alice Walker, "Everyday Use," from *In Love and Trouble: Stories of Black Women* by Alice Walker. Copyright © 1973, renewed 2001 by Alice Walker. Reprinted by permission of Houghton Mifflin Harcourt Publishing Company and the Joy Harris Literary Agency, Inc. All rights reserved.

Index of Authors and Titles